HANDBOOK OF ARTIFICIAL INTELLIGENCE AT WORK

Handbook of Artificial Intelligence at Work

Interconnections and Policy Implications

Edited by

Martha Garcia-Murillo

College of Information Science and Technology, University of Nebraska, Omaha, USA

Ian MacInnes

College of Business Administration, University of Nebraska, Omaha, USA

Andrea Renda

Center for European Policy Studies, Brussels, Belgium

 Edward Elgar
PUBLISHING

Cheltenham, UK • Northampton, MA, USA

Published by
Edward Elgar Publishing Limited
The Lypiatts
15 Lansdown Road
Cheltenham
Glos GL50 2JA
UK

Edward Elgar Publishing, Inc.
William Pratt House
9 Dewey Court
Northampton
Massachusetts 01060
USA

A catalogue record for this book
is available from the British Library

Library of Congress Control Number: 2023949655

This book is available electronically in the **Elgar**online
Political Science and Public Policy subject collection
http://dx.doi.org/10.4337/9781800889972

ISBN 978 1 80088 996 5 (cased)
ISBN 978 1 80088 997 2 (eBook)

Typeset by Cheshire Typesetting Ltd, Cuddington, Cheshire
Printed and bound by CPI Group (UK) Ltd, Croydon, CR0 4YY

Contents

Figures

Tables

Contributors

Andrea Aler Tubella, Department of Computing Science, Umeå University, Sweden

Kosmas Alexopoulos, Laboratory for Manufacturing Systems and Automation, University of Patras, Greece

Gabriela Avila, School of Engineering, National Autonomous University of Mexico

Karim Benyekhlef, Université de Montréal, Canada

Norma Elva Chávez, School of Engineering, National Autonomous University of Mexico

George Chryssolouris, Laboratory for Manufacturing Systems and Automation, University of Patras, Greece

Francesco Corea, Independent researcher, UK

Thomas Cornwell, VillageMD, USA

Rishabh Kumar Dhir, International Labour Office, Switzerland

Steven Dhondt, Netherlands Organisation for Applied Scientific Research, the Netherlands; Catholic University of Leuven, Belgium

Giancarlo Frosio, Queen's University Belfast, UK

Martha Garcia-Murillo, College of Information Science and Technology, University of Nebraska – Omaha, USA

Reinhard Grabler, Institute of Management Science, TU Wien, AT, Austria

David Heatley, Sawtooth Economics, New Zealand

Wayne Holmes, UCL Knowledge Lab, University College London, UK

Bronwyn Howell, Victoria University of Wellington, New Zealand

Sabine T. Koeszegi, Institute of Management Science, TU Wien, Austria

Allison Littlejohn, UCL Knowledge Lab, University College London, UK

Ian MacInnes, College of Business Administration, University of Nebraska – Omaha, USA

Sotiris Makris, Laboratory for Manufacturing Systems and Automation, University of Patras, Greece

Naoko Muramatsu, School of Public Health, University of Illinois Chicago, USA

Alexios Papacharalampopoulos, Laboratory for Manufacturing Systems and Automation, University of Patras, Greece

Uma Rani, International Labor Office, Switzerland

Andrea Renda, Center for European Policy Studies, Belgium

Saiph Savage, Northeastern Civic A.I., USA

Dan Sholler, University of California Santa Barbara, USA

Panagiotis Stavropoulos, Laboratory for Manufacturing Systems and Automation, University of Patras, Greece

Emily Stiehl, School of Public Health, University of Illinois Chicago, USA

Zhe Sun, Beijing University of Technology, USA

Pingbo Tang, Carnegie Mellon University, USA

Andreas Theodorou, Department of Computing Science, Umeå University, Sweden

Michael Walker, Macquarie University, Australia

Jinding Xing, Carnegie Mellon University, USA

Setareh Zafari, Institute of Management Science, TU Wien, Austria

Miloš Žefran, Department of Electrical and Computer Engineering, University of Illinois Chicago, USA

Jie Zhu, Université de Montréal, Canada

1. Introduction to the *Handbook of Artificial Intelligence at Work: Interconnections and Policy Implications*
Martha Garcia-Murillo and Ian MacInnes

Artificial Intelligence (AI) is revolutionizing our lives. As this book is being published, the internet is witnessing another information revolution with the introduction of ChatGPT, a natural language processing tool whose generative pre-trained transformer (GPT) architecture was trained with vast amounts of text to respond to queries. Just two months from its inception, it had already attracted 13 million users; by the start of 2023, the number had surpassed 100 million. This technology is being incorporated into search engines. Companies are using its chat capabilities to respond to a large volume of customer service inquiries, product information questions that support sales teams, and employee inquiries in human resources units. However, this sort of AI use is only one of the many applications of AI we see in many aspects of our lives. This book is a collection of research articles documenting how AI is being created and used and discussing its economic implications. This chapter provides an overview of the content. It starts by defining AI and outlining the ways that AI can affect many areas of human endeavor. Capabilities such as natural language processing, computer vision, and autonomous decision making are revolutionizing fields from healthcare and transportation to finance and education. AI can improve work by automating tasks that are repetitive or time-consuming and it can assist workers in making better decisions using systems that provide real-time data and insights. In the rest of this chapter, we explore the rapidly evolving field of AI and how it is transforming work in various settings.

WHAT DO WE MEAN BY AI?

The field of AI has been in existence almost since the birth of the computer. In the 1950s, Alan Turing proposed a test to determine if a system is convincingly human-like (Nilsson, 2005). In the 2020s, AI is moving closer and closer to human-like capabilities (Ciardo et al., 2022). During the Industrial Revolution, machines overcame the limitations of the human

1

body; today, AI is overcoming the limits of the human mind (Berry & Elliott, 2016). Its current capabilities follow from a long evolutionary path that has produced greater and faster processing capabilities. The development of programming languages and increases in computational power, processing speed, connectivity, and the amount of data generated by humans and devices have made it possible for researchers and machines to process enough data to make productive inferences and forecast outcomes.

Computers today are no longer isolated; they are part of highly interconnected computer networks that can perform parallel computations (Ramesh et al., 2004). Research in AI has benefited from the contributions of multiple disciplines, including computer science, psychology, economics, cognitive science, and mathematics (Norvig & Russell, 2021). Haenlein and Kaplan (2019) defined AI as "a system's ability to interpret external data correctly, to learn from such data, and to use those learnings to achieve specific goals and tasks through flexible adaptation."

From a conceptual perspective, AI is divided into general and specialized or narrow AI. *Artificial general intelligence* powers computers and machines capable of simulating human functions. Such a level of complexity has not yet been achieved, and it will take many years, if ever, before a single computer can work and behave like a human in all respects (Goertzel & Wang, 2007). However, although deep learning requires vast amounts of data to work well, technology is rapidly progressing, making learning easier and faster. In 2022 a Google chatbot, and in 2023 a Microsoft chatbot, could interact with people as if they were "sentient" (Grant & Metz, 2022; Roose, 2023). AI developments demonstrate how vast amounts of data enable a computer to "converse," even if AI only generates narratives from online repositories.

Specialized AI refers to domain-specific systems with narrowly defined tasks, such as face recognition, gaming, navigation, and diagnosis. These narrowly defined capabilities have made it possible for AI to expand into many areas, and in this book we focus on those developments. We identify the tools and processes devised to expand AI capabilities and explore their impact on different sectors and professions.

As we learn more about how AI is being incorporated into work settings and various sectors of the economy, we find that it is a significant area of innovation that can bring great benefits to workers, organizations, and society. However, it can also result in displacement and significant disparities. Hence, there is a double-edged impact associated with the set of technologies that constitute AI. This book explores how AI affects work in several sectors of the economy: agriculture, healthcare, infrastructure, law, education, security, government services, financial services, and the

Table 1.1   Functions of artificial intelligence

Human function	Artificial intelligence function
Sight	Computer vision (object recognition)
Speech	Speech recognition
Body movement	Untiring and stable navigation, manipulation, and transportation of objects
Comprehension	Natural language processing
Conversation	The ability to discourse
Creation	The ability to develop compositions from existing compilations of different types of art and to integrate a variety of numerical and sensory data

Source: Compiled from Frey and Osborne (2013) and Patel et al. (2017).

production of goods. As an illustration of how AI can take on and expand human functions, Table 1.1 maps the human capabilities that have been incorporated in systems that use specialized AI.

Like all information technologies, AI has the potential to impact society positively. It can lead to better use of resources, more efficient production of goods, improved provision of services, and enhanced human experience. The challenge for governments and society is to continually assess the impact of technologies like this because they can also have unexpected or adverse outcomes. In this book, we focus on three aspects of AI in the workplace: (1) challenges and opportunities in the development processes behind AI; (2) the deployment of AI and its impact on different sectors of the economy; and (3) the effects of AI on labor. The effects of AI on work depend on how people and machines support or replace each other. Technology integration has proceeded gradually from mechanical and analytical assistance to intuitive, and lately, empathetic assistance (Huang and Rust, 2018). Table 1.2 provides a schematic of how humans and machines can perform several types of work activities.

Routine or repetitive and predictable tasks are performed regularly and follow set patterns or procedures. Computers can easily substitute for this type of work, which can be done better, more rapidly, and more accurately by machines. It calls for mechanical intelligence, which falls on the spectrum of activity at the end where the device performs repetitive tasks requiring minimal intelligence. The use of technology in these functions belongs to what Davenport and Kirby (2015) call Era Two in automation history. We find these functions to be most commonly deployed in manufacturing. For instance, recently, companies in the transportation sector

Table 1.2   Types and frequencies of artificial intelligence tasks

		Type of activity	
		Predictable	Unpredictable
Frequency of activity	Routine	I Substitute for human labor Mechanical intelligence	II XAI–human agent interaction Hybrid augmented intelligence
	Non-routine	III Augmented general- purpose tools	IV Evolvable hardware Mostly human work Analytical intelligence

have been experimenting with self-driving trucks on long-haul, remote routes (Ackerman, 2021). Other examples are filling out forms through algorithms, writing routine texts about the performance of stocks in the business section of a newspaper (Cortés & Luengo, 2021), and taking advantage of computer vision and more complex AI robots to make pizza dough (Petit et al., 2017). Use of this type of AI is motivated by efficiency and cost reductions, where a computer gradually replaces any job that can be codified (Davenport & Kirby, 2015).

Routine and unpredictable tasks involve actions that are regular but are not done in the same way every time. This type of AI is often called *hybrid augmented intelligence*, where humans "collaborate" with machines (Zheng et al., 2017). There are many areas of the economy where a lot of routine tasks are gradually being handled by AI. Nevertheless, in these processes, there are occasionally situations the AI system cannot handle. In manufacturing, much of the equipment successfully performs routine tasks; however, when a machine fails, humans need to bring it back in line.

Similarly, the monitoring of conditions like light and temperature in smart buildings can be easily done through automated AI systems; however, when service is needed above and beyond routine AI monitoring capabilities, a human must intervene (Wellsandt et al., 2022). We see a similar scenario with police robots capable of handling routine tasks. An example is Cobalt Robotics, whose robots can take care of alarm responses, escort visitors, and conduct roving audits using AI, and then connect to an operator when the robot encounters a rare scenario not anticipated by the machine. Medical emergencies also fall under this type of work. They happen often, but everyone experiences them differently. Doctors need to find the medical solution that fits the unique manifestation in each patient. We called Quadrant II in Table 1.2 "augmented diagnostics" because people in professional fields will need tools to help them understand the nature of an event in every case in order to make accurate inferences and appropriate decisions. AI can enhance human capabilities, apply common sense, and provide flexibility and informed judgment (Autor, 2014).

Non-routine and predictable tasks are done infrequently but follow the same or similar patterns or processes; some examples are yearly company audits, safety inspections, and training sessions for new employees. General-purpose AI tools can support activities like these by providing a basic understanding of a process and automating parts of it; then an experienced and knowledgeable human can provide customization by complementing, answering, clarifying, or addressing the specific circumstances and context of the learning. For example, AI tools can provide general training when onboarding a new employee or upskilling an existing employee; then a colleague can fill in any knowledge gaps with specific examples, specialized tools, or help with systems the employee will use. A lot of training has been developed with AI whereby a system can forward learning from basic to more advanced by deploying different content and by testing to assess the speed and depth of progress. However, because they are more general, these tools cannot provide context nor help a learner apply the content to a specific situation.

Non-routine and non-predictable tasks are those associated with human abilities and skills. We have tended to believe that traits such as judgment, leadership, innovation, entrepreneurship, contextual understanding, and spontaneous responses to events are difficult to replicate in machines. However, the continual evolution of AI has resulted in applications that can simulate intuition and empathy. Robots like Pepper are often found in lobbies welcoming people to premises (Choudhury, 2016). We also see many more devices in the health sector that support the "care" of people with smart speakers and pet-like robots. AI "empathy" can be manifested by fast, interconnected computers with access to massive amounts of data that can perform analysis and provide almost instantaneous responses to human inquiries.

We find that AI will play different roles in different sectors of the economy. In some, it will take care of routine tasks, while in others, it will require more human intervention. The development of AI, however, requires large amounts of data. In some fields, these data are readily available, but in others, human coding is necessary. This book provides a broad view of how AI is being developed, of the challenges developers face when making algorithmic decisions, of the use of AI in different sectors, and of the implications for labor.

The book is organized into three parts. Part I focuses on the developments that led to the creation of AI applications. It explains the uses of AI in commercial settings, such as how business models are constructed, how data are collected to train AI systems, how we give AI responsibility in decision making, and what the weaknesses of our still early realizations of AI are. Part II contains the book's main content and is organized around the different sectors of the economy and how people in each sector are affected by AI. Finally, Part III discusses implications of AI, particularly for workers, and how it may be having disproportionate negative effects on some types of workers while helping others, including its impact on unions. These sections of the book altogether provide a comprehensive overview of how AI is being implemented in various fields.

PART I: CONCEPTUALIZING THE HUMAN WITH THE MACHINE

Because computational power and techniques are evolving rapidly, it has become increasingly difficult for scientists to determine the rationale used by AI to produce the outcome of an analysis. This is the topic of Chapter 2, where Koeszegi, Zafari, and Grabler argue that without a clear understanding of these systems, we risk leaving the entire responsibility to the system, regardless of whether a decision makes sense. They explain the tradeoffs we will create by designing systems that may force us to decide what entity is responsible for AI-related mistakes. An important area is emerging within the decision-making context of AI; the field is further specializing in what scholars call *interpretability* – the ability of a system's decision-making processes and outcomes to be made comprehensible to the user (Miller, 2019). The main thrust of these studies is to introduce knowledge from fields like psychology, philosophy, and cognitive science to facilitate a person's understanding of AI outcomes and forecasting. In a similar vein, considering the significant drawbacks of having a system making decisions, Theodorou and Aler Tubella in Chapter 3 point out factors we should consider when deploying AI. As they argue, we need to build checkpoints to allow stakeholders to understand the output of AI systems. They contend that companies will pretend to follow guidelines regarding AI development, but in reality they may be doing "ethics washing." Rather than using AI they may be using human labor. Ensuring that AI is ethically developed is not an easy task. There are many challenges, and some of the greatest are determining what values are to be embedded in a system, who gets to decide on the values, and what tradeoffs need to be considered and resolved. While this is a difficult process,

Theodorou and Aler Tubella state that such decisions will help to build trust in, and foster the use of, these technologies.

Developing AI is not just about considering values; a crucial component is having access to vast amounts of data. For some AI applications, the required data have been easy to obtain and have been used effectively. There are, however, some areas where much data still need to be collected and where acquiring them still requires human participation. Rani and Kumar Dhir's Chapter 4 describes the practices of some companies that claim to use AI in their business operations when, in fact, they still largely use human labor. These companies take advantage of cheap human labor obtained from crowdsourcing platforms and sell it at a premium, while claiming to be using AI. The chapter reveals that deceptive business practices are taking advantage of cheap labor and contributing to poor working conditions for the people doing these menial tasks at a fraction of the cost of legitimate work. One of the most popular platforms where companies and organizations post human coding projects to collect data that can be used for the development of AI applications is Amazon Mechanical Turk (AMT). Research about the platform (Bergvall-Kåreborn and Howcroft, 2014; Martin et al., 2014) has found that workers, also known as turkers, have little power over the compensation they receive and the unpaid invisible labor they do. On AMT and similar platforms, digital workers who generate the data necessary for AI applications are not compensated for the transaction costs associated with learning tasks, are poorly paid, and have few opportunities for professional growth. Recognizing these injustices, Chapter 5 by Savage and Garcia-Murillo addresses the apps that scholars have developed to help these workers. The authors describe recent trends in the field and tools now available that identify tasks that pay better and offer better experiences that can improve workers' effectiveness and skills. The chapter aims to illustrate how we can improve AI development for individuals whose coding helps to generate the mountains of data we need for AI applications.

Even if much work remains to be done for us to use AI seamlessly, we are already interacting with these technologies. These systems reside in all types of computers, from medical diagnosis systems to large manufacturing machines to personal assistants that can support people's daily lives at all stages of life.

PART II: SECTORAL USES, APPLICATIONS, CHALLENGES, AND OPPORTUNITIES

While the first part of the book focuses on the processes behind AI development, the second part delves into several economic sectors where industries have introduced this technology to support their operations, and identifies how those working in different sectors of the economy are being affected by AI. We begin with Andrea Renda's Chapter 6 on agriculture, one of the most ancient economic activities, which describes how AI can benefit farmers and positively impact the environment. AI can reduce the amount of water, pesticides, and fertilizer used on crops, while significantly increasing productivity. The use of the technology-intensive food-production practices is known as *precision farming*. Drones with visual AI can determine if a crop is mature for harvesting, and real-time market monitoring can measure produce supplies to minimize waste. These technologies are also gradually being used with livestock to monitor the health of animals and changes stemming from different types and amounts of feed given to them. A challenge is the uneven deployment of these technologies around the world. Developing countries that employ a large percentage of their population in agriculture have limited access to basic internet connectivity. These highly automated and more complex tools require digital literacy to conduct data analyses to inform decision making. Hence, a few companies can dominate and abuse their power if the population does not have these skills and resources. As Renda indicates, policymakers can limit these inequities if they invest in connectivity, educate their people working in this sector, and connect to supply chains. AI in agriculture has a bright future but will need some government intervention to succeed globally.

Another traditional economic sector is manufacturing, which has seen an enormous transformation since the early days of the Industrial Revolution. In Chapter 7, Stavropoulos and Chryssolouris describe how AI has transformed manufacturing and how the new capabilities make manufacturing more resilient, enhancing our human capabilities and working conditions while interacting with machines.

In Chapter 8, Xing et al. focus on the use of AI to monitor a country's infrastructure, including bridges, roads, water distribution systems, and power plants, among others. As they indicate, faulty infrastructure can negatively impact a country's economy. Infrastructure involves both construction and maintenance. In Chapter 8, Xing et al. focus on a single aspect of infrastructure, the operations of a nuclear power plant. In operating a plant, AI must consider human capabilities and the reliability of the physical and cyber systems. AI can detect cracks in images and can safeguard procedures by guiding operators through the steps and verifying the status of components. However, data about infrastructure are not always complete, as sensors can fail and data can be misinterpreted if inappropriate algorithms are used. While we are not yet at the stage of complete reliability, these technologies will continue to evolve, providing better data and improving infrastructure diagnostics and operations.

In Chapter 9, Muramatsu focuses on caring for the elderly at home, a specific segment of the healthcare sector where AI-enabled "virtual humans" can support human caregivers. Help from wearable devices, voice-enabled agents, smartphones, and speakers can identify potential medical or mental challenges in time to save the lives of these vulnerable people. Through virtual assistants, family members can schedule medical appointments, program a smart medication dispenser, and monitor blood through sensors. Muramatsu describes in her chapter how fully functional AI at home can support different aspects of elders' independent living.

Education is another ancient profession that has been part of the human experience for centuries. The way we teach and learn has not changed much; however, changes are now being felt as technology becomes incorporated into all areas of our lives. As Holmes and Littlejohn observe in Chapter 10, the most significant change in instruction is the upskilling of employees already in the workplace who need to remain relevant and productive in their workplace. Even with automation, training content will need to be tailored to specific contexts. In this respect, many companies are starting to use AI to support learners through interactive and sometimes gamified experiences. Intelligent tutoring systems are being designed to facilitate independent learning through automated teachers and AI-enabled tutors. This scenario, however, has not yet been fully realized. From the teachers' perspective, some AI has been used to facilitate plagiarism detection, classroom monitoring, assessment, and the curation of materials, but with limited effectiveness. For people to remain competitive throughout their working lives, lifelong learning will have to be customized more effectively for specific roles and responsibilities. AI technologies like chatbots can enhance this training by enabling voice interactions with the system about the material being learned. As Holmes and Littlejohn explain, while we are progressing, much more needs to be done to equip these systems to empower the learner. As in other settings, AI in education will be a complementary rather than a substitute technology.

Financial services are also introducing AI into their operations. In Chapter 11, Corea describes how the financial sector has been transformed by technology. Computers have been ubiquitous in this area for a long time. However, there are some pockets, such as private equity and venture capital, where technology is much less prevalent, and AI has been considered only recently. In many institutions, the decision about whether to fund a start-up has traditionally been made through "a gut feeling" or heuristics. As Corea notes, the smaller venture capital firms have become more willing to take risks and are relying on data more systematically. As he explains, AI is gathering data from social media and the web and generating IP- and product-related insights to help venture capital firms determine the probability of success. The most sophisticated companies use hoards of data to identify promising investments. These more complex models assess the company but also market trends and can match what the company offers to promising demand patterns. While AI use is still in its early stages in this sector, future research will determine how accurately AI algorithms have been able to predict the long-term success of start-ups compared to traditional methods.

In Chapter 12, Frosio describes the challenges AI is creating in the area of intellectual property (IP) rights. AI-generated creativity does not fit the traditional IP standards for personhood, authorship, or originality. AI-generated art programs can produce "original" images almost instantaneously, and it won't be long before AI can generate video. Many artists are worried about this new technological development, and some have filed lawsuits against some art sites. Although current laws allow this type of art production, Frosio's chapter describes many instances where the law may need to be changed for AI-generated creativity to continue.

There has been tremendous progress in AI regarding the identification of information. Search engines today have potent algorithms capable of identifying relevant content. It is thus not surprising that the judicial system, which relies on prior cases, procedures, rules, and regulations, would be affected by the power of these technologies. As Karim Benyekhlef and Jie Zhu describe in Chapter 13, AI will transform the legal profession. It will support cases through "machine learning evidence." It can, for example, reconstruct degraded DNA, and AI-enabled 3D models can trace the path of a bullet. An immersive virtual environment could "recreate" the entire context of a case for a jury. Descriptive and outcome analytics can support the organization of data and information about a case and its potential outcome, and even calculate the compensation for harm. However, as in many other areas where AI is beginning to be used, lawyers and judges need to be alert to the biases that algorithms using prior data will invariably contain. Benyekhlef's chapter highlights areas where a clear identification of values, as described by Theodorou and Aler Tubella in Chapter 3, would be valuable.

In Chapter 14, Savage et al. provide some insights about how AI has been implemented in the military. Perhaps this sector is one of the most difficult to understand, in part because the ways technology gets incorporated into military operations is classified and explaining it can have potentially negative consequences for national security. In this chapter, Savage et al. identify how AI is used in strategic, tactical, and operational functions. They describe the roles that governments and the private sector play in developing and deploying AI in the military. They also invite us to consider new factors, such as pandemics and social media, as part of a national security strategy. Consequently, they indicate that AI in the military will require private, public, and academic coordination with their counterparts in other countries.

The last chapter of Part II is about using AI to provide government services. In Chapter 15, Renda describes the greater productivity, increased accuracy, and cost reductions AI could generate if integrated into government services. For example, governments can use AI for real-time regulation monitoring or for the detection of anomalies in financial transactions. However, Renda also comments on the potential risks of introducing AI into government operations. These risks include a weaker protection of rights, loss of employment due to automation, and reduced quality and access to public services.

PART III: THE LABOR IMPLICATIONS OF ARTIFICIAL INTELLIGENCE AT WORK

The last part of the book focuses on the implications of having greater AI penetration into all sorts of work. In a *Harvard Business Review* article, a tech blogger asks, "How will they [workers] compete against AI?" (Davenport & Kirby, 2015), so in the last few chapters, the focus is on the implications of AI penetration for employment.

We begin this section with Chapter 16 from Heatley and Howell about the impact of AI on employment levels. Their work was motivated by the common belief in academic circles that AI will replace and displace many workers. They question this notion and believe instead that this has historically been a common fear about technology and human experience when new disruptive technologies emerge. Their review of the literature and data from New Zealand labor market indicators suggests that such displacement is not happening, that productivity is down rather than up, and that any increase in unemployment in sectors able to fully automate is taking longer than predicted. Their chapter then explains the fallacies that make us believe technology negatively affects employment.

At a more micro level, in Chapter 17, Sholler and MacInnes highlight some of the nuanced observations offered by the contributors to this book. AI's impacts on different sectors of the economy are not equivalent. In some sectors, AI will be a welcome complement to complex settings where having such technology will facilitate or enhance work. In other sectors,

AI can disempower, dehumanize, and significantly decrease workers' skills. The impact will thus be differential; some will gain from the ways AI can elevate their skills, quality of work, and income, while for others, the opposite will be the case. The authors argue that this will lead to increasing inequality between those in situations where AI improves and increases their productivity and those in situations where it is detrimental. They provide recommendations to minimize these negative impacts.

In the final chapter, Walker analyzes the impact of AI on unions. Because technology in the past has had detrimental effects on workers, there is a need, he argues, for mechanisms that support consultation and joint decision making concerning technology. One challenge to union efforts to minimize the potential negative impact of AI is low levels of union membership. Walker presents cases illustrating how AI affects workers and describes strategies and tools workers can use to address this technology's adverse effects. Paradoxically, new AI technology can empower them to address their concerns.

There are many sectors of the economy where AI will substitute for human labor. In other areas, AI will complement and augment human capabilities to improve the working experience, while enhancing the services and products we use daily. We recognize, however, that in the absence of policies that alleviate the inequalities that can emerge from the introduction of AI, many people will be displaced with no good options. Others will toil in difficult and poorly paid jobs. Despite these risks, we are optimistic that many new jobs will emerge because of the introduction of AI. We believe that future generations of workers will find more meaningful work that will take advantage of their creativity, skills, and talent. The AI-enabled devices that will eventually invade every aspect of our lives will require people who can build, maintain, upgrade, and troubleshoot them. This means that we will need workers in the different sectors of the economy who are knowledgeable about these technologies.

Similarly, people displaced by machines and not interested in working with computers could be in professions involving human interaction such as emotional support, guidance, and personal care of children and adults. Currently these occupations are poorly paid, sometimes despite labor shortages. As more people move into these areas, a question is whether salaries will be sufficient to maintain a similar standard of living for people who would otherwise be in professions where AI has displaced workers. There will be great advantages gained in society as more AI is introduced but there will also be challenges, particularly during the transition.

REFERENCES

Ackerman, E. (2021, January 4). This year, autonomous trucks will take to the road with no one on board. IEEE Spectrum. https://spectrum.ieee.org/this-year-autonomous-trucks-will-take-to-the-road-with-no-one-on-board

Autor, D. (2014). Polanyi's paradox and the shape of employment growth. National Bureau of Economic Research.

Bergvall-Kåreborn, B., & Howcroft, D. (2014). Amazon Mechanical Turk and the commodification of labour. *New Technology, Work and Employment, 29*(3), 213–223.

Berry, B. J. L., & Elliott, E. (2016). The surprise that transforms: An American perspective on what the 2040s might bring. In L. Grinin, T. Devezas, & A. Korotayev (eds), *Kondratieff Waves: Cycles, Crises, and Forecasts* (pp. 82–98). Uchitel.

Choudhury, S. R. (2016). SoftBank's Pepper robot gets a job waiting tables at Pizza Hut. CNBC. www.cnbc.com/2016/05/24/mastercard-teamed-up-with-pizza-hut-restaurants-asia-to-bring-robots-into-the-pizza-industry.html

Ciardo, F., De Tommaso, D., & Wykowska, A. (2022). Human-like behavioral variability blurs the distinction between a human and a machine in a nonverbal Turing test. *Science Robotics, 7*(68), eabo1241.

Cobalt Robotics. (2022). Cobalt Robotics, https://www.cobaltrobotics.com/.

Cortés, H., & Luengo, M. (2021). Data journalism, massive leaks, and investigation. In M. Luengo & S. Herrera (eds), *News Media Innovation Reconsidered* (pp. 105–123). John Wiley & Sons.

Davenport, T. H., & Kirby, J. (2015, June 1). Beyond automation. *Harvard Business Review*. https://hbr.org/2015/06/beyond-automation

Frey, C. B., & Osborne, Michael. (2013). The future of employment: How susceptible are jobs to computerisation? Oxford Martin School. www.oxfordmartin.ox.ac.uk/publications/the-future-of-employment/

Goertzel, B., & Wang, P. (2007). Advances in artificial general intelligence concepts, architectures and algorithms: Proceedings of the AGI Workshop 2006. IOS Press.

Grant, N., & Metz, C. (2022, June 12). Google sidelines engineer who claims its AI is sentient. *New York Times*. www.nytimes.com/2022/06/12/technology/google-chatbot-ai-blake-lemoine.html

Haenlein, M., & Kaplan, A. (2019). A brief history of artificial intelligence: On the past, present, and future of artificial intelligence. *California Management Review, 61*(4), 5–14.

Huang, M.-H., & Rust, R. T. (2018). Artificial intelligence in service. *Journal of Service Research, 21*(2), 155–172.

Martin, D., Hanrahan, B. V., O'Neill, J., & Gupta, N. (2014). Being a turker. *Proceedings of the 17th ACM Conference on Computer Supported Cooperative Work and Social Computing*, 224–235.

Miller, T. (2019). Explanation in artificial intelligence: Insights from the social sciences. *Artificial Intelligence, 267*, 1–38.

Nilsson, N. J. (2005). Human-level artificial intelligence? Be serious! *AI Magazine, 26*(4), 68–68.

Norvig, P., & Russell, S. (2021). Artificial intelligence: A modern approach. http://aima.cs.berkeley.edu/

Patel, A., Patel, R., & Kazi, F. (2017). Vitality of robotics in healthcare industry: An Internet of Things (IoT) perspective. In C. Bhatt, N. Dey, & A. S. Ashour (eds), *Internet of Things and Big Data Technologies for Next Generation Healthcare* (pp. 91–109). Springer.

Petit, A., Lippiello, V., Fontanelli, G. A., & Siciliano, B. (2017). Tracking elastic deformable objects with an RGB-D sensor for a pizza chef robot. *Robotics and Autonomous Systems, 88*, 187–201.

Ramesh, A. N., Kambhampati, C., Monson, J. R. T., & Drew, P. J. (2004). Artificial intelligence in medicine. *Annals of the Royal College of Surgeons of England, 86*(5), 334–338.

Roose, K. (2023, February 16). A conversation with Bing's chatbot left me deeply unsettled. *New York Times.* www.nytimes.com/2023/02/16/technology/bing-chatbot-microsoft-chatgpt.html

Wellsandt, S., Klein, K., Hribernik, K., Lewandowski, M., Bousdekis, A., Mentzas, G., & Thoben, K. D. (2022). Hybrid-augmented intelligence in predictive maintenance with digital intelligent assistants. *Annual Reviews in Control, 53*, 382–90.

Zheng, N.-n., Liu, Z.-y., Ren, P.-j., Ma, Y.-q., Chen, S.-t., Yu, S.-y., Xue, J.-r., Chen, B.-d., & Wang, F.-y. (2017). Hybrid-augmented intelligence: Collaboration and cognition. *Frontiers of Information Technology & Electronic Engineering, 18*(2), 153–179.

PART I

CONCEPTUALIZING THE HUMAN WITH THE MACHINE

2. The computer says no: how automated decision systems affect workers' role perceptions in socio-technical systems

Sabine T. Koeszegi, Setareh Zafari, and Reinhard Grabler

INTRODUCTION

In a sketch by the British television comedy show *Little Britain*, a mother and her five-year-old daughter come to the hospital for an agreed tonsillectomy appointment. Having entered the daughter's data, the receptionist says the child is scheduled for bilateral hip replacement surgery. Despite the objections from the mother, which the receptionist first types into her computer, she keeps responding with the answer: "Computer says no!" This sketch illustrates how "intelligent systems" may absurdly shift the roles and accountabilities of humans and machines. Regardless of how reasonable the mother's objections are and how wrong the computer's statements are, the machine's proposed decision ultimately triumphs. The critical questions are: why does the receptionist rely on the erring system, and how could we prevent such situations in work contexts?

Humans have used model-based and data-based support systems in decision-making for approximately 50 years. With data-driven artificial intelligence (AI) methods, the application of decision support systems has expanded from complex, difficult decisions to simple, frequently occurring everyday choices, in which we can be supported by preselection of suitable alternatives or which we delegate to the system entirely. In many situations, we are not aware of the fact that automated decision systems (ADS) are being used at all. ADS are systems in which algorithms execute decision-making models, and the system wholly or partially replaces human assessment. Hence, the paradigmatic change triggered by technological progress is based on the ever increasing autonomy and the resulting agency of such systems. Decisions we made ourselves in the past are wholly or partially transferred to ADS. In many applications of algorithmic decision-making, the boundaries between automated decision-making and decision-making support are blurred. The capacity of ADS to learn and adjust without human intervention makes it much more complex and unlikely for humans to keep oversight over the process.

So far, research has focused primarily on analyzing the effects of algorithmic decisions on those affected – and has already tempered the high expectations. It turns out that algorithmic choices can also have similar problems as human decisions due to partial or incomplete data, inadequate modelling, and problematic objectives. After all, AI systems are also "just" designed by those error-prone humans that should be replaced – an irony of automation (see Bainbridge, 1983). However, how work changes for users of such systems has received little attention. But what happens when workers are assigned "intelligent" and "autonomous" systems as co-workers with whom they make joint decisions? It is essential to ask whether ADS meet the expectations when deployed in practice, whether users and clients will accept their decisions, and how they change the role of the human in a work environment.

Since the delegation of tasks to ADS results in collaborative work processes, autonomous systems and human agents need to adapt to each other and collaborate in joint decision-making tasks. Users will develop (correct or wrong) expectations about the system's capabilities, may form assumptions about the system's reliability and trustworthiness, and adapt their role and self-perception accordingly in the decision-making process. Hence, we need to take the whole socio-technical system into account, i.e. a framework that, in addition to the technical components of the system, also includes the political, social, and economic context in which the ADS is deployed. The adaptation processes within such a socio-technical system may jeopardize a clear attribution of tasks and accountability within the socio-technical ensemble and present additional and novel challenges for work design (Zafari & Koeszegi, 2018).

In this chapter, we identify the following fundamental changes for the human in the ensemble:

1. the perception of their role;
2. the perception of their competencies and self-efficacy; and
3. their assumption of accountability for the work process and outcomes.

After we give a brief overview of opportunities and challenges associated with ADS, we discuss the fundamental changes in the work organization when ADS are deployed by assessing and the associated risks such as over-reliance on automated systems, reduced autonomy and self-efficacy of users, and ultimately a diffusion of accountability for work processes and outcomes.

OPPORTUNITIES AND CHALLENGES ASSOCIATED WITH ADS

ADS are associated with increased efficiency in decision-making, including lower costs and better outcomes (e.g. Smith et al., 2010; Wihlborg et al., 2016). Indeed, under laboratory conditions, the combination of complementary capabilities of humans and ADS can be shown to improve decision quality. While humans are needed for selecting and developing decision models, setting goals, and interpreting the decision context, ADS can analyze vast amounts of data in a short time and identify correlations and patterns. This requires a well-designed interface between humans and ADS that first automatically sorts, evaluates, and categorizes information from various data channels. If future predictions are subsequently enabled, this reduces the cognitive workload of humans and thus ultimately improves the quality of decision-making. In practice, however, the numerous claims about the advantageousness of ADS must be considered cautiously. In the following, some applications in private and public areas are highlighted, as well as problems and challenges associated with ADS.

Expectations about Economic Benefits of ADS in Business

The primary motivations for implementing ADS applications in business operations are efficiency, reduced costs, and reduced human error. The following cases are examples of the potential benefits of ADS: consolidated communications in call centers and faster resolution and automated validation and diagnosis of customer complaints and problems (Resolve Systems, n.d.a); and ADS reducing waiting times of customers in online shops (Brownells Inc., n.d.). By automating networks' testing, incident resolution, and creating daily communication network health reports, companies can save money on the operation of their infrastructure (Resolve Systems, n.d.b). Furthermore, ADS reduce processing hours and human errors by automating port requests (Campbell, 2021). Analytic, AI-based software for clinical decision-making reduces health care costs, avoids complications, reduces the hospital burden, and enables more patients to receive proper treatment (SAS, n.d.b). ADS are also used to coordinate allocation schemes for organ donations (UK National Health Service Blood and Transplant, n.d.). Automation services are furthermore used in the banking industry, e.g. in the personalization of customer experiences to increase profitability (SAS, n.d.d), in optimizing risk management in credit decisions (SAS, n.d.a), in fraud analytics, thus reducing losses from fraud, supporting anti-money-laundering efforts (SAS, n.d.c), and reducing the number of loan applications requiring review (PNC Financial

Services Group, n.d.). Moreover, Bogen and Rieke (2018) point out that ADS support in hiring processes helps to quickly sort out unqualified candidates and prioritize those qualified for further review, helping make efficient staffing decisions.

Expectations about Better, Fairer, and Faster Decisions of ADS in the Public Sector

Besides business operations, ADS are used in the public sector to automate government–citizen interactions – anticipating improved impartiality (Wihlborg et al., 2016) – and to support decision-makers in finding decision alternatives or assessing risks and providing classifications (HLEG AI, 2019). The New York government uses predictive technologies to protect children from abuse and neglect by introducing software which gives frontline case workers a streamlined overview of the cases to assist their decision-making (NYC Administration for Children's Services, 2018). In the criminal justice system, algorithms are used to resolve crimes by probabilistic genotype matching to sort out DNA strands (Pishko, 2017) and automated techniques are utilized to determine housing options for jail or prison inmates (Berk et al., 2003; Shahabsafa et al., 2017). Furthermore, administrations use algorithms to achieve better assignments in high schools (Roth, 2015), to measure the effectiveness of teachers (RAND Education and Labor, n.d.), to predict where fires could break out in cities (Flood, 2010; Heaton, 2015), to prevent discrimination against low-income renters (Bousquet, 2018), to create a risk assessment of immigrants and assist in the decision of deportation (Sonnad, 2018), and to anticipate where crime could potentially happen and thus deploy police officers accordingly (Levinson-Waldman, 2018). Other applications of ADS in the public sector can be found in the Canadian government, which applied them in 2014 to filter applications of immigration (Kuziemski & Misuraca, 2020), the Chilean Tax Authority, which uses an e-tax system to collect and process information about citizens from sources such as banks and businesses to generate a completed tax form (Smith et al., 2010), and Airborne Early Warning radar systems, where ADS increase decision quality (Huang, 1990).

In summary, attitudes toward ADS seem cautiously optimistic, as Araujo et al. (2018) found in a survey where nearly every second respondent perceived them as applicable to some degree. Especially in an environment with plenty of decisions, ADS can assist with simple choices and suggest critical decisions that a human operator must review. So they can, as a result, focus more on those vital decisions (Huang, 1990). The broad range of ADS applications indicates their actual usefulness in various sectors. This should remind us that such systems are already part of our daily life – wittingly and unwittingly. However, it is also essential to see how ADS fail to meet high expectations.

When ADS Fail

Citron (2007) points out some cases where ADS failed with severe consequences: a benefits management system in Colorado made hundreds of thousands of incorrect decisions as the programmers had implemented rules incorrectly; airline travelers are often mislabeled as terrorists by the data-matching program known as the "No Fly" list – where there is no means to get the entry cleared again; the Terrorist Surveillance Program generates high numbers of false positives, causing many innocents to be on terrorist lists; the Federal Parent Locator Service falsely identified parents owing child support, and as a result, garnished wages and bad credits without notifying the persons concerned. Other examples of failed ADS can be found in Chicago, where the Department of Children and Family Services had to end a data-mining program that was supposed to predict child abuse after several cases of child death were not recognized (Jackson & Marx, 2017). In Queensland, Australia, a coding error in an algorithm led to incorrect results of DNA evidence (Murray, 2015). A school assignment system in Boston elevated existing disparities for the access of black and Latino students to higher-ranked schools (Feijo, 2018). Contracts of teachers in the United States could be terminated if a score they achieved in an evaluation system was too low (Loewus, 2017). There were 34,000 or more individuals falsely accused of unemployment fraud by an algorithm (Charette, 2018). Some errors, such as an incorrect implementation of a set of rules by programmers, Citron (2007) mentions, might not even be recognized if the results are not catastrophic and thus will continue to make wrong decisions for long periods.

Moreover, ADS may perpetuate or even increase social injustice and inequality. Citron and Pasquale (2014) point out the possibilities of extensive data-mining practices which can be used as a basis for a scoring system, e.g. when a consumer's credit risk is derived from payments made for therapy, or algorithmic predictions about health risks based on data a user shares with apps, which could result in higher insurance premiums. Suppose such scores are used for automated decisions in a person's life, e.g. determining their fitness for a job. In that case, it can be a further perpetuation of the gap between privilege and disadvantage, as a bad score could lead to several situations which would even lower the person's score in the future, thus perpetuating existing stereotypes and social segregation (Article 29 Data Protection Working Party, 2018). Unfortunately, as the example of China's Social Credit System shows, even certain governments show interest in using scoring systems, which rightfully triggers controversy. Chinese citizens are assessed on creditworthiness and trustworthiness, determining whether they can access education, markets, and tax deductions (Liang et al., 2018). These scoring systems seem even more counterproductive when considering that algorithms are biased, too. Bogen and Rieke (2018) found numerous examples of how ADS can perpetuate interpersonal, institutional, and systemic biases as a result of discrimination based on gender, race, age, or religion, among others, which is reflected in the data used by the algorithm: individuals named Jared were given higher chances of success; women working in lower-level jobs in the past would be recommended lower-paying jobs despite being qualified; racial differences resulted in unequal scoring, as short distances to the workplace were counted as an advantage, and residential areas strongly correlated with race due to historical disparities. The Berkeley Haas Center for Equity, Gender and Leadership analyzed 133 biased systems across industries from 1988 and 2021, finding that an alarmingly high share of 44.2 percent of the systems demonstrated gender bias and around a quarter of the systems had both gender and racial bias (Smith & Rustagi, 2021).

HOW ADS CHANGE WORK

The state-of-the-art discussion recommends the inclusion of ADS for optimizing and automating tasks. However, the success of ADS deployments depends not only on overcoming technical limitations (e.g. insufficient training data and poor data governance/analysis) and unrealistic expectations on ADS (i.e. one-size-fits-all solution) (Zhang et al. 2019) but also on considering socio-psychological challenges that are associated with changes in the work organization. Over the last decades, a growing body of literature has reflected that technology is shaped by and simultaneously influences the evolution of social structures (Orlikowski, 2007; Zammuto et al., 2007). Organizations need to become aware of the underlying integration process to fully utilize the positive potential of introducing ADS to work processes (Zafari et al., 2021).

Several studies have shown that human–AI collaboration can outperform a group of humans and sophisticated AI systems, e.g. in diagnosing cancer (Wang et al., 2016). The resulting team success can be attributed to the unique advantages that emerge from combining human and AI capabilities in a compatible way (Krüger et al., 2017). While humans are often confronted with information that requires extensive interpretation,

AI systems can be implemented to help them make instant use of all these data and facilitate decision-making (Dragicevic et al., 2020). A well-designed ADS enhances data analysis by promoting the understanding of multimodal information extracted from multiple data channels, e.g. sorting, scoring, or categorizing the data. It reduces the human agents' cognitive workload demand hence improving decision quality. To benefit from the capabilities of AI in decision-making, it is essential to identify the risks and tradeoffs in socio-technical ensembles to solve problems that neither an ADS nor a human agent can solve on its own. In the following section, we identify and discuss the three main areas that may be negatively affected by the deployment of ADS in work contexts.

Roles of Human and Artificial Agents

ADS significantly impact work processes and individuals' tasks and understanding of their roles. In a case study of a Swedish government agency, where an ADS is used to assess the eligibility of applicants for government benefits, the shift in role structure is visible. Whereas previously the staff members made assessments and decisions, they increasingly see themselves reduced to the role of mediator between the system and the applicants. They "just keep the system running," although they are formally responsible for the final decision. Officials point out in interviews that the system proposes a decision based on all the information entered; therefore, there can be no room for doubt about the decision. The assignment of tasks is also linked to corresponding expectations and attributions of competence, while one's ability to act is equally restricted. Hence, Wihlborg et al. (2016, 2911) highlight how decision support users become a "mediator rather than a decision-maker." While self-determined action requires a degree of personal accountability, delegating decisions to automated systems limits this agency and perceived control over the decision-making process.

A large body of literature has investigated the human perception and expectations of AI assistants. A recent study by Zhang et al. (2021) found that people's preferred characteristics of AI teammates are instrumental skills, shared understanding between humans and AI, communication capabilities, and human-like behavior and performance. As systems become more intelligent and agentic, people put higher expectations on ADS that are dramatically out of step with the actual system operation. Overtrusting a decision made by ADS can lead to poor and ineffective results. For instance, when processes are too complex to control, we blindly adopt the results suggested by the software. It is, therefore, necessary to develop proper and more accurate expectations of the ADS and its capacities to adjust the extent we rely on them. Riveiro and Thill (2021) show how explanations should align with user expectations, in which explaining why the system produced a specific output is appropriate when the system's output is in line with user expectations and explaining why the system had one outcome instead of another works better when the results differ from user expectations. Meurisch et al. (2020) explore how human expectations depend on the domains and context of user-centered support and propose assistant systems with controllable proactivity levels. In line with this, Zafari and Koeszegi (2020) conclude that when individuals feel in control and believe that they determine the task outcome and not external factors, they tend to feel more comfortable collaborating with proactive agents. These studies indicate that providing working conditions that preserve a sense of control and efficacy is vital.

Most digitization strategies, however, focus mainly on enhancing machine intelligence and industrial productivity and consider workers as users rather than collaborators of these systems. When ADS restrict human roles to "providing data" for training the systems and "setting goals or boundaries" for satisfactory outcomes, it becomes increasingly difficult for humans to control these systems or take corrective action in the case of a system failure or system errors. Hence, despite the technological enhancements, workers represent a significant factor in the design of socio-technical systems, and their role in joint decision-making processes needs to be strengthened as autonomous agents cannot fully and cost-effectively reproduce human competencies, skills, and qualities.

Perception of Competencies and Self-Efficacy

Required worker skills will change with the deployment of ADS. Smith et al. (2010) point out that even with the implementation of the low-level automation of c-voting machines, the simple task of counting votes now requires technological expert knowledge: the voting systems can be vulnerable on a software or hardware level, transforming the simple task of counting votes into a complex algorithmic and computer security affair. While the intention of switching to the automated system was to reduce human error in counting, it created new challenges due to the different skills needed to operate and oversee it, an irony of automation which Bainbridge (1983) had already pointed out. Moreover, the lack of possibilities to visually verify the votes and thus the inner workings of the system has led to controversies in the past, e.g. Premier Election Solutions' refusal to make their software code available (Smith et al., 2010) and more recently with numerous false claims that voting machines switched votes to favor a candidate in the 2020 United States presidential election (Pennycook & Rand, 2021). It shows that despite the high hopes that automated decisions will increase accuracy, efficiency, and fairness (Simmons, 2018), not understanding how a decision is made is problematic, at least for an unjustified judgment.

On the other hand, the fact that a decision is not made by a human, but is the result of an automated process, lends it certain neutrality and legitimacy and thus weakens the users' sense of competency. It has been argued that algorithmic and automated processes could increase the perceived "neutrality" of the result (Citron & Pasquale, 2014). According to a study by Logg et al. (2019), this is particularly problematic because people who have little or no knowledge in a particular field prefer to trust an algorithm rather than rely on the specialized expertise of humans, while experts are significantly less likely to rely on the credibility of algorithmic predictions. Hence, the tendency to save mental resources when making decisions can lead to automation bias and not questioning the suggested decisions or seeking out additional information while interacting with an ADS that provides wrong recommendations (Parasuraman & Manzey, 2010).

Furthermore, a recently conducted study in which an AI system used facial recognition software to identify not only test subjects' gender, ethnicity, and age but also their emotional state and personality traits demonstrated how impressed laypeople could be even by obviously false results. The readout "must be correct. Because a computer makes the assessment, and computers are better than people at drawing such conclusions" (test subject, quoted in Wouters et al., 2019, 454). This can even get to the point that subjects question their self-image due to a wrong classification by the computer (Wouters et al., 2019).

Moreover, changes in human roles may increase human dependency on assistance systems to the extent that they might not be able to make the decision entirely on their own. Relying on a description of the computational process that determines correlations between the source data and the outcome of the automated decision could inhibit learning opportunities. Only when the system can explain the decision-making process can individuals assess the decision's effect on the outcome, gain new knowledge, and discover new rules and connections in the context (Adadi & Berrada, 2018).

Overall, using ADS may lead to deskilling processes. Humans are no longer acquiring essential expertise or skills – or lose them over time – when replaced by automated systems (Bainbridge, 1983). But evaluating the quality of decisions is challenging. In order to not only evaluate decisions by their outcome (i.e. outcome bias), we need to ensure that users also have access to contextual information. This will entice human agents to critically examine the whole decision-making process by which an outcome is reached.

Accountability and Oversight

Autonomy and self-determined action require a certain degree of (personal) accountability. If the delegation of decisions to algorithmic decision-making systems limits the power of humans to act, there will also be shifts in perceived control. When decisions are automated, questions regarding the attribution of credit or blame for outcomes remain unanswered. There are already disagreements about accountability allocation in collaborative settings and adding an algorithmic decision maker exacerbates this debate.

In general, it seems to be harder to accept ADS as legitimate if they replace humans in critical decisions (Simmons, 2018). Smith et al. (2010) illustrate this in an example where the use of automated fingerprint identification systems affects the decision-making of experts: the experts' final decision is based on a recommendation for the most likely match of the fingerprint, leaving some experts even unable to explain how the decision was derived as it is beyond their comprehension and scrutiny. According to Smith et al. (2010), this shows two dysfunctions of accountability: (1) experts are relying more on outputs by the machine while not understanding the decision process (i.e. overtrust), and (2) experts can be blamed for false accusations of a crime as they make the final decision. Nevertheless, they cannot be blamed entirely as the automated system had a part in it (i.e. diffusion of accountability). Despite the potential conflict regarding accountability, it is evident that using such systems in fingerprint identification has the overwhelming advantage of searching through large databases, which humans cannot compete with.

Recent studies show that as the autonomy of an autonomous AI system increases, people attribute more blame to the system than to themselves (Furlough et al., 2021; Kim & Hinds, 2006). One possible explanation is that people perceive these autonomous agents to have more agency and freedom in deciding and are thus automatically subjected to taking the blame for the choice. However, this is not the case for taking credit. Lei and Rau (2021) found that autonomous AI systems are more blamed than human agents, but they both received similar levels of positive recognition. Thus, introducing autonomous agents to work processes seems to challenge the usual responsibility practices.

Because ADS are so complex and untransparent, their decision-making processes cannot be fully understood by the developers and their users. And yet people tend to have great faith in technology, even if they don't understand precisely how it works. This is especially problematic because the responsibility of the decision always has to be taken by human agents, as AI-based technologies cannot meet the requirements for moral agency and responsibility (Coeckelbergh, 2019; Zafari & Koeszegi, 2018). A human agent's sense of responsibility for ADS depends highly on the extent of their understandability of the "inner workings" and how an ADS makes decisions and effectively manages the decision outcomes. In other words, the lack of understanding behind the system's design and providing recommendations (i.e. the black box problem) can weaken the accountability of the human agents for the work process and outcomes. Therefore, ADS should be capable of filling the knowledge gap, which is also understood as reducing the information asymmetry between the system and the users (Malle et al., 2007).

System transparency increases technology acceptance and reliance (Miller, 2019). Expanding the system transparency enables users to understand better its capacity and the processes that bring the system to a specific decision or prediction (De Graaf & Malle, 2017; Felzmann et al., 2019). However, having only access to data processed by the system is insufficient; ADS outputs need to be accompanied by explanations of how and why a decision was made. It is essential that also non-expert users understand ADS output as plausible, valuable, and trustworthy (Papagni & Koeszegi, 2021a, 2021b; Papagni et al., 2022). Kim and Hinds (2006) found a negative relationship between the transparency of an AI system (in this case a robot) and participants' understanding of the robot's behavior. They found that the offered explanations confused participants even more. Hence, Papagni and Koeszegi (2021b) present a model in which transparency and understanding of an AI system are determined by the plausibility of explanations resulting from contextual negotiations between the parties involved. When a system explains its decision-making process in a language that non-expert users understand, the human agent is enabled to develop a mechanism to determine the causes and premises associated with the decision. Thus, explaining can help human collaborators examine the findings more thoroughly, handle the problem, and thus increase overall accountability.

CONCLUSIONS

The transformation from today's conception of human–AI collaboration into tomorrow's reality in organizational settings requires specific reference models, procedures, standards, and concrete criteria for properly considering human factors in designing and implementing ADS. In other words, creating a socio-technical system requires considering both technical and social aspects of work processes to shed light on how technological and social entities affect one another. To refer back to the sketch on

Little Britain, a potential overtrust in systems needs to be mitigated by a consequently transparent design of such systems.

We need to understand ADS as socio-technical ensembles within socio-technical systems: algorithms are not neutral, and when we speak of ADS or algorithms, we are referring to an undefined network of technical arrangements in which the participation of humans remains hidden in every process step. It is humans who decide on the methods and model design, it is humans who curate and correct the training data, and it is humans who design the algorithms by determining which parameters are relevant in which contexts and which target function is to be achieved. Finally, it is humans who apply ADS for certain tasks in specific contexts. Thus, we have to understand that "these algorithmic systems are not standalone little boxes, but massive, networked ones with hundreds of hands reaching into them, tweaking and tuning, swapping out parts and experimenting with new arrangements ... We need to examine the logic that guides these hands" (Seaver, 2014, 10). Thus, it is necessary to identify further requirements for human-centered technology designs that preserve the control and meaningful role of the employees.

Overconfidence can lead to the point where people question their self-image and self-confidence. Moreover, reliance on technology causes loss of skills and competencies by humans because they are not regularly used and trained. When decision-making processes are not transparent, they do not offer learning opportunities and new experiences and insights for humans. This increases dependency on AI systems even more, which becomes especially problematic when they fail or do not function properly. While it is expected in so-called out-of-the-loop scenarios that humans can step in and take over the systems' tasks again, they then lack the experience and skills to do so – another irony of automation (Bainbridge, 1983).

Hence, accountability for the consequences of using and relying on ADS has to be regulated. Several studies have proposed methods and measures to assess the fairness of ADS (e.g. Kroll et al., 2017; Schoeffer & Kuehl, 2021). For instance, Citron and Pasquale (2014) suggest measures that allow individuals to comment on the collected data, specific indicators, and algorithms used. While these examples and initiatives may be applicable for weak ADS (e.g. simple linear regression in machine learning), a further (empirical) investigation is required to facilitate transparency and explainability of complex ADS. A seminal study in this area is the work of Kraft et al. (2020), which proposes how regulatory mechanisms of dealing with accountability problems can be matched to different applications of ADS based on the risk involved, which results in agency loss. Consequently, before ADS can be used, it must be ensured that possible negative consequences for individuals and society can be ruled out or minimized.

For successful integration of ADS in work organizations, we need to inform and engage with the workers who consequently need to use these technologies in their work rather than putting them in the situation and demanding them to be faster, better, and responsible for the decisions. As individuals gain more experience with ADS, we expect them to develop new mental models of the agents' capabilities, adapt their perceptions of how they fit into the work environment, and make alterations to their use of them to accommodate their needs better.

REFERENCES

Adadi, A., & Berrada, M. (2018). Peeking inside the black-box: A survey on explainable artificial intelligence (XAI). *IEEE Access*, 6, 52138–52160

Araujo, T., De Vreese, C., Helberger, N., Kruikemeier, S., van Weert, J., Bol, N., Oberski, D., Pechenizkiy, M., Schaap, G., & Taylor, L. (2018). Automated decision-making fairness in an AI-driven world: Public perceptions, hopes and concerns. Digital Communication Methods Lab.

Article 29 Data Protection Working Party. (2018). Guidelines on Automated Individual Decision-Making and Profiling for the Purposes of Regulation 2016/679.

Bainbridge, L. (1983). Ironies of automation. *Automatica*, 19(6), S. 775–779.

Berk, R. A., Ladd, H., Graziano, H., & Baek, J. (2003). A randomised experiment testing inmate classification systems. *Criminology & Public Policy*, 2(2), 215–242.

Bogen, M., & Rieke, A. (2018). Help wanted: An examination of hiring algorithms, equity, and bias (United States of America). Report, Upturn. https://apo.org.au/node/210071

Bousquet, C. (2018, February 28). How New York is protecting affordable apartments with analytics. *Data-Smart City Solutions*. https://tinyurl.com/y3cascc7

Brownells Inc. (n.d.). IBM Cloud. https://tinyurl.com/mwdc9kfw

Campbell, J. (2021, March 22). Syniverse Improves Operational Efficiency and Consistently Meets SLAs with Automation. *Resolve Systems*. https://tinyurl.com/2m3dpwtn

Charette, R. N. (2018, January 24). Michigan's MiDAS unemployment system: Algorithm alchemy created lead, not gold. *IEEE Spectrum*. https://tinyurl.com/6vey252h

Citron, D. K. (2007). Technological due process. *Washington University Law Review*, 85, 1249.

Citron, D. K., & Pasquale, F. (2014). The scored society: Due process for automated predictions. *Washington University Law Review*, 89, 1.

Coeckelbergh, M. (2019). Artificial intelligence, responsibility attribution, and a relational justification of explainability. *Science and Engineering Ethics*, 1–18.

De Graaf, M. M., & Malle, B. F. (2017). How people explain action (and autonomous intelligent systems should too). *2017 AAAI Fall Symposium Series*.

Dragicevic, N., Ullrich, A., Tsui, E., & Gronau, N. (2020). A conceptual model of knowledge dynamics in the industry 4.0 intelligent grid scenario. *Knowledge Management Research and Practice*, 18(2), 199–213.

Feijo, S. (2018, July 16). Here's what happened when Boston tried to assign students good schools close to home. *News @ Northeastern.* https://tinyurl.com/yp5neuxn

Felzmann, H., Fosch-Villaronga, E., Lutz, C., & Tamo-Larrieux, A. (2019). Robots and transparency: The multiple dimensions of transparency in the context of robot technologies, *RAM*, 26(2), 71–78.

Flood, J. (2010, May 16). Why the Bronx burned. *New York Post.* https://tinyurl.com/2zj35tsc

Furlough, C., Stokes, T., & Gillan, D. J. (2021). Attributing blame to robots, I: The influence of robot autonomy. *Human Factors*, 63(4), 592–602.

Heaton, B. (2015, June). New York City fights fire with data. *Government Technology.* https://tinyurl.com/4um9n5zm

HLEG AI. (2019). High-level expert group on artificial intelligence. *Ethics Guidelines for Trustworthy AI.*

Huang, C. Y. (1990). Real-time automated decision-making in an advanced airborne early warning system. *IEEE Conference on Aerospace and Electronics*, Dayton, OH, 434–439.

Jackson, D., & Marx, G. (2017, December 6). Data mining program designed to predict child abuse proves unreliable, DCFS says. *Chicago Tribune.* https://tinyurl.com/4wb7yxub

Kim, T., & Hinds, P. (2006). Whom should I blame? Effects of autonomy and transparency on attributions in human-robot interaction. *ROMAN 2006: The 15th IEEE International Symposium on Robot and Human Interactive Communication*, 80–85.

Krafft, T. D., Zweig, K. A., & König, P. D. (2020). How to regulate algorithmic decision-making: A framework of regulatory requirements for different applications. *Regulation & Governance.*

Kroll, J. A., Huey, J., Barocas, S., Felten, E. W., Reidenberg, J. R., Robinson, D. G., & Yu, H. (2017). Accountable algorithms. *University of Pennsylvania Law Review*, 165, 633.

Krüger, M., Weibel, C. B., & Wersing, H. (2017). From tools towards cooperative assistants. Paper presented at HAI, New York, 287–294.

Kuziemski, M., & Misuraca, G. (2020). AI governance in the public sector: Three tales from the frontiers of automated decision-making in democratic settings. *Telecommunications Policy*, 44(6), 101976.

Lei, X., & Rau, P. L. P. (2021). Should I blame the human or the robot? Attribution within a human-robot group. *International Journal of Social Robotics*, 13(2), 363–377.

Levinson-Waldman, R. (2018, January 26). Court: Public deserves to know how NYPD uses predictive policing software. Brennan Center for Justice. https://tinyurl.com/y9tvk23s

Liang, F., Das, V., Kostyuk, N., & Hussain, M. M. (2018). Constructing a data-driven society: China's social credit system as a state surveillance infrastructure. *Policy & Internet*, 10(4), 415–453.

Loewus, L. (2017, October 26). Houston District settles lawsuit with teachers' union over value-added scores. *Education Week.* https://tinyurl.com/yckucffc

Logg, J. M., Minsona, J. A., & Moore, D. A. (2019). Algorithm appreciation: People prefer algorithmic to human judgment. *Organizational Behavior and Human Decision Processes*, 15, 90–103.

Malle, B. F., Knobe, J. M., & Nelson, S. E. (2007). Actor–observer asymmetries in explanations of behaviour: New answers to an old question. *Journal of Personality and Social Psychology*, 93(4), 491.

Meurisch, C., Mihale-Wilson, C. A., Hawlitschek, A., Giger, F., Müller, F., Hinz, O., & Mühlhäuser, M. (2020). Exploring user expectations of proactive AI systems. *Proceedings of the ACM on Interactive, Mobile, Wearable and Ubiquitous Technologies*, 4(4), 1–22.

Miller, T. (2019). Explanation in artificial intelligence: Insights from the social sciences. *Artificial Intelligence*, 267, 1–38.

Murray, D. (2015, March 20). Queensland authorities confirm "miscode" affects DNA evidence in criminal cases. *The Courier Mail*. https://tinyurl.com/mrxkarpw

NYC Administration for Children's Services. (2018, October 30). ACS deploys new technology to help frontline staff protect NYC children from abuse and neglect. NYC Administration for Children's Services. https://tinyurl.com/3trmrmuk

Orlikowski, W. J. (2007). Sociomaterial practices: Exploring technology at work. *Organisation Studies*, 28(9), 1435–1448.

Papagni, G., & Koeszegi S. T. (2021a). A pragmatic approach to the intentional stance: Semantic, empirical and ethical considerations for the design of artificial agents. *Minds and Machines*, 31, 505–534.

Papagni, G., & Koeszegi, S. T. (2021b). Understandable and trustworthy explainable robots: A sensemaking perspective. *Paladyn: Journal of Behavioral Robotics*, 12(1).

Papagni, G., De Pagter, J., Zafari, S., Filzmoser, M., & Koeszegi, S.T. (2022). May I explain? Explainability is a trust support strategy for artificial agents. *Journal of Knowledge, Culture and Communication*.

Parasuraman, R., & Manzey, D. H. (2010). Complacency and bias in human use of automation: An attentional integration. *Human Factors*, 52(3), 381–410.

Pennycook, G., & Rand, D. G. (2021). Examining false beliefs about voter fraud in the wake of the 2020 Presidential Election. *The Harvard Kennedy School Misinformation Review*.

Pishko, J. (2017, November 29). The impenetrable program transforming how courts treat DNA evidence. *Wired*. https://tinyurl.com/yc7wv3e9

PNC Financial Services Group. (n.d.). IBM Cloud. https://tinyurl.com/52x8wdy6Riveiro, M., & Thill, S. (2021). "That's (not) the output I expected!" On the role of end-user expectations in creating explanations of AI systems. *Artificial Intelligence*, 298, 103507.

RAND Education and Labor. (n.d.). Value-added modeling 101. (n.d.). https://tinyurl.com/4ud78rea

Resolve Systems. (n.d.a). Network automation saves consolidated communications $1.3m monthly. https://tinyurl.com/2a9mn45n

Resolve Systems. (n.d.b). T-Mobile saves 40k man hours annually by automating and accelerating network testing. https://tinyurl.com/yrjp2uew

Roth, A. (2015, July 2). Why New York City's high school admissions process only works most of the time. Chalkbeat New York. https://tinyurl.com/43xv3wvj

SAS. (n.d.a). Better reporting yields better understanding of risk management. https://tinyurl.com/vntjtu5b

SAS. (n.d.b). Health care data analytics. https://tinyurl.com/2crzbeja

SAS. (n.d.c). Nationwide reduces fraud losses by 75%. SAS. https://tinyurl.com/2w5ju74k

SAS. (n.d.d). Understanding the needs of banking customers in the digital economy. https://tinyurl.com/bdd8smth

Schoeffer, J., & Kuehl, N. (2021, October). Appropriate fairness perceptions? The effectiveness of explanations in enabling people to assess the fairness of automated decision systems. *Companion Publication of the 2021 Conference on Computer Supported Cooperative Work and Social Computing*, 153–157.

Seaver, N. (2014). Knowing algorithms. *Media in Transition*, 8. https://static1. squarespace.com/static/55eb004ee4b0518639d59d9b/t/55ece1bfe4b030b2e8302 e1e/1441587647177/seaverMiT8.pdf

Shahabsafa, M., Terlaky, T., Gudapati, C., Sharma, A., Plebani, L., Wilson, G., & Bucklen, K. B. (2017). The inmate assignment and scheduling problem and its application in the PA Department of Correction. *Interfaces*, 48(5), 467–483.

Simmons, R. (2018). Big data, machine judges, and the criminal justice system's legitimacy. *UC Davis School of Law: Law Review*, 52, 1067.

Smith, G., & Rustagi, I. (2021, March 31). When good algorithms go sexist: Why and how to advance AI gender equity. *Stanford Social Innovation Review*.

Smith, M. L., Noorman, M. E., & Martin, A. K. (2010). Automating the public sector and organising accountabilities. *Communications of the Association for Information Systems*, 26(1), 1.

Sonnad, N. (2018, June 26). US border agents hacked their "risk assessment" system to recommend detention 100% of the time. *Quartz*. https://tinyurl.com/ yw7jmxt6

UK National Health Service Blood and Transplant. (n.d.). IBM Cloud. https:// tinyurl.com/bd4tc2ms

Wang, D., Khosla, A., Gargeya, R., Irshad, H., & Beck, A. H. (2016). Deep learning for identifying metastatic breast cancer. arXiv:1606.05718

Wihlborg, E., Larsson, H., & Hedström, K. (2016). "The computer says no!": A case study on automated decision-making in public authorities. *49th Hawaii International Conference on System Sciences*, Koloa, HI, 2903–2912.

Wouters, N., Kelly, R., Velloso, E., Wolf, K., Ferdous, H. S., Newn, J., Joukhadar, Z., & Vetere, F. (2019). Biometric mirror: Exploring values and attitudes towards facial analysis and automated decision-making. *Conference on Designing Interactive Systems*, 1145.

Zafari, S., & Koeszegi, S. T. (2018). Machine agency in socio-technical systems: A typology of autonomous artificial agents. *2018 IEEE Workshop on Advanced Robotics and its Social Impacts*, 125–130.

Zafari, S., & Koeszegi, S. T. (2020). Attitudes toward attributed agency: Role of perceived control. *International Journal of Social Robotics*, 1–10.

Zafari, S., Koeszegi, S. T., & Filzmoser, M. (2021). Human adaption in the collaboration with artificial agents. In J. Fritz & N. Tomaschek (eds), *University–Society–Industry: Beiträge zum lebensbegleitenden Lernen und Wissenstransfer*. Konnektivität: Über die Bedeutung von Zusammenarbeit in der virtuellen Welt.

Zammuto, R. F., Griffith, T. L., Majchrzak, A., Dougherty, D. J., & Faraj, S. (2007). Information technology and the changing fabric of the organisation. *Organization Science*, 18(5), 749–762.

Zhang, R., Torabi, F., Guan, L., Ballard, D. H., & Stone, P. (2019). Leveraging human guidance for deep reinforcement learning tasks. arXiv: 1909.09906.

Zhang, R., McNeese, N. J., Freeman, G., & Musick, G. (2021). "An ideal human": Expectations of AI teammates in human–AI teaming. *Proceedings of the ACM on Human–Computer Interaction*, 4(CSCW3), 1–25.

3. Responsible AI at work: incorporating human values

Andreas Theodorou and Andrea Aler Tubella

INTRODUCTION

When looking at the wide variety of guidelines and standards produced for the governance of artificial intelligence (AI), a key aspect emerges: there is a global call for AI technology that *explicitly aligns with human values*. For example, the European Union's "Ethics guidelines for trustworthy AI" call for "ensuring adherence to ethical principles and values" (European Commission, Directorate-General for Communications Networks, Content and Technology, 2019), and the IEEE's guide for ethically aligned design advocates for "systems to remain human-centric, serving humanity's values and ethical principles" (IEEE Global Initiative on Ethics of Autonomous and Intelligent Systems, 2019). These policy and industry responses are evidence of the growing need for technology to not only perform a specific function, but to do so while respecting the legal, social, cultural, and ethical values of its deployment context. Such "ethically aligned" or "value-aligned" AI should not only benefit from the increased social trust, but also make for a more seamless and safe adoption. By understanding how a system fulfils human values, stakeholders are able to *calibrate their trust* (Glass et al., 2008), understand where *responsibility* for the system's behavior lies (Dignum, 2019), and make informed decisions on how the system fits into their organization in relation to their own organizational values. Value-aligned systems, therefore, translate into more reliability, safety, and accountability (Figure 3.1). All these aspects are crucial for the incorporation of AI into the work context, where intelligent systems are only one element of a pipeline where the humans interacting with them must be able to use them safely and correctly.

Incorporating human values in the design and behavior of intelligent systems poses many challenges. To start, values are not universally accepted or understood and are highly context dependent. Furthermore, translating human values into actionable technical requirements on a system requires a specificity that abstract values do not provide. Additionally, it is a topic of discussion who should make these decisions, and where responsibility lies in cases where the system does not perform adequately. In this

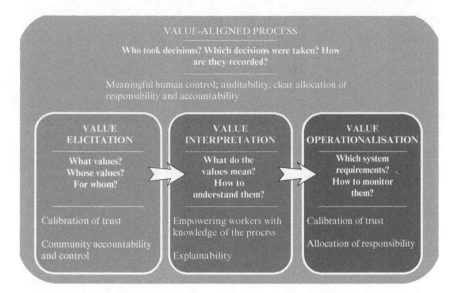

Figure 3.1   Value-aligned process

chapter, we will discuss how to incorporate values into intelligent systems by presenting literature and state-of-the-art tools around three key challenges: (1) recognizing *which* and *whose* values should be considered; (2) operationalizing values and actively including them in an intelligent system's behavior; and (3) ensuring that not only the resulting system, but the design and deployment process as a whole adhere to desirable values.

When it comes to "AI at work," each of these aspects is key for its advancement. Firstly, identifying relevant stakeholders and their values is fundamental for the adoption of modern technology into any organizational process. The idea of values being incorporated in technology design has a long history and is tied to the idea of democracy in the workplace. Approaches such as participatory design (or co-design) (Muller & Kuhn, 1993) emerged to fill this gap specifically in the work context, precisely proposing that all stakeholders should be involved in the design process. Spurred by similar challenges regarding the incorporation of intelligent systems into human workflows, such methodologies have been adapted to AI design, proposing ways in which stakeholders can deliberate and agree on values and their interpretations. Secondly, operationalizing values into specific constraints and behaviors of intelligent systems increases trust (Dignum, 2019), rendering interactions more efficient and safe, therefore helping these tools to fulfil their function seamlessly and empowering workers with the knowledge needed to adequately operate these systems.

Finally, ensuring that design and deployment processes follow values such as transparency and responsibility is of great benefit for organizations and workers, allowing to show due diligence, compliance to governance constraints and auditability (Bryson & Theodorou, 2019), which clarifies the allocation of responsibility and prevents disuse stemming from mistrust.

Overall, this chapter aims to provide a clear overview of how it is possible to incorporate values in the design, deployment, and use of intelligent systems, as well as the challenges associated with it. Throughout the chapter, we focus on a simple claim: incorporating values is not only ethical (and recommended by guidelines), but also provides added value in terms of efficacy, safety, and human empowerment in the context of work.

The chapter is structured as follows. First, we discuss the relationship between values and AI systems, introducing to the reader approaches for participatory design. Then, we present tools on how we should move from abstract policies into concrete solutions. Next, we discuss how even the organizational and governance processes that go around the system's lifecycle need to adhere to values. In the penultimate section, we outline some of the ongoing challenges. We conclude with a summary of the content presented.

VALUES IN AI SYSTEMS DESIGN: WHOSE AND FOR WHOM?

At the time of writing, there are over 700 guidelines and policies regarding AI research and development (OECD, 2021), advocating for the incorporation of high-level values such as *transparency, fairness*, and *accountability* in the design and deployment of intelligent systems. While varied, meta-analyses indicate that these guidelines mostly converge around shared principles. For example, Floridi and Cowls (2019) found that most recommendations fall under the principles of beneficence, non-maleficence, autonomy, justice, and explicability. Thus, when it comes to incorporating values into intelligent systems, this level of convergence is promising. It is, however, far from sufficient for concrete implementations. Indeed, the first challenge when it comes to choosing and implementing values is that while high-level values such as those presented in guidelines and standards provide high-level guidance, they often provide no explicitness on how to interpret and operationalize such values (Theodorou & Dignum, 2020). This generality, which is a strength in terms of their applicability to a variety of settings and future technologies, is however a challenge when it comes to concretizing and implementing specific values into specific systems. Compounding this challenge is the fact that human values are not universally understood across cultures and individuals (Turiel, 2001); instead, they are influenced by the socio-cultural and application context in which systems are deployed (Jakesch et al., 2022). For example, views on social competition and what determines income inequality influence what is considered fair in terms of redistribution of wealth and resources (Alesina & Angeletos, 2005). This lack of absolute definitions and understandings of values necessarily leads to the question: when designing and deploying an intelligent system, how is it possible to determine which values we should follow, how, and for whom (Dignum, 2019)?

The challenges of incorporating socio-ethical values in the design of technology – specifically in the context of work – are not new. Historically, such approaches are born as a means of bringing the technology into the workplace in a democratic way, in which the values and perspectives of the workers which will use the technology are incorporated into its design. An early example is the Norwegian Iron and Metal Workers Union project (1970–1973) to involve workers in the design of a computer-based planning and control system for their workplace (van der Velden & Mörtberg, 2014). This was done in collaboration with researchers from the Norwegian Computing Centre, where design activities with the unions were undertaken to find needs, assess possible solutions, and propose changes to the technology. This project is an example of the *participatory design* approach, which values the skills and expertise of workers (Muller & Kuhn, 1993) and incorporates them throughout the design process in various ways. Relatedly, socio-technical design advocates for considering the optimization both of the technology introduced within an organization and of the organization itself, with special attention to the social factors that come into play (Winby & Mohrman, 2018). While providing different perspectives, these methodologies share two key premises:

1. that the inclusion of users in technology design and deployment can empower "ordinary working people with overall knowledge of the productive process, making them capable of critical and collaborative judgments about production and distribution" (Zuboff, 1989); and
2. that values in technology are only meaningful within the context they are deployed in and must therefore be collected and interpreted within that context.

These provide an answer to the question we posed: it is the stakeholders of the specific system who can provide the necessary context and interpretations of what values mean to them and how they should be interpreted. Especially for the case of technology, these tenets have been adopted and several design methodologies have been developed with a focus on consulting stakeholders and eliciting their interpretations of what values mean (van der Velden & Mörtberg, 2014). For AI specifically, participatory methods, e.g. *value-sensitive design* (Friedman, 1996; Friedman et al., 2006) and *design for values* (van de Poel, 2013) present methods for including stakeholders in the design and development phases. During the development of AI systems, taking a design for values approach means including explicit activities with stakeholders for: (1) the identification of societal values; (2) deciding on a moral deliberation approach (e.g. through algorithms, user control, or regulation); and (3) linking values to formal system requirements and concrete functionalities. It should be noted that they do not replace software engineering approaches, but rather complement them by ensuring the integration of human values and not just product and business requirements (Aldewereld et al., 2015).

When it comes to AI, there are some unique ethical and technical issues to incorporating human values (Umbrello & van de Poel, 2021; van de Poel, 2020). Namely, the non-deterministic and often opaque nature of AI systems can result in a complex emerging behavior as the system interacts with its environment and stakeholders, violating and adhering to values in unforeseen ways as the system's behavior is hard to predict (Theodorou et al., 2017). Suggested extensions of value-sensitive design for AI systems ground the value elicitation and integration with the AI for the social good framework by Floridi et al. (2020). One of the proposed additions is, for example, the constant monitoring of compliance to values, so that undesirable behavior can be immediately identified and addressed, even requiring system redesign.

The idea of incorporating stakeholders' values into technology is particularly highlighted in the context of work, where the acceptance and trust of new technology is key to incentivizing its use and integrating it into organizational processes (Baxter & Sommerville, 2011). In fact, the adoption of a technology is not incentivized simply by demonstrating high performance, but rather by allowing the calibration of trust in the technology (Lee & See, 2004). This trust comes not only through understanding how the technology works, but it is also influenced by the socio-cultural context in which it is deployed – and how much the technology respects it (Straub et al., 1997). Most crucially, participatory approaches that ensure the inclusion of cultural, societal, and organizational values in AI at work align with the idea of empowering the community that will be affected by its deployment. Recent critical work with roots in social activism emphasizes the idea of "nothing about us without us"; i.e. a focus on community accountability and control (Costanza-Chock, 2020).

OPERATIONALIZING VALUES: IMPLEMENTING TRUSTWORTHY AI

Through deliberative approaches, designers, stakeholders, and developers may arrive at a shared understanding of relevant values and their interpretations. Once this crucial step is reached, how is it possible to incorporate them into an intelligent system? When it comes to technical operationalizations to ensure that an AI system adheres to given values, there are two main approaches: *enforcement*, meaning actively constraining a system's behavior to follow specific requirements, and *monitoring*, i.e. observing the behavior of the system so that any non-compliant behavior is flagged and reparatory actions can be taken. For either of these solutions, it is crucial to reach a *concrete and explicit* understanding of what it means for the system to adhere to a value. The biggest aspect of operationalization therefore consists of distilling abstract values into concrete system requirements that can be implemented and checked.

This concretization process is challenging. It is a process that requires continued input from the stakeholders, experts, consideration of what is feasible with the technology, as well as possible trade-offs (van de Poel, 2013). Design for values methodologies account for concretization steps in the design process, where each value is distilled into actionable system requirements and concrete functionalities in an explicit manner (Friedman et al., 2006; Van Den Hoven, 2005). A way to obtain such concreteness is for example to proceed hierarchically (van de Poel, 2013), progressively concretizing each value into more and more concrete norms, ending up with concrete testable requirements (Aler Tubella et al., 2019).

In the context of work, concretizing values into actionable requirements means considering the pipeline within which an intelligent system will be used, considering the humans involved as assets that can provide complementary skills to meet the requirements of the system (Clegg, 2000). For example, it is possible to technically implement oversight with approaches incorporating human intervention (human-in-the-loop), which rely as much on the system as on expert operators that can override it. To exploit the richness afforded by the expertise of human workers, recent methodologies advocate for incorporating values into the socio-technical system formed by an intelligent system together with the humans and the pipeline in which it is deployed (Makarius et al., 2020).

Although concretizing abstract values into technical system requirements is a challenge, much work has been done for specific values in the context of AI, such as fairness, explainability, or privacy. The burgeoning field of fairness for classifier systems, for example, provides quantitative definitions for fairness, which consider elements such as accuracy amongst different groups, false positives, or false negatives (Dwork et al., 2017; Zemel et al., 2013). While still highly contextual, these proposals can serve as a guide for developers and stakeholders to agree and implement specific. operationalizations of the fairness value. This progress comes accompanied with openly available de-biasing methods and tools, e.g. AI Fairness 360 toolkit (AIF360) from IBM (Bellamy et al., 2019), Fairlearn from Microsoft (Bird et al., 2020), and others, which can be used to produce models that provably adhere to given operationalizations of fairness. Although such approaches constitute a big advancement and provide tools for responsible AI designers, they rely on testable, quantifiable definitions of fairness. Critical approaches emphasize that fairness is multi-dimensional and that purely quantitative bias definitions and de-biasing methods can lead to new biases (Aler Tubella et al., 2022) or may be unable to deal with intersectionality (Kearns et al., 2018). Thus, with fairness as with all values, the next research challenge consists of incorporating socio-technical contexts into its operationalization.

Similarly, the field of explainable AI concerns itself with operationalizations of the value of explainability (Miller, 2019). There exist many ways in which one can explain the behavior of an intelligent system, such as text-based functional explanations, image-based heat maps, influence maps of how much each feature influences the outputs of the system, or counterfactual explanations indicating which changes in the input would alter the output. In fact, the purpose of an explanation influences what is acceptable: it is different to provide explanations to a user for the purpose of interacting with a system, to a developer for the purpose of debugging, or to a client to enable contestability of decisions (Aler Tubella et al., 2020). For intelligent systems to be responsibly deployed in the context of work, transparency and explainability are crucial: incorporating systems into a workflow with human actors hinges on the humans being able to assess the system's capabilities and adjusting their trust accordingly, thus being able to determine when the system is appropriate for a task and understand when it is malfunctioning (Miller, 2019; Theodorou et al., 2017). Incorporating transparency and explainability on AI at work therefore means navigating the accuracy–interpretability trade-off, again taking a socio-technical view of the system where workers' understanding of the tools they use takes as much importance as the capabilities of the tools themselves.

Just as for fairness and explainability, whole research areas are devoted to operationalizing values such as privacy, transparency, and human oversight in AI. This explicit transformation of abstract values into concrete requirements brings great benefits to all stakeholders, and is crucial in the context of work, as it becomes clear how the system is interpreting and employing relevant abstract human values. With this understanding, stakeholders (both workers and customers) can *calibrate their trust*, understand where *responsibility* for the system's behavior lies, and make informed assessments of a system's decisions. However, operationalization is not value-free in itself: it consists of design choices and technical decisions that must be documented to guarantee that not only the system, but its design, deployment, and use adhere to responsible practices (Brundage et al., 2020).

BEYOND VALUE-ALIGNED SYSTEMS: VALUE-ALIGNED PROCESSES

Beyond advocating for intelligent systems that respect human values, most standards and guidelines emphasize that the design, deployment, and usage processes should also adhere to certain values, particularly those of responsibility, accountability, and transparency (Dignum, 2019). That is as we should never separate the artefact from the environment in which it is being developed and used (Theodorou & Dignum, 2020). This means that when going through all the work of producing value-aligned systems (as presented in the previous two sections), organizations should keep transparent records of the parties involved and the decisions taken, e.g. which values were prioritized and how they are operationalized.

Transparency is tightly related to *traceability*, i.e. the ability to trace at a point of time or over a period of time what influenced a decision (Holzinger et al., 2019; Winfield et al., 2021). This traceability of systems should never be "just" about the artefact; instead, it should always include the processes and decisions that went around the system's lifecycle. For example, deciding to explicitly embed values, as we championed in the previous section, should be documented. The decisions around *which values* and *how they were interpreted* lead to different behaviors of the artefact – a behavior which may be beneficial for workers in certain countries and damaging to others – and should therefore be traceable. In turn, traceability is fundamental for us to maintain *meaningful human control* over the technology (Methnani et al., 2021; Santoni de Sio & van den Hoven, 2018). Meaningful human control requires taking into consideration not only the artefact but also the relevant human agents and their moral reasons and responsiveness to those reasons. For this, traceability at all points of the development and usage processes is necessary. Otherwise, the lack of traceability leads to misattributing accountability for any subsequent claims and challenges to those claims about a system's performance, behavior, and impact (Brundage et al., 2020).

This issue can be seen as of particular importance in the workplace, where the impact of a system could damage the careers and livelihoods of workers interacting or otherwise affected by the system. Misidentifying or non-assigning accountability at all may propagate inequalities and power imbalances between workers and employers (Roberson et al., 2020; Yang & Liu, 2021).

Keeping an accountable and transparent process also enables *auditability*, where organizations can show that they have done their *due diligence* prior to the deployment or during the use of intelligent systems. Assessing that the entire processes leading to the development and deployment of an AI system adhere to ethical requirements has been brought forward as a way to "close the AI accountability gap" (Brännström et al., 2022; Raji et al., 2020). Audit techniques are also used for certification. Standards, such as the IEEE 7001 on transparency (Winfield et al., 2021), are often *process* standards, i.e. with a focus not on the specifications of the artefact but on the activity or set of activities performed to ensure certain properties. This idea augments the concept of *quality control*, in the sense that the values that should be followed are explicitly stated and audited for, far beyond the technical performance of the system. This transparent process provides clarity when it comes to who is accountable for given decisions and impacts of a system, which is key to the smooth adoption of technology at work, as technology that muddles the allocation of responsibilities often falls into disuse as it fails to be integrated (Baxter & Sommerville, 2011).

Following a transparent – and audited – process fosters trust and is likely to accelerate the acceptance of the technology as stakeholders calibrate their trust to the system due to assurances in the process surrounding it (Schnackenberg & Tomlinson, 2016). By volunteering the disclosure of information, an organization exposes itself to the risk of revealing trade secrets or other information that can be used to hold it accountable. However, by accepting these risks, the organization signals its willingness to act to benefit the receipt of the transparency information and in an overall trustworthy manner (Colquitt et al., 2007; Schnackenberg & Tomlinson, 2016).

Circling back to the idea of participatory design, the incorporation of stakeholders in design decisions facilitates the development of technology that matches their needs. By being explicit on how their feedback was incorporated into the system, stakeholders obtain a clear idea of the system's capabilities, rendering interactions more efficient and safe (Dignum, 2019). Otherwise, we risk "participation washing" where participatory design, marketed as a panacea, is used by organizations to obtain free labor, market data, and, ultimately, conduct "ethics washing"

(Sloane et al., 2020). For example, this can take the form of AI ethics councils without actual power to influence and shape organizational policies, or a shifted focus on user responsibility – placing moderation in the hands of the users rather than facing the risks of the technology itself (Bietti, 2020).

A summary of the different aspects of incorporating values into the design of AI in the work context can be seen in Figure 3.1, where we highlight the different questions posed at each stage, as well as the benefits outlined in this chapter.

OPEN CHALLENGES AND RISKS

When it comes to incorporating values in AI, much work has been devoted to governance and democratic procedures, whereas the specifics of how to bring the high-level values set down in guidelines into real applications remain vague. This distance between theory and practice is referred to as the *operationalization* or *abstraction gap* and it is one of the main current challenges in developing trustworthy AI systems (Mittelstadt, 2019; Theodorou & Dignum, 2020). To effectively operationalize values, tools and methods that translate ethical principles into technical specifications are still needed (Brännström et al., 2022; Morley et al., 2021). However, the challenge of bridging the operationalization gap is augmented by the risk of overcompensating in the other direction, and assuming a purely technical point of view towards complex social or cultural values. This is particularly risky in fields where technical approaches provide seemingly simple "patches," such as fairness or privacy methods. For example, technical de-biasing methods rely on the assumption that all fairness issues can be presented as a statistical distribution, leading to altered distributions in which the same individual may be treated differently at different points in time, or to a focus on problems of distribution of goods, bypassing issues of human dignity and representation (Dolata et al., 2022). While these approaches are essential to produce trustworthy AI, a narrow focus on the technical methods forgets the wider lens on the social and institutional barriers that make these tools necessary in the first place (Dolata et al., 2022). Thus, the remaining challenge is to provide operationalizations of values where the socio-technical perspective prevails, particularly in the work context where organizational practices must adhere to the same values as the systems operating within them.

Furthermore, operationalization decisions are made by the developers of a system, tipping the balance of power in the decision-making process in their favor. This means that even with the best interests of the stakeholders in mind, the ultimate decisions for implementation may be taken without their direct input or knowledge, as they may be too technical for stakeholders to weigh in. This gap between stakeholders and developers creates uncertainty over who is ultimately responsible and accountable for ensuring alignment between values and systems. Clarifying the allocation of responsibilities requires a governance layer, specifying which aspects would fall under the responsibility of the developing team, the deploying organization, or other actors (Georgieva et al., 2022). Again, this challenge gains importance in the context of work, where uncertainty about the allocation of responsibilities with respect to technology leads to systems that are never integrated into organizations (Baxter & Sommerville, 2011).

Finally, the idea of incorporating values into intelligent system design and deployment may be appealing to organizations because of optics. Although it is a good incentive, the associated risk is the practice of "ethics washing" (Floridi, 2019), where organizations can claim to have done due diligence in the design of the intelligent systems deployed within their organizations and thereafter shirk regulation (Bietti, 2020). Thus, it is important to highlight that the methods described in this chapter must take place in conjunction with clear and effective regulatory and auditing frameworks.

CONCLUSION

Embedding values into the intelligent systems that will be deployed at work is a necessity if we aim to produce trustworthy technology that will be safely adopted. Doing so requires a shift from high-level statements to concrete implementable requirements that put such values into practice. In this chapter, we have given an overview on the ideas and techniques leading to operationalizing trustworthy AI: from selecting values and their meaning to implementing them within a system and throughout the entire organizational process. Ensuring these steps means producing systems that fit within organizational processes and can be understood and assessed, therefore boosting efficiency and safety. Ethically and value-aligned technology comes with its challenges. Continued research in this area focuses on closing the operationalization gap and continuing to advocate for a broad, socio-technical perspective on the challenges of accountability and trustworthiness. For AI at work, incorporating stakeholders' values empowers workers to use the tools they are provided with to their full potential, calibrating their expectations and overall accounting for the processes that surround the system.

REFERENCES

Aldewereld, H., Dignum, V., & Tan, Y. (2015). Design for values in software development. In J. van den Hoven, P. E. Vermaas, & I. van de Poel (Eds), *Handbook of Ethics, Values, and Technological Design* (pp. 831–845). Springer Netherlands.

Aler Tubella, A., Theodorou, A., Dignum, F., & Dignum, V. (2019). Governance by glass-box: Implementing transparent moral bounds for AI behaviour. *Proceedings of the Twenty-Eighth International Joint Conference on Artificial Intelligence.*

Aler Tubella, A., Theodorou, A., Dignum, V., & Michael, L. (2020). Contestable black boxes. In *Lecture Notes in Computer Science, 12173 LNCS*, 159–167.

Aler Tubella, A., Barsotti, F., Koçer, R. G., & Mendez, J. A. (2022). Ethical implications of fairness interventions: What might be hidden behind engineering choices? *Ethics and Information Technology, 24*(1), 12.

Alesina, A., & Angeletos, G.-M. (2005). Fairness and redistribution. *American Economic Review, 95*(4), 960–980.

Baxter, G., & Sommerville, I. (2011). Socio-technical systems: From design methods to systems engineering. *Interacting with Computers, 23*(1), 4–17.

Bellamy, R. K. E., Mojsilovic, A., Nagar, S., Ramamurthy, K. N., Richards, J., Saha, D. et al. (2019). AI fairness 360: An extensible toolkit for detecting and mitigating algorithmic bias. *IBM Journal of Research and Development, 63*(4–5).

Bietti, E. (2020). From ethics washing to ethics bashing: A view on tech ethics from within moral philosophy. *Proceedings of the 2020 Conference on Fairness, Accountability, and Transparency*, 210–219.

Bird, S., Dudík, M., Edgar, R., Horn, B., Lutz, R., Milan, V., Sameki, M., Wallach, H., & Walker, K. (2020). Fairlearn: A toolkit for assessing and improving fairness in AI (Issue MSR-TR-2020-32). Microsoft. www.microsoft. com/en-us/research/publication/fairlearn-a-toolkit-for-assessing-and-improving-fairness-in-ai/

Brännström, M., Theodorou, A., & Dignum, V. (2022). Let it RAIN for social good. *IJCAI 2022 Workshop on AI safety.*

Brundage, M., Avin, S., Wang, J., Belfield, H., Krueger, G., Hadfield, G. et al. (2020). Toward trustworthy AI development: Mechanisms for supporting verifiable claims. arXiv: 2004.07213.

Bryson, J. J., & Theodorou, A. (2019). How society can maintain human-centric artificial intelligence. In T. M. & S. E. (Eds), *Human-Centered Digitalization and Services* (pp. 305–323). Springer.

Clegg, C. W. (2000). Sociotechnical principles for system design. *Applied Ergonomics, 31*(5), 463–477.

Colquitt, J., Scott, B., & LePine, J. (2007). Trust, trustworthiness, and trust propensity: A meta-analytic test of their unique relationships with risk taking and job performance. *Journal of Applied Psychology, 92*, 909–927.

Costanza-Chock, S. (2020). Design justice. https://doi.org/10.7551/mitpress/12255.001.0001

Dignum, V. (2019). *Responsible Artificial Intelligence: How to Develop and Use AI in a Responsible Way.* Springer.

Dolata, M., Feuerriegel, S., & Schwabe, G. (2022). A sociotechnical view of algorithmic fairness. *Information Systems Journal, 32*(4), 754–818.

Dwork, C., Immorlica, N., Tauman Kalai, A., & Leiserson, M. (2017). Decoupled classifiers for fair and efficient machine learning. arXiv: 1707.06613.

European Commission, Directorate-General for Communications Networks, Content and Technology. (2019). Ethics guidelines for trustworthy AI. https://doi.org/10.2759/346720

Floridi, L. (2019). Translating principles into practices of digital ethics: Five risks of being unethical. *Philosophy & Technology*, *32*(2), 185–193.

Floridi, L., & Cowls, J. (2019). A unified framework of five principles for AI in society. *Harvard Data Science Review*, *1*(1).

Floridi, L., Cowls, J., King, T. C., & Taddeo, M. (2020). How to design AI for social good: Seven essential factors. *Science and Engineering Ethics*, *26*(3), 1771–1796.

Friedman, B. (1996). Value-sensitive design. *ACM Interactions*, *3*(6), 16–23.

Friedman, B., Kahn, P. H., & Borning, A. (2006). Value sensitive design and information systems. In P. Zhang & D. F. Galletta (Eds), *Human-Computer Interaction and Management Information Systems: Foundations: Foundations* (Vol. 5, pp. 348–372). Routledge.

Georgieva, I., Lazo, C., Timan, T., & van Veenstra, A. F. (2022). From AI ethics principles to data science practice: A reflection and a gap analysis based on recent frameworks and practical experience. *AI and Ethics*. https://doi.org/10.1007/s43681-021-00127-3

Glass, A., McGuinness, D. L., & Wolverton, M. (2008). Toward establishing trust in adaptive agents. *Proceedings of the 13th International Conference on Intelligent User Interfaces*, 227. https://doi.org/10.1145/1378773.1378804

Holzinger, A., Langs, G., Denk, H., Zatloukal, K., & Müller, H. (2019). Causability and explainability of artificial intelligence in medicine. *WIREs Data Mining and Knowledge Discovery*, *9*(4), e1312.

IEEE Global Initiative on Ethics of Autonomous and Intelligent Systems. (2019). Ethically aligned design: A vision for prioritizing human well-being with autonomous and intelligent systems. IEEE Standards Association. https://standards.ieee.org/industry-connections/ec/autonomous-systems.html

Jakesch, M., Buçinca, Z., Amershi, S., & Olteanu, A. (2022). How different groups prioritize ethical values for responsible AI. https://doi.org/10.1145/3531146.3533097

Kearns, M., Neel, S., Roth, A., & Wu, Z. S. (2018). Preventing fairness gerrymandering: Auditing and learning for subgroup fairness. *International Conference on Machine Learning*, 2564–2572.

Lee, J. D., & See, K. A. (2004). Trust in automation: Designing for appropriate reliance. *Human Factors: Journal of the Human Factors and Ergonomics Society*, *46*(1), 50–80.

Makarius, E. E., Mukherjee, D., Fox, J. D., & Fox, A. K. (2020). Rising with the machines: A sociotechnical framework for bringing artificial intelligence into the organization. *Journal of Business Research*, *120*, 262–273.

Methnani, L., Aler Tubella, A., Dignum, V., & Theodorou, A. (2021). Let me take over: Variable autonomy for meaningful human control. *Frontiers in Artificial Intelligence*, *4*, 737072.

Miller, T. (2019). Explanation in artificial intelligence: Insights from the social sciences. *Artificial Intelligence*, *267*, 1–38.

Mittelstadt, B. (2019). Principles alone cannot guarantee ethical AI. *Nature Machine Intelligence*, *1*(11), 501–507.

Morley, J., Elhalal, A., Garcia, F., Kinsey, L., Mökander, J., & Floridi, L. (2021). Ethics as a service: A pragmatic operationalisation of AI ethics. *Minds and Machines*, *31*(2), 239–256.

Muller, M. J., & Kuhn, S. (1993). Participatory design. *Communications of the ACM*, *36*(6), 24–28.

OECD. (2021). National AI policies and strategies. www.oecd.ai/countries-and-initiatives/

Raji, I. D., Smart, A., White, R. N., Mitchell, M., Gebru, T., Hutchinson, B., Smith-Loud, J., Theron, D., & Barnes, P. (2020). Closing the AI accountability gap: Defining an end-to-end framework for internal algorithmic auditing. arXiv: 2001.00973.

Roberson, Q., King, E., & Hebl, M. (2020). Designing more effective practices for reducing workplace inequality. *Behavioral Science & Policy*, *6*(1), 39–49.

Santoni de Sio, F., & van den Hoven, J. (2018). Meaningful human control over autonomous systems: A philosophical account. *Frontiers in Robotics and AI*, *5*, 15.

Schnackenberg, A. K., & Tomlinson, E. C. (2016). Organizational transparency: A new perspective on managing trust in organization–stakeholder relationships. *Journal of Management*, *42*(7), 1784–1810.

Sloane, M., Moss, E., Awomolo, O., & Forlano, L. (2020). Participation is not a design fix for machine learning. *Proceedings of the 37th International Conference on Machine Learning*, 7.

Straub, D., Keil, M., & Brenner, W. (1997). Testing the technology acceptance model across cultures: A three country study. *Information & Management*, *33*(1), 1–11.

Theodorou, A., & Dignum, V. (2020). Towards ethical and socio-legal governance in AI. *Nature Machine Intelligence*, *2*(1), 10–12.

Theodorou, A., Wortham, R. H., & Bryson, J. J. (2017). Designing and implementing transparency for real time inspection of autonomous robots. *Connection Science*, *29*(3), 230–241.

Turiel, E. (2001). *The culture of morality*. Cambridge University Press.

Umbrello, S., & van de Poel, I. (2021). Mapping value sensitive design onto AI for social good principles. *AI and Ethics*, *1*(3), 283–296.

van de Poel, I. (2013). Translating values into design requirements. *Philosophy and Engineering: Reflections on Practice, Principles and Process*, *15*, 253–266.

van de Poel, I. (2020). Embedding values in artificial intelligence (AI) systems. *Minds and Machines*, *30*(3), 385–409.

Van Den Hoven, M. J. (2005). Design for values and values for design. *Information Age*, August/September(2), 4–7.

van der Velden, M., & Mörtberg, C. (2014). Participatory design and design for values. In J. van den Hoven, P. E. Vermaas, & I. van de Poel (Eds), *Handbook of Ethics, Values, and Technological Design: Sources, Theory, Values and Application Domains* (pp. 1–22). Springer Netherlands.

Winby, S., & Mohrman, S. A. (2018). Digital sociotechnical system design. *Journal of Applied Behavioral Science*, *54*(4), 399–423.

Winfield, A. F. T., Booth, S., Dennis, L. A., Egawa, T., Hastie, H., Jacobs, N. et al. (2021). IEEE P7001: A proposed standard on transparency. *Frontiers in Robotics and AI*, *8*, 665729.

Yang, J. R., & Liu, J. (2021, January 19). Strengthening accountability for discrimination: Confronting fundamental power imbalances in the employment

relationship. Economic Policy Institute. www.epi.org/unequalpower/publications/
strengthening-accountability-for-discrimination-confronting-fundamental-power-
imbalances-in-the-employment-relationship/
Zemel, R., Wu, Y., Swersky, K., Pitassi, T., & Dwork, C. (2013). Learning fair
representations. *30th International Conference on Machine Learning*, 1362–1370.
Zuboff, S. (1989). *The Age of the Smart Machine: The Future of Work and Power*
(2nd ed.). Basic Books.

4. AI-enabled business model and human-in-the-loop (deceptive AI): implications for labor
Uma Rani and Rishabh Kumar Dhir

INTRODUCTION

Advances in digital technologies, computing power, machine learning, and artificial intelligence (AI) have reinvigorated concerns over automation's implications for jobs and the labor markets.[1] Despite claims of an impending "AI-driven transition to a post-work world" and a surge in AI-focused start-ups hoping to automate jobs (Bangert, 2022; Toews, 2021), this discourse is increasingly being challenged by researchers. The notion of what is being portrayed as AI is also under scrutiny. According to a group of experts set up by the European Commission, AI has been defined as an "algorithmic system of analysis that, thanks to large amounts of data, is able to extract patterns and make predictions by mimicking functions that humans associate with their own intelligence" (Aloisi & De Stefano, 2022, p. 65). While machine learning can enable an algorithm to be trained to accomplish tasks, including those that may be challenging to codify and automate, there are still non-routine tasks that workers will be required to perform where they hold comparative advantage over AI or machines (Autor, 2015).

The emergence of AI-enabled business models in the digital economy has led to the development of new tools, products, and services that enhance the efficiency and functioning of the digital ecosystem. The growth of these businesses is largely driven by the availability of vast amounts of financial resources from governments, the private sector, and venture capital funds (Nitzberg et al., 2019), as well as low-cost information technology (IT) and cloud infrastructure. This has allowed many entrepreneurs to enter the market with low investment in physical infrastructure and set up AI companies to provide a range of services. Additionally, advances in AI and natural language processing have made it possible for start-ups to

---

[1] The authors would like to thank Marianne Furrer and Nora Gobel for their assistance with data analysis for this chapter.

advertise and sell their services to businesses as AI-enabled. Such services may result in lowering costs for firms through the replacement of workers with AI or it may help in improving productivity through augmentation.

Despite the prevailing discourse of automation associated with AI, research has been highlighting the growing reliance of the AI industry on invisible and often precarious workers, and the need to focus on the human labor needed to produce or service AI (Aloisi & De Stefano, 2022; Casilli, 2021; ILO, 2021; Irani, 2016; Tubaro et al., 2020), as well as on the workers performing the tasks that are portrayed to be performed by AI (Casilli, 2021; ILO, 2021). Such activities are identified as digital labor, which "designates datified and taskified human activities," including on-demand labor, microwork, and crowdworkers (Casilli, 2021, p. 117). Workers are key to the preparation and verification of AI, and many are performing tasks at the back end of what tends to be portrayed as AI in the front end (Ludec et al., 2023; Aloisi & De Stefano, 2022; ILO, 2021; Tubaro et al., 2020). Human workers are also being managed dispassionately through algorithmic management practices and performing simple and repetitive tasks (ILO, 2021). In many sectors, the role of human workers remains vital despite the portrayal of AI as taking over their jobs.

The emergence of AI-enabled business models has three major implications on work and workers. Firstly, it highlights the shift towards contingent work arrangements on digital labor platforms, which provide access to a global pool of digital labor. They may provide flexibility but also lead to precarious working conditions and weaken the bargaining power of workers. Secondly, humans play an important role in generating data and training algorithms, which may lead to the deskilling of workers and the creation of a global sweatshop of digital labor. This trend is concerning as it risks replacing or displacing highly skilled and professionally certified workers in various fields. Thirdly, these AI-enabled models can change the organization of work, and can contribute to lower labor share in income, polarization of the workforce, and increase income inequality.

This chapter examines AI-enabled business models in low-end (such as image annotation, labeling, and content moderation) and high-end services (like translation, legal and medical transcription), and the level of automation and human involvements in these models, based on existing literature. It shows that the human-in-the-loop process remains important in these AI-enabled models as algorithms are not yet accurate and these models rely heavily on human labor for training, development, monitoring, and service of the AI. The chapter will also analyze the impact of this process on workers' working conditions, income, social security, and skill development. Specifically, it will focus on tasks such as labeling, image annotation, transcription, translation, and content moderation, drawing on surveys of workers on microtask platforms conducted in 2017. The chapter concludes with a discussion on how these AI-enabled business models are transforming the nature of employment and its relationship as work is outsourced to crowdworkers on digital labor platforms, raising concerns about the quality of jobs in terms of both working conditions and the content of the task.

EXPLORING THE POTENTIAL FOR AI PENETRATION IN INDUSTRIES AND OCCUPATIONS: WHAT DOES THE EMPIRICAL EVIDENCE SHOW?

There are numerous potential applications of AI across various industries and occupations. This section explores some of these applications and examines the extent to which human labor is involved in the process. According to a study by Tubaro and Casilli (2019), the potential application of AI in the automotive industry includes self-driving cars, on-board virtual assistants with speech interfaces to assist drivers in focusing on the road, safety features that recognize a driver's emotions, and targeted marketing based on a driver's preference and behavior. However, the study notes that many AI applications, like autonomous vehicles, rely on machine-learning algorithms that necessitate large datasets with appropriately labeled and annotated information, such as images of pedestrians, dogs, traffic lights, or other vehicles. This process requires human input, and autonomous vehicle manufacturers often outsource this work to crowdworkers through platforms that fragment tasks into small ones, including image classification, object detection or tagging, landmark detection, and semantic segmentation. Schmidt (2019) adds that automotive firms require large amounts of high-quality AI training data. For example, a full semantic segmentation[2] of an image may take a worker up to two hours to complete. If done in-house, the high demand for high-precision and high-quality data could increase costs for these companies, which is why they often outsource this work to platforms and business process outsourcing companies (BPOs). The need for such high-precision data has also led to the growth of specialized platforms like Mighty AI, Scale AI,

---

[2]   Semantic segmentation requires assigning every dot in an image associated with an object based on a list of relevant types for pixel-level object detection. Images are classified based on different parameters such as quality, content, or setting.

Hive, and Playment that cater specifically to the needs of the automotive industry and AI research (ILO, 2021; Schmidt, 2019). Platforms like Uber also rely on data generated by drivers who are independent contractors and not paid for this data to train its algorithms (ILO, 2021).

Speech interfaces for AI-assisted driving, similar to autonomous vehicles, require microworkers to perform various tasks. Tubaro and Casilli (2019) explain that workers record their voices in order to produce data to train virtual assistants by using different words, short sentences, or asking questions in multiple ways. The audio data require annotation for recognizing them under different scenarios, and human input is required to detect or assess pronunciation, accents, or sentiments. Additionally, there is a need to produce and annotate visual and sound data for monitoring drivers' behavior and offering targeted advertising.

The need for microworkers to assist virtual assistants is not limited to the automotive industry but also extends to other occupations such as secretarial tasks (for instance, scheduling meetings) (ILO, 2021; Tubaro et al., 2020). To train virtual assistants that respond to audio, a large number of workers is required to capture a variety of accents, pronunciations, and sentiments, and they must undertake tasks such as recording the same sentence or asking the same question in multiple ways. Additionally, workers are needed to verify if the virtual assistant understood what was said by the user (Tubaro et al., 2020). This verification involves workers listening to a recording and comparing it with the transcript produced by the virtual assistant. It may also include tasks such as adding tags to parts of the transcribed text to better understand its performance. However, even after the provision of human input, virtual assistants are far from functioning autonomously. As an International Labour Organization (ILO) report (2021) shows, even a simple task such as scheduling a meeting based on an email can be challenging, since AI still struggles to understand the idiosyncratic requirements of clients, such as "Hey, I can do a call next week." This situation thus requires human intelligence, and hence virtual assistants, although marketed as fully automated by start-ups, may operate within a human-in-the-loop system. The ILO report (2021) found that in the case of a workplace virtual assistant start-up for scheduling meetings, microworkers were operating at the back end through a platform. They would extract different parameters from an email regarding setting up a meeting, training the AI, checking if the parameters were being correctly used, and making the required corrections if needed. Similarly, Aloisi and De Stefano (2022) note that while Facebook was testing a virtual assistant that was seen to be effective, it turned out that humans were behind it (see also Wagner, 2015).

French AI companies have been offering automatic checkout machines and automated video surveillance for theft detection which are deployed in the retail industry, and heavily rely on human labour in Madagascar (Ludec et al., 2023). While the computer vision model for the checkout machines is designed in France, the data annotation tasks to train the model is done by workers in Madagascar. Similarly, the AI surveillance system functions based on the thefts detected by the workers in Madagascar in less than a minute based on a livestreamed video, who effectively work as remote security guards, which further feeds into the model. Similarly, consumer goods, such as "vacuum cleaner robots", also often need humans for their training so that they can recognize or avoid obstacles, and often these tasks are outsourced by companies to microworkers in developing countries. For example, a microworker in Brazil spent two days "moving her dog's poop" and took more than 250 photographs in her home so as to generate training data for a vacuum cleaner to avoid animal excrements, while being paid only a few cents for each photograph (Matheus et al., 2023, p. 17).

Another area where AI is gaining popularity is in the field of translation, as machine learning can predict how a human would translate text from one language to another (Agrawal et al., 2019). Machine translation on eBay (eMT) uses statistical models for phrase-to-phrase translations and automatically scraps data from the internet to improve the quality of translations. This helped in a 17.5 percent increase of exports on eBay (Brynjolfsson et al., 2018). The study also notes that human language experts post-edit the outputs using machine-assisted human translation to further improve the quality of translations. While this improves translation quality, eMT generates high-quality translations within milliseconds in real time. Agrawal et al. (2019) argue that AI can augment human labor associated with online buying and selling by providing translation that enhances trading activities.

Kenny (2022) highlights the ongoing relevance of human translators in machine translation. Human translators play a crucial role in training machine translation systems, as well as evaluating and diagnosing issues in their output. Machine translation has become increasingly popular, with applications in expanding search engine capabilities, conversing in different languages, and translating audio-visual content. To reduce errors, evaluation and post-editing of output, as well as pre-editing of source texts to simplify translation, are common practices in the industry. Human translators also utilize computer-assisted translation, including machine translation engines, which can be outsourced to platform workers as microtasks (Garcia, 2017). Some tools, such as KantanLQR (Language Quality Review), aid human evaluators of machine translation output, based on specific quality criteria, and allow them to compare multiple outputs (Rossi & Carré, 2022).

However, there are limits to machine translation. Taivalkoski-Shilov's (2019) research in the context of literary texts suggests that while machine translation may make the translator's work faster, there are concerns regarding translation quality as well as ethical issues such as the risk of altering the meaning of the source text. Additionally, the notion of "voice" in literary texts poses challenges for machine translation, as it may homogenize the style of different authors or heterogenize the style of one author. Machine translation may also result in segmentation and fragmentation, translating without context, and undermining the creativity of the translator (Moorkens et al., 2018).

Moorkens (2022) also notes that while translation is a highly skilled task, many aspects of the workflow have become automated, including "automatic job assignment, the imposition of post-editing, and the repurposing of translation data for tasks that translators may not expect" (p. 132). Further, the large freelance workforce in translation has also resulted in translators having little control over processes and conditions, which are often unilaterally determined by agencies or employers. There is a power imbalance as translators work on a project-by-project basis, and there is a growing disconnect between the workers and the companies.

The field of transcription is also increasingly utilizing AI, given that the core skill of transcribers is "predicting which words to type upon hearing a recording" (Agrawal et al., 2019, p. 48). However, automatic speech recognition (ASR)-based transcription still faces limitations and is more prevalent for well-represented languages such as English or Spanish. Vashistha et al. (2017) discuss the case of Respeak engine, which combines ASR with crowdsourcing. The engine fragments and distributes audio files to workers who listen to the audio, repeat the same words in a quiet environment, and then transcribe the segment with the help of the ASR system. The worker submits the transcript segment, and the Respeak engine combines the outputs from multiple users. The submitted transcript is compared to the best estimation transcript obtained using multiple string alignment and the majority voting system, which determines the worker's reward. Respeak can be used to transcribe audio files in local languages and localized accents.

In the context of music transcription, Samiotis et al. (2021) argue that optical music recognition systems are insufficient for music transcription. They instead recommend a hybrid approach that incorporates workers on microtask platforms to check for the accuracy of the algorithmic results, provide solutions when the algorithm fails, and improve substandard results. They also found that task design was crucial for effective performance by the 144 workers on Amazon Mechanical Turk (AMT) who executed the tasks, even when formal knowledge of music among workers was rare. Worker performance improved when they were provided with audio extracts of the target music score. The authors conclude that "hybrid crowdsourcing workflows" can combine the efficiency of algorithms with the cognitive power and insight of humans (Samiotis et al., 2021, p. 26). Aloisi and De Stefano (2022) also note that audio transcription services are marketed as automatic, despite the fact that these tasks are performed by workers.

The use of AI in the medical sector is gaining prominence, particularly in automating medical transcription and medical image analysis (Gifu, 2022; Ørting et al., 2020). AI-based transcription services are used to transcribe reports in radiology, which have been recorded earlier and sent to a human transcriber (Agrawal et al., 2019). However, there are concerns regarding the accuracy of AI-based tools and errors could have significant consequences for patients (Reader, 2020; Silverberg, 2022). AI methods are more likely to be assimilated in the practice of radiology and, given the complex nature of biology, radiologists are less likely to be replaced (Thrall et al., 2018). AI-based systems have also been proposed for voice-based prescription generation, but medical professionals still need to spend time recalling patient information into a computer (Ghadage et al., 2021). AI-based approaches have shown some important experimental outcomes, particularly in detecting COVID-19 based on CT scan images, which can be utilized to improve the performance of radiologists and increase the speed of diagnosis (Ghayvat et al., 2022). However, challenges remain regarding the availability and size of data needed to train machine-learning algorithms for medical image analysis (Ørting et al., 2020). "Human-based computation" through crowdsourcing has been suggested as a more efficient and cost-effective way to overcome these limitations (Petrović et al., 2020, p. 2447). This study also shows that crowdsourcing can be utilized for annotation, segmentation, and classification of tasks related to medical imaging. These crowd annotators are utilized for training machine-learning algorithms related to medical images.

The use of AI in legal services has potential for both substituting and augmenting tasks. Armour and Sako (2020) suggest a workflow for introducing AI, which involves human input at every step such as problem definition, testing, data preparation, output review, and evaluating implications. The input is required from legal experts, as well as data scientists, software engineers, information security experts, project managers, and design thinkers. However, the adoption of AI is more likely in corporate legal services than in consumer legal services due to the lack of large-scale data availability for machine learning and the high costs associated with labelling training data for legal services. Furthermore, aspects of legal services that require comprehensive interactions with clients or problem solving creatively will be difficult to automate. While AI may feature as part of the workflow in litigation, it will not replace human lawyers. In contrast, AI could be scaled in contract analytics and legal research, with lawyers still labeling legal data points and interpreting results to interface with clients. Yamane (2020) raises ethical concerns about the use of AI in legal services. However, Armour and Sako (2020) show that the growth of new business models within legal services is driven by the use of AI, including legal operations, legal technology, and consulting. Legal process outsourcing (LPO) (Brudenall, 2011) has also emerged as a way to outsource routine tasks to third-party companies, which can reduce costs but may have risks.

More recently, ChatGPT, an AI-powered "virtual assistant" focused on language-based tasks, has gained a lot of attention since its launch in November 2022. It provides information or assistance to users in a conversation format. ChatGPT is a large language model, which is a machine-learning system that "autonomously learns from data" by training on a massive dataset of text to produce sophisticated results (van Dis et al., 2023, p. 224). However, there are concerns that AI technology such as ChatGPT may replace knowledge workers, especially in fields such as content writing, computer programming, coding, and financial analysis (Stahl, 2023). There have been debates regarding the impacts of these AI systems on jobs and occupations, and whether it would lead to automation or augmentation to improve worker productivity (Brynjolfsson et al., 2023; Chui et al., 2023; Dell'Acqua et al., 2023; Gmyrek et al., 2023; Lorenz et al., 2023). Although this technology may free up workers from routine or repetitive tasks, human verification remains crucial for accountability, particularly to prevent human automation bias (van Dis et al., 2023; Zarifhonarvar, 2023). Additionally, despite ChatGPT's strong performance in tasks such as summarization and machine translation, it still exhibits some failures and raises trust issues, especially as it can "hallucinate" to produce incorrect but convincing information (Bang et al., 2023; Lorenz et al., 2023). Therefore, addressing such errors requires human intervention. Moreover, some tasks will always require human judgment and creativity, making it highly unlikely for AI systems to replace humans entirely (Zarifhonarvar, 2023). It has also been argued that in advanced economies in particular, where high skilled jobs are most exposed to AI systems, there may be risks of labour substitution but also the greatest benefits for productivity (Pizzinelli et al., 2023).

However, despite the promise of augmentation and productivity increases from such systems, the strike action in 2023 by the Writer's Guild of America (the union representing screenwriters across the creative industries in the United States) has underlined that issues around such

AI technology are rooted in labour relations. Unions have thus started to raise concerns regarding the augmentation, reclassification and exploitation of human labour by, as well as in the name of such AI systems (Leaver & Srdarov, 2023).

Furthermore, the role of humans remains crucial for the back end of AI systems such as ChatGPT, which also raises concerns about the workers who have enabled the development and operation of such systems. Despite the hype around the automated learning of ChatGPT, its website emphasizes the use of human trainers, stating, "We trained an initial model using supervised fine-tuning: human AI trainers provided conversations in which they played both sides – the user and an AI assistant. We gave the trainers access to model-written suggestions to help them compose their responses" (Open AI, 2022). The growing popularity of such language models has resulted in a greater need for such data that is specific to a country and language, which has led to a demand for crowdworkers in some developing countries to increasingly train such algorithms to generate content, as observed in Brazil (Matheus et al., 2023).

The growth of platforms and the large amount of information circulating online has led to the emergence of content moderation as an important field. Companies have been using AI systems for detecting and removing harmful content, but the power of such automation has been under scrutiny. Humans remain indispensable and continue to play a key role in performing content moderation functions (Whittaker, 2020), often facing serious mental health implications due to the explicit content they have to screen. Despite claims of advances in AI, human judgment is still necessary, and often these workers are hired on contracts rather than as regular full-time employees, lacking any mental health support. Recently, a former content moderator sued Meta and its contractor Sama for providing misleading information about the nature of the work and inadequate psychosocial support (BBC, 2022). Furthermore, although AI tools have been proposed as a means to protect human moderators from harmful content, such systems often lack decisional transparency or accountability. As a result, they risk operating as invisible infrastructure that are not neutral and may instead reinforce existing social or racial inequalities (Gorwa et al., 2020; Siapera, 2022). This is particularly worrisome because platforms rely on automated systems to manage abusive content in order to ensure continued user engagement, rather than address the issues of racism or discrimination faced by marginalized groups on these platforms (Siapera, 2022).

Based on existing literature, AI-enabled businesses provide a variety of AI applications to companies, either fully automated or human-powered, in areas like virtual assistants, legal services, and microtasks such as labeling and image annotation. These businesses typically have two profiles – one for clients and another for crowdworkers. Crowdworkers are fundamental to train AI models to infer patterns correctly, which is initially required for developing the AI, and in the process subsidize AI development across a range of occupations. As a result, the AI systems operate as a human-in-the-loop process, with a worker reviewing the AI analysis and making the final decision. Therefore, the advances in AI and machine learning are not eliminating humans from performing tasks but are transforming and integrating them with machines.

While some argue that AI will never function like humans, others suggest there is a symbiotic relationship between humans and AI that leverages AI's computational power and analytics to enhance collaboration (Jarrahi, 2018). However, scholars have raised important concerns about AI, including their opacity and the risk of biased algorithms due to how they are designed and trained (Aloisi & De Stefano, 2022; Gorwa et al., 2020; Siapera, 2022). Moreover, it is crucial to consider the challenges arising from AI systems, which are intended to replace or augment humans but are developed, improved, and sustained through the exploitation of human labor, often by workers in developing countries. The building, developing, and maintaining of an AI system are highly dependent on invisible crowdworkers, unpaid workers on microtask platforms, and low-paid workers in BPOs. Such workers increasingly form an intrinsic part of the evolving global AI supply chains, where interdependencies are often asymmetric and the cross-border nature of AI production, servicing and deployment can allow companies to minimize legal accountability while maximizing commercial benefits (Cobbe et al., 2023).

WORKERS BEHIND AI AND MACHINE LEARNING: PROFILE OF CROWDWORKERS

The analysis in this section draws on a survey conducted by the ILO between February and May 2017 on five platforms – AMT, CrowdFlower, Clickworker, Microworkers, and Prolific – with a sample of 2,350 respondents. The survey aimed to better understand the type of tasks performed by workers, their motivations for working on these platforms, their socio-demographic backgrounds, and their work histories. The survey also explored workers' working conditions, including hours worked, earnings, work safety, and social protection. The workers on these microtask platforms performed two types of task. The first type related to AI and machine learning, such as data collection, categorization, image annotation, translation, transcription, and audio and image recording. The second type related to promoting products, such as content access, market research, and reviews. In this chapter, the analysis focuses on workers who performed tasks related to AI and machine learning. The sample size for this group is 1,632, which represents almost 70 percent of the total sample. The survey results indicate that this type of work is mainly concentrated in urban areas, with 80 percent of the workers residing in urban or suburban communities. The sample of workers came from 75 countries, with representation from Brazil, India, Indonesia, Nigeria, and the United States, as well as both Western and Eastern Europe (for more details see Berg et al., 2018).

Of these workers, almost 60 percent resided in advanced economies, while 40 percent resided in developing countries. The overall gender balance was quite uneven, with only one out of three workers in the total sample being a woman. However, there was some gender balance in advanced economies, with 54 percent men and 46 percent women. In contrast, in developing countries there was a major gender gap, with only one out of four workers being a woman. Such a gender divide can have implications for bias in an AI system, given that it is trained and serviced with limited data on and participation from women. The average age of workers surveyed was 33.3 years, ranging from 18 to 71 years. In developing countries, the average age was lower, at 31 years old, compared to advanced economies, where the average age was 35 years old. Interestingly, the average age of women (36 years old) was higher than that of men (32 years old).

The crowdworkers performing AI and machine-learning tasks were generally well educated, with only 34 percent having less than a high school education. These proportions were higher in advanced economies (40.5 percent) compared to developing countries (25 percent). Approximately 65 percent of the workers had a bachelor's or post-graduate degree (Figure 4.1). Interestingly, a higher proportion of workers in developing countries (74 percent) had a bachelor's degree or higher compared to advanced economies (59 percent).

The survey findings show that the majority of workers engaged in AI and machine-learning tasks hold bachelor's or post-graduate degrees. A further analysis of this high level of education by different disciplines reveals impressive education profiles and interesting differences between advanced and developing countries (Figure 4.2). Approximately 47 percent of workers are specialized in science and technology (14 percent in medicine and natural sciences, 14 percent in engineering, and 19 percent in IT and computers). While a higher proportion of workers in developing countries have a background in engineering and IT,

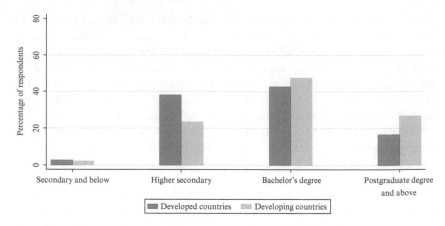

Source: Authors' calculations based on ILO global survey of workers on microtask platforms, 2017.

Figure 4.1   Education level of workers performing AI and machine-learning tasks

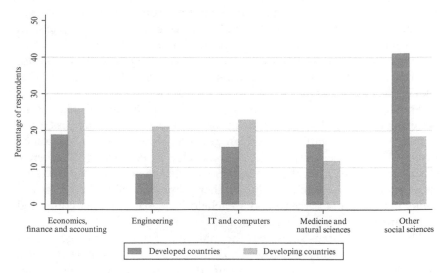

Source: Authors' calculations based on ILO global survey of workers on microtask platforms, 2017.

Figure 4.2   Field of education of workers performing AI and machine-learning tasks

the proportion of workers in medicine and natural sciences is higher in advanced economies. Additionally, 22 percent specialize in economics, finance, and accounting, while the remaining 31 percent have been educated in humanities and other social sciences, which is quite high in advanced economies (Figure 4.2).

TASKS UNDERTAKEN BY WORKERS FOR TRAINING AI-ENABLED BUSINESS MODELS

The tasks performed by highly educated workers on these platforms include categorization (including image annotation), data collection, content moderation, audio and image recording, verification, and translation and transcription. These tasks are typically short and repetitive and are distributed among a large pool of crowdworkers. The tasks require human cognition and have been described as "cognitive piecework" (Irani, 2015) and "human computation" (von Ahn, 2005). While it is possible that some tasks might be automated in the future, others are unlikely to be, as they require human input. Although some tasks like content creation and editing, speech transcription, and translation require higher skill sets, they can also be broken down into smaller microtasks (Cheng et al., 2015), potentially leading to deskilling. According to the ILO global survey of workers, data collection was the most commonly reported task (51 percent), followed by translation and transcription (42 percent) and categorization (35 percent). Workers from developing countries had a higher proportion of data collection (58 percent) and translation and transcription tasks (53 percent) compared to those in developed countries (Figure 4.3). Fewer workers were engaged in content moderation, audio and image recording, and verification.

In addition, many microtask platforms generate new datasets for training AI and machine-learning models using crowdworkers. For example, Clickworker gathers large amounts of high-quality AI training data from the crowd when there is not sufficient data available on the web. This enables the platform to provide its clients with a unique and newly created dataset for a specific project, which can be used for training AI and machine-learning models. Figure 4.4 provides an example of such a task on a microtask platform.

The example in Figure 4.4 shows that the AI training is for a client who provides a 3D authentication security check tool for companies to prevent fraud on the internet. To achieve this, crowdworkers are asked to upload three videos of themselves with a landscape orientation for 10 to 20 seconds each. Workers who accept this job also give the clients the right

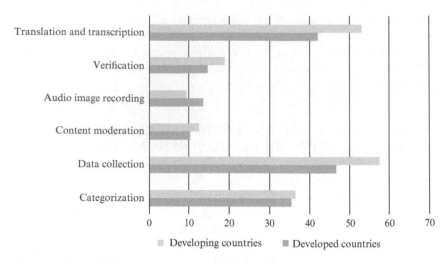

Figure 4.3   AI and machine-learning tasks performed by workers

to save and use the photos containing their personal data to train the AI. Workers are paid €1.50 once the customer validates the uploaded video and the payment is made within 30 days. These tasks are open for a specific period of time (30 days) and the crowd is invited to perform the tasks and is remunerated monetarily. There are potential implications of performing such tasks for workers as well as for their privacy, as workers may be underpaid for their efforts and their personal data could be used without their knowledge or consent in a number of other projects, which may not be mentioned in the advertised task.

Similarly, companies also provide various automated services or AI tools to business clients. One such example is "virtual assistants," which are used for scheduling meetings (ILO, 2021). Despite advancements in technology, automating a virtual assistant is not as easy as one might expect, as AI still requires human-in-the-loop assistance to function effectively. While natural language-processing capabilities are improving, there is still a long way to go before the AI can power the entire workflow process of a particular task and completely replace human workers. Meanwhile, these tasks are outsourced to thousands of invisible workers globally who work on digital labor platforms. An in-depth interview with one of the companies offering this service revealed that human–machine interaction remains critical, and continuous feedback and human judgment are necessary to prompt as well as to review final decisions. Many businesses adopt

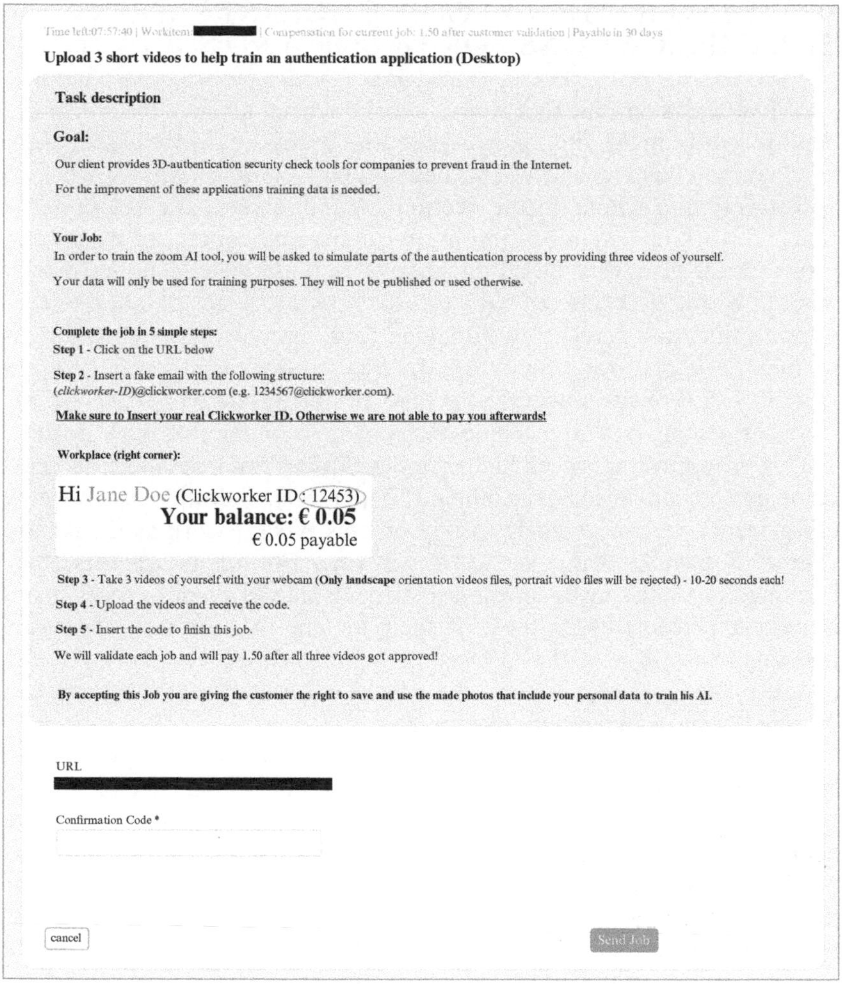

Time left:07:57:40 | Workitem: ███████ | Compensation for current job: 1.50 after customer validation | Payable in 30 days

Upload 3 short videos to help train an authentication application (Desktop)

Task description

Goal:

Our client provides 3D-authentication security check tools for companies to prevent fraud in the Internet.

For the improvement of these applications training data is needed.

Your Job:

In order to train the zoom AI tool, you will be asked to simulate parts of the authentication process by providing three videos of yourself.

Your data will only be used for training purposes. They will not be published or used otherwise.

Complete the job in 5 simple steps:

Step 1 - Click on the URL below

Step 2 - Insert a fake email with the following structure:
(*clickworker-ID*)@clickworker.com (e.g. 1234567@clickworker.com).

Make sure to Insert your real Clickworker ID. Otherwise we are not able to pay you afterwards!

Workplace (right corner):

Hi Jane Doe (Clickworker ID: 12453)
Your balance: € 0.05
€ 0.05 payable

Step 3 - Take 3 videos of yourself with your webcam (**Only landscape** orientation videos files, portrait video files will be rejected) - 10-20 seconds each!

Step 4 - Upload the videos and receive the code.

Step 5 - Insert the code to finish this job.

We will validate each job and will pay 1.50 after all three videos got approved!

By accepting this Job you are giving the customer the right to save and use the made photos that include your personal data to train his AI.

URL
████████████████

Confirmation Code *

cancel   Send Job

Source: Screenshot of a task on Clickworker, posted in March 2023.

Figure 4.4   Example of a video creation task for AI and machine learning on a microtask platform

virtual assistant technology with the belief that AI processes their requests, but these tasks are performed by workers in developing countries. An ILO survey of 300 online home-based workers in the Philippines revealed that around 14 percent of the respondents were working as "virtual assistants" for clients based in Australia, Canada, the Philippines, and the United States (King-Dejardin, 2021).

WORKING IN THE AI LOOP: UNDERSTANDING THE IMPLICATIONS FOR LABOR AND SOCIETY

As AI systems continue to advance, workers from all over the world are deployed to train AI and machine-learning processes, as well as to clean and maintain them regularly. This has significant implications for workers and society as a whole. In this section, we will explore the key implications on working conditions (both job quality and content of work) and future career prospects, based on surveys and interviews conducted with workers by the ILO between 2017 and 2019. Due to a lack of labor market opportunities and access to well-paying jobs, many workers have turned to microtask platforms for work. In fact, a significant proportion of workers (36 percent) reported that their primary source of income came from performing AI and machine-learning tasks on microtask platforms.

This proportion was even higher in developing countries (43.6 percent) compared to advanced economies (32 percent). Additionally, women (40 percent) were more likely to rely on this type of work as their main source of income than men (34.5 percent). For many workers, performing AI-related tasks on these platforms allows them to work from home (31 percent) or supplement their income (41 percent). However, it is important to note that a large percentage of workers in developed countries (46.3 percent) perform these tasks to supplement their income as opposed to those in developing countries.

This section examines the working conditions of workers performing AI-related tasks, including their earnings, working time, social protection, and experience on microtask platforms. While several studies have explored working conditions on specific or multiple microtask platforms (see Berg et al., 2018; Felstiner, 2011; Hara et al., 2018; ILO, 2021), what distinguishes this analysis is the focus on the different categories of AI and machine-learning tasks performed by workers. To understand workers' earnings, we asked them about the time they spent doing paid work (i.e., actual work tasks for which the worker was paid) and unpaid work (i.e., time spent looking for tasks, earning qualifications, communicating with other requesters through online forums, and tasks that were rejected and not paid). This allowed us to estimate hourly earnings considering both paid and unpaid hours, presented in Table 4.1.

On average, workers performing AI and machine-learning tasks earned US$3.4 per hour when considering both paid and unpaid hours, with a median earning of about US$2.1 per hour (Table 4.1). When only paid hours were considered, the average earnings were higher at US$4.6. Workers in developed countries earned an average of US$4.2 per hour, which was twice the amount earned by those in developing countries (US$2.1).

Table 4.1   *Average and median hourly earnings (in US$) by types of task and development status*

AI task	Developed countries		Developing countries		Total	
	Mean	Median	Mean	Median	Mean	Median
Categorization	4.2	3.2	2.0	1.2	3.4	1.2
Content moderation	3.5	2.8	2.3	1.0	3.0	1.0
Data collection	4.3	3.3	1.8	1.2	3.2	1.2
Audio-image recording	4.5	3.8	3.2	1.6	4.1	1.6
Verification	3.7	2.7	1.7	1.0	2.9	1.0
Translation and transcription	4.8	4.0	2.2	1.4	3.7	1.4
All artificial intelligence related tasks	*4.2*	*3.3*	*2.1*	*1.2*	*3.4*	*2.1*

Source: Authors' calculations based on ILO global survey of workers on microtask platforms, 2017.

Figure 4.5 shows the distribution of total average and median hourly earnings for workers in developed and developing countries. The distribution of hourly earnings for workers in developing countries is skewed towards the left, with 58 percent of workers earning below the average wage of US$2.1 per hour, while almost 40 percent earn US$1. In contrast, the earning distribution for workers in developed countries is normally distributed.

Additionally, the median earnings of workers in developing countries were three times lower than those in developed countries, indicating a significant disparity in earnings. The average and median earnings of workers in developed countries were higher than the overall average and median earnings for all tasks performed for training AI. Conversely, the median earnings for workers in developing countries were only US$1.2, which means that 50 percent of the workers earned close to a dollar per hour for these tasks, despite having higher educational levels. Although there were no significant gender differences in overall average earnings for AI-related tasks, women earned 10 to 15 percent less than men in tasks related to content moderation and audio and image recording.

The survey asked respondents to describe up to five different types of task they typically performed on the platforms. The different responses were categorized into different types of task, and the average and median

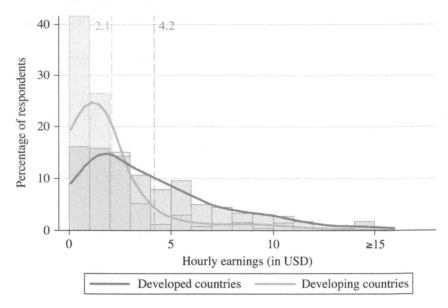

Source: Authors' calculations based on ILO global survey of workers on microtask platforms, 2017.

Figure 4.5   *Average hourly earnings (in US$) of workers performing AI-related tasks, by developed and developing countries*

earnings were calculated for the most frequently performed tasks by the workers. Among the different categories of AI task, workers who performed audio-image recording had the highest average earnings at US$4.1, followed by translation and transcription tasks at US$3.7. Developed-country workers earned more than twice that of developing-country workers for audio-image recording, while it was 1.4 times for translation and transcription tasks (Table 4.1). The variation in earnings between developed- and developing-country workers for audio and image recording, as well as for translation and transcription, could be related to the complexity of tasks. Additionally, clients may assign certain higher-paid tasks to workers from developed countries, as indicated by qualitative responses. However, it is surprising to see that developed-country workers earn almost 2.4 times that of developing-country workers for data collection tasks, where the nature of task does not vary significantly.

The qualitative responses in the survey revealed that workers from developing countries were dissatisfied with their earnings, citing them as too low and unfair. They also noted that workers from certain countries were often excluded from certain tasks, highlighting a differential

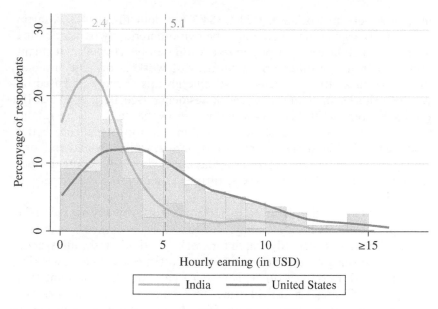

Source: Authors' calculations based on ILO global survey of workers on microtask platforms, 2017.

Figure 4.6   *Average hourly earnings (in US$) of workers performing AI-related tasks, India and the United States*

treatment between workers from developed and developing economies. Another concern raised by workers from developing countries was the mode of payment, with many receiving gift vouchers instead of cash which often could not be utilized, and those receiving cash often received amounts lower than what was initially prescribed due to additional fees they had to pay for money transfer services.

We also examined whether there were differences between workers from different countries on a single platform. As we had a significant number of workers from the United States and India on AMT, we compared their earnings. Figure 4.6 illustrates the total hourly earnings, including paid and unpaid work, of Indian and American workers on AMT. The hourly earnings of Indian workers are highly skewed towards the lower end of the distribution, while those of American workers are more evenly distributed. There is a significant disparity in average wages between American and Indian workers. On average, an American worker on AMT earned more than twice (approximately 2.1 times) as much per hour as an Indian worker.

Pay differentials are even more apparent when examining median wages. The median Indian worker on AMT earned US$1.6, while the median American worker earned US$4.3 per hour (Table 4.2). Martin et al. (2014) argued that there might be two different pay bands existing in this marketplace which pay workers differently. However, it might also stem from the differential treatment of workers on platforms, as they allow tasks to be targeted to specific groups of workers based on various criteria, including country of residence (see Berg et al., 2018; Rani & Furrer, 2019). The survey findings show that tasks, such as audio and image recording, translation and transcription, which are better paid are more often done by American workers, while low-end and low-paying tasks, such as categorization, data collection, and content moderation, are left to Indian workers, further exacerbating the disparities (Table 4.2).

The use of microtask platforms to outsource work globally has led to the development of a 24-hour economy. Due to low wages earned by workers, they are forced to constantly search for work. In addition, the idiosyncrasies of task posting based on client time zones often results in long working hours (Rani & Furrer, 2019). This practice has extended the number of both paid and unpaid hours, blurring the boundaries between work and home. On average, workers spent one-fifth of their time performing unpaid tasks, a trend observed in both developed and developing countries.

Microtask platforms rely on algorithms to manage and supervise tasks, rather than humans, despite humans being responsible for developing the system and outsourcing work. Workers select tasks, but an algorithm oversees the work process, their submissions, and payment. This algorithmic management practice can lead to unfair work rejections, often with no justification for the rejections, causing significant concern for workers.

Table 4.2   *Average and median hourly earnings (in US$) by types of task in India and the United States*

AI task	United States		India	
	Mean	Median	Mean	Median
Categorization	5.4	4.5	2.6	1.6
Content moderation	4.7	3.9	2.4	1.0
Data collection	5.3	4.8	2.2	1.6
Audio-image recording	5.7	4.7	3.1	1.8
Verification	4.6	4.2	1.3	1.0
Transcription	5.6	4.8	2.4	1.7
All artificial intelligence related tasks	5.1	4.3	2.4	1.6

Source: Authors' calculations based on ILO global survey of crowdworkers, 2017.

The workers on these microtask platforms cannot discuss why their task was rejected with the client or requester, which further exacerbates the issue. About 88 percent of the workers reported rejection and not being remunerated. In developing countries, the rejection rate is even higher at 95 percent compared to 83 percent in developed countries. Workers were often frustrated and disappointed, as the reason for rejection was sometimes due to misleading attention checks, unclear instructions, bugs in the tasks, technical errors, or a lack of information from the requester. Rejected work not only results in unpaid labor but also negatively affects a worker's ability to secure new tasks and may even lead to deactivation of their account on the platform if they exceed a certain threshold of rejections. There is a need for a mechanism to inform workers of what went wrong when their work is rejected, to increase transparency and fairness in algorithmic management.

Besides the issue of low wages, workers on microtask platforms have limited social protection coverage. Out of ten respondents, only six had health insurance, while one in five had access to work-related injury benefits and one in six had unemployment benefits. A smaller proportion of workers in developing countries had access to these benefits compared to their counterparts in developed countries. The majority of respondents obtained this coverage from their primary job in the offline labor market, or were dependent on their family members or state-sponsored universal benefits.

The issues associated with working conditions are not limited to workers carrying out AI-related tasks on microtask platforms; they are also prevalent in BPO firms. A Time investigation recently revealed that Open AI utilized Kenyan workers working for the BPO company Sama to address toxicity issues with ChatGPT, such as its violent, sexist, or racist responses (Perrigo, 2023). These workers were paid less than US$2 per hour for filtering toxic content from the data, with some suffering traumatic experiences due to such exposure. Some workers had to work nine-hour shifts and received a commission for meeting performance indicators related to accuracy and speed. This highlights the exploitation of workers, particularly in developing countries, who play a vital role in building, sustaining, and maintaining AI tools that are utilized, to some degree, to replace workers in other locations or improve the productivity of other workers. These workers undertake repetitive or routine tasks, some of which can be harmful, so that the AI system may help some professional workers spend less time doing routine tasks. OpenAI, with US$11 billion in investments (Crunchbase, n.d.), underlined that the outsourcing company Sama was responsible for managing payment and pricing and for the mental health needs of the workers (Perrigo, 2023).

Finally, it is important to note that many workers who perform AI-related tasks and train AI and machine-learning models possess university degrees in specialized fields, and there is no correlation between the level of education and the type of task performed (Rani & Furrer, 2019). These workers are essentially utilized to perform simple, repetitive, and menial tasks that will eventually contribute to the development of more advanced AI systems, which can help to reduce routine tasks for knowledge and other workers. This raises concerns about the impact of this work on future employment prospects for these highly educated workers. In addition, many of the workers feel a sense of insecurity about their work because it is not perceived as serious work by their family and friends (see Rani & Furrer, 2019). There is a risk of not being able to reintegrate into the offline labor market after a sustained period of performing such "dead-end" routine tasks on these platforms, as there are insecurities about how to reflect this work on their resumés. While such AI-related tasks on microtask platforms offer easily accessible work and immediate financial benefits, there are concerns about the content of such work and whether it is a desirable path for the present and future generation of highly educated workers, especially in developing countries where much of the work is outsourced.

This situation is also similar for workers who perform such tasks in call centers, where tasks are outsourced from big tech companies such as Google (part of Alphabet), Facebook (part of Meta), and Microsoft to countries like India, Kenya, and the Philippines. Interviews conducted with call centers in the context of content moderation in India revealed that over 95 percent of the workers comprise IT professionals holding a university degree in engineering or computer science. These workers are primarily responsible for monitoring and removing offensive, obscene, false, or illegal content from social media and other platforms (ILO, 2021). While the tasks generate employment opportunities in these countries, there is no relation to their educational qualifications, and they do not provide any learning or career advancement. On the other hand, tasks such as reviewing disturbing images or videos can have detrimental effects on the mental well-being of the workers who often do not get any psychological support, which can have an adverse effect on their working life.

Another risk of AI-related work is that it could lead to the deskilling of work and replacement of skilled labor with unskilled labor as tasks are broken down into smaller, simpler tasks. Furthermore, some tasks, such as content moderation in social media or more recently ChatGPT, can have negative psychological effects on workers. This technology has led to a race to the bottom for cheaper labor, which is a concern for workers in both advanced economies and developing countries, where public investments in education, particularly in science, technology, engineering and mathematics fields, could be underutilized. Many of these workers have received higher education, especially in science and technology, in urban areas and institutions where the cost of education is quite high and can be a financial burden for households. Governments often provide subsidies or scholarships to promote higher education, but there are concerns that this investment may not be utilized to its fullest potential, especially in developing countries. Therefore, there is a need to have a debate on what these new technologies mean for our societies and how to utilize the technology in a way that brings about a productive transformation and contributes to economic development, while also ensuring the protection and fair treatment of workers. It is crucial to address the concerns of highly educated workers who are performing low-level tasks, to provide them with more meaningful and rewarding work opportunities and to ensure that the benefits of AI and machine learning are equitably shared across society.

CONCLUSIONS

This chapter has illustrated that human labor continues to be crucial to what are often portrayed as automated AI systems. Workers perform a variety of tasks within the AI supply chain, such as data labeling, image annotation, transcription, translation, or content moderation, which are essential to train, develop, monitor, and service AI systems. Although many companies advertise these systems as entirely automated, they continue to rely on a global pool of outsourced and invisible workers at the back end who perform the tasks. This is because AI systems and algorithms are still prone to errors and lack accuracy, requiring human-in-the-loop support to generate meaningful output. Many of the workers are typically located in developing countries and, despite being highly educated, face precarious employment, poor working conditions, and perform routine and repetitive tasks.

The analysis in this chapter raises concerns about the perpetuation and exacerbation of inequalities within the economic system that underpin the development and deployment of AI systems. Workers crucial to the production and sustenance of AI systems remain on the fringes of the digital economy, while some workers, especially those credited with coding, programming, or marketing, are generously rewarded. This stark inequality is a product of the prevailing global economic system, where workers in the global South who provide the materials needed for making clothes struggle to make ends meet, while clothes designers in the global North can become millionaires. There is a need to expand our understanding of digital labor to include all "human-performed work tasks," including affluent workers and not just those on the margins, to better comprehend the dynamics of labor within the digital economy at the supply-chain or sectoral level (Dorschel, 2022, p. 293).

Situating AI systems within this framework of inequality is crucial to better comprehend their broader implications for the world of work and to determine whether such systems can operate through genuine collaboration between AI and humans, rather than through unequal power relationships. The development and deployment of AI systems have significant implications for the labor market, particularly for those who rely on microtask platforms for their livelihoods. It is therefore important to address these issues to ensure fair and equitable opportunities for all workers regardless of gender or location. While AI systems have the potential to augment workers' capacities and enhance productivity, there are some important concerns that require particular attention.

Firstly, the pursuit of enhancing productivity through AI tools must also address the decent work deficits of workers in developing countries who train and service the AI system, and ensure that work opportunities are created that make meaningful contributions towards the socio-economic development of their countries. The exploitation of such workers risks exacerbating inequalities and undermines the innovative and productive potential of highly educated workers in developing countries who are engaged in mind-numbing repetitive tasks in the AI supply chain. This also has broader implications for the development trajectories of countries where human capital tends to be scarce and requires significant investment.

Secondly, there is a risk of creating new forms of inequality between companies and workers from advanced economies, who often have access to costly AI systems that tend to be controlled by a few technology companies, and those from developing countries who have limited resources or training to access such systems. This can exacerbate an already existing technology divide and has major implications for widening gaps between countries, as well as creating challenges for companies in developing countries to compete. Therefore, a transformation in the world of work with the rise of AI systems needs to be rooted in promoting decent work opportunities for all and fostering sustainable enterprise creation.

Finally, there are concerns about workers' data and their privacy. For instance, ChatGPT was trained on publicly available data without the consent of the users who generated that data, which could potentially be used to identify people, their location, contact details, or family members. There are no procedures to ensure that OpenAI does not store people's personal information or to delete such information if necessary (Gal, 2023).

Italy for example, had imposed a temporary limitation on the processing of data of Italian users by OpenAI and had underlined that there was no legal basis underpinning the collection and processing of personal data to train the AI system (OECD, 2023). In addition, there are risks of potential intellectual property rights infringements, and some writers have undertaken legal action against OpenAI and claim that copyrighted material was utilized to train the large language models (David, 2023).

Moreover, there are issues of accountability, particularly due to the "black box" nature of the algorithm and the learning models, which cannot be scrutinized or evaluated for biases. In some cases, the operations of the algorithm in such AI systems are not even adequately understood by the company responsible for its design and operations (Q.ai, 2023; Schoenherr, 2023). The recent conclusion of the strike by the Writers Guild of America has shown that social dialogue will be critical to address many of these emerging concerns from AI systems (Silberling, 2023).

REFERENCES

Agrawal, A., Gans, J. S., & Goldfarb, A. (2019). Artificial intelligence: The ambiguous labor market impact of automating prediction. *Journal of Economic Perspectives, 33*(2), 31–50.

Aloisi, A., & De Stefano, V. (2022). *Your Boss Is an Algorithm: Artificial Intelligence, Platform Work and Labour*. Hart Publishing.

Armour, J., & Sako, M. (2020). AI-enabled business models in legal services: From traditional law firms to next-generation law companies? *Journal of Professions and Organization, 7*(1), 27–46.

Autor, D. H. (2015). Why are there still so many jobs? The history and future of workplace automation. *Journal of Economic Perspectives, 29*(3), 3–30.

Bang, Y., Cahyawijaya, S., Lee, N., Dai, W., Su, D., Wilie, B. et al. (2023). A multitask, multilingual, multimodal evaluation of ChatGPT on reasoning, hallucination, and interactivity. arXiv: 2302.04023

Bangert, V. (2022, January 8). AI is quietly eating up the world's workforce with job automation. VentureBeat. https://venturebeat.com/datadecisionmakers/ai-is-quietly-eating-up-the-worlds-workforce-with-job-automation/

BBC. (2022, May 12). Meta being sued by ex-Facebook content moderator. BBC News. www.bbc.com/news/technology-61409556

Berg, J., Furrer, M., Harmon, E., Rani, U., & Silberman, M. S. (2018). *Digital Labour Platforms and the Future of Work*. International Labour Organization.

Brudenall, P. (2011, September 1). Legal process outsourcing: Opportunities and risks. *Practical Law*. https://uk.practicallaw.thomsonreuters.com/9-508-0134?transitionType=Default&contextData=(sc.Default)&firstPage=true#co_anchor_a747432

Brynjolfsson, E., Hui, X., & Liu, M. (2018). Does machine translation affect international trade? Evidence from a large digital platform. Working Paper 24917. National Bureau of Economic Research.

Brynjolfsson, E., Li, D., & Raymond, L. R. (2023). *Generative AI at work*. NBER Working Paper 31161. National Bureau of Economic Research.

Casilli, A. A. (2021). Waiting for Robots: The ever-elusive myth of automation and the global exploitation of digital labor. *Sociologias, 23*(57), 112–133.

Cheng, J., Teevan, J., Iqbal, S. T., & Bernstein, M. S. (2015). Break it down: A comparison of macro- and microtasks. *Proceedings of the 33rd Annual ACM Conference on Human Factors in Computing Systems*, Seoul, April 18–23, 4061–4064.

Chui, M., Hazan, E., Roberts, R., Singla, A., Smaje, K., Sukharevsky, A., Yee, L., & Zemmel, R. (2023). *The Economic Potential of Generative AI: The Next Productivity Frontier*. McKinsey & Company.

Cobbe, J., Veale, M., & Singh, J. (2023). Understanding accountability in algorithmic supply chains. *Proceedings of the 2023 ACM Conference on Fairness, Accountability, and Transparency (FAccT'23)*, New York, June 12–15, 1186–1197.

Crunchbase. (n.d.). Organization: OpenAI. Crunchbase. www.crunchbase.com/organization/openai

David, E. (2023, September 20). George R.R. Martin and other authors sue OpenAI for copyright infringement. *The Verge*. https://www.theverge.com/2023/9/20/23882140/george-r-r-martin-lawsuit-openai-copyright-infringement

Dell'Acqua, F., McFowland III, E., Mollick, E., Lifshitz-Assaf, H., Kellogg, K. C., Rajendran, S. et al. (2023). *Navigating the jagged technological frontier: Field experimental evidence of the effects of AI on knowledge worker productivity and quality*. Working Paper 24–013. Harvard Business School.

Dorschel, R. (2022). Reconsidering digital labour: Bringing tech workers into the debate. *New Technology, Work and Employment, 37*(2), 288–307.

Felstiner, A. (2011). Working the crowd: Employment and labor law in the crowdsourcing industry. *Berkeley Journal of Employment and Labor Law, 32*(1), 143–203.

Gal, U. (2023, February 8). ChatGPT is a data privacy nightmare. If you've ever posted online, you ought to be concerned. *The Conversation*. https://theconversation.com/chatgpt-is-a-data-privacy-nightmare-if-youve-ever-posted-online-you-ought-to-be-concerned-199283

Garcia, I. (2017). Translating in the cloud age: Online marketplaces. *HERMES – Journal of Language and Communication in Business, 56*, 59–70.

Ghadage, K., Reddy, L., Borate, D., Dalavi, O., & Aundhakar, S. P. (2021). Voice based prescription generation using artificial intelligence. *International Research Journal of Engineering and Technology, 8*(6), 1195–1200.

Ghayvat, H., Awais, M., Bashir, A. K., Pandya, S., Zuhair, M., Rashid, M., & Nebhen, J. (2022). AI-enabled radiologist in the loop: Novel AI-based framework to augment radiologist performance for COVID-19 chest CT medical image annotation and classification from pneumonia. *Neural Computing and Applications*, 1–19.

Gifu, D. (2022). AI-backed OCR in healthcare. *Procedia Computer Science, 207*, 1134–1143.

Gmyrek, P., Berg, J., & Bescond, D. (2023). *Generative AI and jobs: A global analysis of potential effects on job quantity and quality*. ILO Working Paper 96. International Labour Organization.

Gorwa, R., Binns, R., & Katzenbach, C. (2020). Algorithmic content moderation: Technical and political challenges in the automation of platform governance. *Big Data & Society, 7*(1), 1–14.

Hara, K., Adams, A., Milland, K., Savage, S., Callison-Burch, C., & Bigham, J. P. (2018). A data-driven analysis of workers' earnings on Amazon Mechanical Turk. *Association for Computing Machinery Conference on Human Factors in Computing Systems*, Montreal, April 21–26.

ILO. (2021). *World Employment and Social Outlook 2021: The Role of Digital Labour Platforms in Transforming the World of Work.* International Labour Organization.

Irani, L. (2015, January 15). Justice for "data janitors." *Public Books.* www.public books.org/justice-for-data-janitors/

Irani, L. (2016). The hidden faces of automation. *XRDS, an ACM Publication, 23*(2), 34–37.

Jarrahi, M. H. (2018). Artificial intelligence and the future of work: Human–AI symbiosis in organizational decision making. *Business Horizons, 61*(4), 577–586.

Kenny, D. (2022). Human and machine translation. In D. Kenny (Ed.), *Machine Translation for Everyone* (pp. 23–49). Language Science Press.

King-Dejardin, A. M. (2021). *Homeworking in the Philippines: Bad Job? Good Job?* ILO Working Paper 25. International Labour Organization.

Leaver, T., & Srdarov, S. (2023). ChatGPT isn't magic: The hype and hypocrisy of generative artificial intelligence (AI) rhetoric. *M/C Journal, 26*(5).

Lorenz, P., Perset, K., & Berryhill, J. (2023). *Initial policy considerations for generative artificial intelligence.* OECD Artificial Intelligence Papers No. 1. Organisation for Economic Co-operation and Development.

Ludec, C. L., Cornet, M., & Casilli, A. A. (2023). The problem with annotation. Human labour and outsourcing between France and Madagascar. *Big Data & Society, 10*(2), 1–13.

Martin, D., Hanrahan, B. V., O'Neill, J., & Gupta, N. (2014). Being a Turker. *Proceedings of the 17th ACM Conference on Computer Supported Cooperative Work and Social Computing*, Baltimore, MD, February 15–19, 224–235.

Matheus, V. B., Tubaro, P., & Casilli, A. A. (2023). *Microwork in Brazil. Who are the workers behind artificial intelligence?* Research Report DiPLab & LATRAPS.

Moorkens, J. (2022). Ethics and machine translation. In D. Kenny (Ed.), *Machine Translation for Everyone* (pp. 121–140). Language Science Press.

Moorkens, J., Toral, A., Castilho, S., & Way, A. (2018). Translators' perceptions of literary post-editing using statistical and neural machine translation. *Translation Spaces, 7*(2), 240–262.

Nitzberg, M. J., Seppala, T., & Zysman, J. (2019). *The Hype Has Eclipsed the Limitations of Third-Wave Artificial Intelligence.* ETLA.

OECD. (2023). *G7 Hiroshima process on generative artificial intelligence (AI): Towards a G7 common understanding on generative AI.* Report prepared for the 2023 Japanese G7 Presidency and the G7 Digital and Tech Working Group. Organisation for Economic Co-operation and Development.

OpenAI. (2022, November 30). Introducing ChatGPT. OpenAI. https://openai.com/blog/chatgpt

Ørting, S. N., Doyle, A., Hilten, A. van, Hirth, M., Inel, O., Madan, C. R., Mavridis, P., Spiers, H., & Cheplygina, V. (2020). A survey of crowdsourcing in medical image analysis. *Human Computation, 7*, 1–26.

Perrigo, B. (2023, January 18). Exclusive: OpenAI used Kenyan workers on less than $2 per hour to make ChatGPT less toxic. *Time.* https://time.com/6247678/openai-chatgpt-kenya-workers/

Petrović, N., Moyà-Alcover, G., Varona, J., & Jaume-i-Capó, A. (2020). Crowdsourcing human-based computation for medical image analysis: A systematic literature review. *Health Informatics Journal, 26*(4), 2446–2469.

Pizzinelli, C., Panton, A., Tavares, M. M., Cazzaniga, M., & Li, L. (2023). *Labor market exposure to AI: Cross-country differences and distributional implications.* IMF Working Paper WP/23/216. International Monetary Fund.

Q.ai. (2023, February 17). Microsoft's AI Bing chatbot fumbles answers, wants to "be alive" and has named itself – all in one week. *Forbes.* www.forbes.com/sites/qai/2023/02/17/microsofts-ai-bing-chatbot-fumbles-answers-wants-to-be-alive-and-has-named-itselfall-in-one-week/?sh=39d7a4a24475

Rani, U., & Furrer, M. (2019). On-demand digital economy: Can experience ensure work and income security for microtask workers? *Journal of Economics and Statistics (Jahrbuecher Fuer Nationaloekonomie Und Statistik), 239*(3), 565–597.

Reader, R. (2020, November 13). Why Google, Amazon, and Nvidia are all building AI notetakers for doctors. *Fast Company.* www.fastcompany.com/90555218/google-amazon-nvidia-ai-medical-transcription

Rossi, C., & Carré, A. (2022). How to choose a suitable neural machine translation solution: Evaluation of MT quality. In D. Kenny (Ed.), *Machine Translation for Everyone* (pp. 51–79). Language Science Press.

Samiotis, I. P., Lofi, C., & Bozzon, A. (2021). Hybrid annotation systems for music transcription. *3rd International Workshop on Reading Music Systems,* 23–27.

Schmidt, F. A. (2019). *Crowd Production of AI Training Data: How Human Workers Teach Self-Driving Cars How to See.* Hans-Böckler-Stiftung.

Schoenherr, J. R. (2023, March 5). Generative AI like ChatGPT reveal deep-seated systemic issues beyond the tech industry. *The Conversation.* https://theconversation.com/generative-ai-like-chatgpt-reveal-deep-seated-systemic-issues-beyond-the-tech-industry-198579

Siapera, E. (2022). AI content moderation, racism and (de)coloniality. *International Journal of Bullying Prevention, 4,* 55–65.

Silberling, A. (2023, September 27). The writers' strike is over; here's how AI negotiations shook out. *TechCrunch.* https://techcrunch.com/2023/09/26/writers-strike-over-ai/?guccounter=1&guce_referrer=aHR0cHM6Ly93d3cuZ29vZ2xlLmNvbS8&guce_referrer_sig=AQAAAMrSXZPa2PmXAllNiF-HmYLIvD3vLA0Cd9duF_nJYeKGQ3KiA-oq-gEzhhyVQpZbJUk4E9QqwOFRxt4wh0FkwSCeEIfw_UdTkn6ib79NZu8ji5eCX6FW3Fs6doVeESbWoZ4uUU6y6rBKwZCsFFEi-fPkKF_w5sMYBudRFRYk9rei

Silverberg, M. (2022, October 27). Speech recognition technology shows promise for better radiology reports. www.rsna.org/news/2022/october/Speech-Recognition-Technology

Stahl, A. (2023, March 3). Will ChatGPT replace your job? *Forbes.* www.forbes.com/sites/ashleystahl/2023/03/03/will-chatgpt-replace-your-job/?sh=1f37b2f51bed

Taivalkoski-Shilov, K. (2019). Ethical issues regarding machine(-assisted) translation of literary texts. *Perspectives, 27*(5), 689–703.

Thrall, J. H., Li, X., Li, Q., Cruz, C., Do, S., Dreyer, K., & Brink, J. (2018). Artificial intelligence and machine learning in radiology: Opportunities, challenges, pitfalls, and criteria for success. *Journal of the American College of Radiology, 15*(3, Part B), 504–508.

Toews, R. (2021, February 15). Artificial intelligence and the end of work. *Forbes.* www.forbes.com/sites/robtoews/2021/02/15/artificial-intelligence-and-the-end-of-work/?sh=4aa6e3ac56e3

Tubaro, P., & Casilli, A. A. (2019). Micro-work, artificial intelligence and the automotive industry. *Journal of Industrial and Business Economics, 46,* 333–345.

Tubaro, P., Casilli, A. A., & Coville, M. (2020). The trainer, the verifier, the imitator: Three ways in which human platform workers support artificial intelligence. *Big Data & Society, 7*(1), 1–12.

van Dis, E. A. M., Bollen, J., Zuidema, W., van Rooij, R., & Bockting, C. L. (2023). ChatGPT: Five priorities for research. *Nature, 614,* 224–226.

Vashistha, A., Sethi, P., & Anderson, R. (2017). Respeak: A voice-based, crowd-powered speech transcription system. *Proceedings of the 2017 CHI Conference on Human Factors in Computing Systems,* 1855–1866.

von Ahn, L. (2005). *Human Computation.* Dissertation, Carnegie Mellon University.

Wagner, K. (2015, November 3). Facebook's virtual assistant "M" is super smart. It's also probably a human. *Vox.* www.vox.com/2015/11/3/11620286/facebooks-virtual-assistant-m-is-super-smart-its-also-probably-a-human

Whittaker, Z. (2020, May 12). Facebook to pay $52 million to content moderators suffering from PTSD. TechCrunch. https://techcrunch.com/2020/05/12/facebook-moderators-ptsd-settlement/

Yamane, N. (2020). Artificial intelligence in the legal field and the indispensable human element legal ethics demands. *Georgetown Journal of Legal Ethics, 33*(3), 877–890.

Zarifhonarvar, A. (2023). *Economics of ChatGPT: A Labor Market View on the Occupational Impact of Artificial Intelligence.* ZBW – Leibniz Information Centre for Economics.

5. Tools for crowdworkers coding data for AI

Saiph Savage and Martha Garcia-Murillo

INTRODUCTION

The development of artificial intelligence (AI) applications relies on a massive amount of data.[1] Some of that data are collected through the day-to-day interactions people have with machines. However, another type of data needs to be created. This chapter focuses on the people, the so-called crowdworkers, who tag, select, identify, and transcribe among many other tasks, making AI possible in wider contexts. The objective is to provide an understanding of their work, the challenges they face, and then the tools being created to improve salaries, career prospects, and overall working conditions.

Some of the key promises of crowdsourcing markets was that they would reduce the costs associated with integrating human workers into the pipeline of an AI system (Gray & Suri, 2019; Lustig et al., 2020). From the perspective of companies, startups, and academics, crowdsourcing markets provide an effective way to hire and access an on-demand pool of workers, as well as the computational mechanisms needed to easily contract and pay these human workers to get large amounts of work done cheaply (Bernstein et al., 2011; Huang & Bigham, 2017; Lasecki et al., 2013). For workers, these online markets provide access to a central place where they can find work with the flexibility of working from wherever they want (Alkhatib et al., 2017; Martin et al., 2014).

However, recent research has identified that, despite these advantages, crowdsourcing markets are actually creating precarious labor conditions for workers. It is an important issue to understand considering workers play an important role in the development of AI (Gray & Suri, 2019). Crowdsourcing markets offer to reduce operational costs (Gray & Suri, 2019; Lustig et al., 2020), the costs incurred in maintaining the day-to-day operations of a business. You may consider that having to manage multiple employees, especially new ones, would

---

[1] This work was partially supported by NSF grant FW-HTF-19541.

increase the operational costs of any business. Crowdsourcing markets, however, have argued that they will take care of those costs so a business can start to integrate new workers into their pipeline without having to provide full-time employment, and thereby increasing their costs.

In its early days, these costs did not disappear. Operational costs were traditionally absorbed by companies, startups, and academics. Today, however, the operational costs of crowdsourcing platforms have been passed onto the shoulders of workers (Crain et al., 2016). In the context of crowd work, the operational costs include all the recurring costs that workers have to pay within the physical world just to do their jobs (ILO, 2021). Some include such things as electricity, internet charges, and rental space, among other additional costs. The problem is exacerbated because crowdworkers are forced to do unpaid labor. This unpaid labor includes completing work that has been rejected, searching for work and finding tasks they are qualified to complete, figuring out how to complete the paid jobs at hand, managing payments, and weeding out which employers, i.e., requesters, they can trust (Gray & Suri, 2019; ILO, 2021; Kaplan et al., 2018; Rani & Furrer, 2021). Workers in these crowdsourcing platforms generate the data companies need for AI at a minimal cost because they do not account for the time-consuming, unpaid activities done to complete the labor for which the workers are paid (Qiu et al., 2020; Sutherland & Jarrahi, 2018). Current research has identified that a majority of workers are earning less than the minimum hourly wage (Hara et al., 2018). This should concern policymakers because workers fueling the efficiency gains of multi-billion dollar AI technology companies are also contributing to the severe inequalities involved in the creation of the AI industry (Kittur et al., 2013; Su et al., 2012). Precariously paid crowdworkers might label content for the AI system of a large internet company and not recommend posts filled with hate speech or pedophilia (Dang et al., 2018; Gillespie, 2018). Low-paid crowdworkers might also transcribe audio to help Amazon's Alexa better understand users (Bigham et al., 2017a).

Researchers have argued that one of the reasons why companies are paying low wages, as well as forcing workers to absorb operational costs and even conduct unpaid labor, is because crowdworkers remain hidden. It is not easy to understand that these workers exist and hence bring accountability. Note that the unpaid aspect of crowd work is not just due to companies and academics posting work on crowdsourcing platforms; it is rather due to the AI industry as a whole that has hidden these workers behind the scenes while training the AI to be better (Gray & Suri, 2019).

Another problem associated with crowd markets is that they have not been designed to allow workers to improve their skills (Bigham et al., 2017b; Dontcheva et al., 2014; Suzuki et al., 2016; Whiting et al., 2016). Consequently, crowdworkers who wish to improve their abilities and thus their economic prospects must explore ways to train themselves outside the crowdsourcing platforms (Kittur et al., 2013). However, given the low pay of crowd work (Berg, 2015; Durward et al., 2016; Hara et al., 2018; Paolacci et al., 2010; Thies et al., 2011), requiring workers to use additional time and money for skill development seems unreasonable (Alkhatib et al., 2017; Kelliher & Anderson, 2008; Rosenblat & Stark, 2016; van Doorn, 2017).

There is no doubt that these workers play a crucial role in the development of AI applications; however, if we are aiming to create a future where the crowd work that feeds the industry is fair and equitable, we need to ensure that workers receive fair wages and have ways to grow and develop professionally. To achieve a fairer future, we need to understand crowdworkers' current conditions in order to design solutions that will create fairer outcomes for workers. To understand their conditions, researchers have been conducting interviews and surveys with crowdworkers (Rani & Furrer, 2019, 2021), as well as designing tools through which they can quantify the labor conditions (Toxtli et al., 2021). Note that self-reported surveys can experience problems because workers could lie in order to present worse conditions than actually exist. Developing tools to quantify labor conditions affords an advantage in that it can be more objective. Having a third-party tool to do the measuring should ensure and limit workers overestimating the alleged ill treatment they receive (Toxtli et al., 2021). Additionally, the data collected from these quantitative investigations can later be used to design tools to improve workers' labor conditions by providing hints as to the type of work that workers should avoid or digital spaces that might be fairer because overall they treat workers better.

In this chapter we focus on how tools can help identify, quantify, and expose the precarious labor conditions of crowdworkers that create AI data. With that objective in mind, researchers have been conducting surveys as well as developing tools to quantify the amount of unpaid labor that workers have to conduct. The data collected can also be used to guide and help workers grow professionally and develop skills directly on these labor platforms. The next section presents how we and other researchers have designed tools to uncover the problematic conditions that workers are exposed to on crowdsourcing platforms. We then present tools that will help address these unjust conditions.

TOOLS FOR QUANTIFYING AND VISUALIZING CROWD LABOR

This section describes how tools have allowed us to numerically measure crowdsourcing platforms, specifically through artifacts that quantify the conditions that workers experience within digital labor platforms. These digital tools allow us to measure both paid and unpaid labor on these digital labor markets. Shedding light on the labor conditions is important to prevent the exploitation of workers and to bring accountability to the platform (Gray & Suri, 2019). Not understanding what happens inside labor markets can perpetuate precarious labor conditions, given that no one knows what exactly is happening inside the platform (Daniels, 1987; Gray & Suri, 2019).

Motivation for the Development of Tools for Crowdworkers

Researchers have argued that in "capitalist societies" there is a propensity to manage the workforce in ways that will generate profit for those who own the technology, often at the expense of labor (Federici, 1975). In the context of crowdsourcing platforms, beneficiaries are often the large technology companies who own the crowdsourcing market, e.g., Amazon, or the actors who post the labor on platforms, i.e., the "requesters" (D'Ignazio & Klein, 2020). Within this setting, platform owners define what labor is to be counted and paid for, and what labor is not paid for (Daniels, 1987; Davis, 1983). Unpaid work is not new nor unique to crowdsourcing platforms. Much labor still suffers from similar treatment. Understanding how workers themselves and outside activists have dealt with underpaid work can inform the design of tools to address the problem within crowd work.

HISTORICAL CONTEXT

Several labor collectives, researchers, practitioners, and individual citizens have fought to empower workers to gain better recognition for their work (D'Ignazio & Klein, 2020; Frazis & Stewart, 2012). In 2013, several collectives had a breakthrough when labor statisticians agreed internationally to begin measuring in official workforce surveys both paid and unpaid labor (Buvinic & King, 2018; CEPAL, 2015). This inclusion influenced the development of new policies around unpaid labor (Buvinic & King, 2018; CEPAL, 2015). Historically, policymakers have overlooked unpaid labor simply because the work was not included in the official statistics used to define new policies (Buvinic & King, 2018; Weyrauch & Langou, 2011). Its exclusion meant that policymakers could not bring about accountability as they did not understand what was happening around the labor, e.g., the type of wages received or the nature of the work, or even the number of citizens impacted. Today counting and including unpaid labor within the official statistics that policymakers use for decision making enables them to more easily understand poorly paid and situated labor in order to design policies that address these challenges and bring about accountability.

Inspired by the impact of the quantification of unpaid labor in transforming policy within other industries and workplaces, academics and practitioners have argued that we need tools to quantify unpaid labor in digital labor platforms (Toxtli et al., 2021). They argue that through these measurements, policymakers will be able to better regulate digital labor platforms and provide an increase in wages and labor conditions for crowdworkers.

TOOLS TO QUANTIFY DIGITAL LABOR CONDITIONS

To quantify and uncover the labor conditions within crowdsourcing platforms we need computational mechanisms to: (1) detect the different activities a worker does on a crowdsourcing platform, especially differentiating between paid and unpaid labor; and (2) measure how much time a worker invests in these different activities. To address these two points, designers regularly choose to create tools that are browser extensions, i.e., plugins (Toxtli et al., 2021). Such tools are useful because they allow workers to use the tool directly while on the crowdsourcing platform, thus avoiding disrupting their normal work routine. Plugins minimize the time that crowdworkers spend using tutorials or material outside their paid work.

Methods for Quantifying Paid Labor in Crowdsourcing Platforms

Designers and researchers have developed a method to detect and measure with plugins when a crowdworker is completing a paid task, called Human Intelligent Task (HIT), within the Amazon Mechanical Turk (MTurk) platform, one of the most popular crowdsourcing platforms. The tools determine the amount of time the worker has invested in completing the paid task and the daily earnings that workers made from the HIT (Saito et al., 2019). Through these tools, researchers have uncovered that on MTurk, the majority of workers are earning less than the minimum wage, around $2.00 per hour, without considering unpaid labor (Hara et al., 2017).

Methods for Quantifying Unpaid Labor

When studying the labor conditions of crowdsourcing platforms it can be especially important to track and measure the time workers spend on unpaid labor. New research has developed tools to quantify unpaid labor within crowdsourcing platforms (Toxtli et al., 2021).

These tools, designed as plugins, focus on detecting and quantifying all other activities that workers do aside from completing HITs, i.e., the paid tasks that requesters or employers on the crowdsourcing platform pay workers to do. These computational tools detect when a worker is visiting other parts of the crowdsourcing platform different from where workers complete paid tasks, i.e., the HIT page tab on MTurk (https://worker. mturk.com/). For example, the worker can be on the first page of MTurk searching for HITs (https://worker.mturk.com/?filters), or in another section of the platform that allows for communication by sending messages to requesters (https://worker.mturk.com/contact requester). These plugins track the exact time from when a worker enters a page to when they finish. The plugin scrapes and parses the HTML of the page to understand how the worker interacted with the page. It then identifies the intervals of time the worker is active on each of these pages. The tools consider a worker to be active on a page when they have the page in focus and engage in any type of user interaction on that page, e.g., mouse movements, scrolls, clicks, or keyboard typing. The tools do not track what a worker does on these pages, e.g., what workers type. The tool simply detects that a worker is active on a particular page from a crowdsourcing platform.

To accomplish this, the tools generally include a page crawler and a time-driven background process that detects the different browser events happening within the crowdsourcing platform, e.g., that the worker visited another page on MTurk, started typing, or began a new HIT. The page crawler detects the worker's location on the MTurk domain page as well as the status of the page, e.g., that the page is loaded, active, inactive, or closed. The background process detects the HITs the worker is doing at that time and identifies what has been finished.

The background process of the plugins polls workers' task queues on MTurk every 30 seconds. From the task queue, the background process obtains the metadata and status of all HITs the worker has accepted. Note that the page crawler is the primary element used to detect whether a crowdworker is completing paid or unpaid labor. The background process helps the plugin to better detect when the worker is completing paid tasks, which can reside outside the crowdsourcing platform, and also when the worker is multitasking, i.e., doing multiple HITs at the same time.

The setup assumes a context where workers are operating from a web browser with the plugin installed. An example of one of the tools that detect and calculate the time spent in paid and unpaid labor is the plugin available in GitHub (https://github.com/NortheasternAI/Quantifying-Invisible-Labor/tree/main/MTURK). It is important to note that these tools quantify the different aspects of unpaid labor. The tools not only provide ways to quantify the amount of time that people have to invest in finding work on the MTurk platforms, but they also study unpaid labor due to workers not being paid after the work has been completed due to technical problems or glitches, or rejection of the work, or where workers are told half-way through the job that they are not eligible and therefore will not be paid.

Related to this, it is important to highlight that another important aspect of unpaid labor can emerge and that these new tools are currently not quantifying cases where workers are not paid monetarily but with gift vouchers, often not utilized, especially in developing countries, because the workers do not require the product or cannot access it. There is value in further studying unpaid labor in crowdsourcing markets using a cultural lens. This will allow the tools to better address the problems that crowdworkers across different parts of the world and with diverse cultural issues face.

It is important to note that the invisible labor measured by these tools currently focusses only on one platform. Crowdworkers do not generally operate just on one platform such as MTurk; they may work on multiple platforms such as the crowdsourcing market of Toloka. Additionally, workers might do invisible labor on other sites and platforms where they complete work. For instance, some workers are asked to complete surveys or use external platforms that might require them to conduct additional unpaid labor. It is important for future work to think about how unpaid labor is being tracked in these cases. To start to understand the phenomena and design better, adequate tools help to connect with qualitative research that has already started through surveys to study the different types of invisible labor that crowdworkers experience across platforms (ILO, 2021; Rani & Furrer, 2021).

MAIN FINDINGS FROM TOOLS QUANTIFYING CROWDSOURCING PLATFORMS

Researchers who have quantified the labor conditions of crowdsourcing platforms have estimated that workers on MTurk earn a median hourly wage of only $2 per hour, while only 4 percent earned more than $7.25 per hour (Hara et al., 2017). Similarly, research using these tools has uncovered that crowdworkers spent 33 percent of their time daily on the transaction costs of understanding and learning how to complete a HIT, which is unpaid labor. The research has found that the most common unpaid task that takes the most time revolves around workers having to manage their payments. The second most time-consuming unpaid type of labor involves hyper-vigilance, where workers watch requesters' profiles for newly posted work or search for labor. It is likely that workers engage in this activity to readily grab the HITs posted by their favorite requesters (Gray & Suri, 2019). Upon manual inspection of workers' digital traces, we identified those who invested the most time in this activity, i.e., the outliers or workers whose time invested was above the 95th percentile (Hao et al., 2007). These workers appeared to be hunting the profiles of specific requesters, ready to do work, i.e., the workers were "on call." The workers opened the profile pages of multiple requesters and then went through the list, likely inspecting if the requesters had posted anything new.

We believe it is important to cover the critical types of unpaid labor identified and quantified by prior work because this type of work has also been found to be present in other digital workspaces (Hall et al., 2015; Rosenblat, 2018). For example, Uber drivers and passengers organized to check how much a passenger was actually charged for a ride versus how much the driver received. This dynamic emerged after Uber changed its pricing algorithm and did not provide transparency on how it functioned (Chen et al., 2015). The lack of transparency not only led drivers and passengers to engage in this type of invisible labor, it also led them to feel cheated and betrayed by the platform (Rosenblat, 2018). Unpaid labor does not only emerge as the fault of requesters, i.e., passengers. It is important for platforms to see that this type of unpaid labor is likely to emerge out of mistrust and thus has the potential to alienate people from the platform. Related to this, a number of tools for quantifying such unpaid labor on gig platforms, such as Uber and Lyft, have emerged to bring further transparency to gig workers. Such tools are not a substitute for surveys; rather, they offer a way to quantify the labor conditions of gig markets. Policymakers can be organized to take action because they understand that the reports are not an exaggeration; the problems are quantified with numbers (see Table 5.1 for an overview of this section).

TOOLS FOR WORKERS' PROFESSIONAL DEVELOPMENT

Inspired by qualitative research that has identified the difficult working situations of crowdworkers, some researchers have designed tools and

Table 5.1   Overview of crowdworkers' unpaid labor

Unpaid labor activity	Mean (min)	Median (min)	Std (min)	% workers
Doing HITs that eventually time out	32.3	4.5	1.5	37%
Starting HITs but then returning them to the platform	11.2	4.2	12.1	92%
Viewing their worker's dashboard	10.6	2.8	16.3	97%
Sending messages	2.4	1.9	0.7	51%
Watching over requesters' profiles	15.0	1.1	12.9	69%
Searching for general HITs	3.6	0.9	5.6	96%
Managing queued HITs	3.2	0.7	4.6	93%
Previewing HITs	1.5	0.6	1.0	66%
Viewing their earnings	0.9	0.5	0.3	85%
Searching for filtered HITs	3.9	0.5	0.6	46%
Checking worker's qualifications	0.4	0.2	0.0	27%
Logging in to MTurk	0.3	0.1	0.1	64%
Reading HIT information	0.1	0.0	0.0	63%
Reading platform help	0.0	0.0	0.0	0%

Note: This table documents the amount of time workers dedicated to each activity per day, and the percentage of workers who engaged in the activity. HITs that eventually time out was the median most time-consuming activity, while viewing their earnings was the most common activity.

platforms that are worker-centric instead of meeting the needs of platform owners or requesters (Hanrahan et al., 2019; Williams et al., 2019).

However, while an ever increasing number of workers are using worker-centric tools to have better outcomes on crowdsourcing platforms (Kaplan et al., 2018), only a fraction of workers' earnings are well above the minimum wage (Hara et al., 2018). Additionally, despite the tools, crowdworkers have not had clear ways to develop and grow their marketable skills within these platforms (Chiang et al., 2018a; Kaplan et al., 2018; Saito et al., 2019). Professional development within this setting would involve workers learning new skills or becoming "stronger" in existing ones. Skills development would entail becoming faster at certain tasks and completing them with higher quality (Chiang et al., 2018b).

Helping workers to be better and faster should help to increase their hourly wage.

Because other tools used by individual workers have not been effective in helping workers develop new skills, scholars have designed other mechanisms for workers to coordinate their activities on the platform and actively share advice with each other on how to grow professionally on crowd markets. This type of design can: (1) increase workers' wages (Savage et al., 2020); (2) enable workers' skill development (Chiang et al., 2018a); and (3) ensure fairness in employers' evaluations. This type of design opens a new area of research focused on computationally orchestrating shared advice to actively drive positive change in their professional lives.

DESIGNS FOR CROWDWORKERS

Crowd markets offer a wide range of readily available labor for workers (Alkhatib et al., 2017). Those tasks will continue to be a critical component in the development of AI applications. Unfortunately, it is often difficult for workers to know how to best navigate crowd markets to find labor that pays well and could be useful for career growth. It is within this setting that new research on tool development has emerged to help workers better navigate crowd markets and enhance workers' growth, e.g., increase their salaries and facilitate skills development.

New Crowd Work Designs: Crowd Coach

In light of the limited number of tools to support crowdworkers in skills development, the authors developed and deployed a system called Crowd Coach (Chiang et al., 2018a).[2] The Crowd Coach system allows workers to collaborate with other workers to develop skills, i.e., become better and faster at their jobs, which can lead them to increased wages. These skills development tools are thus ways for crowdworkers to gain access to better work environments.

The Crowd Coach considers that some crowdworkers have become efficient in interpreting the vast amount of information available in crowd markets to go after certain professional goals. For instance, some workers may be effective in using transparency information to earn higher wages.

---

[2]   The tool is accessible at https://chrome.google.com/webstore/detail/crowd-coach/gppgnnfijfhlkddbbcmcnnidnfnagkcb

The crowd coach system thus focuses on recruiting workers who have been able to achieve particular professional goals; and it computationally orchestrates them to share advice on how other workers should use available information from crowd markets to reach specific goals, including increasing their wages or developing their skills.

These workers become coaches to other workers. The Crowd Coach system also incorporates techniques from machine learning to garner the type of advice from coaches that is most effective in enabling workers to achieve their desired goal. Thus, workers who are the data engine behind AI can also be the engine that supports their work. The result is that workers can set a skill they wish to develop and then receive concrete guidelines on how to navigate the crowd market to develop the skill, i.e., become faster and better. This brings about a better prospective for workers as it allows them to potentially increase their wages as they learn how to complete particular tasks faster and with higher quality, thus increasing the amount of jobs they can take per hour, and thereby increasing their hourly wage.

Another interesting design paradigm created within the Crowd Coach system is that it defines designs that allow workers to become coaches, i.e., give advice to a collective of other workers without the activity being the main task. Therefore, new paradigms allow for coaching to exist in a manner that is lightweight and does not distract workers from their main job. The coaching becomes a side activity that does not disturb the main task of workers.

In general, the work frames the design of the coaching around: (1) availability: workers should be able to engage in collectively helping each other with a click; (2) low cognitive load: workers should be able to collectively help each other without the task being a distraction from the main work on the crowd market. Finally, given the economically harsh labor conditions that crowdworkers face, the design focuses on enabling: (3) paid training: allowing workers to receive advice from the coaching while earning money, i.e., directly on the crowdsourcing platform.

The main incentive to coach others is that while such payments may be lower than if the person did the task themselves, it is still large enough to motivate participation (Suzuki et al., 2016). Another incentive is for workers to enjoy new career opportunities where they can be hired as managers for novice workers. Workers acting as coaches can do so uncompensated, simply to help their fellow workers have better experiences in the marketplace and improve labor conditions for everyone. The Crowd Coach system allows workers to pursue any performance goals they set with the help of the collective of workers.

Figure 5.1 presents an overview of our Crowd Coach system.

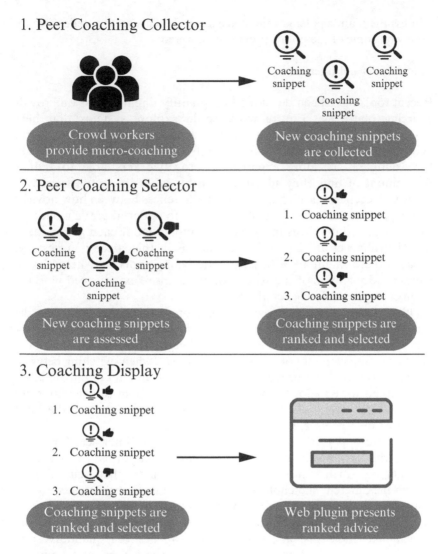

Figure 5.1   Coaching

FINAL REFLECTIONS

In this chapter we have presented an overview of tools for crowd work that focus on: (1) quantifying the labor conditions inside crowdsourcing platforms; and (2) using the knowledge and understanding to then design new tools and systems that can empower crowdworkers by helping them address the main challenges they face at work. This section reflects more deeply on some of the points previously covered.

Future Tools and Interfaces

Recent tools have been developed to quantify unpaid labor on crowdsourcing platforms. Future work could explore systems that help workers limit the amount of time they dedicate to such unpaid work. Within this space are several research opportunities you can ask, for example: Are more experienced crowdworkers able to reduce the amount of time they spend in invisible labor in comparison with novices? Recent research has identified differences between how novices and experts decide what type of paid labor to undertake. We wonder if there are also differences in the type of unpaid labor each group takes on (Hanrahan et al., 2021). More analysis in this space is necessary, because there might be a benefit in designing tools that help novice workers adopt some of the strategies of the more experienced workers (Han et al., 2020; Savage et al., 2020).

Other questions can be intriguing to explore in this space: How does the way workers manage the amount of unpaid labor relate to wages? How exactly does multitasking and context switching relate to unpaid labor? Does a worker's amount of unpaid labor increase when switching between tasks? Do certain tasks or requesters magnify the amount of unpaid labor that workers have to do? Responding to these questions can be important for designing novel tools that can help workers better focus on the work and reach their goals, e.g., increase their wages.

There are opportunities to explore other types of interfaces for quantifying what is happening inside crowdsourcing platforms. For instance, it might be worth exploring transparent interfaces that quantify and inform the different stakeholders of a crowdsourcing marketplace to just how far each stakeholder is fair and respectful of others' values (Chiang et al., 2018b). Within this space, it is important to consider technical and educational challenges, in particular, the gap between qualitative and quantitative researchers who are investigating crowd work, and aiming to shed light on what happens within these platforms. Qualitative researchers might not feel as comfortable deploying tools that study labor markets in a quantified way. Perhaps this is because significant technical knowledge is still required for researchers to adopt and deploy the tools in the wild. However, qualitative researchers might feel more comfortable simply using the quantitative data collected by researchers. There is value in enabling data ecosystems where different stakeholders with different technical skills can make use of the data provided from the quantitative studies of those researchers who deploy tools for quantifying crowd work. Such a setup helps encourage qualitative researchers to study other aspects of crowd work they might not have had access to in the past because they lacked the technical knowledge to collect and access such data.

Governmental Policy Toward Crowdworkers

With the rise of "gig economy" platforms and the growing number of people around the world who work for them, there are ongoing discussions about whether they should be considered formal employees and what labor rights they should have. Policymakers in New Zealand and potentially the United Kingdom have created a new category of workers to attack gig economy problems. This type of worker, often called a "dependent contractor," could be provided with the protection they need and deserve. Nevertheless, this status change could also bring about difficulties for crowd platforms. The policies surrounding the change should be designed carefully so as not to affect the flexibility that many crowdworkers enjoy. It will be highly challenging to take into consideration both the business model of the different crowd platforms and the rights their workers should have.

Cherry and Poster (2016) describe the experiences of Canada in creating new types of workers some decades ago. In Canada, they had success in implementing the dependent contractor status for tradespeople, such as plumbers. This benefited a new class of employees starting in the 1970s. Although, as discussed, it is currently highly challenging to measure the work times of on-demand workers, this is where policymakers can benefit from tools that study how crowdworkers operate across different crowd marketplaces.

In the United States, independent work is one of the fastest-growing labor sectors. It is very challenging to design policies that can protect this workforce as there is no employer-paid health or disability insurance, no retirement fund, to name a few issues. Governments must understand that the work ecosystem is evolving and there is no longer just "traditional work." Policies that help crowdworkers improve their skills could help small businesses grow. Crowdworkers' talent helps close the skill gaps in both small and large businesses. Their service-oriented work prevents independent workers' jobs from being automated.

Policymakers currently have limited ways to understand what is happening inside crowdsourcing markets. Inspired by the impact the quantification of unpaid labor has had in transforming policy within other industries and workplaces, we imagine that in the future with the development of more tools that quantify what happens inside digital labor markets we can help policymakers use the data to bring about new policies that improve the labor conditions of crowdworkers. However, given that the use of data in policymaking is usually an organic, political process (Dhaliwal & Tulloch, 2012), which might not be obvious to outsiders (e.g., workers and their advocates), there is likely value in designing socio-technical mechanisms that guide workers on how to best use the data from our plugin to drive policy innovation (Crewe & Young, 2002).

This could include tools that guide workers on the time to release the data that quantifies unpaid labor on digital labor markets to match the political cycle. Being in tune with the political cycle could help citizens have a better chance to influence policymakers (Weyrauch & Langou, 2011). Similarly, other tools could focus on helping citizens to easily visualize which policymakers might be most influenced if they see statistics from the data collections. There is likely value in tools that can guide workers on how to use our plugin data to gather public support and create pressure on policymakers (Blagescu & Young, 2006; Start & Hovland, 2004).

We imagine that such tools could be used to create pressure on the platforms themselves. For instance, it could help crowdworkers connect with media outlets and create massive social media campaigns where workers can expose the amount of unpaid work they have to do and how this hits their pay check every month. Usually, companies care greatly about branding so this type of dynamic could be effective in creating pressure and helping workers drive positive change on the platform.

Notice that unpaid work is not just the fault of platforms. It can also be due to requesters who might post tasks that time out too soon, which can lead workers to not be paid for their labor or tasks designed incorrectly, so workers spend significant time trying to do the task only to identify that the task was broken. Within this space, we also think about interfaces that could learn to predict when a requester is posting a task that leads to invisible labor. In such a case, the interface could nudge the requester to reconsider the design of the task. This would help requesters to avoid posting tasks that increment the amount of unpaid labor of workers. When thinking about tools that guide requesters, another important type to consider are those that inform requesters about possible privacy violations involving workers, and advise workers of privacy dangers that might exist from doing a certain task.

Finally, we hope this chapter has provided a useful overview of tools to quantify crowd work and how data quantification can be used to inspire a range of positive policy innovations in digital work as well as the creation of new platforms and systems that benefit workers. The chapter sheds much-needed light on the tool movement around crowd work.

REFERENCES

Alkhatib, A., Bernstein, M. S., & Levi, M. (2017). Examining crowd work and gig work through the historical lens of piecework. *Proceedings of the 2017 CHI Conference on Human Factors in Computing Systems*, 4599–4616.

Berg, J. (2015). Income security in the on-demand economy: Findings and policy lessons from a survey of crowdworkers. *Comparative Labor Law and Policy Journal*, 37, 543.

Bernstein, M. S., Brandt, J., Miller, R. C., & Karger, D. R. (2011). Crowds in two seconds: Enabling realtime crowd-powered interfaces. *Proceedings of the 24th Annual ACM Symposium on User Interface Software and Technology*, 33–42.

Bigham, J. P., Kushalnagar, R., Huang, T.-H. K., Flores, J. P., & Savage, S. (2017a). On how deaf people might use speech to control devices. *Proceedings of the 19th International ACM SIGACCESS Conference on Computers and Accessibility*, 383–384.

Bigham, J. P., Williams, K., Banerjee, N., & Zimmerman, J. (2017b). Scopist: Building a skill ladder into crowd transcription. *Proceedings of 14th International Web for All Conference*, April.

Blagescu, M., & Young, J. (2006). *Capacity development for policy advocacy: Current thinking and approaches among agencies supporting civil society organisations*. Overseas Development Institute London.

Buvinic, M., & King, E. M. (2018). Invisible no more? A methodology and policy review of how time use surveys measure unpaid work. United Nations Foundation, Data2X. https://data2x. org/wp-content/uploads/2019/05/Data2X-Invisible-No-More

CEPAL. (2015). Classification of time-use activities for Latin America (cautal). United Nations. www.cepal.org/en/publications/40170-classification-time-use-activities-latin-america-and-caribbean-cautal

Chen, L., Mislove, A., & Wilson, C. (2015). Peeking beneath the hood of uber. *Proceedings of the 2015 Internet Measurement Conference*, 495–508.

Cherry, M. A., & Poster, W. R. (2016). 14 crowdwork, corporate social responsibility, and fair labor practices. *Research Handbook on Digital Transformations*, 291.

Chiang, C.-W., Kasunic, A., & Savage, S. (2018a). Crowd coach: Peer coaching for crowd workers' skill growth. *Proceedings of the ACM on Human-Computer Interaction*, 2(CSCW), 1– 17.

Chiang, C.-W., Betanzos, E., & Savage, S. (2018b). Exploring blockchain for trustful collaborations between immigrants and governments. *Extended Abstracts of the 2018 CHI Conference on Human Factors in Computing Systems*, LBW531.

Crain, M., Poster, W., & Cherry, M. (2016). *Invisible labor: Hidden work in the contemporary world*. University of California Press.

Crewe, E., & Young, M. J. (2002). Bridging research and policy: Context, evidence and links. Overseas Development Institute.

Dang, B., Riedl, M. J., & Lease, M. (2018). But who protects the moderators? The case of crowd-sourced image moderation. arXiv: 1804.10999.

Daniels, A. K. (1987). Invisible work. *Social Problems*, 34(5), 403–415.

Davis, A. (1983). The approaching obsolescence of housework: A working-class perspective. *Women, Race, and Class*, 222–244.

Dhaliwal, I., & Tulloch, C. (2012). From research to policy: Using evidence from impact evaluations to inform development policy. *Journal of Development Effectiveness*, 4(4), 515–536.

D'Ignazio, C., & Klein, L. F. (2020). *Data feminism*. MIT Press.

Dontcheva, M., Morris, R. R., Brandt, J. R., & Gerber, E. M. (2014). Combining crowdsourcing and learning to improve engagement and performance. *Proceedings of the 32nd Annual ACM Conference on Human Factors in Computing Systems*, 3379–3388.

Durward, D., Blohm, I., & Leimeister, J. M. (2016). Crowd work. *Business & Information Systems Engineering*, *58*(4), 281–286.

Federici, S. (1975). *Wages against housework*. Falling Wall Press Bristol.

Frazis, H., & Stewart, J. (2012). How to think about time-use data: What inferences can we make about long- and short-run time use from time diaries? *Annals of Economics and Statistics/Annales d'économie et de statistique*, 231–245.

Gillespie, T. (2018). *Custodians of the internet: Platforms, content moderation, and the hidden decisions that shape social media*. Yale University Press.

Gray, M. L., & Suri, S. (2019). *Ghost work: How to stop silicon valley from building a new global underclass*. Eamon Dolan Books.

Hall, J., Kendrick, C., & Nosko, C. (2015). *The effects of Uber's surge pricing: A case study*. University of Chicago Booth School of Business.

Han, L., Maddalena, E., Checco, A., Sarasua, C., Gadiraju, U., Roitero, K., & Demartini, G. (2020). Crowd worker strategies in relevance judgment tasks. *Proceedings of the 13th International Conference on Web Search and Data Mining*, 241–249.

Hanrahan, B. V., Martin, D., Willamowski, J., & Carroll, J. M. (2019). Investigating the Amazon Mechanical Turk market through tool design. *Computer Supported Cooperative Work*, *28*(5), 795–814.

Hanrahan, B. V., Chen, A., Ma, J., Ma, N. F., Squicciarini, A., & Savage, S. (2021). The expertise involved in deciding which hits are worth doing on Amazon Mechanical Turk. *Proceedings of the ACM on Human-Computer Interaction*, *5*(CSCW1), 1–23.

Hao, L., Naiman, D. Q., & Naiman, D. Q. (2007). *Quantile regression*. Sage.

Hara, K., Adams, A., Milland, K., Savage, S., Callison-Burch, C., & Bigham, J. (2017). A data-driven analysis of workers' earnings on Amazon Mechanical Turk. arXiv: 1712.05796.

Hara, K., Adams, A., Milland, K., Savage, S., Callison-Burch, C., & Bigham, J. P. (2018). A data-driven analysis of workers' earnings on Amazon Mechanical Turk. *Proceedings of the 2018 CHI Conference on Human Factors in Computing Systems*, 449.

Huang, T.-H. K., & Bigham, J. P. (2017). A 10-month-long deployment study of on-demand recruiting for low-latency crowdsourcing. *Fifth AAAI Conference on Human Computation and Crowdsourcing*.

ILO. (2021). The role of digital labour platforms in transforming the world of work. International Labour Organization.

Kaplan, T., Saito, S., Hara, K., & Bigham, J. P. (2018). Striving to earn more: A survey of work strategies and tool use among crowd workers. *Sixth AAAI Conference on Human Computation and Crowdsourcing*.

Kelliher, C., & Anderson, D. (2008). For better or for worse? An analysis of how flexible working practices influence employees' perceptions of job quality. *International Journal of Human Resource Management*, *19*(3), 419–431.

Kittur, A., Nickerson, J. V., Bernstein, M., Gerber, E., Shaw, A., Zimmerman, J., Lease, M., & Horton, J. (2013). The future of crowd work. *Proceedings of the 2013 Conference on Computer Supported Cooperative Work*, 1301–1318.

Lasecki, W. S., Miller, C. D., & Bigham, J. P. (2013). Warping time for more effective real-time crowdsourcing. *Proceedings of the SIGCHI Conference on Human Factors in Computing Systems*, 2033–2036.

Lustig, C., Rintel, S., Scult, L., & Suri, S. (2020). Stuck in the middle with you: The transaction costs of corporate employees hiring freelancers. *Proceedings of the ACM on Human–Computer Interaction*, 4(CSCW1), 1–28.

Martin, D., Hanrahan, B. V., O'Neill, J., & Gupta, N. (2014). Being a Turker. *Proceedings of the 17th ACM Conference on Computer Supported Cooperative Work and Social Computing*, 224–235.

Paolacci, G., Chandler, J., & Ipeirotis, P. G. (2010). Running experiments on Amazon Mechanical Turk. *Judgment and Decision Making*.

Qiu, S., Gadiraju, U., & Bozzon, A. (2020). Improving worker engagement through conversational microtask crowdsourcing. *Proceedings of the 2020 CHI Conference on Human Factors in Computing Systems*, 1–12.

Rani, U., & Furrer, M. (2019). On-demand digital economy: Can experience ensure work and income security for microtask workers? *Jahrbücher für Nationalökonomie und Statistik*, 239(3), 565–597.

Rani, U., & Furrer, M. (2021). Digital labour platforms and new forms of flexible work in developing countries: Algorithmic management of work and workers. *Competition & Change*, 25(2), 212–236.

Rosenblat, A. (2018). *Uberland: How algorithms are rewriting the rules of work.* University of California Press.

Rosenblat, A., & Stark, L. (2016). Algorithmic labor and information asymmetries: A case study of Uber's drivers. *International Journal of Communication*, 10(27).

Saito, S., Chiang, C.-W., Savage, S., Nakano, T., Kobayashi, T., & Bigham, J. (2019). Turkscanner: Predicting the hourly wage of microtasks. *World Wide Web Conference*, 3187–3193.

Savage, S., Chiang, C. W., Saito, S., Toxtli, C., & Bigham, J. (2020). Becoming the super Turker: Increasing wages via a strategy from high earning workers. *Proceedings of the Web Conference 2020*, 1241–1252.

Start, D., & Hovland, I. (2004). *Tools for policy impact: A handbook for researchers.* Overseas Development Institute.

Su, H., Deng, J., & Fei-Fei, L. (2012). Crowdsourcing annotations for visual object detection. *Workshops at the Twenty-Sixth AAAI Conference on Artificial Intelligence*.

Sutherland, W., & Jarrahi, M. H. (2018). The sharing economy and digital platforms: A review and research agenda. *International Journal of Information Management*, 43, 328–341.

Suzuki, R., Salehi, N., Lam, M. S., Marroquin, J. C., & Bernstein, M. S. (2016). Atelier: Repurposing expert crowdsourcing tasks as micro-internships. *Proceedings of the 2016 CHI Conference on Human Factors in Computing Systems*, 2645–2656.

Thies, W., Ratan, A., & Davis, J. (2011). Paid crowdsourcing as a vehicle for global development. *CHI Workshop on Crowdsourcing and Human Computation*.

Toxtli, C., Suri, S., & Savage, S. (2021). Quantifying the invisible labor in crowd work. *Proceedings of the ACM on Human-Computer Interaction*, 5(CSCW2), 1–26.

van Doorn, N. (2017). Platform labor: On the gendered and racialized exploitation of low- income service work in the "on-demand" economy. *Information, Communication & Society*, 20(6), 898–914.

Weyrauch, V., & Langou, G. D. (2011). Sound expectations: From impact evaluations to policy change. *International Initiative for Impact Evaluation Working Paper*, *12*.

Whiting, M. E., Gamage, D., Gaikwad, S. S., Gilbee, A., Goyal, S., Ballav, A. et al. (2016). Crowd guilds: Worker-led reputation and feedback on crowdsourcing platforms. arXiv: 1611.01572.

Williams, A. C., Mark, G., Milland, K., Lank, E., & Law, E. (2019). The perpetual work life of crowdworkers: How tooling practices increase fragmentation in crowdwork. *Proceedings of the ACM on Human–Computer Interaction*, *3*(CSCW), 1–28.

PART II

SECTORAL USES, APPLICATIONS, CHALLENGES, AND OPPORTUNITIES

6. AI and the transformation of agricultural work: economic, social, and environmental implications
Andrea Renda

AI AND AGRICULTURE: TECHNOLOGY MIRACLE, OR TECHNOLOGY TRAP?

There is no doubt, among scholars and market analysts, that agriculture will be massively affected over the coming decade by the development of digital technologies, including artificial intelligence (AI) and in particular machine learning (ML). The nature and magnitude of this impact are however difficult to anticipate, since they will depend on the policies that will be adopted by governments around the world to ensure that the prospective benefits of deploying AI in agriculture are maximized, and the corresponding risks are mitigated. The expected benefits are massive: not surprisingly, the global AI market for agriculture is estimated to grow from USD 820.3 million in 2019 to USD 6,189.75 million in 2030, a compound annual growth of 24.31 percent (Bharat Book Bureau 2020). At the same time, as will be explained in more detail below, the distribution of these benefits across the globe will be extremely unequal in the years to come.

In all respects, agriculture needs digital technology. It is one of the sectors that most dramatically impact climate change, and the one that most evidently operates beyond planetary boundaries (Rockström et al. 2009; Campbell et al. 2017). Agriculture today uses too much land (up to three times the maximum sustainable area) and too much freshwater (75 percent of the total availability); it sprays excessive toxic pesticides; it relies too much on monoculture; it loses or wastes too much food (one third of the total); and it contributes one third of net anthropogenic greenhouse gas (GHG) emissions (including a staggering 58 percent of nitrous oxide) (Renda et al. 2019). The global agri-food chain also features slowing productivity growth and enormous inefficiencies on the side of food distribution and consumption: besides food waste, today approximately 850 million people are undernourished, and even more people are at risk of premature death due to unhealthy diets. In this respect, digital technology is often invoked as the only way (together with advanced use of biotechnology) to reach the projected 70 percent increase in food production needed to feed the future population of the planet (estimated at 9.1 billion by 2050) without having to use even more land and freshwater. This is a challenge that requires an estimated 60 percent increase in productivity in the sector (FAO 2018).

Academics largely agree that agriculture features a series of tasks that are highly susceptible to automation. Among others, Nedelkoska and Qunitini (2018), in an analysis focused on countries of the Organisation for Economic Co-operation and Development, find that the tasks most exposed to automation are likely to be concentrated predominantly in manufacturing and agriculture. This is mostly due to the repetitive nature of many tasks, as well as their relatively low skill requirements. As a matter of fact, the number of use cases for AI deployment in agriculture has skyrocketed over the past years, giving rise to a whole new domain of research labeled AgTech (alternatively, "digital agriculture" or "agriculture 4.0"), mostly drawing on the already known yet increasingly technology-intensive practice of precision farming (Saiz-Rubio & Rovira-Más 2020). As will be shown in the first section, from the use of drones and image recognition to identify ripe fruit and crops to the use of sensors and actuators to monitor the moisture of the soil and dispense fertilizers with optimal timing, to the use of big data and prediction analytics in various phases of the supply chain, AI-enabled innovation is gradually revolutionizing agriculture. Productivity and returns on investment appear equally attractive: already in 2016, in a study focused on the United States, Schimmelpfennig (2017) reported that precision agriculture (including computer mapping, guidance, and variable-rate equipment) was increasing corn farm operating profit by as much as USD 163 per hectare compared to non-adopters, with margins rising to USD 272 depending on the crop.

Against this background, however, there are reasons to doubt that farmers, and in particular the 3 billion people living in roughly 475 million small farm households, working on land plots smaller than 2 hectares, will be ready for the massive transformation required to effectively deploy digital technologies such as AI and the Internet of Things (IoT). First, size matters: economies of scale appear to be extremely significant in agriculture (Duffy 2009). Not surprisingly, in the United States the agriculture sector has experienced a massive wave of concentration over the past decades, encompassing all agricultural inputs (seed, crop protection chemicals, machinery, processing, food manufacturing, and retail). This trend has further accelerated with the introduction of digital technologies: the power of big data, the ability of AI to integrate and process various data sources, and the increasingly digitized value chains inevitably generate massive economies of scale, which giants such as Monsanto, John Deere, and ChemChina are reaping to an extent that smaller producers are unable to replicate.

Moreover, while consolidation and economies of scale have driven productivity increases in agriculture, at least in developed countries, this trend was accompanied by a significant decrease of the share of agriculture in the economy. As of 2018, agriculture only represented 3 percent of the world's gross domestic product (GDP), but still employed almost 30 percent of all workers. This average figure hides enormous differences across regions. In the developed world, agriculture represents around 1 percent of GDP, whereas it accounts for more than 50 percent of GDP in many African and poorer Asian countries. In Africa, as much as 51 percent of workers are employed in agriculture (with peaks of over 80 percent in Somalia), while in Asia the share is 32 percent and in Latin American and the Caribbean it is 16 percent (AfDB et al. 2018). In the United States, it is as low as 1.36 percent. In least developed countries, deteriorating economic conditions also led to a rise in the employment of child labor in agriculture, as shown by a recent ILO and UNICEF study (2021). The same can be said more generally about forced labor (Blackstone et al. 2021).

The fall in the share of agriculture on the overall economy has been constant over the past decades and was partly due to mechanization, as well as the diversification of the economy, now characterized by a dominance of the service economy in high-income countries. Much of the employment formerly found in the agriculture sector has moved to services, creating problems of labor shortage in developed countries, especially when it comes to seasonal employment (Figure 6.1).

Based on these considerations, one would be tempted to draw a rather optimistic conclusion: if AI and related technologies can boost productivity and improve efficiency in agriculture, it may be able to promote growth, especially in those countries in which agriculture has a large share of the economy and labor. However, reality is likely to prove quite different, for several reasons.

As a matter of fact, precision agriculture and AgTech require, first and foremost, connectivity. Unfortunately, however, basic connectivity (let alone sophisticated IoT deployment) is missing exactly in those areas where agriculture is a dominant economic activity. Among others, Mehrabi et al. (2021) show that basic connectivity is still underdeployed especially in countries with high specialization in agriculture. They show that only 24–37 percent of farms of less than 1 hectare in size are served by 3G or 4G services, compared to 74–80 percent of farms larger than 200 hectares; and across many countries in Africa, less than ~40 percent of farming households have internet access, and the cost of data remains

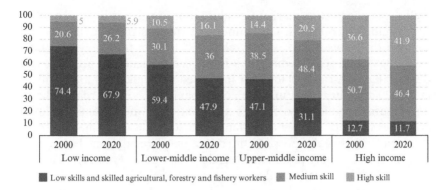

Source: UNCTAD based on data from ILOStat according to the ISCO-08.

Figure 6.1   Share of the labor force employed in agriculture, 2019

prohibitive. McKinsey (2021) estimates that by the end of the decade, enhanced connectivity in agriculture could add more than USD 500 billion to global GDP, a critical productivity improvement of 7 to 9 percent for the industry, but also acknowledges that much of that value will require investments in connectivity that are not being observed in the sector.

Additionally, it must be recalled that connectivity is not the only pre-condition for digital agriculture: equally important are data services, digital literacy, and skills, and these are largely missing in those areas where agriculture is most in need of being digitized. Against this background, UNCTAD (2021b) acknowledges the fear that "the widespread adoption of frontier technologies in developed countries will reduce the labor-cost competitiveness of today's less industrialized economies," and added that the COVID-19 pandemic may further exacerbate this disadvantage for lower-income countries, due to their "fewer resources, lower technological capabilities and less productive industries and agricultural sectors." Market forecasts for AI confirm that the enormous potential benefits of this technology are not expected to spread evenly throughout the world economy: based on estimates by McKinsey (2018), AI's 15.7 trillion USD potential would lead by 2030 to a 26.1 percent in GDP in China, a 14.5 percent rise in the United States, but only a 5 percent increase in Latin America and Africa. In a nutshell, as observed a decade ago by Lybbert and Sumner (2012), the developing regions of the world, with low agricultural productivity and high climate vulnerability, have the greatest need but the lowest access to sustainable agriculture technologies.

Finally, it is important to recall, albeit briefly, geo-economic and geo-political trends that may affect the evolution of the sector in the future, as well as the prospective market size and labor opportunities in agriculture for developing countries. One important trend is the ongoing shortening and diversification of supply chains, which in turn may lead many developed countries to reduce their imports of agricultural products from developing countries and look for increased self-sufficiency and resilience (FAO 2020). This trend may be accompanied by the search for higher agricultural productivity through automation, a move that developing countries may not be able to match, at least within the same timeframe. A second trend is the possible introduction of regulation that ends up restricting the export potential from developing to developed countries: these include, especially in the European Union (EU), whole-of-supply-chain due diligence obligations, and also carbon border adjustment taxes (UNCTAD 2021a). A third trend is the expansion of the Chinese Belt and Road Initiative (BRI) in several developing countries across the Global South, from the Indo-Pacific to Africa and Latin America: the BRI implies a high degree of automation, which may in turn lead to investment in infrastructure, mostly by Chinese private corporations, but at the same time rather limited labor opportunities for smallholders and low-skilled labor.

In summary, the AI–agriculture nexus is complex and potentially problematic, especially for the future of work. In countries and regions where agriculture is being rapidly digitized, one would expect a dramatic rise in productivity and market concentration, and a reshuffling of the job market due to radical task automation. In areas where agriculture will not immediately absorb the full benefits of AI, agriculture jobs will remain part of the production process, but the rising productivity gap may lead production to gradually shift to higher-productivity portions of the globe. In other words, whatever the scenario in terms of technology uptake, jobs in agriculture are at risk, and this calls for a proactive approach by governments. The prospect of low technological absorption led authors to argue that Sub-Saharan Africa is locked in a "technology trap" (Fofack 2008). Factors that may further worsen this prospective scenario include the effects of COVID-19, which is likely to divert resources in developing countries (e.g. from education and infrastructure to debt repayment and population subsidies); and the effects of climate change, which is likely to increase the frequency and intensity of extreme events, generating insecurity and causing damage in both semi-arid and sub-humid and humid areas. A recent study by Ortiz-Bobea et al. (2021) estimated that anthropogenic climate change has reduced global agricultural total factor productivity by about 21 percent since 1961; an effect that is substantially more severe (a reduction of 26–34 percent) in warmer regions such as Africa and Latin America and the Caribbean. Besides, projected temperature increases will reduce the total number of working hours in G20 countries by 1.9 per cent by 2030, with a greater effect on agricultural workers and on workers in emerging countries (ILO 2018).

In the second section, the emerging use cases of AI in agriculture are explored more in depth. The third section then describes the preconditions for entirely automated factories and their impact on productivity and urbanization. The fourth section summarizes the possible impacts of increased AI uptake on the quantity and quality of employment in agriculture. Finally, the chapter concludes by outlining a number of possible policy actions which would bring the digital transformation of agriculture in line with the Sustainable Development Goals (SDGs).

MAIN USE CASES OF AI IN AGRICULTURE AND THE EMERGING TECHNOLOGY STACK

Digital technologies such as AI are revolutionizing agriculture. This is mostly due to a combination of task automation, especially in the case of manual, repetitive tasks such as harvesting and sowing; data collection from a variety of sources, including sensors, drones, and satellite sources, plus direct data communication from other parts of the agri-food chain (e.g. marketplaces, distribution); data storage in the cloud or in more decentralized edge/cloud architectures; and the processing of data through AI, in particular ML. The resulting benefits encompass enhanced efficiency and productivity through automated data collection and sustainability gains through lower use of water, fertilizers, and pesticides. Below, some of the key emerging use cases are briefly illustrated.

- *Continuous data-driven feedback provided to farm systems.* With real-time data exchange and processing, farms can automatically adapt to changing environmental conditions and therefore optimize production. AI-augmented farms can also connect to smart marketplaces and automatically adjust crop quantities, based on supply and demand data coming from food retailers and food service providers downstream. In terms of sourcing products, farmers can benefit from real-time signaling from the market as to which crops are being demanded and at what prices. This, in turn, leads to a reduction in food waste and loss.
- *Precision farming.* Farmers will be able to grow different crops symbiotically, using ML solutions to spot or predict problems and to take appropriate corrective action via robotics. For example, should a corn crop be seen to need a booster dose of nitrogen, an

AI-enabled system (with IoT actuators) could deliver the nutrients. This kind of production could be more resilient to both predicted and unpredictable environmental events.

- *Support to human decisions.* By applying ML to sensor data and satellite data, farm management systems can evolve into real-time AI-enabled programs that provide rich recommendations and insights for farmer decision support and action. Key use cases include (Liakos et al. 2018):
  - *Crop management.* AI and complementary technologies can lead to improvements in yield prediction, which impacts key tasks such as yield mapping, yield estimation, matching crop supply with demand, and crop management to increase productivity. Use of AI also massively improves disease detection, particularly in the area of pest and disease control, where the use of ML allows much better targeting of agro-chemical input in terms of time and place, thus avoiding the uniform spraying of pesticides, and break-throughs in image processing and recognition can enable real-time control of plant infection, as well as real-time plant classification. IoT-enabled systems can help farmers manage diseases and pests more sustainably. Here again, imaging data from remote sensing technology can help identify and classify diseases and pests.
  - *Crop analysis and forecasts.* In terms of data availability, key contributions to the future of farming come from earth observation (including both soil observation and other factors, such as weather monitoring and forecasts), which enables ML applications to yield predictive value, which requires enormous amounts of data to create models, including from weather patterns. It also facilitates the estimate of land fertility by estimating moisture content, soil erosion, parkland forest cover, pest infestation, crop health, irrigated landscape mapping, and potential crop yield.
  - *Precision irrigation.* Agriculture accounts for around 70 percent of global freshwater withdrawals (FAO 2017). Optimizing the use of water is therefore crucial to "increase water-use efficiency across all sectors and ensure sustainable withdrawals and supply of freshwater" (UN 2015). IoT-enabled precision irrigation systems can help achieve just that in roughly three steps: identifying the right data and indicators; building an IoT infrastructure to collect the relevant data; and integrating the data into the broader system to analyze it and make it actionable (Zhang et al. 2018).
  - *Livestock management.* In the field of animal welfare, AI can help the monitoring and classification of behavior based on data from cameras and drones, the recognition of the impacts of

dietary changes (in cattle), and even the automatic identification and classification of chewing patterns (in calves) thanks to data collected by optical sensors. In the area of livestock production, studies have led to the accurate prediction and estimation of farming parameters to optimize the economic efficiency of the production system. Researchers are increasingly able to avoid using RFID tags to recognize and monitor animals, and this removes a source of stress for the animal itself, enabling them to leave their homecages and at the same time reducing costs.

○ *Water management.* ML is applied to the estimation of evapotranspiration, important for resource management in crop production, to the design and management of irrigation systems, and to the prediction of daily dew-point temperature.

○ *Soil management.* ML leads to a more accurate estimation of soil drying, condition, temperature, and moisture content, at the same time dramatically reducing costs. Using high-definition images from airborne systems (e.g. drones), real-time estimates can be made during cultivation periods by creating a field map and identifying areas where crops require water, fertilizer, or pesticides, with consequent resource optimization.

When it comes to connectivity, data availability, and processing, cloud-based solutions in agriculture face several challenges in smart agriculture, mostly related to security (especially since IoT networks enlarge and densify the "attack surface"); speed (data collection and transfer is extremely time consuming); and cost (cloud computing expenses typically depend on the amount of data generated by the "things" and transferred through the network; in addition, they have to be periodically replaced). In this respect, so-called "edge computing" potentially offers a solution by offering the possibility to deploy "agribots" that behave intelligently, for example by calculating the most efficient paths to cover the required area considering the type of task performed, number of vehicles currently in the field, size of implements, etc., and rerouting automatically in case of unexpected obstacles. Similarly, greenhouses or even entire farms can be put on autopilot using IoT edge computing, and regardless of the connection to the main server, take decisions locally based on the data from local sensors. This has the potential to improve process reliability and reduce waste, making agriculture more sustainable. Finally, with edge computing, agriculture IoT systems can take informed decisions about potential environmental hazards or natural disasters.

The resulting technology stack, as explained by Zamora-Izquierdo et al. (2019), is likely to be distributed into three main layers: crop (local) cyber-physical systems (CPS) tier, edge computing tier, and data analytics and smart management at the cloud. The CPS and cloud planes are designed to be respectively deployed at the local crop premises and remote data servers. The intermediate layer for edge computing comprises a set of virtualized control modules in the form of Network Functions Virtualization nodes that can be instantiated along the network path, from the field facilities to the cloud plane on the internet. This increases versatility in the deployment of the solution, while at the same time connectivity performances with the CPS layer are met. At the crop premises, sensors and actuators for automation are deployed and connected with CPS nodes.[1] Additionally, there are emergency reactive actions locally implemented in the CPS nodes that require real-time operation and can be launched without human or edge plane supervision. An example of these is the opening of windows and turning on ventilation if the greenhouse inner temperature reaches a predefined threshold. The data cloud serves as the interface between users and the core platform, which is where the current status of the crop and configuration parameters are maintained. Moreover, special analytics coupled with concrete service needs are performed using the cloud as data source.

The Promise of the Unmanned Farm

The World Economic Forum (2018) observed that smart agriculture has the potential to change agriculture even more, and more rapidly, than mass farming methods did. In particular, AI could enable farms to become almost fully autonomous if complementary technologies such as big data, 5G, or other forms of connectivity and edge/cloud infrastructure are made available.

As a matter of fact, the first pilot projects of entirely unmanned farms have started already, in 2017. As reported by Wang et al. (2021), United Kingdom-based Harper Adams University and Precision Decision jointly launched the Hands-Free Hectare project in 2017, employing automated tractors, exploration vehicles and harvesters, and unmanned aerial vehicles (UAVs) for drawing paths and for positioning. This project reportedly still required some human participation in UAV operation and background monitoring. One year later, in 2018, Keihanna opened the

---

[1]   Examples of sensors are solar radiation, humidity, temperature, carbon dioxide, pH meter, electrical conductivity, liquid consumption (flow meters), or pressure sensors, while some of the actuators considered are soil and water nutrition pumps, valves, and activation of devices (watering and ventilation devices, lighting, or automated windows).

first factory to use Techno Farm™, one of the largest automated vertical farms in the world, leveraging cutting-edge technologies such as robotics and the IoT, where planting, management, and harvesting are controlled by robots. This automated vertical farm achieves remarkable environmental and circular economy goals, such as 98 percent recycling of water resources, alongside a 25 percent increase in production and a 50 percent reduction of labor costs. The use of LEDs to simulate sunshine led to one third energy saving.

Several projects to establish completely unmanned farms have been launched in China since 2020. For example, a 20 hectare rice field in Waigang, Jiading District, employs agricultural vehicles equipped with a BeiDou Navigation Satellite System, which transports produce between a warehouse and the field, automatically avoiding obstacles in the way to carry out harvesting. Activities such as plowing, sowing, field management, and harvesting are entirely automated, and the farming area will be expanded to 1,600 mu (264 acres) in 2022. The impact of full automation on labor costs is reported at USD 15.47 per mu per year, and the income per mu 1,000 yuan higher than traditional farming. Similar projects were launched in Guangzhou's Huangpu district, in Zibo, Shandong province, and in northeast China's Heilongjiang province. One of these projects, led by Luo Xiwen, aims to reduce the labor cost of pig breeding by 30–50 percent, reduce feed consumption by 8–10 percent, and shorten the average slaughter time by 5–8 days, which can reduce the cost of 50 billion yuan a year.[2] In Australia, Wagga Wagga announced in 2021 the launch of the first fully automated farm, which will use robotic tractors, harvesters, survey equipment, and drones, AI that will handle sowing, dressing, and harvesting, new sensors to measure plants, soils, and animals and carbon management tools to minimize the carbon footprint. The farm is already operated commercially and grows a range of broadacre crops, including wheat, canola, and barley, as well as a vineyard, cattle, and sheep.

Farm automation is associated with a number of prospective benefits, beyond profitability. These include accuracy and learning from historical data, improved safety, efficient GPS-enabled digital pasture

---

2   Hands Free Hectare Project Set to Become World's First Fully Automated Crop Cycle, www.fdfworld. com/food/hands-free-hectare-project-set-become-worlds-first-fully-automated-crop-cycle; Unprecedented Productivity through Advanced Robotics, https://technofarm.com/en/innovation/; Unmanned Agricultural Machinery Completes Rice "Farming Management," http://digital paper.stdaily.com/, http_www.kjrb.com/kjrb/html/2020-09/07/content_453125.htm?div=-1; Jingdong Liu Qiangdong Announced: Pig Raising!, www.sohu.com/a/366309070_488608.

management, resource-saving smart irrigation, lower consumer prices, and a reduced environmental footprint. A recent analysis by Microsoft and PwC (Gillham 2020) suggests that agricultural AI applications can help reduce emissions by up to 160Mt CO_2e in 2030 whilst providing more food and using fewer resources. At the same time, it is associated with the gradual elimination of rather unsafe agricultural jobs on farms, and their partial replacement with service-oriented, higher-skilled, mostly off-farm jobs. Given the compelling economics of autonomous farming, it is likely that the AgTech market, especially that for autonomous farming equipment, will boom over the coming years, with initial applications mostly confined to developed countries. Current market forecasts place the global autonomous farm equipment market at USD 115.2 billion by 2024.[3]

Schimmelpfennig (2017) finds that information from precision agriculture "can promote stewardship and increase profits, but in some cases, it may raise operating costs." Balafoutis et al. (2017) confirm that technologies such as variable-rate nutrient application, variable-rate irrigation systems, controlled traffic farming, and machine guidance have substantial emission reduction potential; and that other technologies such as variable-rate pesticide application, variable-rate planting/seeding, and precision physical weeding show lower, but not irrelevant, GHG emission mitigation. A study conducted by OnFarm, as reported by Gorli (2017), found that following the usage of IoT on the average farm, yield rose by 1.75 percent, energy costs dropped USD 7 to USD 13 per acre, and water use for irrigation fell by 8 percent. The United States, where IoT is most widespread, produces 7,340 kg of cereal per hectare of farmland, compared to the global average of 3,851 kg of cereal per hectare. Having these figures in mind, it is easy to expect an uptake in IoT deployment, especially in large farms: IoT device installations in the agriculture world are projected to increase from 30 million in 2015 to 75 million in 2020.

Five Risks of the AgTech Revolution

As often occurs with digital technologies, the current AgTech revolution is likely to bring both opportunities and risks. Among the latter, the following are worth mentioning as they are relevant for the purposes of this chapter, i.e. they can directly affect the ability of this sector to develop in a resilient and sustainable way, creating good-quality jobs over the years to come.

---

[3]   https://markets.businessinsider.com/news/stocks/global-autonomous-farm-equipment-market-to-reach-115-2-billion-by-2024-1030702062

First, as already mentioned, the future of agriculture is connected. And this calls for bridging, wherever possible, the digital divide. This divide is defined by three primary factors: the availability of telecommunications infrastructure (connectivity); education and skills; and financial resources. All of these gaps need to be bridged in order to close the digital divide. According to the GSMA, almost half of the world's population was offline in 2020 and 40 percent will still be offline by 2025.

Second, future data-driven agriculture requires skills in data management. One third of individuals today reportedly lacks basic skills such as copying files or folders using copy and paste tools; only 41 percent have standard digital skills, such as installing or configuring software or using basic spreadsheet formulas; and only 4 percent master specialist computer languages to write computer programming (ITU 2018).

Third, digital technologies in agriculture entail non-negligible costs in order to set up the complex pipeline from data collection to (cloud) infrastructure, to analysis and action. In order to collect data, for example, farmers have to invest in IoT hardware to collect digital data (Figure 6.2). These complex steps can be partially outsourced to service providers, but these maintenance services imply recurring costs for farmers. Investment data show the enormous disparities between venture capital availability in different parts of the world. Funding is a critical input to innovation and the funding stage is also important: early funding is key to getting startups out of incubation and later-stage funding essential to scale a company into a market leader.

Fourth, one of the risks posed by digital solutions for sustainability is the massive energy consumption associated with the deployment of certain technologies at scale. In the specific case of AI and AgTech, possible environmental benefits due to greater resource efficiency and the reduced use of pesticides and fertilizers have to be gauged against the massive energy consumption requirements of data centers and sophisticated AI techniques such as deep learning.[4] In this respect, reliance on edge/cloud partly decentralized architectures may prove essential. For example, Ahvar et al. (2022) find that a distributed architecture, because of not using intra-data center network and large-size cooling systems, consumes between 14 and 25 percent less energy than fully centralized and partly distributed architectures (Uddin et al. 2021). Likewise, the increased use of digital devices

---

[4]   For example, it is estimated that data centers use 200 terawatt hours each year for the manufacturing and operation of information and communications technology infrastructure (International Energy Agency 2017). Also, AI models that use neural networks emit the carbon dioxide equivalent of nearly five times the lifetime emissions of an average American car (Strubell et al. 2019).

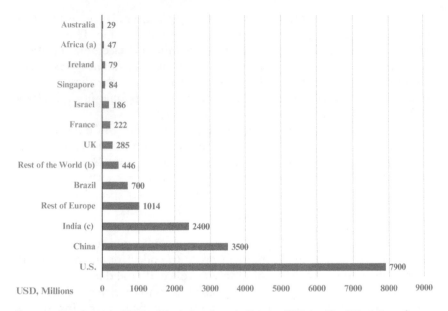

Source: Renda et al. (2019), elaboration from AgFunder 2018 Agrifood Tech Investing
Report; CTA/Dalberg D4Ag Investment Tracker, Disrupt Africa, CEPS analysis.

Figure 6.2   Global AgTech Investment 2018

may lead to growing problems related to e-waste: according to the United
Nations University's second Global E-waste Monitor, 44.7 million Mt of
e-waste was generated worldwide in 2016. It is estimated that, at the rate it
is growing, the e-waste stream will reach 50 million Mt in 2018.

A fifth source of concern is related to the possibility that the digital transformation of agriculture beyond developed countries leads to problems
of market concentration, data hoarding, and imbalances in contractual
power. As observed by Rotz et al. (2019, 117), data-producing equipment
such as smart tractors, UAVs, and sensors require data management to
transform the data into useful outputs for farmers; data management
platforms are being developed by AgTech giants, leading to situations in
which "while farmers still own the fields, they are effectively renting their
data." This places them in a situation of economic dependency, which
translates into weaker bargaining power and, ultimately, an inability to
retain the value generated by agricultural activity. This problem is related
to a more general problem of data ownership and governance, which led
at least some governments to seek to empower farmers vis à vis their contractual counterparties. For example, in the EU a Code of Conduct on
Agricultural Data Sharing by Contractual Arrangement was launched by

a coalition of associations from the EU agri-food chain in April 2018 to facilitate data management in the agri-food chain and attribute ownership to farmers. Such an initiative is unlikely to prove sufficient in protecting the data rights and ownership of farmers generally, and smallholder farmers specifically.

AUTOMATED AGRICULTURE: TOWARDS MASSIVE JOB DISPLACEMENT?

The pace and extent of automation and the lack of adequate skills are likely to create tensions in the job market in the coming years and reinforce the shift from labor to capital. In the original calculations by Frey and Osborne (2013), farm manual labor and pesticide applicators were projected to be most highly automated by 2030 (97 percent), with farm management being the task least likely to be automated (4.7 percent). Rotz et al. (2019) highlight three key tensions that are likely to arise in the domain of agriculture, especially in developing countries. First, rising land costs may induce farmers to speed up the adoption of automation to reduce labor input costs. Second is the possible polarization of the agriculture labor market, with highly qualified jobs becoming strongly demanded, whereas low-skill ones will almost disappear from the market. Third, issues will emerge regarding control over the digital data produced in the context of new digital agriculture business models.

It is extremely difficult to accurately predict the impact of digital agriculture on employment, given the many converging factors that will eventually determine the final outcome. To be sure, existing trends do not guarantee that technology, by itself, will help achieve the relevant SDGs. For example, meeting Target 2.3 of the SDGs would entail doubling agricultural productivity and the incomes of small-scale food producers, particularly women, indigenous peoples, family farmers, pastoralists, and fishers, including secure and equal access to land, other productive resources and inputs, knowledge, financial services, markets, and opportunities for value addition and non-farm employment. Meeting target 8.5 would imply full and productive employment and decent work for all. Against this backdrop, there seem to be important reasons to believe that the future of labor in agriculture will be far from bright. These reasons are related to the quantity of jobs as well as to their nature and quality.

In terms of labor requirements, governments in developed countries expect an increase during the current decade. This is due to the high average age of farmers in these countries (e.g. in Europe, 31 percent of farmers are older than 65 years, whilst only 6 percent are younger than 35; in Canada and the United States, the average age of farmers is 55 and 57.5, respectively), but also due to the need to increase production. For example, in Canada, a report estimated that by 2029 the agriculture sector will need significantly more workers to reach production targets: the sector is expected to see 112,200 workers retire between 2018 and 2029 (37 percent of the workforce), and the sector's labor gap (which already doubled between 2007 and 2017) will nearly double over the next 10 years, reaching 123,000 people by 2029 (CAHRC 2021). And while the top reported recruitment challenge is the difficulty of manual labor, the lack of qualified labor features highly on the list. In Australia, the Department of Agriculture observed that "the workforce is shrinking and aging, which may pose future challenges" and that "labour shortages could pose a significant problem to the industry's future viability" (Wu et al. 2019). In Japan, an ongoing population decline and a shift towards white-collar jobs imply that the average number of farmers will be halved by 2030 compared with 2005 (Yoshikawa 2022).

On the other hand, in developing countries the situation is likely to be different, given the high share of total employment still represented by agriculture. A recent comprehensive report on India confirms that the agricultural workforce will be "smaller, younger, and more feminized" in the future. Giller et al. (2021) highlight worrying trends for the development of the agricultural sector in the Global South, noting slow consolidation of farms in Southeast Asia and India, as well as insufficient conditions for the modernization of agriculture in Africa, where agriculture is expected to remain a prominent source of labor due to the lack of job alternatives in many regions. Absent comprehensive, ad hoc reform and investment, many of the countries in the Global South will be unlikely to catch up with the projected increase in the population, and meanwhile will be harmed by policies implemented by developed countries, the deterioration of land conditions due to climate change, and the gradual abandonment of land due to ongoing urbanization.

Big changes should however be expected in terms of the nature of the work required. Where AI and related technologies will be significantly adopted, one would expect technology to gradually replace workers in the jobs that feature high seasonality and a prevalence of manual, repetitive tasks. As an example, a single strawberry robot harvester has the potential to pick a 25 acre area in 3 days and replace 30 farm workers (Daniels 2018). Initially, the need to train ML systems will determine an increase in short-term employment (data trainers), which is anyway likely to fade away as machines become gradually more accurate. At the same time, off-farm employment in data management, farm management and planning, edge/cloud services, plus specialist skilled work featuring complementary skills to AI/IoT systems deployed on farms is expected to increase.

Another complex issue to be considered is the likely impact of digital technologies on the quality of on-farm and off-farm labor. Here, too, it is reasonable to expect both positive and negative impacts. Positive factors that may have to be considered include health benefits due to the replacement of human manual tasks like hand weeding, which typically put physical strain on workers (Sørensen et al. 2005), and benefits from lower stress (Reissig 2017), lower agrochemical exposure, and the reduction of accidents involving large machinery. The reduction of manual work can also open new opportunities for women participation, provided that adequate access to training is guaranteed. Gillham (2020), in a joint analysis by Microsoft and PwC, estimates that Sub-Saharan Africa and Indo-Pacific regions, due to the prominent share of employment engaged in lower-skilled agricultural work, will see by 2030 net job losses globally of 2.6 percent to 1.7 percent, "with the nature of work, and other economic factors, more directly replacing rather than augmenting employment"; they also add that "while the number of jobs and hours worked may change in different directions in each sector and occupation type, automation of repetitive tasks may also have positive effects on quality of life."

On the negative side, several potential elements need to be factored into the analysis, as explained above. First, the short-term emergence of repetitive jobs such as data cleaning and machine training may lead to rather poor working conditions, as well as lack of job security, as is explained in Chapter 17 of this volume. Second, dependence on AI-enabled machines can lead to gradual deskilling in the sector, even if to date this phenomenon has not been observed (Carolan 2020; Prause 2021). Third, capture of data and value may gradually lead to weaker bargaining power for farmers vis à vis larger tech corporations and a deterioration of working conditions; this phenomenon is exacerbated by AI and robotics, since workers may face a readily available alternative, which reduces their contractual power.

A POLICY MIX TO ENSURE A SUSTAINABLE TRANSITION TO DIGITALLY ENABLED AGRICULTURE

The agriculture sector has been radically transformed during the past century, from a dominant form of production to an almost residual sector in developed countries, and an inefficient yet paramount source of labor and the economy in the Global South. The sector still features extremely high levels of informality, lower-than-average wages, an ageing workforce, and patterns of production (and waste) that largely go beyond planetary boundaries (Steffen et al. 2015), at a time in which the Earth's population is rapidly increasing and the global supply chains that are expected to guarantee food availability are in deep crisis and transformation.

In all this, AI and related digital technologies represent an essential beacon of hope, but will be able to come to the rescue only if certain conditions are verified. Six main actions for policymakers are illustrated below.

1. *Invest in connectivity.* This does not mean pouring money into 5G telecommunications, as for agriculture the connectivity mix may entail the use of legacy 2G/3G networks and LPWA technologies (LoRa, Sigfox). In addition, satellite and space data are being made available for free (e.g. Copernicus data from the EU), and could be usefully employed to unleash the true potential of ML systems. In developing countries the connectivity needs may require a significant upgrade of the infrastructure, even to guarantee good LoRa connectivity, and an assessment of the scalability of LoRa investments into 5G/6G networks at a later stage. In addition, both for small farmers and less developed countries, the issue of technology affordability and accessibility will become essential, potentially triggering proposals for an international agreement on the licensing of key technologies at affordable conditions, as well as the provision of equipment "as a service" with the help of international donors or government actors.
2. *Deploy the full technology stack.* Once connectivity is in place, the whole IoT stack has to be deployed: this, too, may happen at different speeds in different parts of the world. The problem is that while IoT and enhanced connectivity are already being deployed in the United States and in some European countries, in other parts of the world this is far from being a prospect. The deployment of IoT in the fields brings significant positive externalities: suffice it to think that in developing countries, less than 10 percent of all spray applications reportedly hit a sick plant, a weed, or a parasite, and therefore 90 percent of spray is wasted and dispersed in the soil, water, or air (EPRS 2016). An essential part of the technology stack is also the edge/cloud architecture, which may end up depending on a limited number of cloud providers.
3. *Promote innovation and entrepreneurship.* This requires public and private sources of funding, the availability of managerial skills among farmers, access to technology, and knowledge needed to deploy solutions that increase yields, etc. Data-driven farming requires supportive policies and programs (e-government), along with data governance policies and standards, to keep data open and accessible to all

stakeholders, especially farmers. Solving these challenges will enhance the effectiveness of the assistance, making agrifood systems more sustainable globally by providing farmers with more tailored information and advice improving their output, yields, and helping them to move higher up the value chain.

4.   *Promote data aggregation at the community level.* According to OnFarm (a connected farm IoT platform provider), the average farm will generate 4.1 million data points by 2050. Renda et al. (2019) observe that using data to improve production practices could enable a 20 percent increase in income while reducing herbicide and fuel consumption by 10–20 percent. However, small-scale farmers are not yet well equipped to make the best use of data, absent dedicated advisory services and third-party support. Accordingly, new solutions and dedicated services will be needed, possibly leading towards community-led data management, coupled with the provision of basic skills and the gradual handover of responsibility to the local community. Digital technologies provide an obvious case for community-based agricultural support, not only for cost-sharing purposes but also for coordinated data management, as well as due to the spillover effects of connectivity and IoT deployment for the full community. In addition, one of the most compelling aspects of community-based services is the possibility to use equipment such as tractors and drones "as a service," in what is often defined as the "uberization" or "servitization" of assets. Finally, data-intensive business models are optimal when it comes to helping small farmers purchase insurance and establish trusted relationships with potential donors, thanks to enhanced possibilities to control land performance and a variety of indicators (Maru et al. 2018). Finally, aggregating data and creating community-based management of joint resources and information is also an effective way to connect local farmers to global supply chains, and to empower them with greater bargaining power (due to aggregation) in contractual relationships (Poppe et al. 2016; Wolfert et al. 2017).

5.   *Connect smallholders to global supply chains.* Once connectivity, data, and technology have been deployed, small-scale farmers must be connected to global supply chains. There, they will normally find much larger players and often end up in a situation of economic dependency, or weaker bargaining power. Here, governments may intervene to avoid the superior bargaining power of a variety of players, including retailers, food processors, wholesalers, cooperatives, producers' organizations, or individual, powerful producers. This requires the adoption of specific policy instruments, such as legislation on the agri-food supply chain to protect smaller players against large

manufacturers and retailers; or rules on abuse of economic dependence (Renda et al. 2014). Importantly, such rules will not be very effective in least developed countries, or more generally in all countries where the rule of law is weaker. Therefore, work has to be done to generate contractual templates and provide advisory services for both the relationship between farmers and distributors and between farmers and data managers whenever the option of farmer-managed data is unavailable.

6. *Promote the responsible, human-centric, and sustainable development of AI-enabled agriculture solutions.* As mentioned above, AI and IoT deployment can in many circumstances genuinely increase efficiency, productivity, and workers' well-being; however, there are cases in which these technologies may become attractive ways to reduce costs at the expense of social and environmental sustainability, let alone product quality (Acemoglu & Restrepo 2018; Renda & Laurer 2020). It is essential that policymakers incentivize the use of digital technologies when this is consistent with overall sustainable development: this notably entails the compatibility of deepening digital transformation with the goal to achieve full and decent employment, as well as nurturing human capital, reducing inequality, and protecting the environment. While the agriculture sector today produces massive negative externalities in terms of waste, emissions, health impacts, and loss of biodiversity, its digitized version may not necessarily achieve better results.

7. *Identify and implement pathways for the upskilling of agricultural workers.* Based on existing studies, middle-skilled workers include experts of organic farming techniques, agricultural technicians involved in crop diversification, and experts in the application of improved technologies. For high-skilled workers, key profiles include soil and water conservationists, environmental restoration planners (certification specialists, economists), water resource specialists and water/wastewater engineers, and agricultural meteorologists.[5] In general, reskilling may also be needed to fill existing gaps in data science and integration, edge/cloud architecture experts, image recognition experts (e.g. for hyperspectral imaging experts), and more generally ML experts, possibly to be deployed in service of a community of smallholders. Technological skills should aim at training farmers to work with robots, work with processed data, choose appropriate

---

[5]   www.ilo.org/wcmsp5/groups/public/---ed_emp/documents/publication/wcms_732214.pdf.

solutions according to the farming project, and master computer science, advanced machinery (auto-steered equipment, drones), and complex apps (RTK, satellite imagery). Environment skills include understanding legislation, gaining expertise in circular agriculture, gaining knowledge of local ecosystems, and acquiring genetics expertise. Finally, managerial skills include business management, innovation management, entrepreneurship, and marketing. Here, technology can come to the rescue through the use of online courses and distance learning.

CONCLUDING REMARKS

Digital technologies such as AI and the IoT promise to massively revolutionize agriculture. In the quest for efficiency- and productivity-enhancing innovation, several solutions are being deployed, ultimately leading to fully autonomous farms and the shift of most labor from on- to off-farm professions. In the context of highly digitized supply chains, the imperative for most small farms will become "adapt or perish." The consequences for future employment in this sector are massive, and the impact most likely negative. In particular, the sector is currently dominated in many countries by smallholders with limited digital skills. Absent ad hoc strategies to empower these workers with community services, including data stewardship and access to equipment as a service, the overall impact on the workforce may be dramatic. Accordingly, upskilling and reskilling strategies will become of utmost importance in many countries, especially those that chiefly depend on agriculture as a source of income and employment.

REFERENCES

Acemoglu, D., & Restrepo, P. (2018). The wrong kind of AI? Artificial intelligence and the future of labor demand. *Toulouse Network for Information Technology*, special issue.

AfDB, ADB, EBRD, & IDB (African Development Bank, Asian Development Bank, European Bank for Reconstruction and Development, & Inter-American Development Bank). (2018). The future of work: Regional perspectives. www.adb.org/sites/default/files/publication/481901/future-work-re gional-perspectives.pdf

Ahvar, E., Orgerie, A.-C., & Lebre, A. (2022). Estimating energy consumption of cloud, fog and edge computing infrastructures. *IEEE Transactions on Sustainable Computing*, 7(2), 277–288.

Balafoutis, A., Beck, B., Fountas, S., Vangeyte, J., van der Wal, T., Soto, I., Gómez-Barbero, M., Barnes, A., & Eory, V. (2017). Precision agriculture technologies positively contributing to GHG emissions mitigation, farm productivity and economics. *Sustainability*, 9, 1339.

Bharat Book Bureau. (2020). Global AI in agriculture market outlook 2030: Industry insights and opportunity evaluation, 2019–2030. www.bharatbook. com/marketreports/global-ai-in-agriculture-market-outlook-2030-industry-ins ights-opportunity-evaluation-2019-2030/2166703

Blackstone, N. T., Norris, C. B., Robbins, T., Jackson, B., & Decker Sparks, J. L. (2011). Risk of forced labour embedded in the US fruit and vegetable supply. *NatureFood*, 2, 692–699.

CAHRC (Canadian Agricultural Human Resources Council). (2021). How labour challenges will shape the future of agriculture: Agriculture forecast to 2029, at https://cahrc-ccrha.ca/sites/default/files/National%20Report_Final%20-%20 EN%202019%20reduced%20size.pdf

Campbell, B. M., Beare, D. J., Bennett, E. M., Hall-Spencer, J. M., Ingram, J. S. I., Jaramillo, F. et al. (2017). Agriculture production as a major driver of the Earth system exceeding planetary boundaries. *Ecology and Society*, 22(4), 8.

Carolan, M. (2020). Acting like an algorithm: Digital farming platforms and the trajectories they (need not) lock-in. *Agricultural Human Values*, 37, 1041–1053.

Daniels, J. (2018). From strawberries to apples, a wave of agriculture robotics may ease the farm labor crunch. *The Edge*. www.cnbc.com/2018/03/08/wave-of-agriculture-robotics-holds-potential-to-ease-farm-labor-crunch.html

Duffy, M. (2009). Economies of size in production agriculture. *Journal of Hunger & Environmental Nutrition*, 4(3–4), 375–392.

EPRS (European Parliament Research Service). (2016). Precision agriculture and the future of farming in Europe. Scientific Foresight Study. www.euro parl.europa.eu/RegData/etudes/STUD/2016/581892/EPRS_STU(2016)581892_ EN.pdf

FAO. (2017). Water for sustainable food and agriculture: A report produced for the G20 presidency of Germany. www.fao.org/3/i7959e/i7959e.pdf

FAO. (2018). The future of food and agriculture: Alternative pathways to 2050.

FAO. (2020). COVID-19 and the risk to food supply chains: How to respond?

Fofack, H. (2008, March 1). Technology trap and poverty trap in Sub-Saharan Africa. World Bank Policy Research Working Paper No. 4582. https://ssrn.com/ abstract=1149085

Frey, C., & Osborne, M. (2013). The future of employment: How susceptible are jobs to computerization? Working Paper, Oxford Martin. https://doi. org/10.1016/j.techfore.2016.08.019

Giller, K. E., Delaune, T., Silva, J. V., Descheemaeker, K., van de Ven, G., Schut, A. G. T. et al. (2021). The future of farming: Who will produce our food? *Food Security*, 13, 1073–1099.

Gillham, J. (2020). How AI can enable a sustainable future. PWC. www.pwc. co.uk/services/sustainability-climate-change/insights/how-ai-future-can-enable-sustainable-future.html

Gorli, R. (2017). *Future of smart farming with Internet of Things*. MAN TECH Publications.

ILO. (2018). The employment impact of climate change adaptation. Input Document for the G20 Climate Sustainability Working Group.

ILO & UNICEF. (2021). Child labour: Global estimates 2020, trends and the road forward, ILO and UNICEF.

International Energy Agency. (2017). Digitalisation and energy. https://iea.blob. core.windows.net/assets/b1e6600c-4e40-4d9c-809d-1d1724c763d5/Digitalizatio nandEnergy3.pdf

ITU (International Telecommunications Union). (2018). *Measuring the Information Society 2018.*

Liakos, K. G., Busato, P., Moshou, D., Pearson, S., & Bochtis, D. (2018). Machine learning in agriculture: A review. *Sensors*, 18, 2674.

Lybbert, T. J., & Sumner, D. A. (2012). Agricultural technologies for climate change in developing countries: Policy options for innovation and technology diffusion. *Food Policy*, 37(1), 114–123.

Maru, A., Berne, D., Beer, J. D., Ballantyne, P. G., Pesce, V., Kalyesubula, S. et al. (2018). Digital and data-driven agriculture: Harnessing the power of data for smallholders. Global Forum on Agricultural Research and Innovation.

McKinsey. (2018). Notes from the AI frontier: Modeling the impact of AI on the world economy. www.mckinsey.com/featured-insights/artificial-intelligence/ notes-from-the-ai-frontier-modeling-the-impact-of-ai-on-the-world-economy

McKinsey. (2021). Where machines could replace humans—and where they can't (yet). www.mckinsey.com/business-functions/mckinsey-digital/our-insights/ where-machines-could-replace-humans-and-where-they-cant-yet

Mehrabi, Z., McDowell, M. J., Ricciardi, V., Levers, C., Diego Martinez, J. D., Mehrabi, N., Wittman, H., Ramankutty, N., & Jarvis, A. (2021). The global divide in data-driven farming. *Nature Sustainability*, 4, 154–160.

Nedelkoska, L., & Quintini, G. (2018). Automation, skills use and training. *OECD Social, Employment and Migration Working Papers*, 202, OECD Publishing. https://doi.org/10.1787/2e2f4eea-en

Ortiz-Bobea, A., Ault, T.R., Carrillo, C.M., Chambers, R. G., & Lobell, D. B. (2021). Anthropogenic climate change has slowed global agricultural productivity growth. *Nature Climate Change*, 11, 306–312.

Poppe, K., Bogaardt, M. J., & Wal, T. (2016). The economics and governance of digitalisation and precision agriculture. Briefing paper 4. *Precision Agriculture and the Future of Farming in Europe.*

Prause, L. (2021). Digital agriculture and labor: A few challenges for social sustainability. *Sustainability*, 13, 5980.

Reissig, L. (2017). Häufigkeit von Burnouts in der Schweizer Landwirtschaft. *Agrarforschung Schweiz*, 8(10), 402–409.

Renda, A., & Laurer, M. (2020). What can the digital transformation and IoT achieve for Agenda 2030? CEPS. www.ceps.eu/ceps-publications/iot-4-sdgs/

Renda, A. et al. (2014). Study on the legal framework covering business-to-business unfair trading practices in the retail supply chain. European Commission, DG MARKT.

Renda, A., Reynolds, N., Laurer, M., & Cohen, G. (2019). Digitising agrifood. Joint Report of CEPS and the Barilla Centre for Food and Nutrition.

Rockström, J., Steffen, W., Noone, K., Persson, Å., Chapin III, F. S., Lambin, E. et al. (2009). Planetary boundaries: Exploring the safe operating space for humanity. *Ecology and Society*, 14(2), 32.

Rotz, S., Gravely, E., Mosby, I., Duncan, E., Finnis, E., Horgan, M. et al. (2019). Automated pastures and the digital divide: How agricultural technologies are shaping labour and rural communities. *Journal of Rural Studies*, 68, 112–122.

Saiz-Rubio, V., & Rovira-Más, F. (2020). From smart farming towards agriculture 5.0: A review on crop data management. *Agronomy*, 10(2), 207.

Schimmelpfennig, D. (2017). Crop production costs, profits, and ecosystem stewardship with precision agriculture. *Journal of Agricultural and Applied Economics*, 50, 1–23.

Sørensen, C. G., Madsen, N. A., & Jacobsen, B. H. (2005). Organic farming scenarios: Operational analysis and costs of implementing innovative technologies. *Biosystems Engineering*, 91(2), 127–137.

Steffen, W., Richardson, K., Rockström, J., Cornell, S. E., Fetzer, I., Bennett, E. M. et al. (2015). Planetary boundaries: Guiding human development on a changing planet. *Science*, 347(6223), 736–747.

Strubell, E., Ganesh, A., & McCallum, A. (2019). Energy and policy considerations for deep learning in NLP. arXiv: 1906.02243.

Uddin, A., Ayaz, M., Mansour, A., Aggoune, e.-H., Sharif, Z., & Razzak, I. (2021). Cloud-connected flying edge computing for smart agriculture. *Peer-to-Peer Networking and Applications*, 14.

UN. (2015). Resolution adopted by the General Assembly on 25 September 2015. Transforming our world: The 2030 Agenda for Sustainable Development. www.un.org/en/development/desa/population/migration/generalassembly/docs/globalcompact/A_RES_70_1_E.pdf

UNCTAD. (2021a). *A European Union carbon border adjustment mechanism: Implications for developing countries*. Geneva: UNCTAD.

UNCTAD. (2021b). *Technology and innovation report 2021: Catching technological waves innovation with equity*. UNCTAD.

Wang, T., Xu, X., Wang, C., Li, Z., & Li, D. (2021). From smart farming towards unmanned farms: A new mode of agricultural production. *Agriculture*, 11, 145.

Wolfert, S., Ge, L., Verdouw, C., & Bogaardt, M. J. (2017). Big data in smart farming: A review. *Agricultural Systems*, 153, 69–80.

Wu, W., Dawson, D., Fleming-Muñoz, D., Schleiger, E., & Horton, J. (2019). The future of Australia's agricultural workforce. CSIRO Data61.

Yoshikawa, Y. (2022). Combatting Japan's agricultural worker shortage. *East Asia Forum*, March 3.

Zamora-Izquierdo, M. A., Santa, J., Martínez, J., Martínez, V., & Skarmeta, A. F. (2019). Smart farming IoT platform based on edge and cloud computing. *Biosystems Engineering*, 177, 4–17.

Zhang, L., Dabipi, I., & Brown, W., Jr. (2018). Internet of Things applications for agriculture. Institute of Electrical and Electronics Engineers. http://iranarze.ir/wp-content/uploads/2018/10/E9758-IranArze.pdf

7.   AI in manufacturing and the role of humans: processes, robots, and systems

Panagiotis Stavropoulos, Kosmas Alexopoulos, Sotiris Makris, Alexios Papacharalampopoulos, Steven Dhondt, and George Chryssolouris

INTRODUCTION

The definition of artificial intelligence (AI) has changed over time, but certain challenges associated with it have remained stable, such as problems of representation and prediction (Schank, 1987). Technical challenges like these are revisited often and center on specific considerations (Hagendorff & Wezel, 2020) – for example, on differences between human thinking and machine intelligence. Also, the problematics around AI, especially regarding machine skills and their corresponding social repercussions (Long & Magerko, 2020), are especially relevant.

In the current era, AI offers many ways of "learning from experience," and this is highly useful for many companies (Akerkar, 2019). Loureiro et al. (2021) have identified 18 areas of AI use that add value to businesses, including manufacturing and marketing. At the same time, despite the fact that legacy companies view data as an asset (Kiron & Schrage, 2019), they seem to have adopted approaches different from those of AI-ready companies, where resources and organizational readiness are elaborate.

The impact of AI on manufacturing, in particular, is large (Wang, 2019), with quite a few success stories continually being reported (NIST, n.d.). Hence, given the need for human centrality in manufacturing (EC, n.d.), it is necessary to redefine the human role in the decision-making process (in both design and operation). The desired human inclusion, as well as the required resilience, will be part of a successful collaboration between humans and machines. In addition to the social complications, the technical difficulties of decision making (MIT SLOAN, n.d.) may be overcome as well.

In this chapter, a distinction is made between Industry 4.0, which is targeted at networked automation-related agents within a factory, and Industry 5.0, which is characterized by simultaneously addressing sustainability, resilience, and human-centricity. We have organized this chapter according to manufacturing functionalities. The design and operational phases of manufacturing are considered, followed by a discussion of the use of AI at three different levels where it supports manufacturing: (1) the process level, where tools interact with the product; (2) the level of automation and robotics, focusing on the line level; and (3) the systems level, where factories and manufacturing networks are studied on a larger scale.

Design and Operation

In manufacturing, there are two distinct phases, design and operation (Chryssolouris, 2006), each with its own requirements for decision making. In the first phase, the design of processes (Papacharalampopoulos et al., 2021) and overall manufacturing cells (Stavropoulos et al., 2022a) takes place. It can also extend to factory design or networked manufacturing. During this phase, the closest-to-optimum configuration has to be selected for a smooth exchange of materials and information to take place through the high utilization of resources. This involves selecting and utilizing specific key performance indicators (KPI). The operation phase involves the materials and information exchanges themselves. There are decisions to be made at this point that could not have been addressed during the design phase. For instance, scheduling cannot be foreseen beforehand, mainly due to order unpredictability. Flexibility, nevertheless, needs to be addressed in both phases, so that potential changes can be managed.

Decision Making and AI

Ranging from operations research (Gupta et al., 2022) to smooth operations, such as monitoring and control (Stavropoulos et al., 2013), are tens of decision-making points within a factory, where cognition, the quantification of metrics, and the assessment of status need to coexist. To this end, AI can provide the tools (i.e., heuristics, machine learning, and natural language processing) to facilitate procedures in parallel with integrating human capabilities. At the same time, so-called "context awareness" may invoke links to the use phase (Papacharalampopoulos et al., 2020b) or the supply chain, enforcing restrictions and affecting the data management in the value chain.

Human ingenuity and creativity can contribute to this overall optimization. At the same time, data elaborated by AI can be used by humans to make decisions. This has highlighted the need for a multitude of constraints on AI (Kazim et al., 2021; Leikas et al., 2019), such as constraints regarding:

- responsibility;
- privacy;
- transparency;
- explainability;
- robustness;
- security;
- bias; and
- ethics by design.

As per the European Commission's vision (EC, n.d.), Industry 5.0 "complements the existing 'Industry 4.0' approach by specifically putting research and innovation at the service of the transition to a sustainable, human-centric and resilient European industry." So, to this end, it is imperative for each business in manufacturing to adopt technologies and innovations that can move towards achieving this strategy.

Industry 5.0 has been associated with several enabling technologies (Müller, 2020), and all approaches that can facilitate the transition to their use are desirable. AI is at the front of this technological disruption in industry, aiming for full collaboration between technology and humans. Figure 7.1 depicts the anticipated transformation, illustrating the impact at all levels (manufacturing processes, line, automation, systems, human resources, business, and marketing).

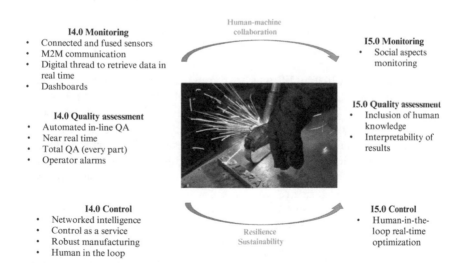

Human-machine collaboration

I4.0 Monitoring
- Connected and fused sensors
- M2M communication
- Digital thread to retrieve data in real time
- Dashboards

I5.0 Monitoring
- Social aspects monitoring

I4.0 Quality assessment
- Automated in-line QA
- Near real time
- Total QA (every part)
- Operator alarms

I5.0 Quality assessment
- Inclusion of human knowledge
- Interpretability of results

I4.0 Control
- Networked intelligence
- Control as a service
- Robust manufacturing
- Human in the loop

I5.0 Control
- Human-in-the-loop real-time optimization

Resilience
Sustainability

Source: Integrated image: www.piqsels.com/en/public-domain-photo-zkaqf.

Figure 7.1   The transformation from Industry 4.0 to Industry 5.0

The Role of Humans

More than is commonly understood, the role of humans is more important in Industry 5.0 development than in Industry 4.0, and certainly in the application of AI in the different dimensions of manufacturing. The way humans interact with technology needs to be understood at the level of individual human needs and at the organizational level.

At the individual level, workers function based on their needs, their experience with technology, their perception of constraints in manufacturing, and their understanding of what businesses requires. Even if there is a major discussion in the social sciences on which human needs are important (objective versus subjective, such as the pyramid of needs; Burnes, 2017), it would be an oversight not to take such needs into account when designing workplaces and functions in organizations.

It is equally important to understand how individuals see technology. Workers' first encounters with AI in the operational environment may be colored by the fact that they have already experienced it in their everyday lives (Manser Payne et al., 2021), including both its benefits and drawbacks, and they may bring this understanding to the workplace. No technology works perfectly. Workers are confronted by several burdens (emotional, mental, biased, manipulative, private, and social; Park et al., 2021) when trying to comply with their job demands. Even if the number of humans in the workplace decreases each year, it does not mean that those who stay are detached from the goals of a business. Workers understand the need for co-creation in business (Saha et al., 2020), and they play an important role in generating innovations (Loureiro et al., 2020).

The logic of Industry 4.0 was to bypass any hindrances to implementation. The slow adoption of Industry 4.0 by companies has been due to a lack of consideration for the needs of individuals in these technological situations (Genz, 2022). In an Industry 5.0 context, there is a need to understand how to deal with these needs, worker engagement, and behavior. For AI to succeed in Industry 5.0, new guidelines are needed to manage the relationship between the individual and technology. In the literature, we can see a shift in AI design guidelines towards good interaction (Amershi et al., 2019). A better understanding is needed of what individuals are thinking in manufacturing. Such an understanding can lead to the integration of guidelines and requirements into mental models (Villareale & Zhu, 2021) for engineers and managers.

Task Modeling and Sociotechnical Design

Industry 5.0 has the task of reviving an understanding of how to design workplaces and organizations. Workplaces need to offer humans opportunities to solve their most basic work issues (Dhondt et al., 2014). The way an organization is designed influences the type of work issues that will arise. Work that is reduced to simple tasks will invariably result in the need for a more complex organization. Humans stuck doing simple and repetitive tasks with no future professional growth are unlikely to succeed. Such simple work, however, is not always easy to automate, even if AI is available, and there are constraints attached to organizational issues due to established workflows. An alternative is to create more complex workplaces where humans can solve work issues on their own. In such contexts, the organizational components would be greatly simplified. These lessons have long been integrated into sociotechnical design (Stavropoulos et al., 2020b) and apply even in the AI era we are entering. Creating interesting organizational working conditions also allows for better workplaces (Mohr & Van Amelsvoort, 2016b). Tools such as TNO's Well-Being During Work help companies to evaluate and improve workplaces (Oeij et al., 2017; Rodijnen, 2021). Human-centricity should be embedded in these sociotechnical design principles.

AI AT THE PROCESS LEVEL

Quality Monitoring

High quality is the main driver of manufacturing to make products appealing in the marketplace. There are many approaches to, and branches of, quality management, with a leading set of operations focusing on process quality monitoring (and control). Methodologies in this area range from data-based techniques (Stavropoulos et al., 2020a) to linking to physics-based models (Stavridis et al., 2018). Figure 7.2 shows an example, illustrating the use of convolutional neural networks for processing thermal videos to assess welding quality. The sampling rate and the amount of data gathered by such applications are quite significant.

In addition to welding quality monitoring, there are applications with similar requirements and setups. One example is tool-wear estimation applications that use non-invasive sensors (Stavropoulos et al., 2016). Finally, there are other applications, such as an application for the selection of optimal scenarios for path planning during processing (Foteinopoulos et al., 2020); additive manufacturing is

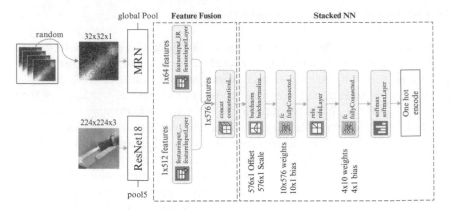

Source: Stavropoulos et al., 2022d.

Figure 7.2   AI use in welding quality monitoring

one example and applications for chatter detection are another (Stavropoulos et al., 2022e).

The goal of all these applications is to use market-available sensors to retrieve useful signals and indirectly predict performance indicators. However, the correlation of the latter with the indicator that one wishes to monitor is not straightforward. Thus, a so-called "black box" must be created that can correlate these two measures. In the process, human knowledge can be of high added value, especially with respect to modeling information to produce an intuitive visualization of the prediction results (Stavropoulos & Papacharalampopoulos, 2022). At the same time, the information flow from AI to humans is also useful, as it can help with training, decision making, human-centricity, and the collaborative operation of manufacturing processes (shared among machines and humans), leading to sustainability. Achieving an efficient prediction system depends mainly on a combination of computational power and human ingenuity.

Extra Applications

Quality monitoring is useless if it is not accompanied by some sort of certification. The latter, however, is not straightforward; each area of manufacturing uses different standards relating to processes, products, and even applications. AI must be able to process these standards. Certification, moreover, does not end with quality monitoring. There are different types of certification, including certification by energy and resource efficiency, origin ("made in X"), and non-financial reporting (Stolowy & Paugam, 2018), in general. Other certifications of interest at the manufacturing process level include certification relating to energy efficiency problems (or sustainability in general; Saxena et al., 2020), process modeling itself (Stavropoulos et al., 2021a), and control (which is part of the discussion below).

Digital Twins

There is a plethora of KPIs (Papacharalampopoulos et al., 2020a) in manufacturing, and with Industry 5.0 there is even an expansion of this list towards quantifying workplace and well-being conditions (Mohr & Van Amelsvoort, 2016a). Therefore, the models facilitating optimization procedure(s) need to be fast enough to solve problems in real time,[1] adaptive enough to integrate data from production, and responsive enough to provide feedback to the physical system. This new, enhanced type of model can then be defined as a digital twin (DT).

In fact, for DTs, there may be more requirements, depending on the application, with Industry 5.0 including still more, such as knowledge management and interaction with humans. All of the above required complex architecture, which led to the development of DTs. Architectures are able to facilitate resilience and robustness (Stavropoulos et al., 2021b) and to integrate many different AI submodules. Technically, however, the integration of AI into DTs appears to present quite a few problems, "drift" being one of them (Mehmood et al., 2021), resulting in the AI model decay with respect to real data.

The use of DTs has been recommended in the literature in many different areas, including robotics (Kousi et al., 2021; Polini & Corrado, 2020), ergonomics (Arkouli et al., 2022), human–robot interaction (Wang et al., 2020), and explainability and interaction (Stavropoulos et al., 2022b). There are even DTs for smart cities (Ruohomäki et al., 2018) and links to product and/or manufacturing lifecycles (Papacharalampopoulos & Stavropoulos, 2022).

Additional AI-related functionalities of the DT can be learning transfer (Sun et al., 2018) and the evolution of meta-learning (Hospedales et al., 2021), to ensure that AI is reapplicable, to allow for federated learning (Li et al., 2020), and to integrate shared but not common knowledge with business applications (Alexopoulos et al., 2020), including in the

---

[1] A soft approach to real time in production could mean "faster than the process cycle time."

management of data and knowledge (Siaterlis et al., 2022). Process planning (Stavropoulos et al., 2022c) may also need networks of DTs that exchange data and information.

Human-in-the-Loop Optimization

The transition to Industry 5.0 (Mourtzis et al., 2022) is not effortless; decision making, collaboration, and jobs need to be re-envisioned in the process of design, considering human actions that range from artistic interventions and creativity (Friesike et al., 2019; Papacharalampopoulos & Balafoutis, 2021) to dexterity (Andronas et al., 2021). Processes function properly if they are designed with humans co-deciding about human–AI interaction. A human-in-the-loop approach helps humans to (co-)govern with algorithmic systems, which increases people's perceptions of the legitimacy of automated decision making (Waldman & Martin, 2022). Humans-in-the-loop goes further than explainable AI, in the sense that humans operate better if they know they can intervene in automated decision making. It is not enough to explain the process by which an autonomous AI operates.

Human Aspects

Humans need to be able to improve on the decisions made by automatic systems. The designers of production systems are always confronted by gaps in their understanding of what is happening in a workplace. The distinction between tacit and non-tacit knowledge has long governed the development of knowledge management systems, because not all knowledge is formalized (Nonaka & Takeuchi, 1995). AI can only perform well if it is also clear in the design what has not been programmed. However, self-learning systems create a new form of non-tacit knowledge, this time created by AI. AI systems that improve work practices or help to innovate products come up with solutions that are not always understood. However, innovation can never become autonomous; engineers, and eventually workers, will need to learn the rules that AI-based machines use to come up with solutions. There will be a need to map how AI systems find new procedures for managing production processes.

AI AT THE AUTOMATION LEVEL AND ROBOTICS

Planning

The design and operation of flexible workplaces involving humans and robots rely substantially on methods for efficient task planning (Evangelou et al., 2021). The main aim of planning is to provide near optimal task assignments to both humans and robots, taking into account the cognitive and physical load of operators while trying to avoid allocating repetitive tasks to humans and working to exploit capabilities like the cognition and dexterity of humans. Figure 7.3 shows such an application, where both human and robot (an automated guided vehicle) coexist in the same space without fences or path restrictions as safety measures. Assembly is the main operation for the corresponding applications.

Human–robot collaborative work cells are designed to enhance the conventional industrial lines by enabling seamless interaction between operators and machines. Shifting away from standard (mainly static) work cells, with operators and machines following strictly defined limits and schedules, the new era of manufacturing introduces versatile workspaces shared by the manufacturing resources.

Knowledge Management

Knowledge management through dedicated platforms (Belkadi et al., 2020) extends the functionality of DTs mainly by linking the semantics of manufacturing tasks to the geometrical representation in the DT. This way, additional submodules of AI can be employed to help process

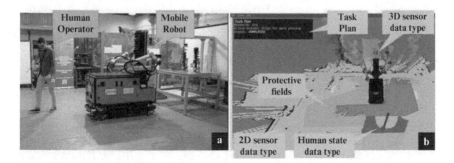

Source: Kousi et al., 2021.

Figure 7.3   Automotive pilot cell: (a) real world; (b) 3D planning scene

additional information and data and thus advance the way machines and robots interact with people. The interaction between human and robots/ AI in such applications is of great importance. Cognitive (Michalos et al., 2010) and physical loads need to be estimated in real time, and AI models can utilize this information and give feedback and/or control to the physical systems and the human operators. Multimodal data are stored and processed to this end, making decisions every fraction of a second with respect to motion and related tasks.

Human–Robot Interaction, Collaboration, and Symbiosis

Human–robot cognitive teaming (Chakraborti et al., 2017) is not straightforward. There are many challenges in both designing and operating such systems. These can be categorized with respect to the functional area; they may involve communication, interactive activity, data processing, decision making, and even modeling. AI and humans take part in every one of these activities. The challenges faced by human-aware AI systems (Kambhampati, 2020) can be addressed through approaches such as augmented reality, explainable AI, and ethics. Even though the roles of the agents (human and AI-based) are distinct, knowledge management (Nikolakis et al., 2019) remains a singular function requiring a lot of attention and contributions from multiple disciplines.

Seamless human–robot collaboration requires equipping robots with cognitive capabilities that give them an awareness of the environment, as well as of the actions that take place inside the assembly cell. One approach (Dimitropoulos et al., 2021) is an AI-based system composed of three modules that can capture the status of the operator, the environment, the process, and the status, and identify the tasks being executed by the operator. The system uses vision-based machine learning and provides customized operator support from the robot side for shared tasks, automatically adapting to the operator's needs and preferences. Moreover, the proposed system can assess the ergonomics of human–robot shared tasks and adjust the robot's position to improve ergonomics, using a heuristics-based search algorithm.

Digital Human Modeling

The modeling of human presence is a mandatory component in a human–robot collaborative assembly system (Tzavara et al., 2021). Human body detection provides detailed information regarding human body posture and positioning in the workspace. 2D and 3D data are fused to map the position of the whole human body and construct a digital human model.

To acquire these data, various vision-based AI methods are used for skeletal point detection and tracking.

In addition to the "existence" of a person on the shop floor, "working task" information is necessary for human modeling. Operators have several degrees of freedom in this respect, which means that the way a task is executed differs from person to person. In addition, operators might make moves such as touching their head or adjusting their uniform. Those common actions are deviations from the predefined order of actions but should not be considered errors. AI-based methods for predicting human intentions and task status take into consideration the different ways a task can be executed and the minor deviations that may occur during execution.

Human Aspects

The design of human–robot interaction is not straightforward, either. Removing the cage around robots does not guarantee a workplace will be more productive. The current design of collaborative robots (cobots) is limited, as the first principle of design is not to inflict pain on humans; consequently, cobots today are not productive enough to transform companies. One way to break this barrier to productivity would be to allow cobots to interact more freely with workers. Looser programming increases risks for workers (Owen-Hill, 2019) but enables them to experiment more with the technology.

The interactions between robots and humans are complex, but so far there has been no reported accident involving cobots and humans (Dhont & Dessers, 2022). One challenge, nevertheless, is that workers do not feel comfortable being near such systems (Kim, 2020). This happens because robot systems do not have standard designs (e.g., cobots vary in hard or flexible actuators), which confuses humans. A lot of research is focused on the different types of human psyches and how they affect the way a person will think and interact with robots and AI (de Vries, 2016).

AI AT THE SYSTEMS LEVEL

Design and Operation Optimization

The systems level, the most inclusive level, requires a number of AI-based solutions to address design and operation optimization, namely in supply-chain management, scheduling, and maintenance. In addition, the modeling of manufacturing systems itself can benefit from empirical models such as the heuristic modeling used in production planning and scheduling (Chryssolouris et al., 2000). An example is dematerialization, where human intuition is involved while data are collected and the system is evolving at the same time (Petrides et al., 2018).

There are many different ways that AI and humans can coexist, depending on the application. Figure 7.4 presents an example of such collaboration – the swapping of batteries in an electric vehicle. An activity like this poses several challenges. Besides quality/energy monitoring and maintenance, this interaction must consider logistics manipulation through heuristics, intellectual property rights (IPR) management through language processing, machine learning for integration optimization, and multimodal safety, among many other considerations. In manufacturing, *networked frugal manufacturing*, which is fabrication using a minimal number of low-cost local processes, can involve both AI and humans, while the product is optimized during the design phase. As stated by Cetinic and She (2022), "in the context of art creation and production, AI technologies are starting to have an ever more important role."

Decision Making under Specific Strategies

For a system that represents a whole factory or a manufacturing network, a set of strategies can be adopted at a holistic level, and this requires overall optimization, besides the local optimizations mentioned in the previous sections. The strategies of energy efficiency (Fysikopoulos et al., 2014), circular economy (Stavropoulos et al., 2021a), zero defect manufacturing, and flexibility and resilience (Stavropoulos et al., 2020b)

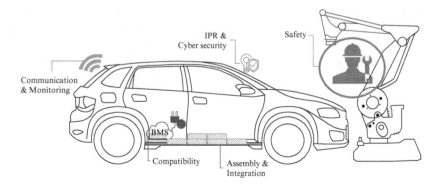

Source: Athanasopoulou et al., 2022.

Figure 7.4   Technical and business challenges involved in swapping batteries in an electric vehicle

can all be used, which entail additional KPIs (criteria) and the use of additional AI modules and models underneath. Human intervention cannot be overlooked; in fact, it can be made mandatory, depending on the sector and strategy. Automation in workflows and decision making, and in optimization itself, has not been fully achieved (due to interoperability among other factors; Leng et al., 2020), and has not been, or cannot be, adopted by many companies (Ozkan-Ozen et al., 2020; Sader et al., 2022).

Knowledge Transfer, Training, Skills, and Competences

At the systems level, AI can support knowledge transfer in various ways. In less formalized settings, it can provide support to map and transfer knowledge. AI is now used extensively to match desirable skills with demand in labor markets and within companies as well (ILO, 2020). AI can also help with knowledge transfer (Mourtzis et al., 2019). More formalized approaches use AI to support learning within a company.

Teaching Factory (Chryssolouris et al., 2016; Mavrikios et al., 2018) is an experiential learning method focused on problem solving and is tailored to match skills development with respect to:

- technology integration;
- soft skills, including:
  - communication/collaboration;
  - creativity;
  - role assignment; and
  - problem solving; and
- digitalization.

The benefits of AI-supported Training Factory experiments are now shared through the Teaching Factory Network (Mavrikios et al., 2019).

Information and Communication Technologies for AI at the Systems Level

DT models have been proposed to accelerate the training phase in machine learning (Alexopoulos et al., 2020). A cyber-physical production system (CPPS) can be formulated along with the DT of the physical system through a data communication channel capable of replicating aspects of the behavior of the CPPS. Both CPPS and DT information stacks can be defined and implemented, based on the same layered architecture approach that adheres to the RAMI 4.0 Reference Architecture (VDI, 2015).

Context-aware smart service systems can be used to provide AI services to blue- and white-collar personnel. Such systems may combine industrial Internet of Things components in the manner of multilayered, service-oriented architecture, which integrates several subsystems, for example, sensors for data acquisition with components for developing AI systems that can be combined with the DT, as per Alexopoulos et al. (2020). This is shown in Figure 7.5. Alexopoulos et al. (2018) suggest industrial Internet of Things context-aware information systems that can support the decision-making processes of mobile or static operators and supervisors, based on the context.

Human Aspects

From a sociotechnical perspective it is useful to map the direction in which human–AI integration should go. Regarding the training dimension covered in the previous section, AI–human interaction is still not very well regulated, so ways to shape this relationship are currently under study. The human dimensions relevant to shaping our future with robots include the management process, communications, information manipulation, and the way technology impacts the decision-making space on the shop floor. The same concerns that were identified at the organizational level (autonomy, solving problems, complexity) also need to be resolved at the systems level.

FUTURE OUTLOOK

For the human–AI relationship to be successful in the future, our thinking needs to change. The thought that Industry 4.0 technologies will replace all work has not proved useful. Progress in manufacturing now relies on adopting the Industry 5.0 perspective, where work and technology need to be human-centric, sustainable, and resilient. The focus in this chapter has been on human centrality and on the relationship between humans and AI. This relationship is far from being regulated in practice. Many dimensions need to be studied to understand how it ought to be defined. The human–AI relationship needs to empower humans in AI manufacturing settings and at company sites and needs to become more resilient. The various technologies that can help in this direction are shown in a non-exhaustive list in Table 7.1.

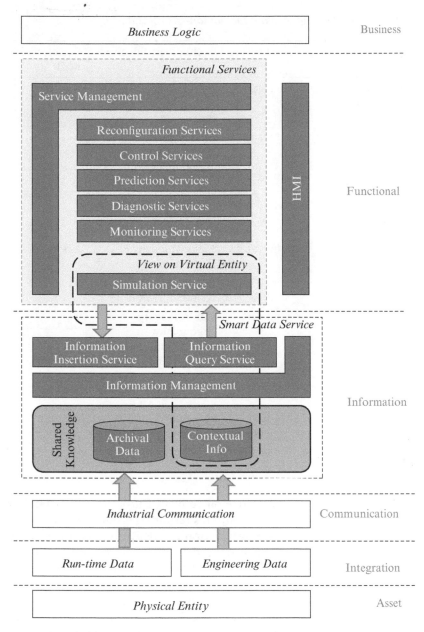

Source: Steindl, 2020, 8903.

Figure 7.5   *Digital twin for the development of machine learning-based applications for smart manufacturing*

Table 7.1   Technologies to aid the human–AI relationship

Target	Target agents	Technologies involved	Sociotechnical need
Knowledge documentation	Human	Mental models Natural language processing	Yes
Interaction at manufacturing processes	AI–human	Machine learning Heuristic algorithms Signal processing Control theory	Yes
Social and human KPI interaction in the assembly process	AI	Machine learning Computer vision	Yes
Knowledge interactions with AI	AI–human	Mental models Explainable AI	Yes
AIs facilitating knowledge transfer	Human	Federation Neural operators	Yes
Natural language processing for guidance generation	AI–human	Control theory Ergonomics Visualization Natural language processing	Yes
Collaborative holistic decision making	AI–human	Machine/deep learning/ Generative Adversarial Networks (GANs)	Yes

Resilience

Industry 5.0 requires a perspective on resilient European production, an emerging concept. This not only requires reshoring production to Europe, but also seeing that European production can deliver the products in the market in the long term. Workers need to be knowledgeable, and they need to trust the AI at work, so that a two-way learning process can take place. AI needs to learn from work practices, while workers need to learn how AI deals with new data. This requires better training and learning situations. It also requires that better metrics be developed, so it is clear when learning happens. Successful collaborative practices need to be shared. By creating these knowledge spillovers, learning networks can support the general resilience of industry.

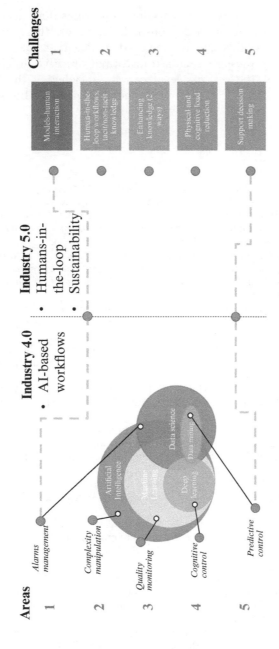

Areas

1 *Alarms management*

2 *Complexity manipulation*

3 *Quality monitoring*

4 *Cognitive control*

5 *Predictive control*

Industry 4.0
- AI-based workflows

Industry 5.0
- Humans-in-the-loop
- Sustainability

Challenges

1 Models-human interaction

2 Human-in-the-loop workflows, tacit/non-tacit knowledge

3 Enhancing knowledge (2 ways)

4 Physical and cognitive load reduction

5 Support decision making

Figure 7.6   Transitioning from Industry 4.0 to Industry 5.0 by introducing extra criteria

Integration of Criteria

The transformation of existing workflows into ones that meet Industry 5.0 criteria has yet to be accomplished. However, there are several indications of how this can be achieved, at least at the application level. Figure 7.6 represents such a transformation. Five different areas of application at the process level can be enriched with challenges pertaining to Industry 5.0, and extra technologies can be utilized to achieve this.

REFERENCES

Akerkar, R. (2019). *Artificial intelligence for business*. Springer.

Alexopoulos, K., Sipsas, K., Xanthakis, E., Makris, S., & Mourtzis, D. (2018). An industrial Internet of Things based platform for context-aware information services in manufacturing. *International Journal of Computer Integrated Manufacturing*, 31(11), 1111–1123.

Alexopoulos, K., Nikolakis, N., & Chryssolouris, G. (2020). Digital twin-driven supervised machine learning for the development of artificial intelligence applications in manufacturing. *International Journal of Computer Integrated Manufacturing*, 33(5), 429–439.

Amershi, S., Weld, D., Vorvoreanu, M., Fourney, A., Nushi, B., Collisson, P. et al. (2019, May). Guidelines for human–AI interaction. *Proceedings of the 2019 Chi Conference on Human Factors in Computing Systems*, 1–13.

Andronas, D., Xythalis, S., Karagiannis, P., Michalos, G., & Makris, S. (2021). Robot gripper with high speed, in-hand object manipulation capabilities. *Procedia CIRP*, 97, 482–486.

Arkouli, Z., Michalos, G., & Makris, S. (2022). On the selection of ergonomics evaluation methods for human centric manufacturing tasks. *Procedia CIRP*, 107, 89–94.

Athanasopoulou, L., Bikas, H., Papacharalampopoulos, A., Stavropoulos, P., & Chryssolouris, G. (2022). An industry 4.0 approach to electric vehicles. *International Journal of Computer Integrated Manufacturing*, 1–15.

Belkadi, F., Boli, N., Usatorre, L., Maleki, E., Alexopoulos, K., Bernard, A., & Mourtzis, D. (2020). A knowledge-based collaborative platform for PSS design and production. *CIRP Journal of Manufacturing Science and Technology*, 29, 220–231.

Burnes B. (2017). *Managing change*. Pearson Education.

Cetinic, E., & She, J. (2022). Understanding and creating art with AI: Review and outlook. *ACM Transactions on Multimedia Computing, Communications, and Applications*, 18(2), 1–22.

Chakraborti, T., Kambhampati, S., Scheutz, M., & Zhang, Y. (2017). AI challenges in human–robot cognitive teaming. arXiv: 1707.04775.

Chryssolouris, G. (2006). *Manufacturing systems: Theory and practice*. Springer Science and Business Media.

Chryssolouris, G., Mavrikios, D., & Rentzos, L. (2016). The teaching factory: A manufacturing education paradigm. *Procedia CIRP*, 57, 44–48.

Chryssolouris, G., Papakostas, N., & Mourtzis, D. (2000). A decision making approach for nesting scheduling: A textile case. *International Journal of Production Research*, 38(17), 4555–4564.

de Vries, J. (2016). *Behavioral operations in logistics*. Doctoral thesis, Erasmus University Rotterdam, No. EPS-2015-374-LIS.

Dhondt. S., & Dessers, E. (2022). *Robot zoekt collega. Waarom we meer artificiële intelligentie nodig hebben op het werk*. Kritak.

Dhondt, S., Delano Pot, F., & O. Kraan, K. (2014). The importance of organizational level decision latitude for well-being and organizational commitment. *Team Performance Management*, 20(7/8), 307–327.

Dimitropoulos, N., Togias, T., Zacharaki, N., Michalos, G., & Makris, S. (2021). Seamless human–robot collaborative assembly using artificial intelligence and wearable devices. *Applied Sciences*, 11(12), 5699.

EC. (n.d.). What is Industry 5.0? https://research-and-innovation.ec.europa.eu/research-area/industrial-research-and-innovation/industry-50_en

Evangelou, G., Dimitropoulos, N., Michalos, G., & Makris, S. (2021). An approach for task and action planning in human–robot collaborative cells using AI. *Procedia CIRP*, 97, 476–481.

Foteinopoulos, P., Papacharalampopoulos, A., Angelopoulos, K., & Stavropoulos, P. (2020). Development of a simulation approach for laser powder bed fusion based on scanning strategy selection. *International Journal of Advanced Manufacturing Technology*, 108, 3085–3100.

Friesike, S., Flath, C. M., Wirth, M., & Thiesse, F. (2019). Creativity and productivity in product design for additive manufacturing: Mechanisms and platform outcomes of remixing. *Journal of Operations Management*, 65(8), 735–752.

Fysikopoulos, A., Pastras, G., Vlachou, A., & Chryssolouris, G. (2014). An approach to increase energy efficiency using shutdown and standby machine modes. Advances in Production Management Systems. Innovative and Knowledge-Based Production Management in a Global-Local World: IFIP WG 5.7 International Conference, APMS 2014, Ajaccio, France, September 20–24.

Genz, S. (2022). The nuanced relationship between cutting-edge technologies and jobs: Evidence from Germany. Policy Brief, Brookings Institution, Center on Regulation and Markets, Washington, DC.

Gupta, S., Modgil, S., Bhattacharyya, S., & Bose, I. (2022). Artificial intelligence for decision support systems in the field of operations research: Review and future scope of research. *Annals of Operations Research*, 1–60.

Hagendorff, T., & Wezel, K. (2020). 15 challenges for AI: Or what AI (currently) can't do. *AI & Society*, 35, 355–365.

Hospedales, T., Antoniou, A., Micaelli, P., & Storkey, A. (2021). Meta-learning in neural networks: A survey. *IEEE Transactions on Pattern Analysis and Machine Intelligence*, 44(9), 5149–5169.

ILO. (2020). *The feasibility of using big data in anticipating and matching skills needs*. ILO.

Kambhampati, S. (2020). Challenges of human–aware AI systems: AAAI presidential address. *AI Magazine*, 41(3), 3–17.

Kazim, E., Koshiyama, A. S., Hilliard, A., & Polle, R. (2021). Systematizing audit in algorithmic recruitment. *Journal of Intelligence*, 9(3), 46.

Kim, W. (2020). The risk analysis for the introduction of collaborative robots in the Republic of Korea. Doctoral dissertation, Iowa State University.

Kiron, D., & Schrage, M. (2019). Strategy for and with AI. *MIT Sloan Management Review Magazine.*

Kousi, N., Gkournelos, C., Aivaliotis, S., Lotsaris, K., Bavelos, A. C., Baris, P. et al. (2021). Digital twin for designing and reconfiguring human–robot collaborative assembly lines. *Applied Sciences*, 11(10), 4620.

Leikas, J., Koivisto, R., & Gotcheva, N. (2019). Ethical framework for designing autonomous intelligent systems. *Journal of Open Innovation: Technology, Market, and Complexity*, 5(1), 18.

Leng, J., Liu, Q., Ye, S., Jing, J., Wang, Y., Zhang, C. et al. (2020). Digital twin-driven rapid reconfiguration of the automated manufacturing system via an open architecture model. *Robotics and Computer-Integrated Manufacturing*, 63, 101895.

Li, L., Fan, Y., Tse, M., & Lin, K. Y. (2020). A review of applications in federated learning. *Computers & Industrial Engineering*, 149, 106854.

Long, D., & Magerko, B. (2020, April). What is AI literacy? Competencies and design considerations. *Proceedings of the 2020 CHI Conference on Human Factors in Computing Systems*, 1–16.

Loureiro, S. M. C., Romero, J., & Bilro, R. G. (2020). Stakeholder engagement in co-creation processes for innovation: A systematic literature review and case study. *Journal of Business Research*, 119, 388–409.

Loureiro, S. M. C., Guerreiro, J., & Tussyadiah, I. (2021). Artificial intelligence in business: State of the art and future research agenda. *Journal of Business Research*, 129, 911–926.

Manser Payne, E. H., Dahl, A. J., & Peltier, J. (2021). Digital servitization value co-creation framework for AI services: A research agenda for digital transformation in financial service ecosystems. *Journal of Research in Interactive Marketing*, 15(2), 200–222.

Mavrikios, D., Georgoulias, K., & Chryssolouris, G. (2018). The teaching factory paradigm: Developments and outlook. *Procedia Manufacturing*, 23, 1–6.

Mavrikios, D., Georgoulias, K., & Chryssolouris, G. (2019). The teaching factory network: A new collaborative paradigm for manufacturing education. *Procedia Manufacturing*, 31, 398–403.

Mehmood, H., Kostakos, P., Cortes, M., Anagnostopoulos, T., Pirttikangas, S., & Gilman, E. (2021). Concept drift adaptation techniques in distributed environment for real-world data streams. *Smart Cities*, 4(1), 349–371.

Michalos, G., Makris, S., Rentzos, L., & Chryssolouris, G. (2010). Dynamic job rotation for workload balancing in human based assembly systems. *CIRP Journal of Manufacturing Science and Technology*, 2(3), 153–160.

MIT SLOAN. (n.d.). Why it's time for "data-centric artificial intelligence." https://mitsloan.mit.edu/ideas-made-to-matter/why-its-time-data-centric-artificial-intelligence

Mohr, B. J., & Van Amelsvoort, P. (2016a). *Co-creating humane and innovative organizations.* Global STS-D Network Press.

Mohr, B. J., & Van Amelsvoort, P. (2016b). Cooperation: A study of the emergence of the Swedish model. *Tiden: Co-Creating Humane and Innovative Organizations*, 200.

Mourtzis, D., Xanthi, F., Chariatidis, K., & Zogopoulos, V. (2019). Enabling knowledge transfer through analytics in industrial social networks. *Procedia CIRP*, 81, 1242–1247.

Mourtzis, D., Angelopoulos, J., & Panopoulos, N. (2022). A literature review of the challenges and opportunities of the transition from Industry 4.0 to Society 5.0. *Energies*, 15(17), 6276.

Müller, J. (2020). Enabling technologies for Industry 5.0. European Commission, 8–10.

Nikolakis, N., Alexopoulos, K., Xanthakis, E., & Chryssolouris, G. (2019). The digital twin implementation for linking the virtual representation of human-based production tasks to their physical counterpart in the factory-floor. *International Journal of Computer Integrated Manufacturing*, 32(1), 1–12.

NIST. (n.d.). Artificial intelligence in manufacturing: Real world success stories and lessons learned. www.nist.gov/blogs/manufacturing-innovation-blog/artifi cial-intelligence-manufacturing-real-world-success-stories

Nonaka, I., & Takeuchi, H. (1995). *The knowledge-creating company: How Japanese companies create the dynamics of innovation*. Oxford University Press.

Oeij, P., Rus, D., & Pot, F. D. (Eds). (2017). *Workplace innovation: Theory, research and practice*. Springer.

Owen-Hill, A. (2019). Are cobots too safe? Samuel Bouchard and Esben Ostergaard discuss. *Blog Robotiq*.

Ozkan-Ozen, Y. D., Kazancoglu, Y., & Mangla, S. K. (2020). Synchronized barriers for circular supply chains in industry 3.5/industry 4.0 transition for sustainable resource management. *Resources, Conservation and Recycling*, 161, 104986.

Papacharalampopoulos, A., & Balafoutis, T. (2021). Systematic design applied in outdoor spatiotemporal lighting. *Designs*, 5(4), 74.

Papacharalampopoulos, A., & Stavropoulos, P. (2022). A manufacturing process digital twin network addressing business added value. Edge Intelligence, Patras University Conference and Cultural Center.

Papacharalampopoulos, A., Tzimanis, K., Sabatakakis, K., & Stavropoulos, P. (2020a). Deep quality assessment of a solar reflector based on synthetic data: Detecting surficial defects from manufacturing and use phase. *Sensors*, 20(19), 5481.

Papacharalampopoulos, A., Giannoulis, C., Stavropoulos, P., & Mourtzis, D. (2020b). A digital twin for automated root-cause search of production alarms based on KPIs aggregated from IoT. *Applied Sciences*, 10(7), 2377.

Papacharalampopoulos, A., Michail, C. K., & Stavropoulos, P. (2021). Manufacturing resilience and agility through processes digital twin: Design and testing applied in the LPBF case. *Procedia CIRP*, 103, 164–169.

Park, H., Ahn, D., Hosanagar, K., & Lee, J. (2021, May). Human–AI interaction in human resource management: Understanding why employees resist algorithmic evaluation at workplaces and how to mitigate burdens. *Proceedings of the 2021 CHI Conference on Human Factors in Computing Systems*, 1–15.

Petrides, D., Papacharalampopoulos, A., Stavropoulos, P., & Chryssolouris, G. (2018). Dematerialisation of products and manufacturing-generated knowledge content: Relationship through paradigms. *International Journal of Production Research*, 56(1–2), 86–96.

Polini, W., & Corrado, A. (2020). Digital twin of composite assembly manufacturing process. *International Journal of Production Research*, 58(17), 5238–5252.

Rodijnen, L. V. (2021). Quality of work in the smart industry; how to measure? A qualitative research on the appropriate aspects for a quality of work measuring instrument in a smart industry environment with the WEBA (Welzijn Bij de Arbeid) as a starting point. Thesis, Radboud University.

Ruohomäki, T., Airaksinen, E., Huuska, P., Kesäniemi, O., Martikka, M., & Suomisto, J. (2018, September). Smart city platform enabling digital twin. *2018 International Conference on Intelligent Systems*, 155–161.

Sader, S., Husti, I., & Daroczi, M. (2022). A review of quality 4.0: Definitions, features, technologies, applications, and challenges. *Total Quality Management & Business Excellence*, 33(9–10), 1164–1182.

Saha, V., Mani, V., & Goyal, P. (2020). Emerging trends in the literature of value co-creation: A bibliometric analysis. *Benchmarking: An International Journal*.

Saxena, P., Stavropoulos, P., Kechagias, J., & Salonitis, K. (2020). Sustainability assessment for manufacturing operations. *Energies*, 13(11), 2730.

Schank, R. C. (1987). What is AI, anyway? *AI Magazine*, 8(4), 59–59.

Siaterlis, G., Franke, M., Klein, K., Hribernik, K. A., Papapanagiotakis, G., Palaiologos, S. et al. (2022). An IIoT approach for edge intelligence in production environments using machine learning and knowledge graphs. *Procedia CIRP*, 106, 282–287.

Stavridis, J., Papacharalampopoulos, A., & Stavropoulos, P. (2018). Quality assessment in laser welding: A critical review. *International Journal of Advanced Manufacturing Technology*, 94, 1825–1847.

Stavropoulos, P., & Papacharalampopoulos, A. (2022). Designing a digital twin for micromanufacturing processes. *Advances in Mechanical Engineering*, 14(6).

Stavropoulos, P., Chantzis, D., Doukas, C., Papacharalampopoulos, A., & Chryssolouris, G. (2013). Monitoring and control of manufacturing processes: A review. *Procedia CIRP*, 8, 421–425.

Stavropoulos, P., Papacharalampopoulos, A., Vasiliadis, E., & Chryssolouris, G. (2016). Tool wear predictability estimation in milling based on multi-sensorial data. *International Journal of Advanced Manufacturing Technology*, 82(1), 509–521.

Stavropoulos, P., Papacharalampopoulos, A., Stavridis, J., & Sampatakakis, K. (2020a). A three-stage quality diagnosis platform for laser-based manufacturing processes. *International Journal of Advanced Manufacturing Technology*, 110(11), 2991–3003.

Stavropoulos, P., Papacharalampopoulos, A., Tzimanis, K., & Lianos, A. (2020b). Manufacturing resilience during the coronavirus pandemic: On the investigation manufacturing processes agility. *European Journal of Social Impact and Circular Economy*, 1(3), 28–57.

Stavropoulos, P., Foteinopoulos, P., & Papapacharalampopoulos, A. (2021a). On the impact of additive manufacturing processes complexity on modelling. *Applied Sciences*, 11(16), 7743.

Stavropoulos, P., Papacharalampopoulos, A., Michail, C. K., & Chryssolouris, G. (2021b). Robust additive manufacturing performance through a control oriented digital twin. *Metals*, 11(5), 708.

Stavropoulos, P., Papacharalampopoulos, A., Athanasopoulou, L., Kampouris, K., & Lagios, P. (2022a). Designing a digitalized cell for remanufacturing of automotive frames. *Procedia CIRP*, 109, 513–519.

Stavropoulos, P., Sabatakakis, K., Papacharalampopoulos, A., & Mourtzis, D. (2022b). Infrared (IR) quality assessment of robotized resistance spot welding based on machine learning. *International Journal of Advanced Manufacturing Technology*, 119(3), 1785–1806.

Stavropoulos, P., Tzimanis, K., Souflas, T., & Bikas, H. (2022c). Knowledge-based manufacturability assessment for optimization of additive manufacturing processes based on automated feature recognition from CAD models. *International Journal of Advanced Manufacturing Technology*, 122(2), 993–1007.

Stavropoulos, P., Papacharalampopoulos, A., & Sabatakakis, K. (2022d). Online quality inspection approach for submerged arc welding (SAW) by utilizing IR-RGB multimodal monitoring and deep learning. *Flexible Automation and Intelligent Manufacturing: The Human–Data–Technology Nexus: Proceedings of FAIM 2022*, June 19–23, 160–169.

Stavropoulos, P., Manitaras, D., Papaioannou, C., Souflas, T., & Bikas, H. (2022e). Development of a sensor integrated machining vice towards a non-invasive milling monitoring system. *Flexible Automation and Intelligent Manufacturing: The Human–Data–Technology Nexus: Proceedings of FAIM 2022*, June 19–23, Detroit, 29–37.

Steindl, G., Stagl, M., Kasper, L., Kastner, W., & Hofmann, R. (2020). Generic digital twin architecture for industrial energy systems. *Applied Sciences*, 10(24), 8903.

Stolowy, H., & Paugam, L. (2018). The expansion of non-financial reporting: An exploratory study. *Accounting and Business Research*, 48(5), 525–548.

Sun, C., Ma, M., Zhao, Z., Tian, S., Yan, R., & Chen, X. (2018). Deep transfer learning based on sparse autoencoder for remaining useful life prediction of tool in manufacturing. *IEEE Transactions on Industrial Informatics*, 15(4), 2416–2425.

Tzavara, E., Angelakis, P., Veloudis, G., Gkournelos, C., & Makris, S. (2021). Worker in the loop: A framework for enabling human-robot collaborative assembly. *Advances in Production Management Systems: Artificial Intelligence for Sustainable and Resilient Production Systems: IFIP WG 5.7 International Conference, APMS 2021*, Nantes, September 5–9, 275–283.

VDI/VDE-Gesellschaft Mess- und Automatisierungstechnik. (2015). Status Report Reference Architecture Model Industrie 4.0 (RAMI4.0). Technical Report.

Villareale, J., & Zhu, J. (2021). Understanding mental models of ai through player–AI interaction. arXiv: 2103.16168.

Waldman, A., & Martin, K. (2022). Governing algorithmic decisions: The role of decision importance and governance on perceived legitimacy of algorithmic decisions. *Big Data & Society*, 9(1).

Wang, L. (2019). From intelligence science to intelligent manufacturing. *Engineering*, 5(4), 615–618.

Wang, Q., Jiao, W., Wang, P., & Zhang, Y. (2020). Digital twin for human–robot interactive welding and welder behavior analysis. *IEEE/CAA Journal of Automatica Sinica*, 8(2), 334–343.

8. Workers and AI in the construction and operation of civil infrastructures
Jinding Xing, Zhe Sun, and Pingbo Tang

DEFINING WORKERS AND AI IN CIVIL INFRASTRUCTURE SYSTEMS ENGINEERING

Civil Infrastructure Systems

Civil infrastructure systems (CIS) support various everyday activities in urban environments. The term "civil infrastructure systems" refers to "the physical components of interrelated systems providing commodities and services essential to enable, sustain, or enhance societal living conditions and maintain the surrounding environment" (Goswami, 2012). CIS include roads and bridges forming ground transportation networks, water distribution systems, water treatment plants and delivery networks, power plants and grids, telecommunication systems, commercial and industrial facilities, and others (Garrett, 2005).

CIS engineering, defined as the design and execution of infrastructure construction and operation processes, is indispensable for ensuring the public has adequate services to support their living needs and carry out business activities. Inadequate civil infrastructure or defective infrastructure construction and operation processes have a cascading impact on the economy, impacting business productivity, gross domestic product (GDP), employment, personal income, and international competitiveness (ASCE, 2021). For example, an economic study estimated that the infrastructure inadequacies in the United States (US) would cause a loss of $10 trillion in GDP (ASCE, 2021). Such inadequacies will lead to a decline of more than $23 trillion in business productivity cumulatively over the next two decades if the US does not close a growing gap in the investments needed for its infrastructure (ASCE, 2021).

Job Responsibilities of Workers

A civil infrastructure project entails five critical stages (Figure 8.1): initiation, planning, construction/operation/maintenance, and decommissioning. The initiation phase investigates if it is feasible to build the civil

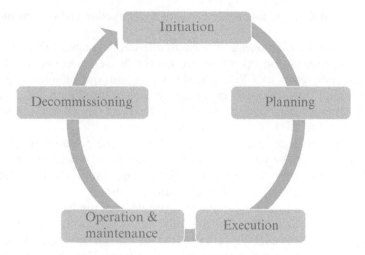

Figure 8.1   Lifecycle of the civil infrastructure systems

infrastructure regarding its economic, social, and environmental impacts on the communities. Then, different stakeholders collaborate to complete the planned project. At the planning stage, the stakeholders identify the scope of the work, the resources needed, and the strategy for producing the civil infrastructure product. In the execution phase, most works are carried out on site. During the operation and maintenance phase, CIS requires active monitoring and maintenance to ensure its structure and function perform correctly. Decommissioning is the process of shutting down the CIS.

CIS construction and operations require considerable manual labor. CIS projects have high labor intensity, long working hours, and hazardous toil. In the CIS industry, a worker refers to someone who performs construction and operational tasks during the execution, operation and maintenance, and decommissioning phases of a construction project. Tearing down buildings, removing hazardous materials, and building highways and roads are examples of construction tasks. A worker's main responsibilities in construction tasks include setting up the construction site (e.g., cleaning and removing debris), building or moving structures (e.g., scaffolding, bridges), operating machinery (e.g., diggers, cranes), moving and preparing materials, and assisting other craftsmen (Go Construct Team, 2022). On the other hand, the operational tasks of workers aim at keeping machines, mechanical equipment, or the structure of a CIS functioning properly. Pipe fitting, machining carpentry, and balancing new equipment are operational tasks.

Challenges in Civil Infrastructure Systems Construction and Operation

CIS are essential components of sustainable development, and their optimum construction and operation are central to socio-economic vitality. Two common goals of CIS execution, operation and maintenance, and decommissioning phases are productivity and safety. Operational safety aims to prevent injury or death during field operations for infrastructure use, construction, or maintenance. In contrast, productivity seeks to achieve the maximum output of the CIS, given the resource and budget constraints. Optimum construction and operation of structures and infrastructure require maximizing availability (i.e., operation over a pre-defined serviceability threshold) and safety at minimum cost.

Figure 8.2 organizes the significant obstacles that hinder the CIS industry from fully realizing the safety and productivity goals into three aspects: (1) physical system reliability; (2) cyber system reliability; and (3) human reliability. These aspects of reliability issues involve interwoven interactions between the operation and management systems' human, physical, and cyber components.

Challenge 1: Physical system reliability

Physical system reliability refers to how physical infrastructure components can function as expected to handle the demands of humans relying on their services. The physical system reliability involves physical

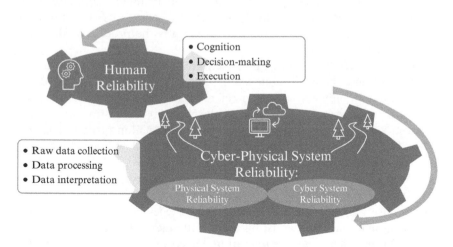

Figure 8.2   Human–cyber physical system reliability for explaining safety and productivity issues in civil infrastructure system construction and operations

infrastructure condition assessment and various physical operation and maintenance activities that change the physical facilities' conditions and real-time changing states. Any given CIS comprises many interconnected components. These components operate under harsh operating and loading conditions and are aging and subject to increasing frequency and severity (Prakash et al., 2021). Gradual and irreversible damage accumulation in these components can lead to failures or degradations of engineered system components. Therefore, routine inspections are necessary to ensure operation safety and productivity of physical facilities of civil infrastructure.

Challenge 2: Human reliability
Human reliability is the likelihood of successfully conducting specific tasks related to equipment repair, equipment or system operation, safety actions, analysis, and other human activities (Calixto, 2016). The human reliability issues refer to the operational risks or inefficiencies that arise when humans engage with the physical environment during field operations, such as infrastructure maintenance activities (Boring, 2014; Kim et al., 2013). The CIS industry is considered a very complex and risky sector (Zhao et al., 2014). In 2019, about 20 percent of job-related fatalities were in the construction industry (OSHA, 2021).

Challenge 3: Cyber system reliability
The cyber system reliability measures how digital technologies used in the CIS industry influence operational safety and efficiency. Various digital technologies used in CIS construction and operation can collect, process, store, and transmit data and digital models generated from raw data. For example, the sensors installed on the roads, bridges, and other ground transportation facilities can collect information regarding the physical state of the civil infrastructures. With the collected physical state information, infrastructure operation personnel conduct maintenance activities that interfere with the infrastructure's physical condition. Unreliable data could lead to incorrect decisions on CIS construction and operation.

AI in Construction and Operation of Civil Infrastructure Systems

AI is a powerful technology with various capabilities. AI methods can automate construction and operation and digitalize processes, thereby enhancing the productivity and safety of CIS construction and operation. AI in CIS construction and operation involves "making intelligence machines and programs that mimic cognitive systems to learn or solve problems" (Baum et al., 2017).

The most common AI methods applied in the CIS industry are: (1) natural language processing; (2) knowledge representation and reasoning; (3) computer vision; (4) robotics; and (5) advanced visualization techniques. Civil infrastructure construction and operations have used these AI methods for addressing physical system reliability, human operational reliability, and cyber system reliability challenges. Existing studies used natural language processing in document management, safety management, compliance checking, and risk management (Cheng et al., 2020). Knowledge representation and reasoning methods adopt symbolic representation of pre-defined rules to enable the computer to understand CIS domain knowledge (Liu et al., 2018). Computer vision works together with image acquisition equipment such as cameras. LiDAR has proven to be a powerful tool for structural health monitoring and construction site monitoring (Atha & Jahanshahi, 2018; Chen et al., 2020). Chong et al. (2022) used robotics in the assembly process of wooden frames. Tsai et al. (2022) used augmented reality for the automatic checking of on-site mechanical, electrical, and plumbing system conflicts.

The following sections provide a detailed review of how these commonly used AI methods benefit workers by improving physical system reliability, human operation reliability, and cyber system reliability.

Motivating Case

The following subsections use the operation of a nuclear power plant (NPP) as a motivating case to demonstrate the challenges of keeping operational safety and productivity for large CIS.

In NPP operations, nuclear field workers' responsibilities include starting and stopping electricity generation equipment as needed, overseeing sensor readings, observing field conditions to know the system's real-time status, and resolving detected equipment problems (de Carvalho et al., 2006). Carrying out these responsibilities involves coordinating many physical, human, and computational processes influencing NPP operational safety and efficiency. The challenges lie in fully considering the interdependencies between human workflows, rapidly changing NPP states, and computational and information-flowing processes for detecting and preventing risks.

Safety issues in the operation of the NPP

The Nuclear Regulatory Commission (NRC) emphasizes safety over competing goals to ensure no worker deaths, disabling injuries, or unfavorable environmental impacts (NRC Web, 2015). The World Association of Nuclear Operators (WANO, 2020) reported that, on average, nearly eight

NPP operation accidents occur every week (WANO, 2020). Operators may be exposed to occupational hazards occurring in NRC-licensed facilities in NPP operations. Such hazards include radiation hazards produced by radioactive materials and facility conditions that affect the safety of radioactive materials. These radiation hazards increase workers' health and safety risks (OSHA, 2013).

Other safety issues also cause various incidents and accidents that lead to injuries and economic losses, such as machine downtime, labor insurance, and facility damages. Industry reports show that finger, head, or neck injuries account for 19 percent of the total reported injuries (International Atomic Energy Agency, 2018). Additionally, the Incident Reporting System collected more than 4,300 event reports from 1981 until 2020. Nearly 50 percent of these events involved radioactive material and hazardous chemical material releasing, while many other consequences also exist (International Atomic Energy Agency, 2020b).

Productivity issues in the operation of the NPP
Operation productivity means no failures or loss of functioning equipment during NPP operations so that the system can achieve high electricity production (Chen et al., 2011; Yu et al., 2020). The operating productivity impacts a given NPP's overall operational costs and capability of producing sufficient electricity with limited resources. The failure or loss of NPP system functions usually occur due to the durability issues of the mechanical and electrical components, computer hardware, or software (International Atomic Energy Agency, 2020a). NPP systems with malfunctioning components can invalidate the system designer's assumptions and intent, leading to suboptimal productivity in producing electricity. More specifically, faulty parts can compromise the plant's operation productivity and result in unplanned automatic NPP shutdowns and reductions in electricity production. Among the event reports collected by the Incident Reporting System in 2020, 64 percent of the events were mechanical component failures or secondary impacts of such failures, and 24 percent were computer hardware/software failures or their secondary effects (International Atomic Energy Agency, 2020b). In 2020, WANO reported an average of two unplanned scrams per year for each NPP. The total operating costs due to efficiency issues of NPPs in the US have been increasing since 2002 (Davis & Hausman, 2016). For example, in 2020, operations with system productivity issues caused nearly a 10 percent loss of the energy generated by NPP worldwide (International Atomic Energy Agency, 2021).

Safety and productivity issues often interweave with human reliability in NPP operations. Human error contributes to more than half of all significant events at NPPs (International Atomic Energy Agency, 2020a).

Table 8.1   Operation error modes

Error mode	Category	Reference
Operation process	Observation of the system state Choice of the hypothesis Testing of the hypothesis Choice of the goal Choice of the procedure Execution of the procedure	Rouse and Rouse, 1983
Cognitive function	Observation error Interpretation error Planning error Execution error	Hollnagel et al., 1998

Action execution	Process structure level:
	  • Omit action
	  • Add action (include repeat action)
	Action level:
	  • Taking action at the wrong time
	  • Taking action of the wrong type
	  • Taking action at the wrong object
		Lee et al., 2011;
		Torres et al., 2018

Other types of human error	Error of omission Error of commission Mistake Slip/lapse Violation	Cho & Ahn, 2019

Cooper et al. (1996) define human error as "divergence between an action performed and the action that should have been performed." Similarly, Rasmussen (1982) views human error as man–machine or man–task misfits. Such misfits or divergence can be classified into different types according to the different factors involved in the cognitive and operation processes. Table 8.1 classifies human errors identified from the literature into error modes relevant to different factors in cognitive and operation processes.

AI FOR PHYSICAL SYSTEM RELIABILITY

Physical System Reliability and AI Application Potential

Physical system reliability refers to how physical infrastructure components can function as expected to handle the demands of humans relying on their services. Any given CIS comprises many interconnected elements. These components operate under harsh operating and loading conditions. Therefore, the physical systems age faster and are subject to the increasing frequency of severe damage (Prakash et al., 2021). Gradual and irreversible damage accumulation in these components can lead to the failure or degradation of engineered system components. Physical infrastructure reliability issues are related to the physical condition assessment during infrastructure operation and maintenance.

Researchers have explored various methods for quantifying and monitoring physical system reliability at the structure level. Many studies examined methods for quantifying the reliability of a structural system (Ditlevsen & Bjerager, 1986). Such studies focus on developing techniques for calculating the reliability of complete structures based on the probability of structural elements' failures and the connections between structural elements (Moses, 1974). Other studies examined the impacts of structural element failures on the loading path changes to predict the consequences of structural element failures (Conte & Zhang, 2007; Gou et al., 2018).

The emergence of AI and machine learning makes physical infrastructure reliability assessment rise to a new level. Machine learning algorithms can use labeled data samples to capture statistically similar features across different data samples and use features related to the labels of the data for classifying new datasets or sequences (e.g., certain objects in images or the particular meaning of a word in a sentence). Machine learning outperforms anomaly detection methods with the power of automatically capturing the features related to specific data labels. For example, conventional image-processing techniques can only detect surface defect features based on salient image region characteristics without leveraging more advanced underlying spatial patterns. In contrast, deep learning methods can learn some in-depth features, dramatically advancing the accuracy of crack detection (Cao et al., 2017). The following section will use crack detection as an example to introduce some applications of AI in the civil infrastructure operation and maintenance domain.

AI for Crack Detection in CIS Operations and Maintenance

Civil structures and infrastructure facilities such as roads, bridges, buildings, and pavements are susceptible to deterioration posed by natural hazards and aggressive environmental conditions (Liong et al., 2019). Concrete develops cracks, and the strength of materials diminishes if the civil structure is exposed to extreme environments for a long time. These cracks can accelerate the deterioration process, weaken the components, reduce their loading capacities, and lead to surface discontinuities

(Dung & Ahn, 2019; Zhang et al., 2016; Zou et al., 2012). A significant concern for the safety and durability of CIS is the cracking of structural components. Early detection of critical cracks can help prevent dangerous trends of structure failing (Oliveira & Correia, 2012). However, undetected cracks can spread through the surface, bring increased failure risks to structural elements, and may subsequently lead to complete collapse, resulting in fatalities, injuries, and financial loss. Manual crack detection methods require experts to examine the structure component visually and use specific tools to identify any deficiency in the component (Oliveira & Correia, 2012). However, manual and visual inspection methods are tedious, labor-intensive, and prone to human error.

Machine learning has become popular in crack detection (Munawar et al., 2021). Crack detection aims to identify the crack type, size, and severity level. Within the scope of cyber-physical system reliability, the basic steps to building a machine learning model for crack detection include data acquisition and model training (Phung et al., 2017). The data acquisition stage acquires two types of data: color and geometry information of the infrastructure surface (Munawar et al., 2021). 3D laser technology is the mainstream method to acquire high-resolution, full-coverage 3D infrastructure surface data for crack detection and condition assessment (Turkan et al., 2018). Some studies have used unmanned aerial vehicles (UAV) as an alternative to collect infrastructure surface image data. Phung et al. (2017) first created a 3D model of the infrastructure and then used the geometric features captured in the 3D model to generate a path for UAV navigation and ensure the coverage of salient geometric features. The UAV then takes images of the suspected surface. The model training stage takes the collected infrastructure surface images as input for training machine-learning models that can find similar features in new images to report cracks. The output of those machine-learning models is the crack type severity and extent in new images that are not part of the training sample (Kalfarisi et al., 2020). Machine-learning models can have different training processes. Table 8.2 shows three machine-learning methods that produce models capable of detecting image defects through three training processes: supervised, unsupervised, and reinforcement learning. The table also summarizes the advantages and limitations of different machine-learning approaches for training crack detection models.

AI FOR HUMAN RELIABILITY

Human reliability research examines human individuals' cognitive, decision-making, and task execution reliabilities. Many studies use AI

Table 8.2 Machine-learning methods for crack detection

Category	Method	Input	Output	Advantages	Limitations	Reference
Unsupervised learning	Gray histogram and Otsu method	2D pavement image	Detected cracks	The unsupervised method does not require a significant amount of data for training	Unable to handle high signal-to-noise ratio images	Akagic et al., 2018
Unsupervised learning	Minimum path-based method	2D pavement image	Crack direction and length	Unsupervised method, robust and precise results in a wide range of situations	Great computation effort	Amhaz et al., 2016
Supervised learning	Deep fully convolutional neural networks	Images of concrete surface	Crack detection accuracy	The pixel-level crack detection model can operate on images of arbitrary size and provide pixel-level detection of the cracks	Requires a large and versatile annotated image dataset, including various crack patterns and background characteristics	Alipour et al., 2019
Supervised learning	Deep learning with a 3D reality mesh model	2D crack image	Crack detection accuracy	Effect and robustness on a wide range of crack images	Requires a large number of labeled crack images	Kalfarisi et al., 2020
Reinforcement learning	Reinforcement learning and deep learning	Road crack dataset	Per-pixel crack predictions	This refinement framework outperforms many current approaches for crack segmentation	Challenging to design a proper reward function; a simple reward function may lead to a suboptimal policy	Park et al., 2021

techniques to characterize and predict human reliability in (1) decision making and (2) action execution.

AI Studies for Comprehending and Predicting Human Decision-Making Reliability

This section uses building system maintenance as the background case to introduce various AI applications and studies addressing human decision-reliability issues. Building systems have become more complex to meet higher energy efficiency and indoor environment comfort demand. However, complex systems do not guarantee reliability and often create complex operational challenges. One survey as early as 1975 reported that 19–64 percent of various building types have defects or faults (Freeman, 1974). Thus, maintaining these systems in good condition is essential (Ma et al., 2020). Items for decision making on facility maintenance include selecting maintenance strategies, prioritization, work order scheduling, etc. Advanced machine-learning techniques enable the maintenance platforms to integrate related maintenance workflows, including proactive maintenance planning, reactive maintenance requesting, work order issuing and tracking, and maintenance performance benchmarking (Sullivan et al., 2010). Table 8.3 shows applications of AI in the civil infrastructure maintenance domain, such as AI for assisting decision making in planning maintenance activities of bridges.

AI Studies for Comprehending and Predicting Human Action Execution Reliability

AI can assist humans in considering changing contexts that influence their ongoing field workflows to ensure efficiency and safety. This section uses the NPP operation to explain recent AI studies in human action execution reliability. Managing NPP operations is challenging because many operational activities occur in a fast-paced and dynamic environment (Germain et al., 2013). NPP operators need to follow well-designed procedures to complete all assigned operational activities. Such well-designed procedures are vital to ensure the safe and reliable operation of NPPs (Oxstrand & Le Blanc, 2017). In practice, such procedures could be classified into three categories: (1) paper-based procedures (PBPs); (2) computer-based procedures (CBPs); and (3) automatic work packages (AWPs).

PBPs are widely adopted by most commercial NPPs in the US to ensure the safe operation of NPPs (Oxstrand & Le Blanc, 2017). Such PBPs offer (1) greater flexibility and resources, (2) capability to view in-progress work

Table 8.3 Machine-learning methods for human reliability

Category	Method	Input	Output	Reference
Cognition reliability	Artificial immune system and extreme gradient boosting algorithm	Fatigue causal network	Fatigue level	Li et al., 2020
Cognition reliability	Hybrid deep neural network	Video of operators performing crane operations	Fatigue level	Liu et al., 2021
Decision-making reliability	Sentiment analysis	Maintenance request	Status of building systems	D'Orazio et al., 2022
Decision-making reliability	Entity embedding with neural network	Bridge inventory, inspection data, damage data, risk data	Condition state, risk level, maintenance advice	Bukhsh et al., 2020

status, (3) performing in-field work package revisions or document additions, and (4) capturing as-found/in-field condition pictures that can be viewed by appropriate support personnel for disposition without requiring plant entry and in real time. Still, such PBPs have limitations, such as (1) the work packages are challenging to develop, implement, control, review, close out, archive, and manage, and (2) filed workers can only access a limited amount of information, so uncertainties exist while deciding on actions.

Table 8.4 summarizes the recent advanced operation support technologies for NPP field operations. Previous studies have demonstrated the potential of using CBPs to significantly increase efficiency and safety by improving how humans interact with the procedures (Oxstrand & Le Blanc, 2017). Such CBPs could (1) guide NPP operators through the logical sequence of the procedure, (2) ease the burden of place-keeping for the operator, (3) alert operators to dependencies between steps, (4) ease the burden of correct component verification for the operator, (5) ease the identification and support assessment of the expected initial conditions, (6) ease the identification and support assessment of the expected plant and equipment response, and (7) include functionality that improves communication. Still, CBPs have some limitations, such as (1) lack of timely, detailed workflow information involving human factors and (2) not supporting reasoning, thus being unable to control ubiquitous hand-offs and emergencies caused by contingencies in NPP operations.

Other studies found that automated work packages (AWPs) can intelligently drive the work process according to rapidly changing NPP conditions, resource-sharing status, and user progress (Rashdan & Agarwal, 2016; Rashdan et al., 2015, 2016). Adaptive and interactive work packages focus on automating the flow of work package processes in specific scenarios during NPP operations (e.g., initiation of work requests, work package creation, scheduling, work package assignment, and sign-off clearance). Such AWPs could (1) provide more frequent feedback on work status than manual methods, (2) guide NPP operators through the logical sequence of the procedure, (3) ease the burden of place-keeping for the NPP operator, (4) make the action steps distinguishable from information-gathering steps, (5) alert operator about dependencies between steps, and (6) ease the burden of correct component verification for the operator. Still, such AWPs have some limitations, such as (1) lack of timely, detailed workflow information involving human factors and (2) not supporting reasoning, thus being unable to control ubiquitous hand-offs and emergencies caused by contingencies in NPP operations. Moreover, these tools demonstrate the limited capability to predict delays

Table 8.4 Advanced field operation support technologies

Operation method/ technology	Description	Benefits	Challenges
Computerized operating support systems	Aid operators in monitoring and controlling the plant	Bolster operator situation awareness, monitoring, diagnosis, prediction, and decision support	Team cooperation, position shift, loss of operation ability
Virtual reality	Planning, man–machine interface, virtual control tables for simulation, training	Cost-saving, easy to understand, evaluate all possible situations	Virtual reality is an isolated, individual experience, with no team cooperation in real workspaces
Augmented reality	Digitizing manual procedures and providing real-time monitoring of hazards presented in an environment	Increase NPP operators' productivity	Hardware, tracking, user–autmented reality interaction, no interaction between virtual and physical objects, no risk-reasoning support

due to human error and evaluate potential delays when implementing different control strategies. An adequately designed communication protocol is imperative in NPP operation control to provide the necessary supervision and reduce time waste.

Interest in implementing AWP allocating systems has improved NPP operational productivity by automating the procedures during NPP operations (i.e., initiation of work requests) (Germain, 2015; Rashdan et al., 2015). Besides, the control room at NPPs is the temporary command center for NPP managers that provides several critical functions for successfully executing the as-planned operation schedule (Germain et al., 2013). The advanced control room implemented in NPP control enables real-time work status updates from automated tools tracking individual workers' workflows (Zhang et al., 2017).

AI FOR CYBER SYSTEM RELIABILITY

Cyber system reliability refers to the uncertainties that could arise during the data collection and analysis for supporting civil infrastructure operations and decision processes (Sun et al., 2020). These uncertainties can impact subject experts' decisions and behavioral reliabilities when they assess and inspect the condition of civil infrastructures through three steps of data analysis: (1) pre-processing of raw data; (2) data processing; and (3) data interpretation. For example, infrastructure maintenance faces one challenge: some data can be missing due to sensor faults. Missing or noisy data make it difficult for engineers to estimate the infrastructure components' conditions and incorrect condition ratings can lead to biased infrastructure system risk analysis and operations decisions.

Table 8.5 defines these three data analyses steps and shows how the three steps have different cyber system reliability issues. The data pre-processing step takes the raw datasets as inputs to transform raw data into structured or semi-structured data that can serve as inputs for the data-processing stage. The data-processing step takes pre-processed data as inputs and extracts features or patterns corresponding to particular objects or events captured in the data. The data interpretation stage derives correlations between features and data patterns extracted by data-processing algorithms and derives behavior and process information representing how objects and events evolve along the timeline. The behavior and process information give engineers meaningful views of objects and events to diagnose the engineered systems or workspaces.

Table 8.5   Three stages of data analysis that derive information from raw data sources and their reliability issues

Step	Purpose	Inputs and outputs	Reliability issues
Data pre-processing	Prepare the raw data in formats that are suitable for reliable feature extraction and pattern recognition	*Inputs*: raw data (images, Excel tables, field notes, and inspection reports) *Outputs*: cleaned and subsampled data, linked or combined data (e.g., cleaned and registered 3D laser-scanning point clouds)	*Losses of object or event details* due to improper data-cleaning actions and sampling rates (Chen et al., 2017; Puttonen et al., 2013) *Errors in linking or combining datasets* due to improper selections of corresponding objects or properties for data linking and integration (Lu et al., 2016; Petricek & Svoboda, 2017)
Data processing	Extract features and data patterns that correspond to objects and changes captured in the spatiotemporal patterns of features	*Inputs*: cleaned, sampled, and linked/combined data. *Outputs*: objects, objects' properties, changes in objects' properties (changes in the locations and strengths of concrete elements), and changing rates (strength deterioration rate of concrete)	*Missing features or feature extraction errors* due to improper feature extraction algorithms (Schneider, 2004; Wang & Chung, 2012) *Errors in the object, event, and change detections* due to mismatches between features/patterns extracted from the pre-processed data and pre-defined features and patterns corresponding to objects, events, and changes (Possegger et al., 2014)
Data interpretation	Analyze relationships between objects and events for interpreting the correlated objects and events into meaningful change information of the facilities and workspaces	*Inputs*: cleaned, sampled, and linked/combined data. *Outputs*: various relationships (e.g., spatiotemporal relationships) between objects and changes in objects (location and material property changes of concrete elements)	*Missing or errors in the detection of relationships between objects and changes* due to improper selection of statistical methods (Chellappa et al., 2009), improper settings of the parameters that are not suitable for the processed data, and data use contexts (Bergstra & Bengio, 2012; Yang et al., 2015), improper use of the statistical metrics in identifying statistically significant relationships between objects and changes (Lorenz et al., 2017)

DISCUSSION

Other Challenges in Civil Infrastructure Engineering

We discussed three major challenges in CIS construction and operations: physical system reliability, human reliability, and cyber reliability. Besides the three major challenges, some other challenges hinder the industry from fully realizing its productivity and safety goals – for example, labor shortage. There is an increase in demand for a skilled workforce in the CIS industry (Kim et al., 2020). Yet, the workforce in the CIS industry has been aging faster than it can replace older workers. In the US, more than 20 percent of construction workers are 55 and older (Sokas et al., 2019). In the European Union, more than 32 percent of construction workers are 55 and older (Coates, 2018). Aged workers are more skilled and reliable yet are experiencing a general decline in physical and cognitive capabilities. The dynamics and complexity characteristics make the CIS industry more susceptible to some force majeure. For example, COVID-19 has significantly and unexpectedly affected the CIS industry (Alfadil et al., 2022). Workers in the CIS industry face challenges working from home due to the large amount of manual labor needed in CIS operation and maintenance projects.

Currently, the construction and operation of the CIS rely heavily on manual visual observations to track task progress, devices, and materials and perform safety planning (Khairadeen Ali et al., 2021). Such manual inspection and progress-tracking methods are time-consuming, labor-intensive, inefficient, and error-prone (Moselhi et al., 2020). To overcome these drawbacks, researchers developed different AI-based remote-working solutions to automate the inspection and tracking of CIS construction and operations. The following paragraphs will review some of the most recent AI-based solutions for supporting remote CIS construction and operation.

Emerging AI technologies use data collected by non-destructive or non-contact methods such as ground-penetrating radars, photogrammetry, laser-scanning technology, infrared thermography, sensors, machine vision, and UAV (Feroz & Abu Dabous, 2021). A UAV, also referred to as a drone, is defined as "an aircraft capable of flying remotely or autonomously over long distances with the aid of a control device transmitting live feed" (Yaacoub et al., 2020). UAV mounted with multiple types of sensors (e.g., visual imagery equipment, infrared thermography, and laser doppler vibrometer) is an effective tool to capture data in unreachable areas (Garg et al., 2019; Liu et al., 2020; Lu et al., 2017). Tan et al. (2021) used UAVs to collect images of high-raised building surfaces for remote quality inspection. Ribeiro et al. (2020) adopted UAV and advanced digital image processing to assess reinforced concrete quality remotely.

Challenges of Adopting AI

AI techniques in the construction sector could boost the sector's automation, productivity, and reliability. Construction practitioners and researchers use AI to identify design conflicts, predict potential risks and human errors in workflows, and learn infrastructure degradation patterns (Chen et al., 2020; Sun et al., 2020). However, integrating emerging AI techniques and algorithms is still challenging for ensuring civil infrastructure projects' safety and productivity.

Despite the remarkable growth of AI-related research in the construction sector, AI techniques have encountered many challenges. Significantly, the major stages (operation and maintenance) in a civil infrastructure project's lifecycle remain severely underdigitized. AI use cases in civil infrastructure construction, operation, and maintenance processes are still relatively nascent (Blanco et al., 2018). For example, enhanced analytics platforms can collect and analyze data from sensors to understand NPP operation anomalies (Jin et al., 2010). Pure AI performs tasks tediously and repetitively, not creatively (Vincent, 2021). Most AI models are "black boxes" that include too many factors and functions that are too complicated for humans to comprehend and interpret (Deng et al., 2019; Rudin, 2019).

Civil infrastructure projects' uniqueness, temporary, and progressive nature require human abstract thinking and creativity to ensure the desired construction product's production and satisfy the operation goals. AI that integrates human and machine intelligence has great potential in the construction sector.

CONCLUSION

CISs constitute physical and cyber systems (e.g., sensing and actuating systems) such as NPPs, which require appropriate and effective operation and maintenance to provide vital services to contemporary society (Sun et al., 2020). Two primary goals in civil infrastructure operations are ensuring operational safety and productivity. The interaction between human and civil infrastructure in the operation process forms a dynamic human–cyber-physical system that gives rise to physical, cyber, and human reliability issues.

The emerging AI techniques and machine-learning algorithms effectively address reliability issues in civil infrastructure operations. AI has served as an efficient and feasible solution to change the traditional role of CIS workers. Recent studies have applied AI techniques and algorithms to assist humans in data collection, processing, analysis, and interpretation in civil infrastructure construction, operation, and maintenance stages in the cyber-physical reliability domain.

REFERENCES

Akagic, A., Buza, E., Omanovic, S., & Karabegovic, A. (2018, May). Pavement crack detection using Otsu thresholding for image segmentation. *41st International Convention on Information and Communication Technology, Electronics and Microelectronics*, 1092–1097.

Alfadil, M. O., Kassem, M. A., Ali, K. N., & Alaghbari, W. (2022). Construction industry from perspective of force majeure and environmental risk compared to the COVID-19 outbreak: A systematic literature review. *Sustainability*, 14(3), 1135.

Alipour, M., Harris, D. K., & Miller, G. R. (2019). Robust pixel-level crack detection using deep, fully convolutional neural networks. *Journal of Computing in Civil Engineering*, 33(6), 04019040.

Amhaz, R., Chambon, S., Idier, J., & Baltazart, V. (2016). Automatic crack detection on two-dimensional pavement images: An algorithm based on minimal path selection. *IEEE Transactions on Intelligent Transportation Systems*, 17(10), 2718–2729.

ASCE. (2021). Failure To Act/Economic impacts of status quo investment across infrastructure systems. https://infrastructurereportcard.org/the-impact/failure-to-act-report/

Atha, D. J., & Jahanshahi, M. R. (2018). Evaluation of deep learning approaches based on convolutional neural networks for corrosion detection. *Structural Health Monitoring*, 17(5), 1110–1128.

Baum, S., Barrett, A., & Yampolskiy, R. V. (2017). Modeling and interpreting expert disagreement about artificial superintelligence. *Informatica*, 41(7), 419–428.

Bergstra, J., & Bengio, Y. (2012). Random search for hyper-parameter optimization. *Journal of Machine Learning Research*, 13, 281–305.

Blanco, J. L., Fuchs, S., Parsons, M., & Ribeirinho, M. J. (2018). Artificial intelligence: Construction technology's next frontier. *Building Economist*, September, 7–13.

Boring, R. L. (2014, September). Top-down and bottom-up definitions of human failure events in human reliability analysis. *Proceedings of the Human Factors and Ergonomics Society Annual Meeting*, 58(1), 563–567.

Bukhsh, Z. A., Stipanovic, I., Saeed, A., & Doree, A. G. (2020). Maintenance intervention predictions using entity-embedding neural networks. *Automation in Construction*, 116, 103202.

Calixto, E. (2016). *Gas and oil reliability engineering: Modeling and analysis*. Gulf Professional Publishing.

Cao, H., Tian, Y., & Lei, J. et al. (2017). Deformation data recovery based on compressed sensing in bridge structural health monitoring. *Structural Health Monitoring*, 1, 888–895.

Chellappa, R., Sankaranarayanan, A. C., Veeraraghavan, A., & Turaga, P. (2009). Statistical methods and models for video-based tracking, modeling, and recognition. *Found Trends Signal Process*. https://doi.org/10.1561/2000000007

Chen, C., Zhu, Z., & Hammad, A. (2020). Automated excavators activity recognition and productivity analysis from construction site surveillance videos. *Automation in Construction*, 110, 103045.

Chen, J., Zhang, C., & Tang, P. (2017). Geometry-based optimized point cloud compression methodology for construction and infrastructure management. *Proceedings of the Congress on Computing in Civil Engineering*.

Chen, K. Y., Chen, L. S., Chen, M. C., & Lee, C. L. (2011). Using SVM based method for equipment fault detection in a thermal power plant. *Computers in Industry*, 62(1), 42–50.

Cheng, M. Y., Kusoemo, D., & Gosno, R. A. (2020). Text mining-based construction site accident classification using hybrid supervised machine learning. *Automation in Construction*, 118, 103265.

Cho, W. C., & Ahn, T. H. (2019). A classification of electrical component failures and their human error types in South Korean NPPs during last 10 years. *Nuclear Engineering and Technology*, 51(3), 709–718.

Chong, O. W., Zhang, J., Voyles, R. M., & Min, B. C. (2022). BIM-based simulation of construction robotics in the assembly process of wood frames. *Automation in Construction*, 137, 104194.

Coates, S. (2018). Migrant labour force within the construction industry. ONS. www.ons.gov.uk/peoplepopulationandcommunity/populationandmigration/internationalmigration/articles/migrantlabourforcewithintheconstructionindustry/2018-06-19

Conte, J. P., & Zhang, Y. (2007). Performance based earthquake engineering: Application to an actual bridge-foundation-ground system. *12th Italian National Conference of Earthquake Engineering*, Pisa, 1–18.

Cooper, S. E., Ramey-Smith, A. M., Wreathall, J., & Parry, G. W. (1996). A technique for human error analysis. No. NUREG/CR-6350. Nuclear Regulatory Commission.

Davis, L., & Hausman, C. (2016). Market impacts of a nuclear power plant closure. *American Economic Journal: Applied Economics*, 8(2), 92–122.

de Carvalho, P. V. R., dos Santos, I. L., Gomes, J. O., da Silva Borges, M. R., & Huber, G. J. (2006, November). The role of nuclear power plant operators' communications in providing resilience and stability in system operation. *2nd Symposium on Resilience Engineering*, Juan-les Pins.

Deng, S., Zhang, N., Zhang, W., Chen, J., Pan, J. Z., & Chen, H. (2019). Knowledge-driven stock trend prediction and explanation via temporal convolutional network. *Companion Proceedings of the 2019 World Wide Web Conference*, 678–685.

Ditlevsen, O., & Bjerager, P. (1986). Methods of structural systems reliability. *Structural Safety*, 3, 195–229.

D'Orazio, M., Di Giuseppe, E., & Bernardini, G. (2022). Automatic detection of maintenance requests: Comparison of human manual annotation and sentiment analysis techniques. *Automation in Construction*, 134, 104068.

Dung, C. V., & Anh, L. D. (2019). Autonomous concrete crack detection using deep fully convolutional neural network. *Automation in Construction*, 99, 52–58.

Feroz, S., & Abu Dabous, S. (2021). UAV-based remote sensing applications for bridge condition assessment. *Remote Sensing*, 13(9), 1809.

Freeman, I. L. (1974). Failure patterns and implications in building defects and failures. Paper presented at a Joint Seminar by Building Research Establishment and Institute of Building, November, London.

Garg, P., Moreu, F., Ozdagli, A., Taha, M. R., & Mascareñas, D. (2019). Noncontact dynamic displacement measurement of structures using a moving laser Doppler vibrometer. *Journal of Bridge Engineering*, 24(9), 04019089.

Garrett, Jr., J. H. (2005). Advanced infrastructure systems: Definitions, vision, research and responsibilities. *Computing in Civil Engineering*. https://doi.org/10.1061/40794(179)4

Germain, S. S. (2015). Use of collaborative software to improve nuclear power plant outage management technologies. Idaho National Laboratory.

Germain, S. S., Farris, R., & Medema, H. (2013). Development of methodologies for technology deployment for advanced outage control centers that improve outage coordination. *Problem Resolution and Outage Risk Management*.

Go Construct Team. (2022). What is a construction worker (definition, roles). Go Construct. www.goconstruct.org/construction-careers/what-is-a-construction-worker/

Goswami, S. (2012). Role of social infrastructure in the economic development of India. *Research Journal of Humanities and Social Sciences*, 3(4), 530–531.

Gou, H., Long, H., Bao, Y. et al. (2018). Stress distributions in girder-arch-pier connections of long-span continuous rigid frame arch railway bridges. *Journal of Bridge Engineering*, 23, 1–13.

Hollnagel, E. (1998). *Cognitive reliability and error analysis method (CREAM)*. Elsevier.

International Atomic Energy Agency. (2018). Industrial safety guidelines for nuclear facilities. IAEA.

International Atomic Energy Agency. (2020a). Nuclear power plant operating experience, IAEA.

International Atomic Energy Agency. (2020b). Operating experience from events reported to the IAEA/NEA fuel incident notification and analysis system (FINAS), IAEA-TECDOC-1932. IAEA.

International Atomic Energy Agency. (2021). Operating experience with nuclear power stations in member states. IAEA.

Jin, X., Guo, Y., Sarkar, S., Ray, A., & Edwards, R. M. (2010). Anomaly detection in nuclear power plants via symbolic dynamic filtering. *IEEE Transactions on Nuclear Science*, 58(1), 277–288.

Kalfarisi, R., Wu, Z. Y., & Soh, K. (2020). Crack detection and segmentation using deep learning with 3D reality mesh model for quantitative assessment and integrated visualization. *Journal of Computing in Civil Engineering*, 34(3), 04020010.

Khairadeen Ali, A., Lee, O. J., Lee, D., & Park, C. (2021). Remote indoor construction progress monitoring using extended reality. *Sustainability*, 13(4), 2290.

Kim, J. H. K. J. H., Thang, N. D. T. N. D., Kim, T. S. K. T. S., Voinea, A., Shin, J. H., & Smith, K. (2013). Virtual reality history, applications, technology and future. *Digital Outcasts*, 63, 92–98.

Kim, S., Chang, S., & Castro-Lacouture, D. (2020). Dynamic modeling for analyzing impacts of skilled labor shortage on construction project management.
Journal of Management in Engineering, 36(1).

Lee, S.J., Kim, J., & Jang, S.C. (2011). Human error mode identification for NPP
main control room operations using soft controls. *Journal of Nuclear Science
and Technology*, 48(6), 902–910.

Li, F., Chen, C. H., Zheng, P., Feng, S., Xu, G., & Khoo, L. P. (2020). An explora-
tive context-aware machine learning approach to reducing human fatigue risk of
traffic control operators. *Safety Science*, 125, 104655.

Liong, S. T., Gan, Y. S., Huang, Y. C., Yuan, C. A., & Chang, H. C.
(2019). Automatic defect segmentation on leather with deep learning. arXiv:
1903.12139.

Liu, P., Chi, H. L., Li, X., & Guo, J. (2021). Effects of dataset characteristics on the
performance of fatigue detection for crane operators using hybrid deep neural
networks. *Automation in Construction*, 132, 103901.

Liu, W., Zhao, T., Zhou, W., & Tang, J. (2018). Safety risk factors of metro tunnel
construction in China: An integrated study with EFA and SEM. *Safety Science*,
105, 98–113.

Liu, Y. F., Nie, X., Fan, J. S., & Liu, X. G. (2020). Image-based crack assessment
of bridge piers using unmanned aerial vehicles and three-dimensional scene
reconstruction. *Computer-Aided Civil and Infrastructure Engineering*, 35(5),
511–529.

Lorenz, R., Hampshire, A., & Leech, R. (2017). Neuroadaptive Bayesian optimization and hypothesis testing. *Trends in Cognitive Science*.

Lu, M., Zhao, J., Guo, Y., & Ma, Y. (2016). Accelerated coherent point drift for
automatic three-dimensional point cloud registration. *IEEE Geoscience and
Remote Sensing Letters*, 13, 162–166.

Lu, Y., Golrokh, A. J., & Islam, M.D. (2017). Concrete pavement service condition assessment using infrared thermography. *Advances in Materials Science and
Engineering*.

Ma, Z., Ren, Y., Xiang, X., & Turk, Z. (2020). Data-driven decision-making for
equipment maintenance. *Automation in Construction*, 112, 103103.

Moselhi, O., Bardareh, H., & Zhu, Z. (2020). Automated data acquisition in construction with remote sensing technologies. *Applied Sciences*, 10(8), 2846.

Moses, F. (1974). Reliability of structural systems. *Journal of Structural Division*,
100.

Munawar, H. S., Hammad, A. W., Haddad, A., Soares, C. A. P., & Waller, S. T.
(2021). Image-based crack detection methods: A review. *Infrastructures*, 6(8),
115.

NRC Web. (2015). Safety culture policy statement. www.nrc.gov/about-nrc/saf
ety-culture/sc-policy-statement.html

Oliveira, H., & Correia, P.L. (2012). Automatic road cracks detection and characterization. *IEEE Transactions on Intelligent Transportation Systems*, 14,
155–168.

OSHA. (2013). Worker protection at facilities licensed by the NRC. Occupational
Safety and Health Administration. www.osha.gov/laws-regs/mou/2013-09-06

OSHA. (2021). eTool: Electric power generation transmission distribution – hazard
assessment and job briefing. Occupational Safety and Health Administration.
www.osha.gov/etools/electric-power/hazard-assessment-job-briefing/job-brief
ing-best-practices

Oxstrand, J., & Le Blanc, K. (2017). Supporting the industry by developing a design guidance for computer-based procedures for field workers. *10th International Topical Meeting on Nuclear Plant Instrumentation, Control, and Human–Machine Interface Technologies*, 2, 1282–1292.

Park, J., Chen, Y. C., Li, Y. J., & Kitani, K. (2021, September). Crack detection and refinement via deep reinforcement learning. *2021 IEEE International Conference on Image Processing*, 529–533.

Petricek, T., & Svoboda, T. (2017). Point cloud registration from local feature correspondences: Evaluation on challenging datasets. *PLoS One*, 12, 1–16.

Phung, M. D., Hoang, V. T., Dinh, T. H., & Ha, Q. (2017). Automatic crack detection in built infrastructure using unmanned aerial vehicles. arXiv: 1707. 09715.

Possegger, H., Mauthner, T., Roth, P. M., & Bischof, H. (2014). Occlusion geodesics for online multi-object tracking. *Proceedings of the IEEE Computer Society Conference on Computer Vision and Pattern Recognition*.

Prakash, G., Yuan, X. X., Hazra, B., & Mizutani, D. (2021). Toward a big data-based approach: A review on degradation models for prognosis of critical infrastructure. *Journal of Nondestructive Evaluation, Diagnostics and Prognostics of Engineering Systems*, 4(2), 021005.

Puttonen, E., Lehtomäki, M., Kaartinen, H. et al. (2013). Improved sampling for terrestrial and mobile laser scanner point cloud data. *Remote Sensors*, 5, 1754–1773.

Rashdan, A., & Agarwal, V. (2016). Automated work package: Initial wireless communication platform design, development, and evaluation. ANS Annual Meeting, Idaho National Laboratory.

Rashdan, A., Oxstrand, J., & Agarwal, V. (2015). Automated work package prototype: Initial design, development, and evaluation. *10th International Topical Meeting on Nuclear Plant Instrumentation, Control and Human Machine Interface Technologies*, July.

Rashdan, A., Oxstrand, J., & Agarwal, V. (2016). Automated work package: Conceptual design and data architecture. OSTI OAI (US Department of Energy Office of Scientific and Technical Information). https://doi.org/10.2172/ 1364774

Rasmussen, J. (1982). Human errors: A taxonomy for describing human malfunction in industrial installations. *Journal of Occupational Accidents*, 4(2–4), 311–333.

Ribeiro, D., Santos, R., Shibasaki, A., Montenegro, P., Carvalho, H., & Calçada, R. (2020). Remote inspection of RC structures using unmanned aerial vehicles and heuristic image processing. *Engineering Failure Analysis*, 117, 104813.

Rouse, W. B., & Rouse, S. H. (1983). Analysis and classification of human error. *IEEE Transactions on Systems, Man, and Cybernetics*, 4, 539–549.

Rudin, C. (2019). Stop explaining black box machine learning models for high stakes decisions and use interpretable models instead. *Nature Machine Intelligence*, 1(5), 206–215.

Schneider, K. M. (2004). Using information extraction to build a directory of conference announcements. *Lecture Notes on Computer Science*. https://doi. org/10.1007/978-3-540-24630-5_65

Sokas, R. K., Dong, X. S., & Cain, C. T. (2019). Building a sustainable construction workforce. *International Journal of Environmental Research and Public Health*, 16(21), 4202.

Sullivan, G., Pugh, R., Melendez, A. P., & Hunt, W. D. (2010). Operations and maintenance best practices: A guide to achieving operational efficiency. https://doi.org/10.2172/1034595

Sun, Z., Xing, J., Tang, P., Cooke, N. J., & Boring, R. L. (2020). Human reliability for safe and efficient civil infrastructure operation and maintenance: A review. *Developments in the Built Environment*, 4, 100028.

Tan, Y., Li, S., Liu, H., Chen, P., & Zhou, Z. (2021). Automatic inspection data collection of building surface based on BIM and UAV. *Automation in Construction*, 131, 103881.

Torres, E. S., Celeita, D., & Ramos, G. (2018, October). State of the art of human factors analysis applied to industrial and commercial power systems. *2nd IEEE International Conference on Power Electronics, Intelligent Control and Energy Systems*, 33–38.

Tsai, L. T., Chi, H. L., Wu, T. H., & Kang, S. C. (2022). AR-based automatic pipeline planning coordination for on-site mechanical, electrical and plumbing system conflict resolution. *Automation in Construction*, 141, 104400.

Turkan, Y., Hong, J., Laflamme, S., & Puri, N. (2018). Adaptive wavelet neural network for terrestrial laser scanner-based crack detection. *Automation in Construction*, 94, 191–202.

Vincent, V. U. (2021). Integrating intuition and artificial intelligence in organizational decision-making. *Business Horizons*.

Wang, Z., & Chung, R. (2012). Recovering human pose in 3D by visual manifolds. *Proceedings: International Conference on Pattern Recognition*.

WANO. (2020). Performance indicators. www.wano.info/resources/performance-indicators

Yaacoub, J. P., Noura, H., Salman, O., & Chehab, A. (2020). Security analysis of drones systems: Attacks, limitations, and recommendations. *Internet of Things*, 11, 100218.

Yang, D., Liu, Y., Li, S. et al. (2015). Gear fault diagnosis based on support vector machine optimized by artificial bee colony algorithm. *Mechanism and Machine Theory*. https://doi.org/10.1016/j.mechmachtheory.2015.03.013

Yu, Y., Peng, M. J., Wang, H., Ma, Z. G., & Li, W. (2020). Improved PCA model for multiple fault detection, isolation and reconstruction of sensors in nuclear power plant. *Annals of Nuclear Energy*, 148, 107662.

Zhang, C., Tang, P., Cooke, N., Buchanan, V., Yilmaz, A., Germain, S., Boring, R., Akca-Hobbins, S., & Gupta, A. (2017). Human-centered automation for resilient nuclear power plant outage control. *Automation in Construction*, 82(October), 179–192.

Zhang, L., Yang, F., Zhang, Y.D., & Zhu, Y.J. (2016). Road crack detection using a deep convolutional neural network. *Proceedings of the International Conference on Image Processing*, Phoenix, September 25–28, 3708–3712.

Zhao, D., Thabet, W., McCoy, A., & Kleiner, B. (2014). Electrical deaths in the US construction: An analysis of fatality investigations. *International Journal of Injury Control and Safety Prevention*, 21, 278–288.

Zou, Q., Cao, Y., Li, Q., Mao, Q., & Wang, S. (2012). CrackTree: Automatic crack detection from pavement images. *Pattern Recognition Letters*, 33, 227–238.

9. AI-based technology in home-based care in aging societies: challenges and opportunities

Naoko Muramatsu, Miloš Žefran, Emily Stiehl, and Thomas Cornwell

INTRODUCTION

Globally, the number and proportion of older adults in the population is increasing rapidly (World Health Organization, n.d.).[1] The population aging heightens expectations for technology to fill the growing societal needs to care for older adults. Artificial intelligence (AI) holds high promise as a core enabling technology to extend older adults' daily activity functions, empower caregivers, and expand healthcare providers' abilities to address heterogeneous needs of older adults, the caregiving burden, and healthcare workforce shortages.

AI is "the capacity of a machine to imitate intelligent human behavior" (Merriam-Webster, 2022), such as learning, visual perception, speech recognition, reasoning, judgment, and decision-making. These abilities are essential for working with people who need assistance with daily activities such as walking, bathing, and cooking. Currently, the hope and expectations for AI exceed its reality in care provision (Bhattacharya et al., 2019; Emanuel & Wachter, 2019; Matheny et al., 2019, 2020). AI has improved clinical diagnosis, health monitoring, surgery, and clinical outcome prediction using image recognition, wearable devices, robotics, and big data such as electronic health records (EHR) (Jiang et al., 2017; Yu et al., 2018). However, there remains a large gap in AI's capacity to translate AI-powered recognition and decision-making into physical actions (Haque et al., 2020). This is

[1] Research reported in this publication was partly supported by the National Institute on Aging of the National Institutes of Health under Award Number R01AG035675 (PI: Muramatsu) and the National Science Foundation under Award Number IIS1705058 (PI: Žefran). The content is solely the responsibility of the authors and does not necessarily represent the official views of the National Institutes of Health or the National Science Foundation.

an important gap in AI applications to healthcare, because physical assistance constitutes a major aspect of caring for adults aging with functional limitations in their homes.

Healthcare is increasingly delivered in the home setting (Feinglass et al., 2018; Muramatsu et al., 2007). *Home-based care* can be medical services, social services (commonly referred to in the United States (US) as home and community-based services), and paid or unpaid (e.g., family) care. Home-based medical services in the US mainly consist of *home-based primary care* (HBPC) services done by physicians, nurse practitioners, and physician assistants, commonly referred to as the "modern-day house call." There has been a dramatic increase in HBPC over the past two decades (Schuchman et al., 2018), which recently accelerated as a response to COVID-19. The other main US home-based medical services are *home health services* (HHS) provided by nurses and therapists under the orders of physicians, nurse practitioners, and physician assistants. HHS are principally paid for by the government's Medicare and Medicaid programs (Medicaid, n.d.; Medicare, n.d.). There are also more advanced medical services such as "hospital at home" that have accelerated in response to COVID-19. Advancing AI applications for home-based care is a major area of opportunity and challenge in aging societies.

The goal of this chapter is to present the current state, opportunities, and challenges related to AI applications for home-based care work. This chapter addresses the following three questions. (1) What are some important factors that need to be considered in developing and deploying AI applications for home-based care? (2) What is the current state of AI applications for home-based care? What opportunities and challenges are there? (3) How would AI applications affect home-based care work? We address these questions by integrating a HBPC case story with the author team's experiences, research, and expertise in HBPC clinical practice, organizational behavior, robotics, and home- and community-based services for diverse aging populations.

HOME-BASED CARE WORK

The *home* is broadly defined here as the hub of daily activities (e.g., eating, bathing, grooming, relaxing, sleeping). Most people prefer to stay home as they age (Davis, 2021). The home is where various health habits (e.g., eating, physical activity) are formed, performed, maintained, and resumed. As people develop age-related disabilities, their activities increasingly center around their home.

Care work is broadly defined in this chapter as an activity or task of caring for others paid or unpaid in the home or in markets (England, 2005). Care encompasses physical, emotional, cognitive, and healthcare tasks. *Home-based care work* is care work provided in or around the home of care recipients who need care. In the US and throughout the world, home-based care is provided mainly by family members and sometimes by close friends or volunteers. This kind of unpaid care is also known as *informal care*. However, home-based care is increasingly provided by paid caregivers, or *formal care* providers, including non-medical or custodial care providers (e.g., home care aides, personal care assistants, privately hired caregivers, and other social service providers) and licensed clinicians (e.g., nurses, therapists).

Home-based formal care is delivered and financed differently across societies. Medicare, federal health insurance for people 65 or older established in 1965, is a major payer of home-based care in the US. Since its inception, Medicare has covered HHS provided by nurses, therapists, social workers, and aides under the orders of a physician (Centers for Medicare & Medicaid Services, 2021; Vladeck & Miller, 1994), targeting short-term restoration of patients' health and function. Medicaid, health insurance for low-income families jointly funded by states and the federal government established in 1965, has become the US's largest payer of long-term care provided in the home or nursing home.

Home-Based Primary Care

HBPC, or "modern-day house calls," is a model of healthcare delivery that moves primary care back to the home of patients with medical needs (Totten et al., 2016). Growing evidence in the US indicates that HBPC improves patient outcomes and reduces healthcare costs, especially for homebound older adults with multiple chronic diseases and functional limitations (De Jonge et al., 2014; Edes et al., 2014; Rotenberg et al., 2018).

The primary care function differentiates HBPC from Medicare HHS. Primary care serves as the first contact point for the patient to enter the healthcare system and then continues to provide and coordinate various medical and social services that the patient needs to maintain or improve their health. When encountering a new patient with new healthcare needs, HBPC can initiate medical treatment, including ordering HHS (Muramatsu & Cornwell, 2003). There are no Medicare restrictions on who can receive HBPC. In contrast, Medicare restricts HHS. Restrictions include requiring provider orders, needing the skilled care of a nurse or therapist (such as for a wound), or a new diagnosis (such as heart failure or a stroke); the patient cannot require only custodial care such as bathing. The patient must also meet Medicare's homebound definition

(Muramatsu et al., 2004). Direct observation of home environments (e.g., food in the refrigerator, untouched prescriptions, fall hazards, mementos, unsanitary conditions) helps HBPC offer caregiving tips or health habit recommendations. HBPC practice models vary, as do available services, within the US and across countries. HBPC access is still limited, especially in rural areas in the US (Yao et al., 2016, 2018), but it is expected to improve as telehealth and telemedicine continue to grow.

Overall, HBPC is rapidly increasing because of the aging of the US population, the increase in technology, and the change in payment models. The biggest accelerant is the payment model shifting from "fee-for service" that pays separately for every visit and procedure and incentivizes volume of services but not quality, to "value-based care" that pays based on better outcomes. Value-based payment models are the economic engine behind HBPC, because HBPC is a low-volume business but has been shown to produce better outcomes such as improving patient and caregiver quality of life while reducing hospitalizations.

The following case story, based on a real-life HBPC practice, illustrates how HBPC works with formal and informal care providers to maximize the patient's function and health (Figure 9.1).

A Case Story

Linda Smith was age 81 when she started HBPC. Linda was homebound with multiple chronic conditions (diabetes, heart failure, hypertension, emphysema, depression, osteoarthritis, urinary incontinence that was worse after taking her water pill, chronic diarrhea after having part of her colon removed secondary to diverticulitis, and cerebral vascular accident with left-sided weakness). David, her 85-year-old husband, is the primary caregiver. The couple's adult daughter, Jennifer, lives 10 hours away. Concerned about her parents but busy with work and her own family, Jennifer arranged for a paid caregiver, Chris, to help David care for Linda.

Before receiving HBPC services, Linda was on 17 medications. She needed assistance with bathing and dressing. She could transfer to a chair, walk about 20 feet with a walker, and do toileting independently, but with difficulties. Because of her weakness and depression, Linda spent most of her time in bed. Her cognitive status was fine. In the year before enrolling in HBPC, Linda had 17 emergency department visits and 13 hospitalizations (69 hospital days), often followed by rehabilitation in a skilled nursing facility before being discharged to home with HHS nurses and therapists. HHS would discharge Linda once she reached her maximal function. When her condition worsened, she would go back to the emergency department, which often resulted in hospital readmission

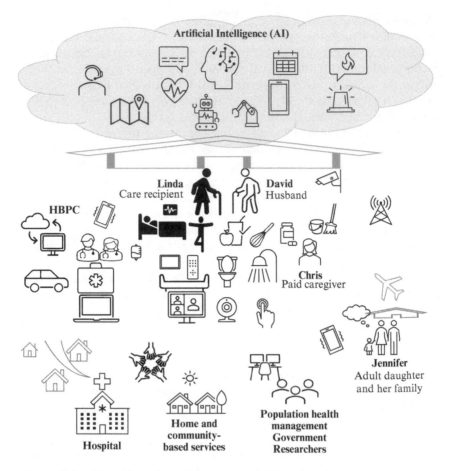

Figure 9.1   Home-based primary care and AI applications

and subsequent short-term HHS. Finally, considering the patient not being able to access her primary care physician's office, a HHS nurse in consultation with the patient's primary care physician referred Linda to an HBPC program where a physician went out to care for Linda in her home.

Linda showed significant improvement in just a couple of months. On their first visit, the HBPC team (the physician and medical assistant) did a thorough medication review, assessment of all medical conditions, a home safety and nutrition assessment, and reviewed Linda's goals of care. Linda stated that no one had ever asked her what her goals were. The top goals included affording her medication, getting stronger and more independent to lessen the burden on her husband, and avoiding the hospital and further aggressive care. When her time came, she wanted to die at home. Outcomes of the first few visits to improve her health and quality of life that focused on the patient's goals of care included:

- Linda was found to have poor inhaler technique and was switched to nebulized medications. This improved her emphysema and reduced medication cost by $650 per month. She was also on a $350 per month lung medication that had limited efficacy. The pros and cons were discussed with the patient who desired to discontinue it, which was done successfully further reducing medication costs.
- To help Linda be more independent and less of a burden on her husband, exercises were recommended along with HHS physical therapy. A hospital bed with a trapeze was ordered to make transfers easier without assistance.
- Linda was on a heart medication and a medication for diabetic neuropathy that had a side-effect of leg swelling. These were discontinued and her leg swelling improved, enabling her water pill to be reduced which decreased her urinary incontinence. Linda's diarrhea was controlled with regular use of antidiarrheal medication that eliminated her fecal incontinence. This added dignity to Linda and reduced burden on the husband who no longer had to clean up accidents. Linda was immensely appreciative of her improved function and independence.
- Linda was started on an antidepressant that dramatically improved her mood over time.
- A nutritional assessment including reviewing foods in the kitchen showed a large quantity of processed food with high sodium, and soda with a high quantity of sugar. Food labels were reviewed with Linda and her husband and daughter (remotely), and over a short period of time there was a significant improvement in her diet.
- Remote patient monitoring was started that included a scale, pulse oximeter, and blood pressure cuff, along with a central hub that transmitted the data and enabled virtual telehealth visits. This alerted the HBPC team of early decompensation to make quick adjustments and immediately reach out to the patient virtually.
- Throughout Linda's care, blood tests were drawn in the home and spun down in the centrifuge in the car prior to transport to the lab. Chest X-rays were ordered and done in the home as needed. All the above enabled high-quality care in the home and prevented the need for hospitalization.
- When Linda's health declined two years later, hospice was called out and supported Linda and her family in her last four months of life. Remote patient monitoring is normally removed when hospice

starts so as not to burden the patient and family. Linda said the remote monitoring gave her a sense of control over her illnesses and desired it to continue, which was done.

● Throughout, HBPC supported and educated Linda's husband David, daughter Jennifer, and caregiver Chris. Because of his caregiver role, David was not going to his primary care doctor, so HBPC started to see him. The HBPC team regularly communicated with the office-based primary care physician via the shared EHR. Except for one short hospitalization two weeks after the first HBPC visit, Linda was not hospitalized for the last 2.5 years of her life. Her goals of affording medication, getting stronger and being less of a burden on her husband, avoiding the hospital, and dying at home were all achieved.

WHAT ASPECTS OF HOME-BASED CARE SHOULD AI APPLICATIONS CONSIDER?

The above case story illustrates HBPC stakeholders' characteristics that should be considered for AI applications to home-based care.

Care Recipients

● Care recipients experience short-term and long-term health changes with occasional flare-ups of acute episodes as they age.
● Care recipients with multiple chronic conditions are diverse. They may have unique sets of physical, mental, cognitive, social, and economic needs all intertwined. However, these are often uncoordinated in healthcare.
● Older, frail care recipients tend to be vulnerable physically, mentally, financially, and socially with limited technology proficiency.

Care Workers

● Care workers (e.g., informal/family caregivers, paid caregivers, clinicians, social service providers, staff) are diverse in terms of care work training and experiences, sociodemographic and cultural backgrounds, and personal attributes and resources available to them, including technology infrastructure.
● Care workers' health and function change as they age.
● Care workers need to be able to respond to unexpected situations appropriately (e.g., adverse health events in the care recipient or other residents in the home).

The Home Environment

- The home of the care recipient is the workplace of home-based care workers.
- Most home-based care activities and care environments cannot be directly observed, monitored, or supervised without the consent of the care recipient and the homeowner.
- Anticipatory guidance, or proactively assessing and addressing risks for avoidable injuries or diseases in the home setting, can optimize the health of care recipients and care workers as they age. For example, guidance for monitoring and fixing poor lighting or loose carpets can prevent falls in care recipients and those who care for them (McDonald et al., 2016; Muramatsu et al., 2018).

AI Concerns for Home-Based Care Work

- Care recipients' diverse needs, changes in health and function, and vulnerability require AI applications to adapt, monitor consumers carefully (both physiological measures and assessments for cognition, depression, nutrition, falls risk, isolation, etc.), align disconnected systems, and generate trust in the user by being transparent about what they are doing or not doing.
- Care providers' diversity, own risks for illness and injury, and responsibility to address unexpected emergencies require user-friendly, adaptable AI applications as well as assistive devices to protect providers' own health and safety, and seamless data collection for supporting and enhancing their decision-making and care effectiveness.
- Home-based care activities are rarely captured as electronic data partly because of privacy issues and partly because of the limited technology infrastructure. Home-based care lacks "big data."

CURRENT STATE, OPPORTUNITIES, AND CHALLENGES

Home-based care presents opportunities and challenges for AI application and deployment. Table 9.1 summarizes home-based care functions that present opportunities for AI applications (e.g., communication, monitoring, decision-making), examples (e.g., smartphones, assistive devices, websites), AI technologies involved (e.g., machine learning, speech recognition, robotics), and challenges by user/stakeholder groups: (1) care recipients and informal care providers; (2) non-medical formal care providers; (3) medical home-based care providers; (4) administrators; and (5) those who engage in population health management (e.g., policy makers, local and national government entities, payers, researchers, staff members).

Current State and Opportunities: AI Applications to Home-Based Care

Care recipients and informal care providers
AI is ubiquitous in American lives. In the HBPC case story above, the care recipient (Linda) and her family members (David, the husband who co-resides, and Jennifer, the daughter who lives far away) were already using smartphones, tablets, and computers with AI-powered applications. However, the extent and ease of use vary with age. Consumers currently aged 80+ may or may not be familiar with the range of functions offered by electronic devices, because of the digital divide across age, ethnic/ racial groups, and geographic areas (Mitchell et al., 2019). In addition, age-related changes in functional or cognitive abilities can make it difficult to use these devices. David has difficulties using his fingers because of his stroke, and smartphone screens are sometimes too small for him. Jennifer is tech savvy and leverages technology to be assured of her parents' safety and health. Jennifer taught her parents how to use virtual assistant apps on their smartphones and tablets to communicate with each other, schedule medical appointments, and arrange transportation through ride-sharing apps. Jennifer arranged a smart medication dispenser that alerted Linda when to take her medication. For safety, the dispenser recognized Linda's face and released the pills only to Linda. Jennifer also looked for an effective diabetes patient self-management tool (e.g., AI-powered glucose sensors, activity- and dietary-tracking devices). Jennifer is now searching for an effective, non-intrusive fall prevention app or device for her father (Wong-Shing, 2022). Jennifer knew that Chris, the paid caregiver, had been overwhelmed from caring for David and Linda. Chris was aging, and Jennifer cared about Chris. Jennifer would like to introduce AI-powered devices to lessen the daily burden on Chris for continuing to care for David.

Although the care recipient (Linda) and her family (David, Jennifer) and caregiver (Chris) communicated regularly to coordinate care, AI applications could offer opportunities to improve collaboration and alignment of effort. For instance, AI applications could serve to reinforce the technology training that Jennifer gave to her parents, offering reminders to David about how to use their virtual assistant apps, occasionally prompting them to initiate video calls with Jennifer, or scheduling medical appointments.

Table 9.1 *Examples of AI applications to home-based care for stakeholder groups*

User group/stakeholder characteristics	Current status and opportunities			Challenges
	Functions and tasks	Examples of applications	Technology	
Care recipients • Diverse, aging • Interrelated needs (physical, mental, cognitive, social, economic needs) • At risk for short-term and long-term health changes	Doing daily activities Communication, scheduling, transportation Health/mood monitoring Health risk assessment, e.g., nutrition Disease prevention and management Medication management Rehabilitation Recreational activities Assisting daily activities (physical, psychological, and cognitive support) Work accommodation Work–life balance	Smartphones, tablets, computers, and websites with AI-powered applications Wearables Assistive devices, e.g., bed with a trapeze Diabetes prevention and management Medication dispenser Evaluation of services via social media Ride-sharing applications	Machine learning, Natural language processing Speech recognition Chatbots Ambient intelligence Robotics Computer vision Virtual reality headsets Deep learning	Privacy Costs Usability Data ownership and consent Explainability Trustworthiness Diversity, equity, and inclusion
Informal care Families, friends, volunteers • Diverse, aging • At risk for illness, injuries				
Formal, non-medical care Home-based care providers • Diverse, aging • At risk for illness, injuries	Care needs assessment Care plan Communication, scheduling Learning and training Transportation Assisting daily activities (physical, psychological, and cognitive support) Reporting, documentation	Smartphones, tablets, computers, websites with AI-powered applications Devices and wearables Assistive devices Global Positioning Systems	Machine learning Natural language processing Robotics Deep learning	Inequitable technology infrastructure Privacy Explainability Trustworthiness Diversity, equity and inclusion

Table 9.1 (*continued*)

User group/stakeholder characteristics	Current status and opportunities			Challenges
	Functions and tasks	Examples of applications	Technology	
Medical home-based care HBPC providers: physicians, physician assistants, nurse practitioners Home-health nurses, therapists, aides • Diverse, aging • At risk for illness, injuries	Diagnosis, treatment Ordering services Assessment, early detection, prediction Communication, scheduling Transportation Referrals, follow-ups Care coordination Documentation, reporting, consulting Learning and training Education for patients and families	Smartphones (function as an electrocardiogram (EKG) machine, ultrasound console, drug database, remote scanner) Laptops, tablets, smartphones (EHR access, order tests, referrals, medical guidelines, diagnosis/decision aid) Diagnostic equipment (X-rays, EKGs, ultrasounds) Therapeutic equipment (smart IV pumps, home dialysis) Devices and wearables Websites	Machine learning Natural language processing Deep learning	Trustworthiness Explainability Usability

Administrators of home-based care providers	Communication, coordination Risk stratification Coding (e.g., ICD-10) and billing Resource allocation, financing Fraud detection, cybersecurity Physician/personnel management Quality assurance and management Strategic planning	Devices and wearables Smartphone, tablet, and laptop apps Electronic health records system Medical billing system Enterprise software system	Machine learning Natural language processing Deep learning	Inequitable distribution of technologies across and within service sectors Interoperability
Population health management (e.g., policy makers, local and national government entities, healthcare systems, payers, researchers)	Needs assessment, risk identification Resource allocation and coordination Policy development and monitoring Genomics Disease prediction, discovery Communication and dissemination	Public health surveillance systems Social media/mobile data tracking systems National COVID Cohort Collaborative (N3C)	Machine learning Natural language processing Deep learning	Issues of data ownership Privacy Missing data Biased data

AI applications could additionally relieve some of the monitoring and/or reporting burdens from Chris by automatically monitoring prescription compliance and/or health metrics (e.g., blood glucose levels, heart rate) and reporting any outliers to the clinical team automatically. Further, AI systems could serve to interact with the older adults directly, providing some level of social connection, including simple conversation, but also updates on news, hobbies, or local events in which the older adults could participate.

Formal, non-medical care
AI applications to the tasks of public or private home care workers or staff (e.g., care needs assessment, care planning, assistance with daily activities) may involve smartphones, and tablets that assist care workers and staff with various tasks (e.g., communication, scheduling, care needs assessment, documentation, staff training). AI-powered virtual nurse assistants, chatbots or conversational agents, and remote patient monitoring are increasingly being developed to address the social and emotional needs of older adults and care workers, facilitating care work.

Medical home-based care
Technological advances have reduced the size of medical equipment (e.g., blood centrifuge, portable lab instruments, X-rays, EKGs, pulmonary function testing, ultrasounds), making them portable enough to travel to patients' homes. Powered by AI, light-weight laptops, tablets, and smartphones with high-speed internet access and global positioning systems enable the HBPC team to access patients' EHR safely. The EHR, which has largely replaced paper-based medical records, facilitate providers and staff to write notes, review medical histories and services received (e.g., prescriptions, test results), and receive notes from specialists. A smartphone alone can function as an EKG machine, ultrasound console, drug database, and remote scanner, as well as a tool to communicate with the patient and healthcare team. These technologies have facilitated HBPC to make diagnoses, initiate immediate medical treatment, provide clinical decision support, order tests, make referrals, and coordinate medical and social services in the home (Cornwell, 2019; Yao et al., 2018, 2021).

AI applications offer opportunities to continuously improve home-based medical care functions, such as monitoring patients, educating patients and family members, training clinicians, identifying trustworthy services for referrals, and enhancing interprofessional collaboration and coordination across home, community, and institutional settings to address patients' acute and long-term health needs.

It could also automate tasks involved in quality HBPC. Currently there are systems to notify when a patient is admitted or discharged from a hospital to enable prompt transitional care management that is crucial in value-based care to improve quality and reduce costs. Pharmacy systems sync with EHR medication lists to update them when a new medication is ordered. Systems are created to automate scheduling and improve routing by visiting patients in proximity to one another on the same day. Ultimately, AI could take a list of historical and physical symptoms and suggest possible diagnoses and treatment plans.

Administrators of home-based care provider organizations
Machine learning, natural language processing, and deep learning extend the healthcare organization's capacities in multiple areas: communication and reporting; risk stratification (e.g., identifying people at risk for hospitalization or a certain medical condition); coding for diagnosis (ICD-10) and billing; resource allocation; fraud detection; cybersecurity; physician and personnel management (e.g., hiring, evaluation, and training); quality assurance and management; and strategic planning).

Recently, healthcare organizations and companies like NowPow have developed new platforms for managing social service referrals. Some of those platforms allow healthcare providers to track whether their patients have followed through on their referrals, and sometimes to track outcomes. These tools have begun to connect sources of data that have previously been disconnected. Home-based care sectors could benefit from connecting with data systems that would allow AI applications to track patients' healthcare journeys across platforms to improve care coordination and care management for pools of patients with similar care needs.

The ongoing healthcare shift from fee-for-service to value-based payment systems mentioned above constitutes a business case for home-based care provider organizations to invest in technologies to demonstrate the value of their services through AI-powered data-capturing, management, and analytics systems.

Population health management
Progress in AI theory, methods, and models and in data sciences will continue to improve complex data management and integration to address important questions for policy makers, government entities, payers, health plans, and researchers. This ongoing progress provides an opportunity for home-based care to be integrated into AI-powered data systems. Big data, such as EHR combined with other sources of data (e.g., billing, administrative records, surveillance data, social media analytics, mobile data, and data from wearable devices), are increasingly used to estimate

the incidence and prevalence of specific diseases, identify risk factors at person, provider, community, and state levels, and predict emergency department use and hospitalizations (Pfaff et al., 2022).

Challenges

While presenting unprecedented opportunities to transform care for the aging population, AI applications need to address challenges related to data, technology, design, costs and market incentives, and ethical issues.

Data-related challenges

The value-based payment requires collection and management of data that lead to actions to improve the quality of care. EHR constitute a critically important data source in healthcare sectors. However, current EHR systems are limited in terms of usability and data quality, especially for social determinants of health such as race and ethnicity (Cook et al., 2021; Melnick et al., 2020). EHR data are not always standardized and are difficult to quickly parse; EHR can overwhelm healthcare providers. In contrast to healthcare sectors that are data rich, social service sectors have limited resources and electronic data, which presents challenges as well as opportunities for AI applications to home-based care.

Technological challenges

AI and machine-learning algorithms learn from data. Automatically developing an AI system requires an initial set of data for training machine-learning algorithms as a foundation for further application and utilization. However, the complex interactions and coordination involved in home-based care are seldom captured in data, especially in non-medical care provided by family members and paid caregivers in the home. In the absence of such data, coordination activities need to be explicitly coded by a human, a process that is quite often not scalable.

AI excels at mapping data to labels, or symptoms to risks. However, AI is not skilled in coordinating multiple domains of care. A major weakness of current AI lies in its limited ability to translate AI-enhanced information and decision-making into AI-powered physical actions. This weakness poses a major challenge for AI applications to home-based care, because physical assistance constitutes a core dimension of care work (e.g., assisting with daily activities such as lifting, cooking, eating, transferring, bathing, toileting, and with prescriptions provided by healthcare professionals).

In addition, technology's ability to adapt to older persons' short-term and long-term changes in health and function is still limited. Technology also needs to adapt to social norms, values, and preferences that vary across persons and their communities.

Costs and market incentives

Many older adults and their caregivers have no or limited access to the internet, email, and devices that feed data for AI (Mitchell et al., 2019). Expensive technology and devices face potential problems of scalability and cost effectiveness. Furthermore, long-term social service-related data are usually not integrated with healthcare data, making it difficult for deep-learning algorithms to identify the full set of social and healthcare needs of older adults with functional limitations. This drawback limits AI's ability to extend care providers' and healthcare professionals' work.

AI systems in support of home-based care would likely benefit from data that could be potentially provided by other smart devices in the home. For example, smart electricity meters can provide a wealth of data on where the older adult spends most of the day and how they use their home appliances. This information can be used to help with adjusting habits and improving health outcomes. However, given the cost of such devices, the challenge is how to make them affordable for consumers. Internet connectivity and other services that enable the functioning of AI systems could also be unaffordable for underprivileged communities. Who should bear the cost of those devices and services? This is an important question to address, especially if providing non-health-related data to AI systems can help optimize the health and function of older adults and care providers.

A related concern is that there is currently a low market demand for devices that target older adults. In the absence of a potential customer base, the manufacturers are not willing to invest in the development of specialized products for this market segment. But with a limited range of options on the market, the older consumers fail to see how the devices can address their needs, thus creating a predicament that is difficult to escape.

Design considerations

Perhaps the single most important issue in the design of AI applications to home-based care is the user interface. The fact that many of the devices that are the best platforms for developing AI applications (e.g., tablets and smartphones) are not designed specifically for older adults, and that older adults are not included in the design process, is one of the main obstacles to the wider adoption of AI technology both by care recipients and older caregivers. Devices designed for the general population without considering older adults' characteristics (e.g., finger dexterity impairment) have been singled out as the main impediment to older adults using technology

(Mitzner et al., 2010). Issues with the use of touchscreens and styli are an example of this disconnect.

The design for older adults has been studied extensively (Hawthorn, 2000; Nurgalieva et al., 2019; Zajicek, 2001). Contrary to popular beliefs, older adults are interested in using the technology (Kurniawan, 2008). AI applications need to be designed with older adults (both care recipients and care providers) in mind to gain their acceptance. That means that older adults need to be an integral part of the design process. Rather than taking a device developed for the general population and trying to adapt it for a particular application relevant to older adults, these potential users need to be consulted on what their needs are, and how these needs are currently serviced (Lee & Kim, 2020; Singh et al., 2018). Universal design (Czaja et al., 2019; Steinfeld & Maisel, 2012) provides a template for how AI applications targeted at the older population should be designed. Device manufacturers should also consider the Americans for Disabilities Act as a framework for improving the accessibility of their products.

During the COVID-19 pandemic, devices that enable communication and social interaction (e.g., smart speakers) were extensively used by older adults to communicate with their loved ones and members of their care teams. Even though these devices served a crucial need and were used in much larger numbers by older adults, they were used *despite* their designs, not because of them.

Ethical issues and privacy

Ethics of AI and data privacy are issues of general concern that are hotly debated (UNESCO, n.d.). AI applications to human behavior in the context of home-based care inevitably face safety, privacy, legal, and ethical issues. Home-based care work involves multiple parties that generate and consume data. While ideally the interests of all stakeholders are aligned, conflicts of interests will naturally arise. Such conflicts require serious investigation. For example, who owns patient data and who can use it? These questions are not easy to answer (Bourke & Bourke, 2020; Liddell et al., 2021). The wish of the older adult to preserve their privacy often conflicts with the desire of the family and care providers to be aware of what the older adult is doing. AI can automatically alert family members or care providers in the event of a fall or in an emergency, but the problem is how to define what constitutes an emergency. Similarly, an older adult with diabetes may not wish to disclose to their healthcare provider that they enjoyed a piece of cake after lunch or had a glass of wine.

Resources for developing and adopting AI applications are inequitably distributed across and within healthcare sectors. Existing data used to train AI often do not sufficiently include people with high needs, such as frail older adults with disabilities, or underrepresented people, organizations, and sectors. Machine learning that relies on existing observational data generally amplifies existing behavior and societal biases, resulting in unintended adverse effects on health inequity (Benjamin, 2019; McCoy et al., 2020; Obermeyer et al., 2019; Wiens et al., 2019).

HOW WOULD AI APPLICATIONS AFFECT HOME-BASED CARE WORK?

Given the challenges described above, AI systems and robots with AI elements are not likely to replace humans to perform care work in the foreseeable future. We should think about how AI applications could support or supplement care providers' work.

Potential Benefits of AI for Care Work

Caring for older adults with functional limitations can be physically, emotionally, and cognitively demanding (Muramatsu et al., 2019). Formal and informal caregivers tend to experience burnout, loneliness, and physical injury. AI could provide assessments, such as the Zarit Caregiver Burden Interview (Zarit et al., 1980), and based on the score make recommendations. AI applications could provide caregivers with informational and cognitive support (e.g., reminders about daily schedules, medication, diet restrictions, preferences, etc.) or emotional support (e.g., facilitating social connections, playing favorite music, encouraging caregivers to rest and relax). AI applications could also provide instrumental support or direct assistance with care work (e.g., automatically monitoring, recording, and reporting changes in the care recipients' health; responding to people with dementia who repeatedly ask the same questions). Eventually, AI may be able to advise on safe lifting or moving (e.g., sensing whether an older adult is ready to be safely transferred) or to supplement systems that could provide physical assistance to older adults.

Such informational, cognitive, emotional, or instrumental support from AI should help the caregiver focus on the aspects of care where humans are irreplaceable, like human contacts, or swiftly respond to signs of changes in the care recipients or their environments. AI should as much as possible relieve the caregiver of tedious tasks to shift their focus to what is important.

AI-enhanced care work would also have the added benefit of allowing the care to be better documented and tracked. The resulting data can be used to assess what works best for the older adult or to synthesize information about the care recipients, which allows the care worker to focus on providing high-quality socio-emotional care. The data can also help improve communication between the care recipient and the caregiver, alert the caregiver when an intervention is needed, and inform the care recipient of the progress of care and what the caregiver is doing. More broadly, data can help train care providers and professionalize their work, which could potentially increase pay, status, or influence in the care team.

Effects of AI on Care Flow and Work

Care work usually extends beyond a dyad of care recipient and a provider. Instead, care is generated and spread among several dyads or collectives of caregivers and care recipients (e.g., among groups of caregivers, among care recipients, and also with individuals outside the initial caring encounter) (Kahn, 1993; Stiehl et al., 2018). Care flow, defined as a process through which care is generated and spread at multiple levels of an organization (e.g., dyads, groups, units, and the entire organization) to address members' needs, involves three stages: *anticipation*, where care providers and care recipients prepare for the interaction, *co-production*, where providers and recipients contribute to the provision of care, and *replenishment*, where both care providers and recipients recover and reflect on the caring encounters (Stiehl et al., 2018).

AI can improve care flow and care work in three ways. First, it can increase caregivers' abilities to anticipate their care recipients' needs by assisting with the acquisition, organization, and analysis of care recipients' data along with the prediction of the care process and outcomes. Second, AI can enhance the coordination of care and hand-offs between multiple caregivers and care recipients by improving monitoring and communication systems. Finally, AI can provide caregivers and care recipients with time and support to reflect on the caring encounter and to decide how best to recharge after caring interactions. To produce positive effects of AI on care flow, it is critical for stakeholders to participate in the process of designing, developing, and disseminating the AI systems. Trustworthy, explainable AI is a prerequisite for integrating AI users and stakeholders into the process.

The effects of AI on care work can extend beyond home-based care and permeate into health and non-health sectors. According to a recent report, nearly one in five Americans are unpaid caregivers for adults (AARP & National Alliance for Caregiving, 2020). The majority (61 percent) of family caregivers are also working. Almost one in four Americans reported that caregiving worsened their own health. Caregiving demands affect all levels of workers, including those in leadership positions. AI-enhanced care work can potentially reduce caregiver stress, enhance workers' quality of life, and improve worker productivity and company profitability.

DISCUSSION

AI is ubiquitous in American lives. AI holds high promise for enhancing home-based care work in both medical and social service sectors. AI applications to home-based care are rapidly evolving. However, the expectations for AI far exceed its reality. AI applications are not likely to replace human care providers for people with complex medical and social care needs aging in their home. We argue that AI should not replace but augment the work of human care providers. AI applications for home-based care must be co-produced by their users (care recipients, their families, caregivers) and healthcare providers.

The COVID-19 pandemic and associated social distancing policies have elevated the role of the home as the location of healthcare delivery, as the workplace for home-based care providers, and as the office for those with flexible job arrangements allowing remote work from home. COVID-19 has dramatically enhanced the hope and expectations for AI to address social, psychological, economic, and health needs in societies. Telehealth has enabled patients to receive healthcare in their homes while minimizing the risk of COVID-19 transmission among care recipients and providers (Monaghesh & Hajizadeh, 2020). The pandemic simultaneously accelerated the increase in demand for home-based care services and the growth of workforce shortages in home-based care.

User interface is a major gap in AI applications' abilities to complement home-based care by humans. Today's older adults did not grow up with electronic devices. For example, those who were born in 1937 (i.e., aged 85 in 2022) were 46 years old when the internet was officially born in 1983; they were 63 years old when Wi-Fi started to become widely available at home in 2000. These older adults' homes (i.e., their care workers' workplace) may not be equipped with high-speed internet that enables AI-based applications. The digital divide across birth cohorts also varies across racial, social, and regional communities.

Currently, AI successes are generally limited to areas that are data rich. The advances in AI applications have mainly been lacking for tasks that are complex, unstandardized, or performed without technology infrastructure, like caring for older adults with complex medical and social care needs in their homes. Integrating medical and social services in the financing and delivery of home-based care has been long recognized as a key driver of quality care for adults with multiple chronic conditions and functional limitations, but progress has been slow. AI holds great promise in coordinating different types of care providers and entities, such as families, friends, and volunteers; primary care, specialty clinics, hospitals, subacute care, social services; end-of-life care; housing, long-term care facilities; private and public payers, local and national public health, aging, and social policy agencies.

CONCLUSION

We propose three premises for AI-based technology in home-based care in aging societies. First, the home, broadly defined as a hub of daily activities and social interactions, is the fundamental environment in which AI and related technologies work together to help people maximize their remaining abilities and age in place. Second, technologies need to have built-in mechanisms to adapt themselves to changes in persons' physical, emotional, cognitive, and sensory abilities in their living environments. Third, technologies should facilitate effective partnerships with care providers, instead of threatening their livelihood. Developing and designing AI technologies must involve users (aging individuals, families, paid caregivers, and healthcare professionals) and community- and healthcare-based stakeholders in urban and rural areas, including low-resourced communities, from the outset. It must also inform and be driven by state-of-the-art AI research that can be applied to the needs of people aging in their homes, including methods to help users understand technologies' risks and benefits and operate them safely and effectively.

There is an urgent need to address the gaps that limit AI technologies' promise for maximizing the health and well-being of older adults and their care workers, and for promoting health equity among diverse aging populations. To advance AI applications for care recipients and providers, we need to address the needs of care recipients and care providers holistically, rather than separate AI development from human actors and their living spaces. We urge AI applications to prioritize diversity, equity and inclusion, and social justice for diverse older adults aging with or into disabilities. We are now in the uncharted territory of population aging and care workforce shortage in the backdrop of unprecedented growth of AI-powered technologies and inequity in the distribution of income, wealth, and resources. Home-based care recipients, providers, and technology designers and disseminators should learn from each other to grow as a learning home-based care system, where "science, informatics, incentives, and culture are aligned with continuous improvement and innovation" (Matheny et al., 2019, p. xv).

REFERENCES

AARP & National Alliance for Caregiving. (2020). Caregiving in the United States 2020. https://doi.org/10.26419/ppi.00103.001

Benjamin, R. (2019). *Race after technology: Abolitionist tools for the New Jim Code*. Polity.

Bhattacharya, S., Pradhan, K., Bashar, M., Tripathi, S., Semwal, J., Marzo, R., Bhattacharya, S., & Singh, A. (2019). Artificial intelligence enabled healthcare: A hype, hope or harm. *Journal of Family Medicine and Primary Care*, *8*(11), 3461–3464.

Bourke, A., & Bouke, G. (2020, August 6). Who owns patient data? The answer is not that simple. *The BMJ*. https://blogs.bmj.com/bmj/2020/08/06/who-owns-patient-data-the-answer-is-not-that-simple/

Centers for Medicare & Medicaid Services. (2021, December 1). Home health PPS. www.cms.gov/Medicare/Medicare-Fee-for-Service-Payment/HomeHealthPPS

Cook, L. A., Sachs, J., & Weiskopf, N. G. (2021). The quality of social determinants data in the electronic health record: A systematic review. *Journal of the American Medical Informatics Association*, *29*(1), 187–196.

Cornwell, T. (2019). Home-based primary care's perfect storm. www.hccinstitute.org/app/uploads/2017/10/Web-HCCI-Perfect-Storm-White-Paper.pdf?x85650

Czaja, S. J., Boot, W. R., Charness, N., & Rogers, W. A. (2019). *Designing for older adults: Principles and creative human factors approaches* (Third edition). Taylor & Francis.

Davis, M. R. (2021, November 18). New AARP survey reveals older adults want to age in place. www.aarp.org/home-family/your-home/info-2021/home-and-community-preferences-survey.html

De Jonge, K. E., Jamshed, N., Gilden, D., Kubisiak, J., Bruce, S. R., & Taler, G. (2014). Effects of home-based primary care on Medicare costs in high-risk elders. *Journal of the American Geriatrics Society*, *62*(10), 1825–1831.

Edes, T., Kinosian, B., Vuckovic, N. H., Olivia Nichols, L., Mary Becker, M., & Hossain, M. (2014). Better access, quality, and cost for clinically complex veterans with home-based primary care. *Journal of the American Geriatrics Society*, *62*(10), 1954–1961.

Emanuel, E. J., & Wachter, R. M. (2019). Artificial intelligence in health care: Will the value match the hype? *Journal of the American Medical Association*, *321*(23), 2281–2282.

England, P. (2005). Emerging theories of care work. *Annual Review of Sociology*, *31*(1), 381–399.

Feinglass, J., Norman, G., Golden, R. L., Muramatsu, N., Gelder, M., & Cornwell, T. (2018). Integrating social services and home-based primary care for high-risk patients. *Population Health Management*, *21*(2), 96–101.

Haque, A., Milstein, A., & Fei-Fei, L. (2020). Illuminating the dark spaces of healthcare with ambient intelligence. *Nature*, *585*(7824), 193–202.

Hawthorn, D. (2000). Possible implications of aging for interface designers. *Interacting with Computers*, *12*(5), 507–528.

Jiang, F., Jiang, Y., Zhi, H., Dong, Y., Li, H., Ma, S., Wang, Y., Dong, Q., Shen, H., & Wang, Y. (2017). Artificial intelligence in healthcare: Past, present and future. *Stroke and Vascular Neurology*, *2*(4), 230.

Kahn, W. A. (1993). Caring for the caregivers: Patterns of organizational caregiving. *Administrative Science Quarterly*, *38*(4), 539.

Kurniawan, S. (2008). Older people and mobile phones: A multi-method investigation. *International Journal of Human-Computer Studies*, *66*(12), 889–901.

Lee, L. N., & Kim, M. J. (2020). A critical review of smart residential environments for older adults with a focus on pleasurable experience. *Frontiers in Psychology*, *10*. www.frontiersin.org/article/10.3389/fpsyg.2019.03080

Liddell, K., Simon, D. A., & Lucassen, A. (2021). Patient data ownership: Who owns your health? *Journal of Law and the Biosciences*, *8*(2), lsab023.

Matheny, M. E., Israni, S. T., Ahmed, M., & Whicher, D. (2019). *Artificial intelligence in health care: The hope, the hype, the promise, the peril*. National Academy of Medicine.

Matheny, M. E., Whicher, D., & Thadaney Israni, S. (2020). Artificial intelligence in health care: A report from the National Academy of Medicine. *JAMA*, *323*(6), 509–510.

McCoy, L. G., Banja, J. D., Ghassemi, M., & Celi, L. A. (2020). Ensuring machine learning for healthcare works for all. *BMJ Health & Care Informatics*, *27*(3).

McDonald, E. M., Mack, K., Shields, W. C., Lee, R. P., & Gielen, A. C. (2016). Primary care opportunities to prevent unintentional home injuries: A focus on children and older adults. *American Journal of Lifestyle Medicine*, *12*(2), 96–106.

Medicaid. (n.d.). Mandatory and optional Medicaid benefits. www.medicaid.gov/medicaid/benefits/mandatory-optional-medicaid-benefits/index.html

Medicare. (n.d.). Home health services coverage. www.medicare.gov/coverage/home-health-services

Melnick, E. R., Dyrbye, L. N., Sinsky, C. A., Trockel, M., West, C. P., Nedelec, L., Tutty, M. A., & Shanafelt, T. (2020). The association between perceived electronic health record usability and professional burnout among US physicians. *Mayo Clinic Proceedings*, *95*(3), 476–487.

Merriam-Webster. (2022). Artificial intelligence. www.merriam-webster.com/dictionary/artificial%20intelligence.

Mitchell, U. A., Chebli, P. G., Ruggiero, L., & Muramatsu, N. (2019). The digital divide in health-related technology use: The significance of race/ethnicity. *The Gerontologist*, *59*(1), 6–14.

Mitzner, T. L., Boron, J. B., Fausset, C. B., Adams, A. E., Charness, N., Czaja, S. J., Dijkstra, K., Fisk, A. D., Rogers, W. A., & Sharit, J. (2010). Older adults talk technology: Technology usage and attitudes. *Computers in Human Behavior*, *26*(6), 1710–1721.

Monaghesh, E., & Hajizadeh, A. (2020). The role of telehealth during COVID-19 outbreak: A systematic review based on current evidence. *BMC Public Health*, *20*, 1193.

Muramatsu, N., & Cornwell, T. (2003). Needs for physician housecalls: Views from health and social service providers. *Home Health Care Services Quarterly*, *22*(2), 17–29.

Muramatsu, N., Mensah, E., & Cornwell, T. (2004). A physician house call program for the homebound. *Joint Commission Journal on Quality and Safety*, *30*(5), 266–276.

Muramatsu, N., Yin, H., Campbell, R. T., Hoyem, R. L., Jacob, M. A., & Ross, C. O. (2007). Risk of nursing home admission among older Americans: Does states' spending on home- and community-based services matter? *Journal of Gerontology, Series B: Psychological Sciences and Social Sciences, 62*(3), S169–S178.

Muramatsu, N., Sokas, R. K., Chakraborty, A., Zanoni, J. P., & Lipscomb, J. (2018). Slips, trips, and falls among home care aides: A mixed-methods study. *Journal of Occupational and Environmental Medicine, 60*(9), 796–803.

Muramatsu, N., Sokas, R. K., Lukyanova, V. V., & Zanoni, J. (2019). Perceived stress and health among home care aides: Caring for older clients in a Medicaid-funded home care program. *Journal of Health Care for the Poor and Underserved, 30*(2), 721–738.

Nurgalieva, L., Jara Laconich, J. J., Baez, M., Casati, F., & Marchese, M. (2019). A systematic literature review of research-derived touchscreen design guidelines for older adults. *IEEE Access, 7*, 22035–22058.

Obermeyer, Z., Powers, B., Vogeli, C., & Mullainathan, S. (2019). Dissecting racial bias in an algorithm used to manage the health of populations. *Science (American Association for the Advancement of Science), 366*(6464), 447–453.

Pfaff, E. R., Girvin, A. T., Bennett, T. D., Bhatia, A., Brooks, I. M., Deer, R. R. et al. (2022). Identifying who has long COVID in the USA: A machine learning approach using N3C data. *The Lancet Digital Health, 4*(7), e532–e541.

Rotenberg, J., Kinosian, B., Boling, P., Taler, G., & Group. (2018). Home-based primary care: Beyond extension of the independence at home demonstration. *Journal of the American Geriatrics Society, 66*(4), 812–817.

Schuchman, M., Fain, M., & Cornwell, T. (2018). The resurgence of home-based primary care models in the United States. *Geriatrics, 3*(3), 41.

Singh, D., Psychoula, I., Kropf, J., Hanke, S., & Holzinger, A. (2018). Users' perceptions and attitudes towards smart home technologies. In M. Mokhtari, B. Abdulrazak, & H. Aloulou (Eds), *Smart homes and health telematics, designing a better future: Urban assisted living* (Vol. 10898, pp. 203–214). Springer International Publishing.

Steinfeld, E., & Maisel, J. L. (2012). *Universal design creating inclusive environments*. John Wiley & Sons.

Stiehl, E., Kossek, E. E., Leana, C., & Keller, Q. (2018). A multilevel model of care flow: Examining the generation and spread of care in organizations. *Organizational Psychology Review, 8*(1), 31–69.

Totten, A. M., White-Chu, E. F., Wasson, N., Morgan, E., Kansagara, D., Davis-O'Reilly, D.-O., & Goodlin, S. (2016). Home-based primary care interventions: NCBI bookshelf. Agency for Healthcare Research and Quality. www-ncbi-nlm-nih-gov.proxy.cc.uic.edu/books/NBK356253/?report=reader

UNESCO. (n.d.). Recommendation on the ethics of artificial intelligence. https://en.unesco.org/artificial-intelligence/ethics#recommendation

Vladeck, B. C., & Miller, N. A. (1994). The Medicare home health initiative. *Health Care Financing Review, 16*(1), 7–16.

Wiens, J., Saria, S., Sendak, M., Ghassemi, M., Liu, V. X., Doshi-Velez, F. et al. (2019). Do no harm: A roadmap for responsible machine learning for health care. *Nature Medicine, 25*(9), 1337–1340.

Wong-Shing, K. (2022). Best medical alerts of 2022: CNET. www.cnet.com/health/medical/best-medical-alerts/

World Health Organization. (n.d.). Ageing. www.who.int/health-topics/ageing

Yao, N., Ritchie, C., Camacho, F., & Leff, B. (2016). Geographic concentration of home-based medical care providers. *Health Affairs (Project Hope)*, *35*(8), 1404–1409.

Yao, N., Ritchie, C., Cornwell, T., & Leff, B. (2018). Use of home-based medical care and disparities. *Journal of the American Geriatrics Society*, *66*(9), 1716–1720.

Yao, N., Mutter, J. B., Berry, J. D., Yamanaka, T., Mohess, D. T., & Cornwell, T. (2021). In traditional Medicare, modest growth in the home care workforce largely driven by nurse practitioners: Study examines the characteristics of the workforce providing home-based medical care for traditional (fee-for-service) Medicare beneficiaries. *Health Affairs*, *40*(3), 478–486.

Yu, K.-H., Beam, A. L., & Kohane, I. S. (2018). Artificial intelligence in healthcare. *Nature Biomedical Engineering*, *2*(10), 719–731.

Zajicek, M. (2001). Interface design for older adults. *Proceedings of the 2001 EC/NSF Workshop on Universal Accessibility of Ubiquitous Computing: Providing for the Elderly*, 60–65.

Zarit, S. H., Reever, K. E., & Bach-Peterson, J. (1980). Relatives of the impaired elderly: Correlates of feelings of burden. *The Gerontologist*, *20*(6), 649–655.

10. Artificial intelligence for professional learning
Wayne Holmes and Allison Littlejohn

INTRODUCTION

Artificial Intelligence (AI) is changing the workplace – in the areas of productivity, administration, human resources and recruitment, research and development, logistics, manufacturing, services and relationships with sellers and suppliers, to name just a few (Fleming, 2020). As AI replaces some job roles and changes others, work practices evolve. This means that professionals have to be able to learn and work with AI systems and other digital technologies (Bughin et al., 2017). For example, an IBM study emphasised the need to scale professional learning to maintain a skilled workforce able to adapt (LaPrade et al., 2019). Meanwhile, AI systems have also been seen as a way to scale professional learning (Edlich et al., 2019). For example, in some places AI is already being used to recommend content to workers as a way (so it is argued) to 'personalise learning' or to 'shorten the learning journey', depending on the prior knowledge and specific skills set of each worker (e.g., Area9 Lyceum, 2022).

So, the consensus is clear: (1) AI is having a growing but uncertain impact on businesses, at every level, in every sector and worldwide, such that (2) business leaders and workforces need to better understand what AI is, its potential and challenges, and how it might best be leveraged for profit, while maintaining the highest ethical standards; and (3) the judicious deployment of AI-assisted educational applications might help organisations deal with changes in job roles and professional practice. However, the context of professional learning differs significantly from formal educational contexts (such as schools and universities). Accordingly, in this chapter, we explore the impact of AI on workplace learning. We begin by critiquing the hyperbole of AI and then introducing workplace learning, differentiating it from formal education. We then examine the application of AI in formal educational settings, and the application of AI to support workplace learning, before concluding by speculating some future possibilities.

ARTIFICIAL INTELLIGENCE

As is well known, it is notoriously difficult to define AI. However, the definition provided by UNICEF is refreshingly helpful:

> AI refers to machine-based systems that can, given a set of human-defined objectives, make predictions, recommendations, or decisions that influence real or virtual environments. AI systems interact with us and act on our environment, either directly or indirectly. Often, they appear to operate autonomously, and can adapt their behaviour by learning about the context. (UNICEF, 2021)

As explained elsewhere (Holmes & Porayska-Pomsta, 2023; Holmes & Tuomi, 2022), this definition is preferred for several reasons. For example, while it accommodates data-driven AI techniques such as artificial neural networks and deep learning, it does not depend on data and therefore also includes rule-based or symbolic AI, as well as any new paradigm of AI that might emerge in future years (such as 'neuro-symbolic' AI; Susskind et al., 2021). It also highlights that AI systems necessarily depend on human objectives and sometimes 'appear to operate autonomously' rather than do operate autonomously: 'it is people who are performing the tasks to make the systems appear autonomous' (Crawford, cited in Corbyn, 2021). This is important given the critical role of humans at all stages of the AI development pipeline.

AI often suffers from exaggeration and hyperbole (Berryhill et al., 2019). For example, AI systems failed to live up to their promise in the COVID-19 pandemic ('Our review [of 2,212 studies] finds that none of the models identified are of potential clinical use'; Roberts et al., 2021, p. 199). In addition AI systems may be biased, because the data on which they are trained are biased, or the algorithms that drive them are biased (Ledford, 2019). They can also be brittle: a small change to a road sign can prevent an AI image recognition system recognising it (Heaven, 2019). Meanwhile, the AI large language models (LMs), such as OpenAI's GPT-3 and Google's Lamda which have recently made dramatic headlines (GPT-3, 2020; Tiku, 2022), often generate nonsense (Hutson, 2021; Marcus & Davis, 2020) and can present real-world risks of harm, especially given:

> the tendency of training data ingested from the Internet to encode hegemonic worldviews, the tendency of LMs to amplify biases and other issues in the training data, and the tendency of researchers and other people to mistake LM-driven performance gains for actual natural language understanding. (Bender et al., 2021, p. 616)

In any case, despite its history and the dominant narrative, AI should not be thought of in purely technical terms. Instead, AI is a complex sociotechnical artefact that needs to be understood as something that is constructed through complex social processes (Eynon & Young, 2021). In other words, when we consider AI, we must consider both the human dimension and the technological dimension in symbiosis.

PROFESSIONAL LEARNING

In contrast with learning that takes place in formal educational settings such as schools and universities, professional learning includes both formal learning (in real or virtual classrooms) and informal learning (learning that is contextualised within the workplace environment), both of which can be important for the development and maintenance of expertise in the modern workplace (Cacciattolo, 2015; Eraut, 2012; Milligan & Littlejohn, 2014). Formal learning (in schools and universities, and for professional learners) is usually designed around predefined learning goals and is driven by participation in a structured curriculum. Informal or 'workplace learning', on the other hand, ranges from more behavioural in orientation such as 'on-the-job' training or observing how an expert colleague carries out a task, to the more knowledge-oriented, such as engaging in strategic discussions with colleagues or asking a manager for advice. Accordingly, workplace learning has a different emphasis, structure, and environment compared with formal learning. It is more guided by immediate work needs and facilitated through work experiences, and is shaped by both *what* is learned and *where* the learning takes place. For all these reasons, the outcomes of workplace learning are less predictable than those in formal learning (Tynjälä, 2008).

Boud and Garrick propose workplace learning is associated with two outcomes. First, 'the development of individuals through contributing to knowledge, skills and the capacity to further their own learning both as employees and citizens in wider society', and second, 'the development of the enterprise through contributing to production, effectiveness and innovation' (2012, p. 6). Thus, while in formal learning the learning is separated *from* work, workplace learning combines learning *with* work. This integration of work and learning raises issues of self-regulation, the social mediation of learning, and human agency, all of which any related application of AI ought to address.

Self-Regulated Learning

Informal professional learning, workplace learning, is dependent on each individual having the internal drive to plan, facilitate, and reflect upon their own learning through self-regulation (Enos et al., 2003). It is enhanced when professionals are motivated by and interested in their learning, when they are able to plan their learning goals in ways that help them achieve their work goals (Sitzmann & Ely, 2011), when they are able to adapt the ways by which they approach their learning, and when they self-evaluate their learning in efficacious ways (Littlejohn et al., 2016a). Such 'self-regulated' learning is influenced by a combination of psychological (cognitive and affective), behavioural, and environmental factors that form its foundation (Bandura, 1991; Pintrich, 2000; Zimmerman, 2002).

Zimmerman's influential model of self-regulated learning provides a framework for analysis of the ways learners set and attain their learning goals (Zimmerman, 2006). The model proposes a number of affective, cognitive, and behavioural constructs that influence learning, which Littlejohn and colleagues explored through a series of studies that examined how professionals self-regulate their learning using digital platforms (Fontana et al., 2015; Littlejohn et al., 2015; Margaryan et al., 2013; Milligan et al., 2014). The following constructs were identified as important (see Table 10.1): the learner's confidence in their learning capacity; their ability to set and adapt their learning goals; their ability to use a

Table 10.1   Self-regulated learning constructs that are important for professional learning

Self-regulated learning construct	Description
Self-efficacy	Confidence in learning capacity
Goal setting	Ability to use and adapt goals to plan learning
Task strategy	Ability to plan learning and adopt a repertoire of learning approaches
Task interest	Interest and readiness to determine the wider value of a learning task
Learning strategy	Ability to integrate new with existing knowledge
Help seeking	Seeking help from other people or resources
Self-satisfaction and evaluation	Readiness to compare own performance against an external goal and satisfaction from this comparison
Learning challenge	Resilience to challenge

repertoire of learning approaches and to alter these when they are not effective; their readiness to think critically about how they can apply learning to other potential areas of application; their ability to integrate new knowledge; their readiness to seek help; their ability to compare their own performance against others and to experiencing a sense of achievement when learning; and their resilience to challenge.

The Social Mediation of Learning

Workplace learning has to take into consideration not only the needs of the individual, but also the social dimension of the collective, since workplace learning goals are socially mediated through interactions with others. To address this issue, Littlejohn and colleagues (2012) proposed that in digital environments, analysis of data should support both self-regulation and social mediation of learning through a process they termed 'charting'. Charting is a process designed to support learners drawing on digital tools, resources, people, and environments to self-regulate their learning and, in doing so, contribute to collective knowledge online. It is based on four broad processes. When the learner charts a learning goal, they draw on technology to (1) *connect* with people and resources that are related to the goal. As they (2) use (or *consume*) these resources, they (3) *create* new resources that they (4) *contribute* back to the collective. Thus, charting involves the processes of connecting, consuming, creating, and contributing resources back to the collective in ways that can be used by others. Charting may also be used to connect learners to others with similar goals, creating networks of people who may support each other, while each learner's goals and motivations are continually reviewed as a form of self-regulated learning.

Human Agency

Human agency is a set of abilities that are nurtured throughout a human's life, which involve the human capability to influence what they do through their own actions (Bandura, 2006). Personal agency is the ability of a learner to maintain an interest in expanding their knowledge, to be willing to invest effort in learning and to be able to adapt their learning orientation as they engage in learning (Bandura, 1986; Pintrich, 2000; van den Boom et al., 2004; Zimmerman, 2000). Behaviours such as setting goals and adapting approaches to learning are characteristics that each learner can improve through practice. Constructs, such as interest, motivation, self-evaluation, and self-satisfaction, can also be influenced by the learner themselves, though this is more challenging for learners to change without support (Winne, 1995; Zimmerman, 2000). The personal agency needed for informal professional learning (workplace learning) is different than the agency needed to engage in formal learning (courses and training) where goals have been predetermined and learning is scaffolded by a teacher (Littlejohn et al., 2016b).

Interagency is also important for workplace learning (Collin, 2008; Fuller & Unwin, 2011). Work environments are complex sites representing divergent interests that are accommodated through processes of negotiation and accommodation (Engeström, 2004). Professionals have to engage with resources, both physical and digital, people, and knowledge immediately available to them to support their learning (Argyris & Schon, 1974). As they do so, professionals develop the 'capacity to work relationally with others on complex problems' (Edwards, 2010, p. 8).

THE APPLICATION OF ARTIFICIAL INTELLIGENCE IN EDUCATION

The application of AI in formal education is increasingly being fêted as an 'altogether new way of spreading quality education across the world' (Seldon & Abidoye, 2018, p. 4). According to a leading AI entrepreneur, Kai-Fu Lee (formerly a senior executive at Google, Microsoft, SGI, and Apple):

> We know the flaws of today's education ... AI can play a major part in fixing these flaws ... AI will make learning much more effective, engaging, and fun ... I believe this symbiotic and flexible new education model can ... help every student realize his or her potential in the Age of AI. (Lee & Qiufan, 2021, p. 118)

Meanwhile, international organisations are loudly proclaiming that AI will 'give learners greater ownership over what they learn, how they learn, where they learn and when they learn' (OECD, 2021, p. 3); and that AI 'helps teachers realize impressive outcomes' (IBM, 2018), especially 'given its ability to provide content tailored to students' learning needs' (World Bank, 2022). In short, so the argument goes, AI will 'transform education' (OECD, 2020, p. 7). As a consequence of this enthusiasm, and despite there being limited evidence for the veracity of these claims, AI for education was one of the top three AI venture capital investment areas in 2020 (Zhang et al., 2022).

While the application of AI to support teaching and learning (AIED) has been researched for more than 40 years, almost as long as AI itself, it is only in the last 10 years or so that it has emerged from the research lab to be taken up widely in schools, higher education institutes, and other formal learning contexts. It is also being extensively commercialised, creating a market expected to become worth more than US$20 billion within five years (GMI, 2022), that was only accelerated by the school shutdowns necessitated by the COVID-19 pandemic. Nonetheless, it remains unclear for educators how to take pedagogical advantage of this still emerging educational technology, and how it can actually impact meaningfully on teaching and learning (Holmes et al., 2019; Miao & Holmes, 2021; Zawacki-Richter et al., 2019). Inevitably, over the years, AIED research has diverged, creating and researching AIED tools that may be grouped in three distinct but overlapping categories: learner-supporting AI, teacher-supporting AI, and institution-supporting AI. These categories have been extended to a taxonomy of AIED (Holmes & Tuomi, 2022; Holmes et al., 2019).

Learner-Supporting AI

The focus of most AIED research and commercialisation has been on learner-supporting AI, usually for subjects such as mathematics or other non-interpretative subjects like physics or computer science. The Holmes and Tuomi taxonomy (2022) identifies (in order of availability, from 'commercially available', through 'researched', to 'speculative') the following types of learner-supporting AI: so-called *intelligent tutoring systems* (ITS; e.g., Spark from Domoscio, 2022), *AI-assisted apps* (e.g., Photomath, 2022; translation software from SayHi, 2022; and homework-answering apps, Dan, 2021), *AI-assisted simulations* (e.g., augmented reality, Behmke et al., 2018; virtual reality, McGuire & Alaraj, 2018; and games-based learning, LaPierre, 2021), *AI to support learners with disabilities* (e.g., Alabdulkareem et al., 2022; Anuradha et al., 2010; Barua et al., 2022; Benfatto et al., 2016; and StorySign by Huawei, 2022), *automatic essay writing*, often supported by generative AI tools such as ChatGPT (Sharples, 2022), *chatbots* (e.g., Hussain, 2017), *automatic formative assessment* (Foster, 2019; Metz, 2021), *learning network orchestrators* (e.g., Lu et al., 2018), *dialogue-based tutoring systems* (which use a dialogic Socratic-approach to teaching and learning, e.g., Nye et al., 2014), *exploratory learning environments* (Mavrikis et al., 2018), and *AI-assisted lifelong learning assistants* (Holmes et al., 2019).

The most prominent learner-supporting AI are ITS, which are now offered by large numbers of multi-million-dollar-funded corporations around the world (Holmes et al., 2019; Miao & Holmes, 2021). With ITS, the learner engages with an online system that delivers some standardised content, an activity, and possibly a quiz. The learner's individual responses (where they click and what they answer) then determines the next piece of information, activity, and quiz they are given. In this way, each learner follows their own adapted pathway through the material to be learned. In summary, the aim of ITS is to enable learners to learn independently of teachers, which is achieved by attempting to automate teacher functions in the form of an artificial personal tutor.

However, while the AIED research community has long demonstrated the efficacy of ITS (and some other learner-supporting AI tools), in short studies researched in limited contexts (e.g., Beal et al., 2007; Ma et al., 2014; Vanlehn et al., 2005), there is surprisingly little to justify its wide use in well-resourced classrooms, other than the marketing materials and mostly unsubstantiated hopes expressed by many policymakers. Robust, independent evidence remains scarce (Miao & Holmes, 2021), and claims that AI will dramatically improve the way learners learn (e.g., OECD, 2021) remain aspirational or speculative (Holmes et al., 2019; Nemorin, 2021, cited in Miao & Holmes, 2021).

Meanwhile, ITS and similar tools have been criticised (Holmes & Porayska-Pomsta, 2023; Holmes & Tuomi, 2022; Holmes et al., 2019) for undermining student agency (students have no choice but to do what the AI requires), disempowering teachers (turning them all too often into mere technology facilitators), and missing out on learning through social engagement; as well as for being focused on pathways leading to the homogenisation of learners rather than on outcomes such as developing self-regulation skills or leading to self-actualisation; and for being solutions- rather than problem-driven. In particular, ITS tend to embody a naïve approach to teaching and learning, involving spoon-feeding prespecified standardised content, adapted to the individual's achievements, while aiming to avoid failure. In other words, despite suggestions to the contrary, the approach is effectively behaviourist or instructionist, and ignores more than 60 years of pedagogical research and development. Typical ITS overlook, for example, *deep learning* (Entwistle, 2000), *guided discovery learning* (Gagné & Brown, 1963), *productive failure* (Kapur, 2008), *project-based learning* (Kokotsaki et al., 2016), and *active learning* (Matsushita, 2018). This *de facto* behaviourist approach, especially spoon-feeding, prioritises remembering over thinking, and knowing facts over critical engagement, thus undermining robust learning.

Teacher-Supporting AI

Over the same 40-year period, there has been relatively little focus on AI designed specifically to support teachers (aside from the dashboards that are common in educational technologies; Jivet et al., 2017).

Recently, however, there has been some research and some, often controversial, commercial products. The Holmes and Tuomi taxonomy (2022) lists (again in order of availability) *plagiarism detection* (e.g., Turnitin, 2022), *smart curation of learning materials* (Perez-Ortiz, 2020), *classroom monitoring* (Lieu, 2018; Moriarty-Mclaughlin, 2020; Poulsen et al., 2017), *automatic summative assessment* (which was tried, then abandoned, by the Australian government; Hendry, 2018), *AI teaching and assessment assistants* (Guilherme, 2019; Holmes et al., 2019; Selwyn, 2019), and *classroom orchestration* (e.g., Song, 2021).

Institution-Supporting AI

Finally, institution-supporting AI is quietly growing behind the scenes, despite there being limited research in this area. The Holmes and Tuomi taxonomy (2022) lists in order of availability AI-assisted *admissions* (e.g., Marcinkowski et al., 2020; Pangburn, 2019; Waters & Miikkulainen, 2014), *course planning* (e.g., Martinez-Maldonado et al., 2021), *scheduling and timetabling* (e.g., Lantiv, 2022), *school security, identifying 'dropouts' and 'students at risk'* (e.g., Baker et al., 2020; Lykourentzou et al., 2009), and *e-proctoring* (Chin, 2020; Henry & Oliver, 2021; Kelley, 2021). Again, some of these developments – especially *e-proctoring* (Chin, 2022) – are controversial.

THE APPLICATION OF ARTIFICIAL INTELLIGENCE IN WORKPLACE LEARNING

So how might AI contribute to workplace learning? Already, many workplaces are using AI applications, mainly with the aim of improving productivity by automating routine and repetitive tasks or by using business analytics with the aim of improving efficiency and supporting humans to focus on complex and creative tasks. In addition, AI-assisted analytic systems are being deployed to provide insights into the working patterns of employees.

Meanwhile, as we have seen, to date almost all applications of AI focus on providing support for learners in formal learning settings in subjects such as mathematics or other non-interpretative subjects like physics or computer science. For workplace learners who have different needs and who only rarely sit in classrooms, a virtual AI-powered tutor (perhaps instantiated on their mobile phone) might have potential. Nonetheless, currently there are very few learner-supporting tools developed specifically for adult learners outside the classroom.

One AI-assisted tool that has been developed for professional learners is Area9 Lyceum (2022). However, Area9 sits alongside work activities, rather than being embedded within them, and is effectively an ITS of standardised content. A key problem with such applications, ones that sit alongside work rather than embedded within it, is that the learner also needs to learn how to apply the new knowledge and skills learned in the classroom to their work setting, which requires significant extra cognitive effort (Markauskaite & Goodyear, 2017).

Other applications of AI to support professional learning tend to focus on matching employees with training opportunities (e.g., eightfold, 2022) or enabling professionals to access information faster (e.g., Chubb et al., 2021). While this may be helpful in terms of work efficiency, it does not reduce the need for teaching support to provide feedback and to scaffold learning. In addition, virtual assistants and bots are being used to support training and mentoring in the workplace (e.g., Khandelwal & Upadhyay, 2021), though these systems are not able to replace the complex forms of support that an experienced teacher or mentor can offer. However, possible future co-working relationships between humans and machines open up opportunities to circumvent this problem by supporting professional learning while people work. For example, people working alongside robots on a car assembly line in future may receive feedback from the robots about the ways in which they work. There are other potential feedback opportunities via so-called smart assistants, healthcare management systems, social media monitoring, and by tapping into other applications of AI. However, it is important to note that to take advantage of these and other future workplace learning opportunities each professional will have to use personal agency to empower them to engage in learning (Enos et al., 2003; Sitzmann & Ely, 2011).

Littlejohn and colleagues have set out an argument for a reframing of AIED for workplace learning focused on participation, where learning goals are set by the professionals themselves and are defined by work priorities and individual agency, rather than by a curriculum (Littlejohn et al., 2012). The proposed approach was based on a series of empirical studies that interrogated the choices professionals made when they decided what they needed to learn and how they went about their learning. These studies took place in the energy sector (Margaryan et al., 2009) and finance sector (Milligan et al., 2015). Effective learning in the finance sector, which was self-reported based on improved work practices and processes, was associated with the capacity to self-regulate learning.

As we have noted, currently there are few innovative or targeted examples of the application of AI to support workplace learning. Accordingly, we end this chapter by speculating on three brief possibilities (the Holmes and Tuomi taxonomy, 2022, might be used to identify others), grounded in existing research but yet to be widely available for workplace learning.

Responsive Open Learning Environments

As we have seen, AIED systems are often designed to deliver relevant and standardised content to learners, depending on their profile and stage of learning. However, in job roles with a high degree of specialism (e.g., research scientists, finance professionals, or design engineers), the professionals themselves are best placed to decide on and plan their learning needs, rather than drawing from a standardised curriculum (Kroop et al., 2015). These professionals may be working at the boundaries of knowledge beyond standard curricula. In these cases, an AI-assisted system (building on ITS) might support the learner by offering them options from which they can choose (something that no existing ITS currently offers). For example, *Responsive Open Learning Environments*[1] is a prototype digital system in which the professionals themselves define the new practices they need to learn (Kirschenmann et al., 2010) (while ITS almost always work towards prespecified fixed learning outcomes). They then plan their own learning by browsing and selecting a set of web-based resources and tools to support their learning. The system is based on conventional forms of AI that use demographic data and recommender analytics to provide content that is sequenced and structured for specific job roles. However, the learners can alter these structures in ways that make sense to them. Since the system is based on machine learning, the more the system is used, the better it 'learns' specific combinations of content appropriate for specific roles – in other words, these sequences of content and activities continually change as learners use the system. Currently, we are not aware of any such systems being widely available.

Chatbots

Chatbots – applications that support text or voice conversations with an AI-assisted agent – analyse questions posed by the learner and respond in a conversational way. These systems perhaps supported by generative AI tools such as ChatGPT, could be used to allow organisational 'know-how' and 'know-who' to be shared with and used by employees during their day-to-day work (Casillo et al., 2020). For example, when a new employee begins work, chatbots might help them to orient themselves faster into

---

[1]   https://premium.golabz.eu/about/projects/role

the organisation by answering routine questions such as 'where can I find information about x' or 'how do I do y'. In fact, there is already some evidence that chatbots can improve onboarding of new employees (e.g., Casillo et al., 2020). However, case examples and commercial offerings tend to focus on the transfer of simple information (e.g., 'where do I find the organisation's training manual') rather than transforming practice (e.g., learning how to manage more effectively).

Institution-Supporting AIED and the Workplace

Changing work processes or practices can be difficult if the organisational environment is not changed at the same time. There are a number of reasons why these changes are demanding: ingrained practices make it difficult for people to incorporate emerging forms of practice into their work; new practices may change the ways employees interrelate, for example if they work remotely (at a distance); and groups of employees may work in silos and organisations have to develop systematic ways to work across these diverse groups (Littlejohn et al., 2019). This means that new processes and practices can only be introduced when work is reconsidered and restructured. To overcome this issue, employees need to be supported to reflect on their workplace and to restructure the environment if needed. This situation is very different from learning in formal education, and again no existing AI-assisted educational tools are designed to or capable of helping professionals learn and transfer their new knowledge to the workplace – although there is potential for an AI-assisted system that supports teams in considering whether and how to restructure work.

THE FUTURE OF AI AND WORKPLACE LEARNING

As we have seen, so far almost all AIED applications have been designed for formal settings, including a few designed for formal professional learning. There are few examples of AI-assisted tools to support specifically and effectively informal professional or workplace learning.

Even in formal settings, while many AI applications gather and analyse data representing learner behaviours that might inform teachers, they cannot replicate the work of accomplished human teachers or trainers who use their experience and questioning to assess the cognitive ability and affective state of each learner and to support and scaffold learning (Holmes et al., 2019). There are various other issues: AI-assisted educational tools failing to leverage social engagement learning opportunities, leading to homogenisation rather than self-actualisation, or perpetuating poor pedagogic practices. In addition, AI-assisted systems are not able to model or teach *how to learn* affective characteristics such as confidence and persistence. Similarly, while some AI-assisted systems (such as those using augmented reality) might be helpful for modelling behavioural and some cognitive expertise, it is clear that professional education, whether formal or informal, cannot be replicated by AI-assisted systems – now or in the foreseeable future, despite the marketing claims.

A key issue for informal workplace learning in particular is that it is (or, at least, it almost always should be) the learner – rather than a teacher or curriculum designer or commercial AI company – who decides what is to be learned, why, and how. In these contexts, AI-assisted systems ideally would support learner agency to actively plan, perform, self-regulate, and reflect on their learning. Currently, as this chapter has highlighted, no AI-assisted systems have been designed to support agency. On the contrary, most such systems actively undermine both student agency and self-regulation skills (or, at least, none have been identified that address the self-regulation skills identified in Table 10.1). Similarly, no such systems support the processes of charting in workplace learning.

However, this chapter does not suggest that AI-assisted applications can never support informal workplace learning, only that few current systems do, and that there needs to be a radical shift in trajectory to prioritise the human learners if we are to take advantage of the power of AI. Future imaginaries include:

- *AI to support authentic assessment of work tasks*. For example, a trainee technician uses augmented reality visualised through safety goggles to learn how to replace a broken starter unit in an engine. The engine starts working and the data are automatically sent to an expert technician who signs off accreditation, indicating that this task has been successfully completed by the trainee.
- *AI to orchestrate network building and collaborative knowledge creation*. A number of engineers in diverse job roles across a large organisation are working on broadly similar tasks. Their work is facilitated by a digital platform that uses AI technologies to support the forming of a network of professionals, to share critical tasks identified by the engineers and to mutually learn and build knowledge together.
- *AI adaptive learning to facilitate student charting, agency, and self-actualisation*. Individual workers on a gig economy platform might learn new skills such as collaboration, critical thinking, confidence, and persistence by means of an AI-assisted system that facilitates

charting and prioritises both personal and inter-agency and self-actualisation. This would be especially beneficial for workers who have little opportunity to be in direct contact with colleagues.

As we have shown, the trajectory of AI developments for professional learning needs to be redirected – towards the design of AI-assisted informal learning applications that support agency, social and mutual learning, self-regulation and human rights, and that embody ethical-by-design AI techniques and innovative pedagogies. Only if we achieve that will we unleash the power of AI to enhance – and not compromise – professional learning.

REFERENCES

Alabdulkareem, A., Alhakbani, N., & Al-Nafjan, A. (2022). A systematic review of research on robot-assisted therapy for children with autism. *Sensors, 22*(3), 944.

Anuradha, J., Ramachandran, V., Arulalan, K. V., & Tripathy, B. K. (2010). Diagnosis of ADHD using SVM algorithm. *Proceedings of the Third Annual ACM Bangalore Conference*, 1–4.

Area9 Lyceum. (2022). Personalized adaptive learning in four dimensions. https://area9lyceum.com/

Argyris, C., & Schon, D. A. (1974). *Theory in practice: Increasing professional effectiveness*. Jossey-Bass.

Baker, R. S., Berning, A. W., Gowda, S. M., Zhang, S., & Hawn, A. (2020). Predicting K-12 dropout. *Journal of Education for Students Placed at Risk, 25*(1), 28–54.

Bandura, A. (1986). The explanatory and predictive scope of self-efficacy theory. *Journal of Social and Clinical Psychology, 4*(3), 359.

Bandura, A. (1991). Social cognitive theory of self-regulation. *Organizational Behavior and Human Decision Processes, 50*(2), 248–287.

Bandura, A. (2006). Toward a psychology of human agency. *Perspectives on Psychological Science, 1*(2), 164–180.

Barua, P. D., Vicnesh, J., Gururajan, R., Oh, S. L., Palmer, E., Azizan, M. M., Kadri, N. A., & Acharya, U. R. (2022). Artificial intelligence enabled personalised assistive tools to enhance education of children with neurodevelopmental disorders: A review. *International Journal of Environmental Research and Public Health, 19*(3), 1192.

Beal, C. R., Walles, R., Arroyo, I., & Woolf, B. P. (2007). On-line tutoring for math achievement testing: A controlled evaluation. *Journal of Interactive Online Learning, 6*(1), 43–55.

Behmke, D., Kerven, D., Lutz, R., Paredes, J., Pennington, R., Brannock, E., Deiters, M., Rose, J., & Stevens, K. (2018). Augmented reality chemistry: Transforming 2-D molecular representations into interactive 3-D structures. *Proceedings of the Interdisciplinary STEM Teaching and Learning Conference, 2*(1).

Bender, E. M., Gebru, T., McMillan-Major, A., & Shmitchell, S. (2021). On the dangers of stochastic parrots: Can language models be too big? *Proceedings of the 2021 ACM Conference on Fairness, Accountability, and Transparency*, 610–623.

Benfatto, M. N., Seimyr, G. Ö., Ygge, J., Pansell, T., Rydberg, A., & Jacobson, C. (2016). Screening for dyslexia using eye tracking during reading. *PLOS ONE*, *11*(12), e0165508.

Berryhill, J., Kok Heang, K., Clogher, R., & McBride, K. (2019). Hello, World: Artificial intelligence and its use in the public sector. OECD Working Papers on Public Governance No. 36. https://doi.org/10.1787/726fd39d-en

Boud, D., & Garrick, J. (2012). Understandings of workplace learning. In *Understanding learning at work* (pp. 1–11). Routledge.

Bughin, J., Hazan, E., Ramaswamy, S., Chui, M., Allas, T., Dahlström, P., Henke, N., & Trench, M. (2017). Artificial intelligence: The next digital frontier? McKinsey Global Institute. www.mckinsey.com/~/media/mckinsey/industries/advanced%20electronics/our%20insights/how%20artificial%20intelligence%20can%20deliver%20real%20value%20to%20companies/mgi-artificial-intelligence-discussion-paper.ashx

Cacciattolo, K. (2015). A critical review of the impact of workplace learning on individual and organisational performance. www.researchgate.net/publication/281114700_A_Critical_Review_of_the_Impact_of_workplace_learning_on_Individual_and_Organisational_Performance

Casillo, M., Clarizia, F., D'Aniello, G., De Santo, M., Lombardi, M., & Santaniello, D. (2020). CHAT-Bot: A cultural heritage aware teller-bot for supporting touristic experiences. *Pattern Recognition Letters*, *131*, 234–243.

Chin, M. (2020, April 29). Exam anxiety: How remote test-proctoring is creeping students out. *The Verge*. www.theverge.com/2020/4/29/21232777/examity-remote-test-proctoring-online-class-education

Chin, M. (2022, August 23). University can't scan students' rooms during remote tests, judge rules. *The Verge*. www.theverge.com/2022/8/23/23318067/cleveland-state-university-online-proctoring-decision-room-scan

Chubb, J., Cowling, P., & Reed, D. (2021). Speeding up to keep up: Exploring the use of AI in the research process. *AI & SOCIETY*. https://doi.org/10.1007/s00146-021-01259-0

Collin, K. (2008). Development engineers' work and learning as shared practice. *International Journal of Lifelong Education*, *27*(4), 379–397.

Corbyn, Z. (2021). Microsoft's Kate Crawford: 'AI is neither artificial nor intelligent'. *Guardian*. www.theguardian.com/technology/2021/jun/06/microsofts-kate-crawford-ai-is-neither-artificial-nor-intelligent

Dan, Z. (2021). Ministry removes homework help apps, citing impact on student learning. *Global Times*. www.globaltimes.cn/page/202112/1241383.shtml.

Domoscio. (2022). Include AI-powered solutions in your educational environment. https://domoscio.com/en/domoscio-spark-2/

Edlich, A., Jogani, R., Phalin, G., & Kaniyar, S. (2019). Driving impact at scale from automation and AI. McKinsey. www.mckinsey.com/~/media/McKinsey/Business%20Functions/McKinsey%20Digital/Our%20Insights/Driving%20impact%20at%20scale%20from%20automation%20and%20AI/Driving-impact-at-scale-from-automation-and-AI.ashx

Edwards, A. (2010). Relational agency: Working with other practitioners. In *Being an expert professional practitioner* (Vol. 3, pp. 61–79). Springer Netherlands.

eightfold. (2022). Single AI platform for all talent. https://eightfold.ai/

Engeström, Y. (2004). New forms of learning in co-configuration work. *Journal of Workplace Learning, 16*(1/2), 11–21.

Enos, M. D., Kehrhahn, M. T., & Bell, A. (2003). Informal learning and the transfer of learning: How managers develop proficiency. *Human Resource Development Quarterly, 14*(4), 369–387.

Entwistle, N. (2000). Promoting deep learning through teaching and assessment: Conceptual frameworks and educational contexts. *TLRP Conference, Leicester.* www.tlrp.org/pub/acadpub/Entwistle2000.pdf

Eraut, M. (2012). Transfer of knowledge between education and workplace settings. In H. Daniels, H. Lauder, & J. Porter (Eds), *Knowledge, values and educational policy* (pp. 75–94). Routledge.

Eynon, R., & Young, E. (2021). Methodology, legend, and rhetoric: The constructions of AI by academia, industry, and policy groups for lifelong learning. *Science, Technology, & Human Values, 46*(1), 166–191.

Fleming, M. (2020). AI is changing work – and leaders need to adapt. *Harvard Business Review.* https://hbr.org/2020/03/ai-is-changing-work-and-leaders-need-to-adapt.

Fontana, R. P., Milligan, C., Littlejohn, A., & Margaryan, A. (2015). Measuring self-regulated learning in the workplace. *International Journal of Training and Development, 19*(1), 32–52.

Foster, S. (2019). What barriers do students perceive to engagement with automated immediate formative feedback. *Journal of Interactive Media in Education,* 1. https://eric.ed.gov/?id=EJ1228614

Fuller, A., & Unwin, L. (2011). Workplace learning and the organization. In M. Malloch (Ed.), *The SAGE handbook of workplace learning*, 46–59. SAGE.

Gagné, R. M., & Brown, L. T. (1963). Some factors in the programming of conceptual learning. *Journal of Experimental Psychology, 62*(4), 313.

GMI. (2022). AI in education market size and share, growth forecast 2022–2030. Global Market Insights. www.gminsights.com/industry-analysis/artificial-intelligence-ai-in-education-market

GPT-3. (2020, September 8). A robot wrote this entire article. Are you scared yet, human? *The Guardian.* www.theguardian.com/commentisfree/2020/sep/08/robot-wrote-this-article-gpt-3

Guilherme, A. (2019). AI and education: The importance of teacher and student relations. *AI & Society, 34*(1), 47–54.

Heaven, W. D. (2019). Why deep-learning AIs are so easy to fool. *Nature, 574*(7777), 163–166.

Hendry, J. (2018). Govts dump NAPLAN robo marking plans. *ITnews.* www.itnews.com.au/news/govts-dump-naplan-robo-marking-plans-482044

Henry, J. V., & Oliver, M. (2021). Who will watch the watchmen? The ethico-political arrangements of algorithmic proctoring for academic integrity. *Postdigital Science and Education.* https://doi.org/10.1007/s42438-021-00273-1

Holmes, W., & Porayska-Pomsta, K. (Eds). (2023). *The ethics of AI in education: Practices, challenges, and debates.* Routledge.

Holmes, W., & Tuomi, I. (2022). State of the art and practice in AI in education. *European Journal of Education.*

Holmes, W., Bialik, M., & Fadel, C. (2019). Artificial intelligence in education: Promises and implications for teaching and learning. Center for Curriculum

Redesign. https://drive.google.com/file/d/1lmzlbhKvYyRB6J0USCndqXitmVg sfTbI/view

Huawei. (2022). StorySign: Helping deaf children to learn to read. https://con sumer.huawei.com/uk/campaign/storysign/

Hussain, A. (2017). Ada: Bolton College's latest digital assistant. www.aftabhus sain.com/ada.html

Hutson, M. (2021). Robo-writers: The rise and risks of language-generating AI. *Nature, 591*(7848), 22–25.

IBM. (2018). IBM Watson Education Classroom helps teachers deliver personalized learning that can improve student outcomes. CT555. IBM Corporation. www.ibm.com/products/us/en/

Jivet, I., Scheffel, M., Drachsler, H., & Specht, M. (2017). Awareness is not enough: Pitfalls of learning analytics dashboards in the educational practice. In É. Lavoué, H. Drachsler, K. Verbert, J. Broisin, & M. Pérez-Sanagustín (Eds), *Data driven approaches in digital education* (pp. 82–96). Springer International Publishing.

Kapur, M. (2008). Productive failure. *Cognition and Instruction, 26*(3), 379–424.

Kelley, J. (2021, June 22). A long overdue reckoning for online proctoring companies may finally be here. *Electronic Frontier Foundation.* www.eff.org/ deeplinks/2021/06/long-overdue-reckoning-online-proctoring-companies-may-finally-be-here

Khandelwal, K., & Upadhyay, A. K. (2021). The advent of artificial intelligence-based coaching. *Strategic HR Review, 20*(4), 137–140.

Kirschenmann, U., Scheffel, M., Friedrich, M., Niemann, K., & Wolpers, M. (2010). Demands of modern PLEs and the ROLE approach. *European Conference on Technology Enhanced Learning,* 167–182.

Kokotsaki, D., Menzies, V., & Wiggins, A. (2016). Project-based learning: A review of the literature. *Improving Schools, 19*(3), 267–277.

Kroop, S., Mikroyannidis, A., & Wolpers, M. (2015). *Responsive open learning environments: Outcomes of research from the ROLE project.* Springer Nature.

Lantiv. (2022). LANTIV™ 2023: Academic and school scheduling software. https://lantiv.com/

LaPierre, J. (2021, January 18). Educational games and AI. *Filament Games.* www. filamentgames.com/blog/educational-games-and-ai/.

LaPrade, A., Mertens, Janet, Moore, T., & Wright, A. (2019). The enterprise guide to closing the skills gap Strategies for building and maintaining a skilled workforce. IBM Institute for Business Value. www.ibm.com/downloads/cas/ EPYMNBJA

Ledford, H. (2019). Millions of black people affected by racial bias in health-care algorithms. *Nature, 574*(7780), 608–609.

Lee, K.-F., & Qiufan, C. (2021). *AI 2041: Ten visions for our future.* WH Allen.

Lieu, J. (2018). Eyes to the front camera: Chinese facial recognition tech targets inattentive students. *Mashable.* https://mashable.com/article/chinese-facial-rec ognition-class.

Littlejohn, A., Milligan, C., & Margaryan, A. (2012). Charting collective knowledge: Supporting self-regulated learning in the workplace. *Journal of Workplace Learning, 24*(3), 226–238.

Littlejohn, A., Papathoma, T., Smidt, S., Jelfs, A., Bridgman, S., & Coe, A. (2015, September 1). Driving disruptive innovation: Analysis of changes in professional practice through the production of an OU module (S309). Open University Insight. http://oro.open.ac.uk/53042/

Littlejohn, A., Hood, N, Milligan, C., & Mustain, P. (2016a). Learning in MOOCs: Motivations and self-regulated learning in MOOCs. *The Internet and Higher Education, 29*, 40–48.

Littlejohn, A., Milligan, C., Fontana, R. P., & Margaryan, A. (2016b). Professional learning through everyday work: How finance professionals self-regulate their learning. *Vocations and Learning, 9*(2), 207–226.

Littlejohn, A., Jaldemark, J., Vrieling-Teunter, E., & Nijland, F. (2019). Networked professional learning: An introduction (pp. 1–11). In *Networked professional learning*. Springer.

Lu, Y., Chen, C., Chen, P., Chen, X., & Zhuang, Z. (2018). Smart Learning Partner: An Interactive robot for education. In C. Penstein Rosé, R. Martínez-Maldonado, H. U. Hoppe, R. Luckin, M. Mavrikis, K. Porayska-Pomsta, B. McLaren, & B. du Boulay (Eds), *Artificial intelligence in education* (pp. 447–451). Springer International Publishing.

Lykourentzou, I., Giannoukos, I., Nikolopoulos, V., Mpardis, G., & Loumos, V. (2009). Dropout prediction in e-learning courses through the combination of machine learning techniques. *Computers & Education, 53*(3), 950–965.

Ma, W., Adesope, O. O., Nesbit, J. C., & Liu, Q. (2014). Intelligent tutoring systems and learning outcomes: A meta-analysis. *Journal of Educational Psychology, 106*(4), 901–918.

Marcinkowski, F., Kieslich, K., Starke, C., & Lünich, M. (2020). Implications of AI (un-)fairness in higher education admissions: The effects of perceived AI (un-)fairness on exit, voice and organizational reputation. *Proceedings of the 2020 Conference on Fairness, Accountability, and Transparency*, 122–130. https://doi.org/10.1145/3351095.3372867

Marcus, G., & Davis, E. (2020). GPT-3, Bloviator: OpenAI's language generator has no idea what it's talking about. *MIT Technology Review*. www.technologyreview.com/2020/08/22/1007539/gpt3-openai-language-generator-artificial-intelligence-ai-opinion/

Margaryan, A., Milligan, C., & Littlejohn, A. (2009). Self-regulated learning and knowledge sharing in the workplace: Differences and similarities between experts and novices. International Conference on Researching Work and Learning RWL6, Copenhagen. www.rwlconferences.org/events/rwl6-denmark-2009

Margaryan, A., Littlejohn, A., & Milligan, C. (2013). Self-regulated learning in the workplace: Strategies and factors in the attainment of learning goals. *International Journal of Training and Development, 17*(4), 245–259.

Markauskaite, L., & Goodyear, P. (2017). Epistemic fluency and professional education. *Innovation, Knowledgeable Action and Actionable Knowledge*.

Martinez-Maldonado, R., Echeverria, V., Mangaroska, K., Shibani, A., Fernandez-Nieto, G., Schulte, J., & Buckingham Shum, S. (2021). Moodoo the tracker: Spatial classroom analytics for characterising teachers' pedagogical approaches. *International Journal of Artificial Intelligence in Education*. https://doi.org/10.1007/s40593-021-00276-w

Matsushita, K. (2018). An invitation to deep active learning. In K. Matsushita (Ed.), *Deep active learning: Toward greater depth in university education* (pp. 15–33). Springer.

Mavrikis, M., Holmes, W., Zhang, J., & Ma, N. (2018). Fractions lab goes east: Learning and interaction with an exploratory learning environment in China. In C. Penstein Rosé, R. Martínez-Maldonado, H. U. Hoppe, R. Luckin, M. Mavrikis, K. Porayska-Pomsta, B. McLaren, & B. du Boulay (Eds), *Artificial intelligence in education* (Vol. 10948, pp. 209–214). Springer International Publishing.

McGuire, L. S., & Alaraj, A. (2018). Competency assessment in virtual reality-based simulation in neurosurgical training. In A. Alaraj (Ed.), *Comprehensive healthcare simulation: Neurosurgery* (pp. 153–157). Springer.

Metz, C. (2021, March 15). Who is making sure the A.I. machines aren't racist? *The New York Times.* www.nytimes.com/2021/03/15/technology/artificial-intel ligence-google-bias.html

Miao, F., & Holmes, W. (2021). AI and education: Guidance for policy-makers. UNESCO. https://unesdoc.unesco.org/ark:/48223/pf0000376709

Milligan, C., & Littlejohn, A. (2014). Supporting professional learning in a massive open online course. *International Review of Research in Open and Distributed Learning, 15*(5), 197–213.

Milligan, C., Littlejohn, A., & Margaryan, A. (2014). Workplace learning in informal networks. In A. Littlejohn & C. Pegler (Eds), *Reusing open resources* (pp. 115–125). Routledge.

Milligan, C., Fontana, R. P., Littlejohn, A., & Margaryan, A. (2015). Self-regulated learning behaviour in the finance industry. *Journal of Workplace Learning.*

Moriarty-Mclaughlin, F. (2020). More colleges eye AI to track, monitor students. *The College Fix.* www.thecollegefix.com/more-colleges-eye-ai-to-track-monitor-students/

Nye, B. D., Graesser, A. C., & Hu, X. (2014). AutoTutor and family: A review of 17 years of natural language tutoring. *International Journal of Artificial Intelligence in Education, 24*(4), 427–469.

OECD. (2020). Trustworthy AI in education: Promises and challenges. www.oecd. org/education/trustworthy-artificial-intelligence-in-education.pdf

OECD. (2021). OECD digital education outlook 2021: Pushing the frontiers with artificial intelligence, Blockchain and robots. https://doi.org/10.1787/589b283f-en

Pangburn, D. J. (2019). Schools are using AI to help pick students. What could go wrong? *Fast Company.* www.fastcompany.com/90342596/schools-are-quietly-turning-to-ai-to-help-pick-who-gets-in-what-could-go-wrong

Perez-Ortiz, M. (2020). *An AI-powered learning algorithm providing inclusive, multimodal, cross-lingual and quality lifelong learning opportunities for all.* AI4T.

Photomath. (2022). *Math explained, step-by-step.* Photomath. https://photomath. com/en.

Pintrich, P. R. (2000). Issues in self-regulation theory and research. *Journal of Mind and Behavior,* 213–219.

Poulsen, A. T., Kamronn, S., Dmochowski, J., Parra, L. C., & Hansen, L. K. (2017). EEG in the classroom: Synchronised neural recordings during video presentation. *Scientific Reports, 7,* 43916.

Roberts, M., Driggs, D., Thorpe, M., Gilbey, J., Yeung, M., Ursprung, S. et al. (2021). Common pitfalls and recommendations for using machine learning to detect and prognosticate for COVID-19 using chest radiographs and CT scans. *Nature Machine Intelligence, 3*(3), 199–217.

SayHi. (2022). SayHi translate: Voice translation for iOS and Android. www. sayhi.com/en/translate/

Seldon, A., & Abidoye, O. (2018). *The fourth education revolution: Will artificial intelligence liberate or infantilise humanity?* University of Buckingham Press.

Selwyn, N. (2019). *Should robots replace teachers? AI and the future of education (digital futures)*. Polity.

Sharples, M. (2022, May 17). New AI tools that can write student essays require educators to rethink teaching and assessment. *Impact of Social Sciences*. https:// blogs.lse.ac.uk/impactofsocialsciences/2022/05/17/new-ai-tools-that-can-write-student-essays-require-educators-to-rethink-teaching-and-assessment/

Sitzmann, T., & Ely, K. (2011). A meta-analysis of self-regulated learning in work-related training and educational attainment: What we know and where we need to go. *Psychological Bulletin, 137*(3), 421.

Song, Y. (2021). A review of how class orchestration with technology has been conducted for pedagogical practices. *Educational Technology Research and Development, 69*(3), 1477–1503.

Susskind, Z., Arden, B., John, L. K., Stockton, P., & John, E. B. (2021). Neuro-symbolic AI: An emerging class of AI workloads and their characterization. http://arxiv.org/abs/2109.06133

Tiku, N. (2022). Google fired Blake Lemoine, the engineer who said LaMDA was sentient. *The Washington Post*. www.washingtonpost.com/technology/2022/07/22/google-ai-lamda-blake-lemoine-fired/

Turnitin. (2022). Empower students to do their best, original work. https://turnitin.com/

Tynjälä, P. (2008). Perspectives into learning at the workplace. *Educational Research Review, 3*(2), 130–154.

UNICEF. (2021). Policy guidance on AI for children. www.unicef.org/globalinsight/media/2356/file/UNICEF-Global-Insight-policy-guidance-AI-children-2.0-2021.pdf.pdf

van den Boom, G., Paas, F., van Merriënboer, J. J. G., & van Gog, T. (2004). Reflection prompts and tutor feedback in a webbased learning environment: Effects on students' self-regulated learning competence. *Computers in Human Behavior, 20*, 551–567.

Vanlehn, K., Lynch, C., Schulze, K., Shapiro, J. A., Shelby, R., Taylor, L., Treacy, D., Weinstein, A., & Wintersgill, M. (2005). The Andes physics tutoring system: Lessons learned. *International Journal of Artificial Intelligence in Education, 15*(3), 147–204.

Waters, A., & Miikkulainen, R. (2014). GRADE: Machine learning support for graduate admissions. *AI Magazine, 35*(1), 64–64.

Winne, P. H. (1995). Inherent details in self-regulated learning. *Educational Psychologist, 30*(4), 173–187.

World Bank. (2022). In Ecuador, artificial intelligence makes learning math easier. www.worldbank.org/en/news/feature/2022/02/10/en-ecuador-aprender-matematicas-es-mas-facil-con-inteligencia-artificial-nivelacion-remediacion-academica

Zawacki-Richter, O., Marín, V. I., Bond, M., & Gouverneur, F. (2019). Systematic review of research on artificial intelligence applications in higher education – where are the educators? *International Journal of Educational Technology in Higher Education, 16*(1).

Zhang, D., Maslej, N., Brynjolfsson, E., Etchemendy, J., Lyons, T., Manyika, J. et al. (2022). The AI index 2022 annual report. arXiv: 2205.03468/

Zimmerman, B. J. (2000). Attaining self-regulation: A social cognitive perspective. In M. Boekaerts, P. R. Pintrich, & M. Zeidner (Eds), *Handbook of self-regulation* (pp. 13–39). Academic Press.

Zimmerman, B. J. (2002). Becoming a self-regulated learner: An overview. *Theory into Practice, 41*(2), 64–70.

Zimmerman, B. J. (2006). Development and adaptation of expertise: The role of self-regulatory processes and beliefs. In K. A. Ericsson, N. Charness, P. J. Feltovich, & R. R. Hoffman (Eds), *The Cambridge handbook of expertise and expert performance* (pp. 705–722). Cambridge University Press.

11. Smart automation in entrepreneurial finance: the use of AI in private markets
Francesco Corea

CAN ARTIFICIAL INTELLIGENCE MAKE YOU A BETTER INVESTOR?

One of the major paradoxes for the financial industry is that it has always been both very resistant to change as well as having deep enough pockets to experiment and test new technologies as they become available. The problems faced in the sector are difficult and, when they fail, they are felt widely in society. Thus, market players are always looking for the most efficient and cheapest solutions (Bajulaiye et al., 2020).

Surprisingly, players at the forefront of innovations are usually not big institutional investors, but rather small companies that are more agile, and thereby able to seize emerging opportunities without facing significant sunk costs, or too rigid business models. In other words, banks, pension funds, and endowments do not innovate either because they are too big to adapt quickly and follow external stimuli or because they do not know how (or do not want) to change long-standing business practices. The cost of mistakes can also be incredibly high. This is not simply true in industry but also in academia, where until 20 years ago there were no relevant contributions in the financial sector (Frame & White, 2002). Cohen and colleagues (1989, 1995) analyzed more than 600 different articles and books in the domain of financial services and found that none of them was related to financial innovation.

Over the past few years things have gradually changed, but even in the age of pervasive artificial intelligence (AI), especially in private markets, the topic remains largely under-researched.

This chapter will explore the implications of the use of machine learning in company evaluation and assessment, as well as how using data could improve the investment process for the private equity and venture ecosystem.

AI IN PRIVATE EQUITY AND VENTURE CAPITAL

Since the early 2000s, the democratization of infrastructure services and the lowering in cost of technology stacks made it easier for first-time entrepreneurs to create new companies. With the increase of potential opportunities, capital had to follow. There are now venture capitalists (VCs), who are comfortable in assuming a very different risk profile (i.e., higher) from other institutional investors, and therefore capable of backing companies with fewer financial data points. Ewens and colleagues (2018) have theoretically shown that disruptive digital technologies (in other words, new inventions or radical innovations) have lowered the cost of experimentation to such a level that the *real option* (i.e., the possibility of starting a new company) written on risky projects becomes increasingly attractive for venture investors, which in turn explains why many more start-ups get funded.

Even if this high-risk, high-return model, dominated by a power law distribution (where only few companies are successful and drive most of the financial returns), is not fully efficient, authors have argued that finding a superior alternative setting is difficult (Neumann, 2019). Investing in private companies is hard, in particular when no data are available to support the investment process. This is normal for early-stage VCs, who often end up relying on gut feeling or heuristics to reach a decision.

This potentially biased process tends to result in two major problems: identification and mispricing. Identification happens when a VC either does not source the right start-up deals or correctly assess the opportunity, while mispricing concerns paying too much to finance a new company. Gornall and Strebulaev (2020) have shown that most VCs fell into this trap, with deals overvalued at up to 100 percent of their fair value.

Even if AI has not proven to be useful so far to address this issue, it has been instead used to optimize for the identification problem (Hunter et al., 2018). In other words, intelligent systems are supporting today's investors to not rely merely on their gut feeling and heuristics, but rather to seek greater assurance from information and data (such as fundraising information, social media presence, web activity, and intellectual property protection).

This is easier said than done, as many VC investors are quite traditional in their approach to investment decisions and do not embrace the power of AI for evaluating new opportunities. A few forward-looking investors (likely no more than 30 worldwide; see Corea, 2019) are actively trying to incorporate machine learning into their workflows, some of them to find acquirers for portfolio companies, others to spot new trends and areas to invest in, and others to match co-investors and deals, or for portfolio management. Most of them use several types of data points, including descriptive information, fundraising, product-related insights, company scores, and estimates of the probability of success of such ventures through mergers and acquisitions.

So far, the most interesting application lies in using machine learning to identify determinants of success for start-ups, not only because it is one of the main activities a venture investor is benchmarked on, but also because it is one of the aspects that highlights the quality of an early-stage investor.

USING DATA SCIENCE FOR COMPANY EVALUATION

The desire to identify and understand the features that make a company successful is certainly not new. Several examples already exist both in academia as well as in the industry. Da Rin et al. (2013), Tykvová (2018), and Corea et al. (2021) mapped with detailed reviews all the applications in the field, showing that until a few years ago a more holistic (multi-variable) approach to the identification problem was still missing (Bai & Zhao, 2021).

Initially, a lot of data analysis was used to try to spot personal traits of entrepreneurs (Ng & Stuart, 2016) as well as of the founding team that could explain the success of certain companies against competitors. Founders, primarily men in their 30s or early 40s (Azoulay et al., 2020), that scored highly on ability tests were more likely to succeed (Frick, 2014; McKenzie & Paffhausen, 2017; McKenzie & Sansone, 2017; Wadhwa et al., 2008). Bengtsson and Hsu (2015) and Sunesson (2009) complemented those earlier studies with other demographic information, such as ethnicity and academic background, while Miettinen and Littunen (2013) focused more on civil status and previous employment status.

Investors suffer from *similarity bias*, which results in investing in founders with similar professional and educational backgrounds (Franke et al., 2006) and in successful serial entrepreneurs (Gompers et al., 2010), which also get better valuation terms (Hsu, 2007).

Data are also useful in debunking myths, such as the one about possessing an MBA being a prerequisite for success (Hoberg et al., 2009) or that passion is enough to build a successful business (Chen et al., 2009). Although focus is necessary, it seems that the ability of engaging in multiple tasks at the same time is a positive trait for management teams of new ventures (Souitaris & Maestro, 2010), and sometimes original founders are not the best positioned to guide the company to future success (Ewens & Marx, 2017), contrary to conventional wisdom.

On the other hand, what seems to be true is that grit (defined as long-term perseverance) has some predictive power of success in building a business (Mueller et al., 2017). Being optimistic and resourceful (Baum & Locke, 2004) and having an internal locus of control (Ayala & Manzano, 2010, 2014) also contribute positively. Finally, the team composition was found to have a significant impact on the final outcome, both because of the type of skills possessed by the co-founders and the diversity of the team (Eesley et al., 2014; First Round Capital, 2015; Jin et al., 2017; Mueller & Murmann, 2016). Diversity increases the likelihood of success.

The diffusion of AI in other sectors is pushing further the frontier in the financial sector. It is even tapping into social networks for data as a source of insight for investor evaluation. Having ties with reputable investors increases the chance to raise funds and with more favorable terms (Hsu, 2004; Liang & Yuan Soe-Tsyr, 2013, 2016; Shane & Stuart, 2002). In the same space, both a personal network (Littunen & Niitykangas, 2010) and a professional one (Gloor et al., 2011, 2013; Nann et al., 2010) are positively correlated with the likelihood of success of a company.

All the aspects and characteristics analyzed so far focus primarily on personal traits of the founders and the team. Financial criteria are equally important though, and many empirical studies as well as industry analysis show that VC-backed companies are more likely to achieve successful exits intended as successful IPOs, acquisitions, or mergers (Bertoni et al., 2011, 2013; Chemmanur et al., 2011; Gompers et al., 2009; Gulati & Higgins, 2003; Hsu, 2006; Hull, 2018; Inderst & Mueller, 2009; Nahata, 2008; Nanda et al., 2020; Ozmel et al., 2013a; Puri & Zarutskie, 2012; Ragozzino & Blevins, 2015; Sorensen, 2007; Zarutskie, 2010).

Even if the contribution of external capital is clearly an asset for the company, the way in which this capital is provided also has a strong impact on potential success. The presence of debt (Cole & Sokolyk, 2018; Robb & Robinson, 2014) and degree of control by investors (Cumming, 2008) can determine whether and to what extent the company will be successful. The number of investors in the round (Das et al., 2011; Tian, 2011) and board members (Coats, 2018) can also affect its success. It seems that more investors or board members are not necessarily better for the company, while an optimal number appears to exist.

Finally, after having checked for personal traits and financial features, the last factor that deserves some examination is the operational one. Whether because of patents (Catalini et al., 2019; Cockburn & MacGarvie, 2009; Hsu & Ziedonis, 2011; Mann & Sager, 2007) or due to strategic alliances (Baum & Silverman, 2004; Hoenig & Henkel, 2015; Lindsey, 2008; Ozmel et al., 2013b), start-ups that invest in business capabilities (through specific business functions, roles, etc.) are more likely to succeed.

More comprehensive models highlighted other operational variables (Arroyo et al., 2019; Guzman & Stern, 2020; Kirsch et al., 2009; Lussier & Halabi, 2010; Marom & Lussier, 2014; Song et al., 2008; Teng et al., 2011; Zhao et al., 2012). Table 11.1 summarizes the factors identified in the literature.

Table 11.1   Taxonomy of success factors

Variable	Reference
Track record	Gompers et al. (2010); Hsu (2007); Kirsch et al. (2009)
Patents and trademark	Baum and Silverman (2004); Cockburn and MacGarvie (2009); Guzman and Stern (2020); Hsu and Ziedonis (2011); Mann and Sager (2007)
Control rights	Cumming (2008)
Debt	Cole and Sokolyk (2018); Robb and Robinson (2014)
Strategic alliances	Baum and Silverman (2004); Hoenig and Henkel (2015); Lindsey (2008); Ozmel et al. (2013b)
School	Sunesson (2009)
Syndicate	Das et al. (2011); Tian (2011)
Team diversity	Eesley et al. (2014); First Round Capital (2015); Jin et al. (2017)
Network	Gloor et al. (2011, 2013); Nann et al. (2010)
VC support	Bertoni et al. (2011, 2013); Catalini et al. (2019); Chemmanur et al. (2011); Croce et al. (2013); Gulati and Higgins (2003); Hoberg et al. (2009); Hsu (2006); Inderst and Mueller (2009); Nahata (2008); Nanda et al. (2020); Ozmel et al. (2013a); Puri and Zarutskie (2012); Ragozzino and Blevins (2015); Sorensen (2007)
Founders' age	Azoulay et al. (2020); Frick (2014); McKenzie and Paffhausen (2017); McKenzie and Sansone (2017); Wadhwa et al. (2008)
Marital status	Miettinen and Littunen (2013)
Previous employment	Miettinen and Littunen (2013)
Founders' replacement	Ewens and Marx (2017)
Equity share	Miettinen and Littunen (2013)
Board composition	Coats (2018)
Psychological features (grit, resilience, internal locus of control, polychronicity)	Ayala and Manzano (2010, 2014); Baum and Locke (2004); Mueller et al. (2017); Souitaris and Maestro (2010)

The traditional investment process is inefficient, slow, and potentially biased. Investors manually look for companies or they get referred to founders; they benchmark those entrepreneurs and respective businesses against what they believe is the top-notch performance in that specific space, to price the company only qualitatively. The hope is that AI could eventually help investors de-risk the way they source and assess new ventures. However, a series of structural issues need to be solved first.

Up to this point we have extensively referred to the notion of success without defining it because it has multiple meanings and possible definitions. One of the complications is related to the lack of transparency in the industry, and the long time to exit does not ease the analysis. It is difficult to establish a direct correlation between a factor and the successful sale of a company that may happen ten years later. Also, the lack of data and its inaccuracy makes any system difficult to implement. Finally, even though we showed that the VC investments have a positive impact on the likelihood of success of a company, we do not know why this is the case. Is it due to some additional value brought to the table or simply because of the extra capital injection? An answer to this question could open up a new entrepreneurial wave.

In addition to the lack of transparency in the data, modeling techniques are also a concern. Even though the popular neural networks can be successfully used in this context (see Ciampi & Gordini, 2013, as well as the work done by EQT Ventures), many studies and industry practitioners are concerned about the lack of transparency of such models. It seems that other classes of models like tree-based ones are more practical and less obscure, and often preferred by researchers (Bhat & Zaelit, 2011; Krishna et al., 2016).

DATA-DRIVEN FUNDS: A DIGRESSION ON INDUSTRY PLAYERS

The factors mentioned above are not simply theoretical correlations, but actual variables used by several funds to build predictive models and invest in start-ups at any stage. Using a data-driven approach is becoming more common these days across different geographies and venture funds, even though each entity has developed its own approach and optimizes for slightly different objectives.

Correlation Ventures is likely the first fund to examine historical data to draw a lesson from the hedge fund industry. They started using data to make investment decisions in less than two weeks, without taking board seats, participating actively in the company activities, or leading deals investing most of the capital. EQT Ventures instead designed its Motherbrain tool, which uses more than 40 data sources and convolutional neural networks to help the team sourcing new deals. SignalFire is the last fund worth mentioning here because it has been with Correlation and EQT a pioneer using AI not only for screening but also to provide market intelligence and talent-matching services to its own portfolio companies.

New smaller funds like InReach Ventures as well as Connetic Ventures have also strengthened their data skills. InReach created a full stack-sourcing engine from scratch and Connetic an automated machine learning due diligence platform to better assess companies while decreasing investment bias.

Other funds are currently experimenting with different methods, and many more are starting to do so. The point here is not about listing all the different nuances or names of investment vehicles that are trying their way into machine learning, but rather highlighting the emergence of a trend. The future of the venture space is data-driven, and AI and machine learning have a role to play in this.

CONCLUDING REMARKS

Currently, less than 5 percent of all VC funds worldwide use AI and machine learning for their investment activities (Houser & Kisska-Schulze, 2023). The relevance of these tools, however, is becoming more prevalent every day because it not only improves the potential investment outcome but also makes the whole process more robust, less biased, and more efficient.

This explains why an increasing number of venture firms are hiring and developing internal data science practices, creating jobs that did not exist in this industry before. The intent is not to make the traditional investor role obsolete, but rather to give it superpowers. AI will be used not to displace old-fashioned investors but instead to create a new data-driven VC who is able to better source, fairly assess, and more effectively help the companies chosen for investment.

In contrast to the fully automated systems developed by hedge fund managers to trade in public exchanges, this new wave of AI systems for private markets would likely generate tools in support of the VC and achieve the greatest bond between humans and machines. It will not be a situation where machines replace human jobs but rather augment the skills of a traditional investor.

The increased deployment of machine learning in the venture space can also provide important benefits to the overall ecosystem: founders would be able to get more and better funding, more jobs would be created, and more problems would be eventually solved by VC-backed companies.

Policy makers and regulators would need to ensure that the use of AI in private markets is consistent with promoting ecosystem development, reducing inequalities, and promoting competition. Their role is also paramount to supporting innovation while protecting consumers from market failures, inaccurate data collection, and incorrect implementation of automated systems.

Finally, given the peculiarity of the times we are living in, it is curious to note how the pandemic has somehow accelerated the demand for using machine learning and data in ventures. Given the impossibility for many funds to source and identify potential investments in traditional ways (e.g., through conferences and networking events), many investment professionals ended up spending more time online and started thinking more about using data to identify new opportunities. As a result, in the last two years, many more institutions have been interested in different types of datasets, and are now thinking about how to create systems that can help them navigate the challenges they have faced during the pandemic and into the future.

REFERENCES

Arroyo, J., Corea, F., Jimenez-Diaz, G., & Recio-Garcia, J. A. (2019). "Assessment of machine learning performance for decision support in venture capital investments." *IEEE Access*, 7 (1): 124233–124243.

Ayala, J. C., & Manzano, G. (2010). "Established business owners' success: Influencing factors." *Journal of Developmental Entrepreneurship*, 15 (3): 263–286.

Ayala, J. C., & Manzano, G. (2014). "The resilience of the entrepreneur: Influence on the success of the business. A longitudinal analysis." *Journal of Economic Psychology*, 42: 126–135.

Azoulay, P., Jones, B., Kim, J. D., & Miranda, J. (2020). "Age and high-growth entrepreneurship." *American Economic Review Insights*, 2 (1): 65–82.

Bai, S., & Zhao, Y. (2021). "Startup investment decision support: Application of venture capital scorecards using machine learning approaches." *Systems*, 9: 55.

Bajulaiye, O., Fenwick, M., Skultetyova, I., & Vermeulen, E. P. M. (2020). "Digital transformation in the hedge fund and private equity industry." *Lex Research Topics in Corporate Law & Economics*, Working Paper No. 2020-1.

Baum, J. R., & Locke, E. A. (2004). "The relationship of entrepreneurial traits skill and motivation to subsequent venture growth." *Journal of Applied Psychology*, 89 (4): 587–598.

Baum, J. A., & Silverman, B. S. (2004). "Picking winners or building them? Alliance, intellectual, and human capital as selection criteria in venture financing and performance of biotechnology start-ups." *Journal of Business Venturing*, 19: 411–436.

Bengtsson, O., & Hsu, D. (2015). "Ethnic matching in the US venture capital market." *Journal of Business Venturing*, 30(2): 338–354.

Bertoni, F., Colombo, M. G., & Grilli, L. (2011). "Venture capital financing and the growth of high-tech start-ups: Disentangling treatment from selection effects." *Research Policy*, 40 (7): 1028–1043.

Bertoni, F., Colombo, M. G., & Grilli, L. (2013). "Venture capital investor type and the growth mode of new technology-based firms." *Small Business Economics*, 40 (3): 527–552.

Bhat, H. S., & Zaelit, D. (2011). "Predicting Private Company Exits Using Qualitative Data." In Huang, J. Z., Cao, L., & Srivastava, J. (eds), *Advances in knowledge discovery and data mining*. Springer.

Catalini, C., Guzman, J., & Stern, S. (2019). "Hidden in plain sight: Venture growth with or without venture capital." Working Paper.

Chemmanur, T. J., Krishnan, K., & Nandy, D. K. (2011). "How does venture capital financing improve efficiency in private firms? A look beneath the surface." *Review of Financial Studies*, 24 (12): 4037–4090.

Chen, X., Yao, X., & Kotha, S. (2009). "Entrepreneur passion and preparedness in business plan presentations: A persuasion analysis of venture capitalists' funding decisions." *Academy of Management Journal*, 52 (1): 199–214.

Ciampi, F., & Gordini, N. (2013). "Small enterprise default prediction modeling through artificial neural networks: An empirical analysis of Italian small enterprises." *Journal of Small Business Management*, 51 (1): 23–45.

Coats, D. (2018). "Too many VC cooks in the kitchen?" https://medium.com/correlation-ventures/too-many-vc-cooks-in-the-kitchen-65439f422b8

Cockburn, I., & MacGarvie, M. (2009). "Patents, thickets and the financing of early-stage firms: Evidence from the software industry." *Journal of Economics and Management Strategy*, 18: 729–773.

Cohen, W. (1995). "Empirical studies of innovative activity." In Stoneman, P. (Ed.), *Handbook of the economics of innovation and technological change*. Blackwell, pp. 182–264.

Cohen, W., & Levin, R. (1989). "Empirical studies of innovation and market structure." In Schmalensee, R., & Willig, R. (Eds), *Handbook of industrial organization*, Vol. 2. North-Holland, pp. 1059–1107.

Cole, R., & Sokolyk, T. (2018). "Debt financing, survival, and growth of start-up firms." *Journal of Corporate Finance*, 50: 609–625.

Corea, F. (2019). *An introduction to data: Everything you need to know about AI, big data and data science*. Springer International Publishing.

Corea, F., Bertinetti, G., & Cervellati, E. M. (2021). "Hacking the venture industry: An early-stage startups investment framework for data-driven investors." *Machine Learning with Applications*, 5 (15).

Croce A., Marti J., & Murtinu S. (2013). "The impact of venture capital on the productivity growth of European entrepreneurial firms: 'Screening' or 'value added' effect?" *Journal of Business Venturing*, 28 (4): 489–510.

Cumming, D. (2008). "Contracts and exits in venture capital finance." *Review of Financial Studies*, 21: 1947–1982.

Da Rin, M., Hellmann, T., & Puri, M. (2013). "A survey of venture capital research." *Handbook of the Economics of Finance*, 2: 573–648.

Das, S. R., Hoje, J., & Yongtae, K. (2011). "Polishing diamonds in the rough: The sources of syndicated venture performance." *Journal of Financial Intermediation*, 20: 199–230.

Eesley, C. E., Hsu, D. H., & Roberts, E. B. (2014). "The contingent effects of top management teams on venture performance: Aligning founding team composition with innovation strategy and commercialization environment." *Strategic Management Journal*, 35 (12): 1798–1817.

Ewens, M., & Marx, M. (2017). "Founder replacement and startup performance." *Review of Financial Studies*, 31 (4): 1532–1565.

Ewens, M., Nanda, R., & Rhodes-Kropf, M. (2018). "Cost of experimentation and the evolution of venture capital." *Journal of Financial Economics*, 128 (3): 422–442.

First Round Capital. (2015). "10 years project." http://10years.firstround.com/

Frame, W. S., & White, L. J. (2002). "Empirical studies of financial innovation: Lots of talk, little action?" Working Paper, Federal Reserve Bank of Atlanta, N. 2002–12.

Franke, N., Gruber, M., Harhoff, D., & Henkel, J. (2006). "What you are is what you like-similarity biases in venture capitalists' evaluations of start-up teams." *Journal of Business Venturing*, 21 (6): 802–826.

Frick, W. (2014). "How old are Silicon Valley's top founders? Here's the data." *Harvard Business Review*.

Gloor, P. A., Dorsaz, P., & Fuehres, H. (2011). "Analyzing success of startup entrepreneurs by measuring their social network distance to a business networking hub." *Proceedings 3rd International Conference on Collaborative Innovation Networks Coins*: 8–10.

Gloor, P., Dorsaz, P., Fuehres, H., & Vogel, M. (2013). "Choosing the right friends: Predicting success of startup entrepreneurs and innovators through their online social network structure." *International Journal of Organisational Design and Engineering*, 3 (1): 67–85.

Gompers, P., Kovner, A., & Lerner, J. (2009). "Specialization and success: Evidence from venture capital." *Journal of Economics and Management Strategy*, 18: 817–844.

Gompers, P., Lerner, J., Scharfstein, D., & Kovner, A. (2010). "Performance persistence in entrepreneurship." *Journal of Financial Economics*, 96: 18–32.

Gornall, W., & Strebulaev, I. A. (2020). "Squaring venture capital valuations with reality." *Journal of Financial Economics*, 135 (1): 120–143.

Gulati, R., & Higgins, M. C. (2003). "Which ties matter when? The contingent effects of interorganizational partnerships on IPO success." *Strategic Management Journal*, 24 (2): 127–144.

Guzman, J., & Stern, S. (2020). "The state of American entrepreneurship: New estimates of the quantity and quality of entrepreneurship for 15 US states, 1988–2014." *American Economic Journal Economic Policy*, 12 (4): 212–243.

Hoberg, G., Goldfarb, B., Kirsch, D., & Triantis, A. (2009). "Does angel participation matter? An analysis of early venture financing." Robert H. Smith School Research Paper 06–072.

Hoenig, D., & Henkel, J. (2015). "Quality signals? The role of patents, alliances, and team experience in venture capital financing." *Research Policy*, 44 (5): 1049–1064.

Houser, K., & Kisska-Schulze, K. (2023). "Disrupting venture capital: Carrots, sticks and artificial intelligence." *U.C. Irvine Law Review*.

Hsu, D. (2004). "What do entrepreneurs pay for venture capital affiliation?" *Journal of Finance*, 59: 1805–1844.

Hsu, D. (2006). "Venture capitalists and cooperative start-up commercialization strategy." *Management Science*, 52: 204–219.

Hsu, D. (2007). "Experienced entrepreneurial founders, organizational capital, and venture capital funding." *Research Policy*, 36: 722–741.

Hsu, D., & Ziedonis, R. (2011). "Strategic factor markets and the financing of technology startups: When do patents matter more as signaling devices?" Unpublished working paper.

Hull, T. J. (2018). "The effect of venture capitalists straying from their industry comfort zones." 2nd Emerging Trends in Entrepreneurial Finance Conference.

Hunter, D. S., Saini, A., & Zaman, T. (2018). "Picking winners: A data driven approach to evaluating the quality of startup companies." arXiv: 1706.04229.

Inderst, R., & Mueller, H. M. (2009). "Early-stage financing and firm growth in new industries." *Journal of Financial Economics*, 93 (2): 276–291.

Jin, L., Madison, K., Kraiczy, N. D., Kellermanns, F. W., Crook, T. R., & Xi, J. (2017). "Entrepreneurial team composition characteristics and new venture performance: A meta- analysis." *Entrepreneurship Theory and Practice*, 41 (5): 743–771.

Kirsch, D., Goldfarb, B., & Gera, A. (2009). "Form or substance: The role of business plans in venture capital decision making." *Strategic Management Journal*, 30 (5): 487–515.

Krishna, A., Agrawal, A., & Choudhary, A. (2016). "Predicting the outcome of startups: Less failure, more success." IEEE 16th International Conference on Data Mining Workshops.

Liang, E. Y., & Yuan Soe-Tsyr, D. (2013). "Investors are social animals: Predicting investor behavior using social network features via supervised learning approach." Proceedings of the Workshop on Mining and Learning with Graphs (MLG-2013), Chicago.

Liang, E. Y., & Yuan Soe-Tsyr, D. (2016). "Predicting investor funding behavior using Crunchbase social network features." *Internet Research*, 26 (1): 74–100.

Lindsey, L. (2008). "Blurring firm boundaries: The role of venture capital in strategic alliance." *Journal of Finance*, 63: 1137–1168.

Littunen, H., & Niitykangas, H. (2010). "The rapid growth of young firms during various stages of entrepreneurship." *Journal of Small Business and Enterprise Development*, 17 (1): 8–31.

Lussier, R. N., & Halabi, C. E. (2010). "A three-country comparison of the business success versus failure prediction model." *Journal of Small Business Management*, 48 (3): 360–377.

Mann, R., & Sager, T. (2007). "Patents, venture capital, and software start-ups." *Research Policy*, 36: 193–208.

Marom, S., & Lussier, R. N. (2014). "A business success versus failure prediction model for small businesses in Israel." *Business and Economic Research*, 4 (2): 63–81.

McKenzie D., & Paffhausen A. L. (2017). "Small firm death in developing countries." World Bank Policy Research Working Paper 8236.

McKenzie, D., & Sansone, D. (2017). "Man vs. machine in predicting successful entrepreneurs: Evidence from a business plan competition in Nigeria." World Bank Policy Research Working Paper 8271: 1–66.

Miettinen, M. R., & Littunen, H. (2013). "Factors contributing to the success of startup firms using two-point or multiple-point scale models." *Entrepreneurship Research Journal*, 3 (4): 449–481.

Mueller, B. A., & Murmann, M. (2016). "The workforce composition of young firms and product innovation:Complementarities in the skills of founders and their early employees." Centre for European Economic Research Discussion Paper 16–074.

Mueller, B. A., Wolfe, M. T., & Syed, I. (2017). "Passion and grit: An exploration of the pathways leading to venture success." *Journal of Business Venturing*, 32 (3): 260–279.

Nahata, R. (2008). "Venture capital reputation and investment performance." *Journal of Financial Economics*, 90: 127–151.

Nanda, R., Samila, S., & Sorenson, O. (2020). "The persistent effect of initial success: Evidence from venture capital." *Journal of Financial Economics*, 137 (1): 231–248.

Nann, S., Krauss, J. S., Schober, M., Gloor, P. A., Fischbach, K., & Führes, H. (2010). "The power of alumni networks:Success of startup companies correlates with online social network structure of its founders." MIT Sloan Research Paper: 4766–4710.

Neumann, J. (2019). "Why do VCs insist on only investing in high-risk, high-return companies?" http://reactionwheel.net/2019/01/why-do-vcs-insist-on-only-investing-in-high-risk-high-return-companies.html

Ng, W., & Stuart, T. (2016). "Of hobos and highfliers: Disentangling the classes and careers of technology-based entrepreneurs." Unpublished Working Paper.

Ozmel, U., Reuer, J., & Gulati, R. (2013a). "Signals across multiple networks: How venture capital and alliance networks affect interorganizational collaboration." *Academy of Management Journal*, 56 (3): 852–866.

Ozmel, U., Robinson, D. T., & Stuart, T. E. (2013b). "Strategic alliances, venture capital, and exit decisions in early stage high-tech firms." *Journal of Financial Economics*, 107: 655–670.

Puri, M., & Zarutskie, R. (2012). "On the lifecycle dynamics of venture-capital- and non-venture capital-financed firms." *Journal of Finance*, 67 (6): 2247–2293.

Ragozzino, R., & Blevins, D. P. (2015). "Venture-backed firms: How does venture capital involvement affect their likelihood of going public or being acquired?" *Entrepreneurship Theory and Practice*, 40 (5): 991–1016.

Robb, A. M., & Robinson, D. T. (2014). "The capital structure decisions of new firms." *Review of Financial Studies*, 27 (1): 153–179.

Shane, S., & Stuart, T. (2002). "Organizational endowments and the performance of university start-ups." *Management Science*, 48: 154–170.

Song, M., Podoynitsyna, K., Van Der Bij, H., & Halman, J. I. M. (2008). "Success factors in new ventures: A meta-analysis." *Journal of Product Innovation Management*, 25 (1): 7–27.

Sorensen, M. (2007). "How smart is smart money? A two-sided matching model of venture capital." *Journal of Finance*, 62 (6): 2725–2762.

Souitaris, V., & Maestro, B. M. M. (2010). "Polychronicity in top management teams: The impact on strategic decision processes and performance of new technology ventures." *Strategic Management Journal*, 31 (6): 652–678.

Sunesson, T. (2009). "Alma mater matters: The value of school ties in the venture capital industry." Unpublished working paper.

Teng, H., Singh Bhatia, G., & Anwar, S. (2011). "A success versus failure prediction model for small businesses in Singapore." *American Journal of Business*, 26 (1): 50–64.

Tian, X. (2011). "The causes and consequences of venture capital stage financing." *Journal of Financial Economics*, 101: 132–159.

Tykvová, T. (2018). "Venture capital and private equity financing: An overview of recent literature and an agenda for future research." *Journal of Business Economics*, 88 (3): 325–362.

Wadhwa, V., Freeman, R., & Rissing, B. (2008). "Education and tech entrepreneurship." Kauffman Foundation Brief.

Zarutskie, R. (2010). "The role of top management team human capital in venture capital markets: Evidence from first-time funds." *Journal of Business Venturing*, 25: 155–172.

Zhao, Y. L., Song, M., & Storm, G. L. (2012). "Founding team capabilities and new venture performance: The mediating role of strategic positional advantages." *Entrepreneurship Theory and Practice*, 37 (4): 789–814.

12. The artificial creatives: the rise of combinatorial creativity from DALL-E to ChatGPT
Giancarlo Frosio

INTRODUCTION

In *The Expanse*, a futuristic novel series set in the twenty-third century, most of humanity is on 'basic' salary income because low-skilled jobs have been taken over by intelligent machines.[1] Artificial intelligence (AI) might be a fundamentally disruptive revolution for human work. Intelligent machines are coming in multiple shapes to serve diverse purposes, replacing humans potentially everywhere. Apparently, AI shows potential for replacing even those activities that are more inherently human. Although most creatives do not fear yet being replaced by robots (Pfeiffer, 2018) – but increasingly disgruntled reactions have been voiced by comic book creators, for example, following the recent AI art explosion (Johnston, 2022) – a major field where AI seems to be increasingly proficient is creativity. AI writes poems, novels, and news articles, composes music, edits photographs, creates video games, and makes paintings and other artworks. In a recent book, *The Artist in the Machine*, Arthur Miller argues that computer creativity will surpass human creativity (Miller, 2019). Whether that will be the case it is still hard to predict. What might instead be easier to predict is that intelligent machines might take over the market for commissioned mass-produced creativity that involves low levels of artistry, as technology such as DALL-E might show (Goldman, 2022; Nicholas, 2022; OpenAI, 2021).

In this context, the adaptation of the intellectual property (IP) system to AI-generated creativity – and the challenges that it brings about – is a topic of critical interest. In particular, the increasing use of machines in creating music, literature, and art raises issues of authorship, ownership, and infringement in machine-generated works and challenges conventional notions. Genuine issues have emerged regarding the protectability

---

[1] Wikipedia, *The Expanse* (novel series), https://en.wikipedia.org/wiki/The_Expanse_(novel_series).

of so-called AI-generated creativity, which might not meet the traditional copyright standards of legal personhood, authorship, and originality. Whether AI-generated creativity is protectable matters very much when considering the impact of AI on the creative market, given that creative work is affected by the incentives we provide at work or through the law. Practical considerations might question the opportunity of introducing incentives to bolster innovation and commercialisation of AI-generated creativity, considering the impact it can have on human creations. Therefore, the question to be determined is whether expansion of current copyright protection to computer-generated works is useful or instead will create negative externalities for the human creatives' market.

ARTIFICIAL CREATIVES AND THE 4TH INDUSTRIAL REVOLUTION

DALL-E, Jasper, and ChatGPT are artificial creatives. They create commissioned works for clients. They are extremely good at their job, so good that they might soon take over the market and kick their competitors out of business. DALL-E is a portmanteau of WALL-E, the robot protagonist of a 2008 animation movie, and Salvador Dalí. DALL-E is an AI to which visual creative works can be commissioned by merely providing a short textual description of the subject (Newton, 2022; OpenAI, 2021). Meanwhile, Jasper can act as your personal copywriter and, from the headline of an article, can generate content that already competes with professional writers (Simonite, 2022). Similarly, ChatGPT, which took the world by storm with its second iteration, is a state-of-the-art generative language model that can generate human-like responses to text-based prompts. Soon, more artificial creatives might join the market, such as MusicLM, a generative model developed by Google for creating high-fidelity music from text descriptions such as 'a calming violin melody supported by a distorted guitar riff' (Saha, 2023). Once again, it won't be long before the market is disrupted by the arrival of AI-generated videos from text, similar to how DALL-E generates images, as demonstrated by ongoing projects like Meta's Make-A-Video and Google's Imagen Video (Wilkins, 2022).

As the case of DALL-E, Jasper, and ChatGPT might prove, intelligent machines are coming in multiple shapes to serve diverse purposes, replacing humans potentially everywhere (ITU, 2018; Pricewaterhouse Coopers, 2017). Apparently, AI shows potential for replacing even those activities that are more inherently human. Although so far most creatives do not fear being replaced by robots (Pfeiffer 2018), actually, a major field where AI seems to be increasingly proficient is creativity. Most creative industries, such as audiovisual (Baujard et al., 2019; EAO, 2020), music (BPI, 2016; Strum et al., 2019), news (Trapova & Mezei, 2022), or publishing (Lovrinovic & Volland, 2019), will be substantially affected (New European Media, 2019; Pfeiffer, 2018).

The recent surge of artificial creatives has brought to mainstream attention a development that has been in the making for several decades. The first book ever written by a computer goes by the title *The Policeman's Beard Is Half Constructed: Computer Prose and Poetry by Racter* (Racter, 1984). It was 1984 and Racter's prose was still rather obscure and unpolished. Since then, things have been changing. The quality of AI-generated creativity has improved dramatically, to the extent that a novella written by a machine made the first rounds of a literary competition in Japan, beating in the process thousands of human authors (Lewis, 2016), or *Sunspring*, a sci-fi film written entirely by an AI, which placed in the top ten at Sci-Fi London's annual film festival (Craig & Kerr, 2019). Meanwhile, AIVA – as well as Amper and Melodrive – runs an AI that composes music, which is marketed to accompany audiovisual works, advertisements, or video games. Z-Machines, a Japanese robot band, perform music, changing the pace of their performance according to actions taken by their audience as well as by people who access their website (Bakare, 2014), while Sony's Flow Machine can interact and co-improvise with a human music performer (Deltorn & Macrez, 2018). As shown by DALL-E or Midjourney, visual art is also a creative field where AI excels. The AI-generated *Portrait of Edmond de Bellamy* sold at Christie's for an astounding $432,500 (Craig & Kerr, 2019). Soon, AIs will generate video from text in the same way DALL-E generates images, as showcased by the ongoing projects Make-A-Video and Imagen Video (Wilkins, 2022).

The emergence of AI creatives has been made possible by a mix of technological advancements, including massive data availability, enhanced computational resources, and novel deep learning-based architectures (Goodfellow et al., 2016). Tightly connected to these advancements, a fundamental development of AI-generated creativity has been caused by the advent of the generative adversarial network (GAN) (Svedman, 2020). This is quite a recent development. In June 2014, Ian Goodfellow published a paper entitled 'Generative adversarial networks' and posted the code on GitHub under a BSD licence (Goodfellow et al., 2014). The paper describes a generative process that uses an adversarial model for machine learning (ML). In this scenario, two neural networks contest with each other in a game. Given a training set, this technique learns to generate new data with the same statistics as the training set. This became a wildly popular method for training AI with large datasets. The technology further evolved into creative adversarial network (CAN) systems, which build over GANs and 'generate art by looking at art and learning about style; and becomes creative by increasing the arousal potential of the generated art by deviating from the learned styles' (Elgammal et al., 2017). GANs and CANs were deployed by the Paris-based Obvious arts collective to generate the *Portrait of Edmond de Bellamy* and a series of generative images called *La Famille de Belamy*. Finally, as in the case of DALL-E, Stable Diffusion, Midjourney, Jasper, ChatGPT, and MusicLM, large text-to-image, text-to-music, or text-to-text models achieved a remarkable leap in the evolution of AI, enabling high-quality and diverse synthesis of images, music, and text from a given text prompt.

AI-GENERATED CREATIVITY AND THE IP REGIME

The adaptation of the IP system to AI-generated creativity is a topic of critical interest. On one side, of course, existing IP regimes, including copyright law, trade secrets, and patent law, can protect software on which AI technology is based (Calvin & Leung, 2020). On the other side, however, the protection afforded to the software does not extend to the output possibly generated by the AI. Whether this protection is available depends on the construction of the present copyright framework. The question is at least threefold. A distinction should be made first between computer-assisted creativity, which is copyrightable as long as the user contribution is original (Clark et al., 1997; Denicola, 2016; *Payer Components South Africa*, 1995), and computer-generated creativity proper, where users' interaction with a computer prompts it to generate its own expression. A related scenario emerges, finally, in the case of works co- or jointly authored, rather than assisted, by human intelligence and AI.

The next few pages will investigate the second scenario. Dissecting the legal regime that might apply to AI-generated creativity implies necessarily to consider at least three critical issues. Next to the question of the A(I) uthor, focusing on protectability of AI-generated creative works under the present copyright system, there are two other fundamental questions: the questions of the (machine) learner and the (A)Infringer. They refer to whether an AI can infringe copyright through the machine-learning process and training that enables the AI to generate creativity and whether an AI can infringe copyright by creating an infringing output. Both issues will affect the role of humans in an AI environment by casting potential liability for copyright infringement on parties training AI to generate creative outputs or using AI tools to assist their own creative process or to generate creativity independently.

The Machine Learner

A first set of questions pertains to the input data that must be fed to ML and other AI processes (Gerber, 2019) for AI learning and development to occur. Data and big data processing is indeed a fundamental portion of ML (Ottolia, 2017). On one side, data ownership is a critical issue. Developing AI and ML systems generally involves training it using large datasets, so the system can continuously improve its decision-making abilities. Who owns the datasets which are used to train the system? If intermediate data are generated by AI/ML during training, should there be intellectual property rights (IPR) over them? On the other side, a critical question emerges regarding the potential copyright infringement that might occur via ML and the role of data mining-related exemptions and database protection in this context.

As per the ownership of training data, one of the basic and fundamental principles of copyright law is that data as such are not protected; copyright only protects the creative form not the information incorporated in the protected work (Hugenholtz, 1989). This follows from the fact that copyright law does not protect data but only original expressions within copyright-protected subject matters. Copyright, thus, is not a viable legal tool to protect data created by ML processes. Meanwhile, database protection never reaches the protection of data as such, also in those jurisdictions that provide so-called *sui generis* protection (e.g. Directive 1996/9/EC). Under general copyright protection of databases, the law protects only the original arrangement of a database (CJEU, C-604/10, para. 45). Instead, under *sui generis* regimes, the protection pertains to the investment to obtain, vary, or preserve the content of a database, but never to the 'created' data (CJEU, C-203/02, para. 31). In this context, there is an increasing push for data propertisation and new *sui generis* rights (Frosio, 2020; Ritter & Mayer, 2018; Samuelson, 1999). In a recent interview, World Intellectual Property Organization Director Francis Gury believed that 'we will see intellectual property moving to areas like data' (Gury, 2019). Also, additional legal tools, such as competition law, unfair competition doctrines, and trade secret law, might be deployed for regulating reuse of data input in ML and other AI processes.

A second legal question pertains to the lawfulness of ML and data-mining processes from an IP/copyright perspective (Caspers & Guibault, 2016; Ducato & Strowel, 2019; Geiger et al., 2018, 2019; Hugenholtz, 2019; Rosati, 2019; Toth 2019; Triaille et al., 2014). ML techniques in which 'algorithms are trained to infer certain patterns based on a set of data in order to determine the actions needed to achieve a given goal' (European Commission, 2020, p. 16) are based on automated computational analysis of digital content known as text and data mining (TDM). TDM refers to a research technique to collect information from large amounts of digital data through automated software tools (Han et al., 2011). It works by: (1) identifying input materials to be analysed, such as works, or data individually collected or organised in a pre-existing database; (2) copying substantial quantities of materials – which encompass (a) pre-processing materials by turning them into a machine-readable format compatible with the technology to be deployed for the TDM so that structured data can be extracted and (b) possibly, but not necessarily, uploading the pre-processed materials on a platform, depending on the TDM technique to be deployed; (3) extracting the data; and (4) recombining it to identify patterns in the final output (e.g. McDonald & Kelly, 2012; Triaille et al., 2014; Weiss et al., 2010).

As is already apparent, there might be a tension between IP protection and TDM techniques. Data as such are not protected by copyright law. Thus, TDM should in principle not be a use covered by any exclusive IPR. However, the chain of activities enabling TDM research can involve some activities encroaching on the exclusive rights provided by copyright and database protection. TDM usually involves some copying of protected subject matter, which even in the case of limited excerpts, at least in some jurisdictions such as the European Union (EU), might infringe the right of reproduction (CJEU, C-5/08, paras 54–55). Basically, IPR can be affected whenever mining involves IP-protected subject matters. Only TDM tools involving minimal copying of a few words or crawling through data and processing each item separately could be operated without running into a potential liability for copyright infringement, as these actions do not involve subject matters protected by copyright or *sui generis* rights (Directive 2019/790/EU, Recital 8). Instead, any reproductions resulting in the creation of a copy of a protected work along the chain of TDM activities might trigger copyright infringement. In this respect, pre-processing to standardise materials into machine-readable formats might trigger infringement of the right of reproduction (Directive 2001/29/EC, Art. 2). Likewise, the uploading of the pre-processed material on a platform – which might occur or not depending on whether the TDM technique adopted makes use of a TDM software crawling data to be analysed directly from the source (Triaille et al., 2014) – might also violate the right of reproduction. Mining – that stage of the TDM process where data are finally extracted – can also infringe upon the right of reproduction depending on the mining software deployed and the character of the extraction. Again, TDM might involve the reproduction, translation, adaptation, arrangement, and any other alteration of a database protected by copyright, which means the original selection and arrangement of the database's content (Directive 1996/9/EC, Art. 5(a–b); Stamatoudi, 2016). For example, pre-processing for extraction might cleanse from a database portions and data that are irrelevant for data analysis. In this respect, pre-processing might violate both the right of reproduction and the right to make adaptations and arrangements (Directive 1996/9/EC, Art. 5(a–b); Stamatoudi, 2016; Triaille et al., 2014). Moreover, TDM might infringe *sui generis* database rights, in particular the extraction – and to a minor extent the re-utilisation – of substantial parts of a database. In this context, even if extraction does occur without reproduction of the original materials, extraction itself would infringe upon the exclusive rights provided to the database owner (Directive 1996/9/EC, Art. 7). In this regard, the Court of Justice of the EU has provided that the transfer of data from one medium to another and its integration into the new medium constitutes an act of extraction (Directive 1996/9/EC, Arts. 2(a), 7(1), 7(2)(b); CJEU, C-203/02; Stamatoudi, 2016).

Whether the actions mentioned above actually infringe IP laws and make TDM unlawful largely depends on differing national approaches in the application of exceptions and limitation and fair uses to copyright law (Fiil-Flynn et al., 2022). Exceptions and limitations – and fair uses – allow for copyrighted works to be used without a license from the copyright owner because that use serves some important public interest and fundamental rights, in particular freedom of expression (Geiger, 2009). Obviously, application of exceptions and limitations to TDM techniques when they are invasive enough to trigger IP infringement have been repeatedly claimed as such application would foster 'public interest, notably in scientific progress ... and economic development' (Quintais, 2017, pp. 197–205). In Europe, several exceptions within the mandatory and voluntary list provided by Directive 2001/29/EC and Directive 2006/115/EC have been selected as possible candidates to screen TDM from IP infringement, such as the temporary acts of reproduction exception, the research exception, the private use exception, the normal use of a database exception, and the extraction of insubstantial parts of a database exception (Geiger et al., 2019). Given the legal uncertainty on applying any of these exceptions, however, in 2019 the Copyright in the Digital Single Market Directive introduced a specific TDM exception (Directive 2019/790/EU, Arts 3–4). Unfortunately, this exception can either be opted out by right holders or can be enjoyed without limitations only by public research institutions doing TDM for research purposes. This arrangement put at a disadvantage private AI industry that cannot freely run TDM processes for ML purposes. Similar restrictions are common in most civil law jurisdictions (Fiil-Flynn et al., 2022). Elsewhere, in particular in some common law jurisdictions such as the United States (US), Canada, United

Kingdom (UK), Australia, and New Zealand, opening clauses or fair use models have been deployed to the end of making TDM lawful (Fiil-Flynn et al., 2022). In the US, for example, TDM is apparently covered by the fair use defence to copyright infringement (Lemley & Casey, 2021). Starting with *Baker v Selden*, courts argued that protected subject matter can be used when it 'must necessarily be used as an incident to' using unprotected materials (*Baker v Selden*, 1879). Once applied to TDM, this case law would imply that in order to mine text and data – which are itself unprotected – a user might lawfully reproduce protected materials. In Google Books, more recently, TDM the entire corpus of human knowledge in order to create a relational database was found a transformative use, hence fair under §107 of the US Copyright Act (*Authors Guild v Google*, 2015; *Authors Guild v HathiTrust*, 2014). To sum up, differing approaches in regulating TDM and ML processes create an unequal playing field for the AI industry, in particular private, operating in jurisdictions with more restrictive laws and more expansive IP protection. However, at the same time, such restrictive approaches provide stronger protection to creatives and make it easier to protect their market share for being overtaken by AI technologies.

The A(I)uthor

The second question – that of the A(I)uthor – investigates whether AI-generated creativity can be protected under the current copyright regime. This investigation must look at three major conditions for copyright protection of creative works: (1) legal personality; (2) authorship; and (3) originality.

Although some theoretical thinking has been supporting the idea of legal personality of intelligent machines (Bostrom, 2014; Solum, 1992), especially future hypothetical strong AI that are autonomous, intelligent, and conscious (Zimmerman, 2017; Ballardini & van den Hoven van Genderen, 2021; European Parliament, 2017), legal personality of machines is certainly unavailable under the present legal framework (Frosio, 2022). Scholarship has consistently stressed how any hypothesis of granting AI robots full legal personhood has to be discarded for now (Banteka, 2020; Mik, 2021; Pagallo, 2018). Caution against construing AI as a legal person for IP protection purposes in particular emerges also from a 2020 Resolution of the European Parliament (European Parliament, 2020).

The question of the A(I)uthor requires also to consider whether an AI is an author according to traditional copyright standards. To put it bluntly, is a human author an intrinsic requirement for authorship? International treaties do not include a definition of author that can provide a definitive answer; however, textual references to human creation in the Berne Convention, such as the life of the author as a term of protection, and 'Berne's humanist cast' might exclude AI from the scope of the notion of author (Berne Convention, Arts 3, 7; Ginsburg, 2018). A close review of EU law would most likely lead to similar conclusions, both by looking at the definition of authorship in legislation and case law, given the multiple references to author as a person, and the doctrinal interpretation (Frosio, 2022; Hugenholtz & Quintais, 2021), although there is no transversal definition in statutory law of the notion of authorship. Also, EU national legislation confirms this approach by referring to authors as a person, to work as creation of the mind or to the intellectual and personal relationship between the author and the work. The US legal system would also leave little room for mechanical authors, although absent an express statutory definition of authorship, some commentators have argued that, textually, the Statute does not limit authorship to human authors (Bridy, 2012; Denicola, 2016; Samuelson, 1986). However, both additional textual references and the Supreme Court's case law apparently exclude the possibility of construing non-human agents as authors under the statute (e.g. 17 U.S.C. § 101; *Community for Creative Non-Violence v Reid*, 1989; *Feist Publications v Rural Telephone Service*, 1990; *Trade-Mark Cases*, 1879; *Burrow-Giles Lithographic Co. v Sarony*, 1884). Finally, *Naruto v Slater*, discussing the potential authorship of two selfies taken by a seven-year-old crested macaque 'Naruto' when wildlife photographer David Slater left his camera unattended in one of his visits to Indonesia, might have put the matter to rest by confirming that animals – and machines by analogy – cannot serve as authors for the purpose of the Copyright Act and own a copyright (*Naruto v David Slater*, 2018). Also as a response to the *Naruto* case, the Third Edition of the Compendium of US Copyright Office Practices has included specifically a 'Human Authorship Requirement' and listed among the 'Works that Lack Human Authorship' those created by a machine or by a mechanical process without intervention from a human (US Copyright Office, §306). In at least two instances already, the US Copyright Office has rejected registration of comic books apparently generated via AI, as in the case of *Zarya of the Dawn* created by Kris Kashtanova via Midjourney and Stephen Thaler's AI-generated painting, 'A Recent Entrance to Paradise' (Cronin, 2022). Finally, Chinese courts have discussed AI authorship in particular. Both *Beijing Feilin Law Firm v Baidu Corporation* (2018) and *Shenzen Tencent v Yinxun* (2019) denied copyright protection to works created solely by machines and confirmed that copyright protection requires human authorship. Instead the courts granted protection only to the original contributions from human agents reworking AI-generated creativity (Frosio, 2022).

Even if a textual anthropocentric construction of authorship is disregarded, also originality as a condition for copyright protection seems to prevent protection of AI-generated creativity. Actually, textual references and case law construe originality via an anthropocentric model that emphasises self-consciousness. Originality is widely defined in most jurisdictions in light of a so-called personality approach that describes an original work as a representation of the personality of the author (Frosio, 2022; see in the EU, CJEU, C-5/08, para. 45; CJEU, C-145/10, para. 94; CJEU, C-604/10, para. 42; Rosati, 2013; in the US, *Burrow-Giles*, 1884; *Feist Publications*, 1990; *Lindsay*, 1999; in the UK, Rahmatian, 2013). The notion of originality is consistently construed via an anthropocentric vision positing that a work is original if it is a representation of 'self', a representation of the personality of the author. Of course, only a sentient self-conscious being would be capable of representing 'self' through a work. Absent any creator's self-consciousness, the originality requirement as representation of the personality of the author – thus representation of 'self' – would be beyond the reach of present machine-generated creativity (Deltorn & Macrez, 2018; Gervais, 2019b; Mezei, 2020; Ramalho, 2017). Unless machines achieve self-consciousness – which might be the case of futuristic hypothetical strong AI – AI-generated creativity cannot meet the originality requirement under the present copyright legal framework.

The (A)Infringer

Can an AI infringe copyright by generating an output that is identical or substantially similar to a protected work? The short answer would be: 'yes, of course'. Although the answer is dependent on judicial doctrines that vary from jurisdiction to jurisdiction, in the US, for example, copyright infringement is a strict liability offense, meaning that it does not depend on any element of culpability on the side of the infringer. Three requirements must be fulfilled to infringe the right of reproduction: that there is an act of copying, rather than independent creation; that the copy made is fixed in tangible medium of expression; and that the act of copying resulted in improper appropriation of protected content. While the second requirement might be more peculiar to US law and less relevant to our investigation, the first and second requirements are commonly applied also in other jurisdictions and merit some specific consideration. As per copying, any infringer can copy by making a mechanical reproduction, by creating a work which is substantially similar to a protected one, and by translating a work to a different medium of expression. Copying does not depend on the mental state of the infringer and whether it is done knowingly or not, as 'it is no excuse that memory played a trick' (*Fisher v Dillingham*, 1924).

Innocent copying is no excuse to infringement as 'intention to infringe is not essential to the copyright act' to the extent that copyright infringement can even be subconscious (*Bright Tunes v Harrison*, 1976), as long as access to the allegedly copied work can be proven (*Three Boys Music v Michael Bolton*, 2000) or there is sufficiently striking similarity between unusual aspects of the two works, in which case not even access to the work needs to be proven for a finding of infringement (e.g. *Selle v Gibb*, 1984). So, as long as the work allegedly copied by a substantially similar work was included in the learning database of a machine, proof of infringement is available as well as if the output generated by the machine is strikingly similar to a protected work.

Improper appropriation depends on the character and amount of the material taken and can occur via comprehensive copying, fragmented literal similarity, or comprehensive non-literal similarity, meaning respectively that the entire work has been copied, quantitatively and qualitatively important parts of the works have been copied, or no literal portion of the work has been copied but the works are substantially similar (Bracha, 2018; Gervais, 2019a). In this case, again, as long as the final output generated by a machine has taken too many literary parts of the work or enough to make the output substantially similar to a protected work, the machine has improperly appropriated, and the AI-generated output will be infringing existing copyrights.

Instead, if the use is transformative, the obvious question that arises is whether using AI to generate images of protected works is considered fair use or not (Newton, 2022). The answer should be obviously positive as transformative use of copyright protected works is excused by the fair use clause (17 USC § 107) and does not trigger copyright infringement (Leval, 1990; Liu, 2019).

This might help answer one critical question: can the rights to the imagery and the people, places, and objects within the imagery that these models were trained on be infringed upon by the final output generated by a machine? The answer would be again 'yes, of course', but only if that protected content is copied by the generated output, not if it remains a source of inspiration that is not copied in an identical or substantially similar manner by the AI-generated output but only used in a quantitatively or qualitatively *de minimis* manner (Bracha, 2018; Gervais, 2019a) or used in a transformative manner (Leval, 1990; Liu, 2019). At least US copyright law has a long judicial tradition confirming that copying protected content, as in the case of the hundreds of millions of images used to train AI text-to-image generators (Growcoot, 2022b), to make a lawful use, as in the case of a transformative use or a *de minimis* use, does not trigger copyright infringement (*Authors Guild v Google*, 2015; *Baker v Selden*, 1879). In this scenario, the AI would not be copying content in copyright terms but using it much the same way human artists do when they study past artists and learn from their works to create their own.

Recently, issues have been raised by AI apps like DALL-E, Stable Diffusion, and Stability AI generating output in the style of famous artists. The new update of Stability AI has actually removed the ability to generate pictures in the style of specific artists, such as Greg Rutkowski, the most popular artist used to generate AI images and well known for producing fantastical high-quality images (Growcoot, 2022b). Rutkowski showed concern for the mass copying of individual styles by AI (Bastian, 2022; Heikkilä, 2022) by noting 'right now, when you type in my name, you see more work from the AI than work that I have done myself, which is terrifying for me. How long till the AI floods my results and is indistinguishable from my works?' (Growcoot, 2022b). Other creatives, especially comic book artists, share Rutkowski's concerns, to the extent that many equate AI art to theft (Baio, 2022; Johnston, 2022). These concerns, however, might be misplaced from a copyright infringement perspective (copying of style could amount instead to plagiarism that is not sanctioned by copyright law but only via social norms). Copyright law generally does not protect styles as such. Instead, as mentioned already, copyright law protects the expression of ideas, and not the ideas themselves. This means that copyright law would not protect the style of a work, no matter how distinct, but would protect the specific expression of that style in a particular work. Courts stated that style is merely one ingredient of expression, but absent substantial similarity between the original work and the new, there cannot be infringement (e.g. *Steinberg v Columbia Pictures*, 1987; *Cummins v Vella*, 2002). In *Dave Grossman Designs v Bortin*, the Court addresses the point even more directly by noting:

> For example, Picasso may be entitled to a copyright on his portrait of three women painted in his Cubist motif. Any artist, however, may paint a picture of any subject in the Cubist motif, including a portrait of three women, and not violate Picasso's copyright so long as the second artist does not substantially copy Picasso's specific expression of his idea. (*Dave Grossman Designs v Bortin*, 1972, p. 1156)

In conclusion, if an AI generates a work that is similar in style to the work of an artist whose images were fed into the AI generator, the AI's work would not be infringing on the artist's copyright unless the AI's work was substantially similar to the artist's work in a way that constituted copying of the artist's protected expression. This is because the 'expression that copyright protects is a combination of multiple factors, including composition, content, style, framing, colour, narrative, artistic intent that pieced together according to the author's free and independent choices represent the personality of the author and, thus, make the work original (*Feist Publications*, 1991; see also CJEU, C-145/10, para 99). One particular piece of that expression taken alone, such as style, is not enough to warrant protection.

ARTIFICIAL CREATIVES AND INCENTIVES

Given the apparent unprotectability of AI-generated, rather than assisted, creativity, under the present copyright framework (Mezei, 2020; Aplin & Pasqualetto, 2019; Gervais, 2019a; Svedman, 2020; Huson, 2019; Palace, 2019; Clifford, 2018; Ramalho, 2017), as per our earlier review, a number of alternative policy options have certainly been emerging. In fact, future policy directions depend heavily on the application of alternative – and competing – IP theoretical approaches. Incentive theory or utilitarianism (Fisher, 2001), which is dominant in the US and common law jurisdictions, have included discussions as to whether not granting protection to AI-generated creativity would be a suboptimal solution. Incentive theory is less concerned with the humanity of the author than personality theories, influencing instead civil law jurisdictions (Kaminski, 2017). This provides more room for arguments in favour of non-human authorship and protectability of AI-generated creativity. According to the incentive theory approach, 'providing financial incentives in order to encourage the growth and development of the AI industry and ensure the dissemination of AI generated works is arguably the ultimate goal of assigning copyright to human authors' (Hristov, 2017, p. 444). Although a computer does not need an incentive to produce its output, the incentive may be useful for the person collaborating with the computer (Hristov, 2017; Miller, 1993). In particular, authors argue that there should be some additional incentive to encourage industry to invest the time and money that it will take to teach machines to behave intelligently (Abbott, 2016; Butler, 1981; Farr, 1989; Kasap, 2019; Milde, 1969) or to reward users with training and instructing AI generating content (Brown, 2019; Denicola, 2016; Ralston, 2005; Samuelson, 1986).

In contrast, most civil law jurisdictions might be less responsive to welfare and incentive arguments and prefer to value systemic balance, thus rejecting any departure from the personality theory approach that shapes the civil law copyright perspective – and its notion of originality. In addition, although AI-generated creations may justify incentives to bolster innovation and commercialisation, the necessity of such incentives is questionable considering the impact it can have on human creations (Craglia et al., 2018). For example, granting protection for these works could devalue human authorship and existing jobs in the field as providing the same protection to AI works would boost their competitive advantage on the market for commissioned works, considering that AI generative capacity is immeasurably greater, speedier, and cheaper (Bonadio & McDonagh, 2020), hamper creativity as it could discourage artists from publishing their creations due to fear of infringing AI-generated protected material (De Cock Buning, 2018; Deltorn, 2017), or clog the creative ecosystem with standardised and homogenised AI-generated output, impacting cultural diversity and identity politics.

Therefore, the policy question to be determined is whether expansion of current copyright protection to computer generated works is useful. The current legal framework might already provide enough protection through patent and copyright law to the underlying software, *sui generis* protection to databases, or other legal mechanisms, such as competition law, to protect automated works without extending the existing copyright regime to non-human authors (Deltorn & Macrez, 2018). As suggested, the questions should be investigated from a law and economics perspective before favouring any solutions (Craglia et al., 2018; Ginsburg, 2018; Ginsburg & Budiardjo, 2019).

COMBINATORIAL CREATIVITY AND THE DEMYSTIFICATION OF ORIGINALITY: A POLICY ARGUMENT AGAINST PROTECTION OF AI-GENERATED CREATIVITY

As neuroscientist Henning Beck shows, brains are imperfect, non-deterministic, and partially analogue (Beck, 2019). Therefore, humans represent things as concepts rather than just pure data. When thinking about some object, humans do not recall the actual object itself but rather a conceptual idea of what the object is. In this regard, human and auto-mated creative processes might be functioning in the opposite manner. For Beck, the human brain's mistakes, missteps, and flows are actually proof of our superiority to computers and AI. ML allows computer programs to compute things in a manner similar to the human brain. The key, however, to machines' lack of true creativity lies in the word compute. Each of these demonstrations of the creative prowess of AI utilises a carefully constrained algorithm to achieve a very specific end goal. At its core, these algorithms are simply manipulating symbols then concatenating the results in a meaningful way. As John Searle argued in

Minds, Brains, and Programs (1984) this does not represent understanding. True machine creativity cannot be derived from a system that solely takes input, performs mathematical functions, and presents an output to the eager programmer that created it. As long as this is the case, the threat of machines completely displacing the human labour force is non-existent (Wulff, 2019).

In this context, it might be worth reflecting on the fact that creativity generated by machines is cumulative and combinatorial par excellence. There are genuine questions emerging on whether AI art is always inherently borrowed or stolen, pointing to the fact that AIs cannot be creative without art (Cooper, 2022). A machine would be always reusing mechanical reproductions of previous works that was originally copied and processed during a ML process. In light of what neuroscience explained, machines do not create by reworking the conceptual idea into a new expression, but always recall and derive their creativity from the actual objects – or data – previously processed via their ML process, as if any AI-generated creativity always originated from a mechanical reproduction of previous potentially protectable works. Actually, copying and recombination remain the sole character of the algorithmic generative process, which can never be original, at least according to the present copyright notion that construes originality as expression of the personality of the author or 'self'.

Therefore, the advent of algorithmic creativity, in fact, might support changes in copyright policies along arguments that have been made in the context of human creativity as well. In my book *Reconciling Copyright with Cumulative Creativity: The Third Paradigm*, I make a historical review of creativity policies, demystifying the 'myth of originality' and making the case of the fundamental nature of creativity as 'combinatorial creativity' (Frosio, 2018). There, I argued that Internet 2.0 and user-generated creativity have re-emphasised cumulative and collaborative mechanics of creativity that characterised most of human pre-modern cultural history. The re-emergence of these creative mechanics, I argued, might justify a renewed emphasis on inclusive, rather than exclusive, rights in copyright policies. In repurposing my framework for reconsidering copyright policies in light of the advent of AI-generated creativity, I would argue how algorithmic creativity proceeds further in completely demystifying the notion of 'absolute originality' upon which modern post-Romantic copyright has been predicated. This theoretical observation would strongly discourage policy solutions aiming at expanding exclusive rights over AI-generated creativity. Instead, AI-generated creativity should be free for anyone to use, reassemble, and remix.

CONCLUSIONS

The fear of the machines stealing our jobs is actually nothing new. Luddite rebellions against the mechanisation of the textile industry were perhaps some of the first examples of human resistance to machines (Thompson, 2017). Regulating AI – in multiple contexts and in the creative market in particular – is a matter of weighting positive and negative externalities for society as a whole, in particular given that international approaches might be very fragmented. This is a type of policy question we have already answered through history. Cars displaced horses, coaches, and coachmen but that proved to be good for society. Mechanisation already displaced human labour but that again, all in all, proved to be good for society. The question that is still unanswered for now, though, is whether the fourth industrial revolution might bring about more inequality, especially in the short/medium term, in the footsteps of a trend already highlighted by recent fundamental scholarship (Piketty, 2017). What we might see in the near future is AI raising the bar for high-skilled and talented jobs in the industry, leaving many behind and consolidating the revenue stream from low-skilled creativity in the hands of the few, in particular if legal reform will attach exclusive rights to AI-generated creativity.

At the moment, the tools might fail to achieve human-level quality immediately; instead they might take days/weeks/months of prompt-engineering, fine-tuning on your own data, and stacking models together (Shynkarenka, 2022). Today, AI creativity generators still largely remain tools that can produce substitutes to commercial products only if handled by qualified creatives, therefore serving as an aid to creatives' work rather than displacing their market share. In light of this, the field is still fundamentally divided between those creatives that see AI technology as an opportunity for greater artistic productivity rather than a competitor (Knight, 2022) and neo-luddites fiercely opposing the new technology (Baio, 2022; Growcoot, 2022a; Johnston, 2022). However, soon enough, AI-generated art might undermine the economic sustainability of being a creative not because art will be replaced by AI as a whole but because mass-consumed creativity will be so much cheaper and good enough for most customers. Rachel Hill, Head of the Association of Illustrators, for example, acknowledges that AI platforms may appeal to art directors seeking a quick and potentially cheaper option for illustrations. However, she believes that human illustrators still have a major advantage as they not only produce the final image, but also play a crucial role in helping clients formulate the initial concepts (ENGTalks, 2022). This advantage might soon disappear given the very fast pace of AI development in the field.

In conclusion, it is worth acknowledging that AI-generated creativity has the potential to significantly disrupt the market for creative jobs, especially in areas such as graphic design, music composition, and copywriting. This is because AI algorithms can generate high-quality creative outputs much faster and at a lower cost than human creatives. Also, the potentialities and the learning curve and pace of AI are 'singular'. Therefore, without the necessary solutions in place, disruption generated by AI is just a matter of time. I reckon that a valid argument based on historical evidence might suggest that long-term readjustment should most likely occur. Still, this does not justify the sustainability of short- and mid-term disruption, which should still be avoided in light of sound policy making. In addition, blindly embracing disruption just because it proved to be positive for society in the long term in the past does not justify following the same path today as the consequences of the present AI disruption on the labour market are in fact unpredictable a priori.

However, to avoid the disruptive effects of AI-generated creativity on the creative market, several solutions can be considered. First, one such solution is to provide a regulatory framework that disincentivises the development of AI that can replace human creativity, rather than augment it. For example, AI can be used to generate ideas and suggestions, but the final creative output should still be the result of human effort. Another solution is to focus on developing AI that has a unique style and tone, rather than just generating outputs that are indistinguishable from human-created content.

Second, another important step to avoid disruption is to protect the value of human creativity. This can be achieved in particular via copyright regulation. On one side, no exclusive IP rights should be attached, as proposed, to AI-generated creativity. If human creatives own – and can transfer – a copyright, they will maintain a market advantage. As I mentioned before, it follows from the wholly combinatorial nature of AI-generated creativity that it belongs to the public domain. On the other side, to account for the market substitution of human creations by AI-generated creativity – and its mentioned wholly combinatorial nature – AI productions should generate money for human literary and artistic projects via a levy system and collective management of revenues that might proceed from this creativity (Senftleben, 2022). Statutory remuneration models (e.g. Geiger, 2014), for example, can be attached to text- and data-mining exceptions, as those recently enacted in articles 3 and 4 of the Copyright in the Digital Single Market Directive. Possibly, these statutory remunerations could be attached only to certain categories of works or rightsholders on the basis of an empirical review of the creative markets more directly affected by the disruptive effects of AI-generated creativity. These 'permitted but paid' models (Ginsburg, 2014) would allow AI-generated creativity to continue being available, while sharing with the entire human community that feeds the machine's combinatorial creativity a portion of the new revenue stream generated.

Finally, the creative industry should embrace new business models that leverage AI-generated creativity. For example, instead of competing with AI, creatives can use AI to help scale their businesses, reach new audiences, and create new revenue streams. By doing so, the creative industry can harness the full potential of AI, while still preserving the value of human creativity. As with President Roosevelt's New Deal for the Arts, with disruption comes opportunity. AI still remains a tool. As such, it is neutral and can produce positive externalities if handled appropriately. Dynamite can kill but also open new paths. Rather than unleashing emotional reactions against a new technology – and seeking protections that were never enjoyed before, such as against text and data mining or the use of a certain artistic style – creatives should harness the power of AI to enhance their own creativity and productivity and regulators should put in place the necessary safeguards to minimise negative externalities for the creative market, while supporting an ethical advancement of AI research and applications.

REFERENCES

Abbott, R. (2016). I Think, Therefore I Invent: Creative Computers and the Future of Patent Law. *Boston College Law Review* 57(4), 1079.

Aplin, T., & Pasqualetto, G. (2019). Artificial Intelligence and Copyright Protection. In Ballardini, R. M., Kuoppamäki, P., & Pitkänen, O. (Eds), *Regulating Industrial Internet through IPR, Data Protection and Competition Law*. Kluwer Law International.

Authors Guild v Google, 804 F.3d 202 (2nd Circ. 2015).

Authors Guild v HathiTrust, 755 F.3d 87 (2nd Cir. 2014).

Baio, A. (2022, 1 November). Invasive Diffusion: How One Unwilling Illustrator Found Herself Turned into an AI Model. *Waxy*. https://waxy.org/2022/11/invasive-diffusion-how-one-unwilling-illustrator-found-herself-turned-into-an-ai-model

Bakare, L. (2014, 4 April). Meet Z-Machines, Squarepusher's New Robot Band. *The Guardian*. www.theguardian.com/music/2014/apr/04/squarepusher-z-machines-music-for-robots

Baker v Selden, 101 U.S. 99, 104 (1879).

Ballardini, R., & van den Hoven van Genderen, R. (2021). Artificial Intelligence and IPR: The Quest or Pleading for AI as Legal Subjects. In Pihlajarinne, T., Alen-Savikko, A., & Havu, K. (Eds), *AI and the Media: Reconsidering Rights and Responsibilities*. Edward Elgar Publishing.

Banteka, N. (2020). Artificially Intelligent Persons. *Houston Law Review* 58, 537.

Bastian, M. (2022, 26 November). Stable Diffusion v2 Removes NSFW Images and Causes Protests. *The Decoder*. https://the-decoder.com/stable-diffusion-v2-removes-nude-images-and-causes-protests

Baujard T. et al. (2019). Entering the New Paradigm of Artificial Intelligence and Series: A Study Commissioned by the Council of Europe and Eurimages. Council of Europe. https://rm.coe.int/eurimages-entering-the-new-paradigm-051219/1680995331

Beck, H. (2019). *Scatterbrain: How the Mind's Mistakes Make Humans Creative, Innovative, and Successful*. Greystone Books.

Beijing Feilin Law Firm v Baidu Corporation, Beijing Internet Court, (2018) Beijing 0491 Minchu No. 239, 26 April 2019.

Berne Convention for the Protection of Literary and Artistic Works.

Bonadio, E., & McDonagh, L. (2020). Artificial Intelligence as Producer and Consumer of Copyright Works: Evaluating the Consequences of Algorithmic Creativity. *Intellectual Property Quarterly* 2, 112.

Bostrom, N. (2014). *Superintelligence: Paths, Dangers, Strategies*. Oxford University Press.

BPI. (2016). Music's Smart Future: How Will AI Impact the Music Industry. British Phonographic Industry. www.musictank.co.uk/wp-content/uploads/2018/03/bpi-ai-report.pdf

Bracha, O. (2018). Not de Minimis: (Improper) Appropriation in Copyright. *American University Law Review* 68, 139.

Bridy, A. (2012). Coding Creativity: Copyright and the Artificially Intelligent Author. *Stanford Technology Law Review* 5, 1.

Bright Tunes v Harrison, 420 F. Supp. 177 (SDNY 1976).

Brown, N. (2019). Artificial Authors: A Case for Copyright in Computer-Generated Works. *Columbia Science and Technology Law Review* 9, 1.

Burrow-Giles Lithographic Co. v Sarony 111 U.S. 53 (1884).

Butler, T. (1981). Can a Computer Be an Author? Copyright Aspects of Artificial Intelligence. *American Journal of Communications and Entertainment Law* 4(4), 707.

Calvin, N., & Leung, J. (2020). *Who Owns Artificial Intelligence? A Preliminary Analysis of Corporate Intellectual Property Strategies and Why They Matter*. University of Oxford's Future of Humanity Institute. www.fhi.ox.ac.uk/wp-content/uploads/Patents_-FHI-Working-Paper-Final-.pdf

Caspers, M., & Guibault, L. (2016). *Baseline Report of Policies and Barriers of TDM in Europe*. FutureTDM. https://project.futuretdm.eu/wp-content/uploads/2017/05/FutureTDM_D3.3-Baseline-Report-of-Policies-and-Barriers-of-TDM-in-Europe.pdf

CJEU, C-145/10, *Eva Maria Painer*, 2011, EU: C:2011:239:121.

CJEU, C-203/02, *The British Horseracing Board Ltd and Others v William Hill Organization Ltd*, 9 November 2004, ECLI:EU:C:2004:695.

CJEU, C-5/08, *Infopaq International A/S v Danske Dagblades Forening*, 16 July 2009, ECLI:EU:C:2009:465.

CJEU, C-604/10, *Football Dataco Ltd and Others v Yahoo! UK Ltd and Others*, 1 March 2012, ECLI:EU:C:2012:115.

Clark, R., Smyth, S., & Hall, N. (1997). *Intellectual Property Law in Ireland*. Butterworths.

Clifford, R. (2018). Creativity Revisited. *IDEA: The IP Law Review* 59, 25.

Community for Creative Non-Violence v Reid, 490 U.S. 730 (1989).

Cooper, D. (2022, 27 July). Is DALL-E's Art Borrowed or Stolen? Creative AIs Can't Be Creative without Our Art. *Engadget*. www.engadget.com/dall-e-gener ative-ai-tracking-data-privacy-160034656.html

Craglia, M. et al. (2018). Artificial Intelligence: A European Perspective. Joint Research Centre, Publications Office of the European Union. https://publications. jrc.ec.europa.eu/repository/bitstream/JRC113826/ai-flagship-report-online.pdf

Craig, C., & Kerr, I. (2019). The Death of the AI Author. *Osgoode Legal Studies Research Paper*.

Cronin, B. (2022, 21 December). AI-Created Comic Has Been Deemed Ineligible for Copyright Protection. CBR. www.cbr.com/ai-comic-deemed-ineligible-cop yright-protection

Cummins v Vella [2002] FCAFC 218.

Dave Grossman Designs v Bortin, 347 F. Supp. 1150 (N.D. Ill. 1972).

De Cock Buning, M. (2018). Artificial Intelligence and the Creative Industry: New Challenges for the EU Paradigm for Art and Technology by Autonomous Creation. In Barfield, W., & Pagallo, U. (Eds), *Research Handbook on the Law of Artificial Intelligence*. Edward Elgar Publishing.

Deltorn, J.-M. (2017). Deep Creations: Intellectual Property and the Automata. *Frontiers in Digital Humanities* 8. www.frontiersin.org/articles/10.3389/fdigh. 2017.00003/full

Deltorn, J.-M., & Macrez, F. (2018). Authorship in the Age of Machine Learning and Artificial Intelligence. *Center for International Intellectual Property Studies Research Paper No. 2018–10*. https://papers.ssrn.com/sol3/papers.cfm?abstract_ id=3261329

Denicola, R. (2016). Ex Machina: Copyright Protection for Computer-Generated Works. *Rutgers University Law Review* 69, 251–287.

Directive 1996/9/EC of the European Parliament and of the Council of 11 March 1996 on the Legal Protection of Databases, 1996 O.J. L 77.

Directive 2001/29/EC of the European Parliament and of the Council of 22 May 2001 on the Harmonisation of Certain Aspects of Copyright and Related Rights in the Information Society, 2000 O.J. L 167.

Directive 2019/790/EU of the European Parliament and of the Council of 17 April 2019 on Copyright and Related Rights in the Digital Single Market and Amending Directives 96/9/EC and 2001/29/EC, 2019 O.J. L 130.

Ducato, R., & Strowel, R. (2019). Limitations to Text and Data Mining and Consumer Empowerment: Making the Case for a Right to 'Machine Legibility'. *International Review of Intellectual Property and Competition Law* 50(3), 649–684.

EAO. (2020). Artificial Intelligence: Summary of Observatory Workshop on AI in the Audiovisual Industry. European Audiovisual Observatory. https://rm.coe. int/summary-workshop-2019-bat-2/16809c992a

Elgammal, A. et al. (2017). CAN: Creative Adversarial Networks Generating 'Art' by Learning about Styles and Deviating from Style Norms. arXiv: 1706.07068.

ENGTalks. (2022, 30 June). We Are Training AI Twice as Fast This Year as Last. *IEEE Spectrum*. www.enggtalks.com/news/217757/we-re-training-ai-twice-as- fast-this-year-as-last?c=2859

European Commission. (2020). White Paper on Artificial Intelligence: A European Approach to Excellence and Trust. COM(2020) 65.

European Parliament. (2017, 16 February). Civil Law Rules on Robotics: European Parliament Resolution with Recommendations to the Commission

on Civil Law Rules on Robotics, 2015/2103(INL). www.europarl.europa.eu/
doceo/document/TA-8-2017-0051_EN.pdf

European Parliament. (2020, 24 April). Draft Report on Intellectual Property Rights
for the Development of Artificial Intelligence Technologies, 2020/2015(INI).

Farr, E. (1989). Copyrightability of Computer-Created Works. *Rutgers Computer
and Technology Law Journal* 15, 63.

Feist Publications v Rural Telephone Service 499 U.S. 340 (1990).

Fiil-Flynn, S. et al. (2022). Legal Reform to Enhance Global Text and Data Mining
Research: Outdated Copyright Laws around the World Hinder Research.
Science 378(6623), 951–953.

Fisher v Dillingham, 298 F. 145 (SDNY 1924).

Fisher, W. (2001). Theories of Intellectual Property. In Munzer, S. (Ed.), *New
Essays in the Legal and Political Theory of Property*. Cambridge University
Press, pp. 168–200.

Frosio, G. (2018). *Reconciling Copyright with Cumulative Creativity: The Third
Paradigm*. Edward Elgar Publishing.

Frosio, G. (2020). Sharing or Platform Urban Mobility? Propertization from Mass
to MaaS. In Finck, M., Lamping, M., Moscon, V., & Richter, H. (Eds), *Smart
Urban Mobility: Law, Regulation, and Policy*. Springer, pp. 163–189.

Frosio, G. (2022). Four Theories in Search of an A(I)uthor. In Abbott, R. (Ed.),
Research Handbook of Artificial Intelligence and Intellectual Property. Edward
Elgar Publishing, pp. 156–177.

Geiger, C. (2009). Copyright's Fundamental Rights Dimension at EU Level. In
Derclaye, E. (Ed.), *Research Handbook on the Future of EU Copyright*. Edward
Elgar Publishing.

Geiger, C. (2014). Challenges for the Enforcement of Copyright in the Online
World: Time for a New Approach. In Torremans, P. (Ed.), *Research Handbook on
the Cross-Border Enforcement of Intellectual Property*. Edward Elgar Publishing.

Geiger, C., Frosio, G., & Bulayenko, O. (2018). Text and Data Mining in the
Proposed Copyright Reform: Making the EU Ready for an Age of Big Data?
International Review of Intellectual. Property and Competition Law 49(7), 814–844.

Geiger, C., Frosio, G., & Bulayenko, O. (2019). Text and Data Mining: Articles 3
and 4 of the Directive 2019/790/EU. In Saiz García, C., & Evangelio Llorca, R.
(Eds), *Propiedad intelectual y mercado único digital europeo*. Tirant lo blanch.

Gerber, O. (2019). Artificial Intelligence and Machine Learning. Background
Paper. 50th EPRA Meeting, Athens. www.epra.org/attachments/athens-ple
nary-2-artificial-intelligence-machine-learning-background-paper

Gervais, D. (2019a). Improper Appropriation. *Lewis and Clark Law Review* 23(2),
600.

Gervais, D. (2019b). The Machine as Author. *Iowa Law Review* 105, 1.

Ginsburg, J. (2014). Fair Use for Free, or Permitted-but-Paid? *Berkeley Technology
Law Journal* 29, 1446.

Ginsburg, J. (2018). People Not Machines: Authorship and What It Means in the
Berne Convention. *International Review of Intellectual Property and Competition
Law* 49, 131.

Ginsburg, J., & Budiardjo, L. (2019). Authors and Machines. *Berkeley Technology
Law Journal* 34(2), 343.

Goldman, S. (2022, 26 July). Will OpenAI's DALL-E 2 Kill Creative Careers? *The
Machine: Making Sense of AI*. https://venturebeat.com/ai/openai-will-dall-e-
2-kill-creative-careers

Goodfellow, I. et al. (2014). Generative Adversarial Networks. arXiv: 1406. 2661.

Goodfellow, I., Bengio, Y., & Courville, A. (2016). *Deep Learning.* MIT Press.

Growcoot, M. (2022a, 28 November). AI Image Generator Stable Diffusion Releases Controversial New Version. *PetaPixel.* https://petapixel.com/2022/11/28/ai-image-generator-stable-diffusion-releases-controversial-new-version

Growcoot, M. (2022b, 21 December). Midjourney Founder Admits to Using a 'Hundred Million' Images without Consent. *PetaPixel.* https://petapixel.com/2022/12/21/midjourny-founder-admits-to-using-a-hundred-million-images-without-consent

Gury, F. (2019, 14 October). IP Horizon 5.0 Conference. *Twitter.* https://twitter.com/EU_IPO/status/1183694801071423489

Han, J., Kamber, M., & Pei, J. (2011). *Data Mining: Concept and Techniques.* Morgan Kaufmann.

Heikkilä, M. (2022, 16 September). This Artist Is Dominating AI-Generated art. And He's Not Happy about It. Greg Rutkowski Is a More Popular Prompt Than Picasso. *MIT Technology Review.* www.technologyreview.com/2022/09/16/1059598/this-artist-is-dominating-ai-generated-art-and-hes-not-happy-about-it

Hristov, K. (2017). Artificial Intelligence and the Copyright Dilemma. *IDEA: The Intellectual Property Law Review* 57, 431.

Hugenholtz, B. (2019). The New Copyright Directive: Text and Data Mining (Articles 3 and 4). *Kluwer Copyright Blog.* http://copyrightblog.kluweriplaw.com/2019/07/24/the-new-copyright-directive-text-and-data-mining-articles-3-and-4

Hugenholtz, B., & Quintais, J. P. (2021). Copyright and Artificial Creation: Does EU Copyright Law Protect AI-Assisted Output? *International Review of Intellectual Property and Competition Law* 52, 1190.

Hugenholtz, P. B. (1989). *Auteursrecht op informatie.* Kluwer.

Huson, G. (2019). I, Copyright. *Santa Clara High Technology Law Journal* 35, 54.

Johnston, R. (2022, 6 December). Comic Book Creators React to AI Artificial Intelligence Art Explosion. *Bleeding Cool.* https://bleedingcool.com/comics/comic-book-creators-react-to-ai-artificial-intelligence-art-explosion

ITU. (2018). Assessing the Economic Impact of Artificial Intelligence. International Telecommunications Union. www.itu.int/dms_pub/itu-s/opb/gen/S-GEN-ISSUEPAPER-2018-1-PDF-E.pdf

Kaminski, M. (2017). Authorship, Disrupted: AI Authors in Copyright and First Amendment Law. *UC Davis Law Review* 51, 589.

Kasap, A. (2019). Copyright and Creative Artificial Intelligence (AI) Systems: A Twenty-First Century Approach to Authorship of AI-Generated Works in the United States. *Wake Forest Intellectual Property Law Journal* 19(4), 335.

Knight, W. (2022, 13 July). When AI Makes Art, Humans Supply the Creative Spark. *Wired.* www.wired.com/story/when-ai-makes-art

Lemley, M., & Casey, B. (2021). Fair Learning. *Texas Law Review* 99(4), 743.

Leval, P. (1990). Toward a Fair Use Standard. *Harvard Law Review* 103, 1105.

Lewis, D. (2016, 28 March). An AI-Written Novella Almost Won a Literary Prize. *Smithsonian Magazine.* www.smithsonianmag.com/smart-news/ai-written-novella-almost-won-literary-prize-180958577

Lindsay v The Wrecked and Abandoned Vessel R.M.S. Titanic, 52 U.S.P.Q.2d 1609 (S.D.N.Y. 1999).

Liu, J. (2019). An Empirical Study of Transformative Use in Copyright Law. *Stanford Technology Law Review* 22, 163.

Lovrinovic, C., & Volland, H. (2019). The Future Impact of Artificial Intelligence on the Publishing Industry. Gould Finch and Frankfurter Buchmesse. https://bluesyemre.files.wordpress.com/2019/11/the-future-impact-of-artificial-intelligence-on-the-publishing-industry.pdf

McDonald, D., & Kelly U. (2012). The Value and Benefit of Text Mining to UK Further and Higher Education. Digital Infrastructure. *JISC*. http://bit.ly/jisc-textm

Mezei, P. (2020). From Leonardo to the Next Rembrandt: The Need for AI-Pessimism in the Age of Algorithms. *UFITA* 84(2), 390–429.

Mik, E. (2021). AI as Legal Person? In Hilty, R., & Kung-Chung, L. (Eds), *Artificial Intelligence and Intellectual Property*. Oxford University Press.

Milde, K. (1969). Can a Computer Be an 'Author' or an 'Inventor'? *Journal of the Patent Office Society* 51, 378.

Miller, A. (1993). Copyright Protection for Computer Programs, Databases, and Computer-Generated Works: Is Anything New Since CONTU? *Harvard Law Review* 106, 977.

Miller, A. (2019). *The Artist in the Machine: The World of AI-Powered Creativity*. MIT Press.

Naruto v David Slater, F.3d 418 (9th Cir., 2018).

New European Media. (2019). AI in Media and Creative Industries. arXiv: 1905.04175.

Newton, C. (2022, 10 June). How DALL-E Could Power a Creative Revolution. *The Verge*. www.theverge.com/23162454/openai-dall-e-image-generation-tool-creative-revolution

Nicholas, J. (2022, 9 June). DALL-E 2 Mini: What Exactly Is 'AI-Generated Art'? How Does It Work? Will It Replace Human Visual Artists? *The Guardian*. www.theguardian.com/culture/2022/jun/09/what-exactly-is-ai-generated-art-how-does-it-work-will-it-replace-human-visual-artists

OpenAI. (2021, 5 January). DALL-E: Creating Images from Text. *OpenAI Blog*. https://openai.com/blog/dall-e

Ottolia, A. (2017). *Big Data e Innovazione Computazionale*. Giappichelli.

Pagallo, U. (2018). Vital, Sophia, and Co.: The Quest for the Legal Personhood of Robots. *Information* 9(9), 230.

Palace, V. (2019). What if Artificial Intelligence Wrote This: Artificial Intelligence and Copyright Law. *Florida Law Review* 71(1), 217.

Payer Components South Africa Ltd v Bovic Gaskins [1995] 33 IPR 407.

Pfeiffer, A. (2018). Pfeiffer Report: Creativity and Technology in the Age of AI. www.pfeifferreport.com/wp-content/uploads/2018/10/Creativity-and-technology-in-the-age-of-AI.pdf

Piketty, T. (2017). *Capital in the Twenty-First Century*. Harvard University Press.

Pricewaterhouse Coopers. (2017). Sizing the Prize: PwC's Global Artificial Intelligence Study: Exploiting the AI Revolution. www.pwc.com/gx/en/issues/data-and-analytics/publications/artificial-intelligence-study.html

Quintais, J. P. (2017). Rethinking Normal Exploitation: Enabling Online Limitations in EU Copyright Law. *AMI* 6, 197–205.

Racter. (1984). *The Policeman's Beard Is Half Constructed: Computer Prose and Poetry by Racter: The First Book Ever Written by a Computer*. Warner Books.

Rahmatian, A. (2013). Originality in UK Copyright Law the Old 'Skill and Labour' Doctrine under Pressure. *IIC* 44, 4–34.

Ralston, W. (2005). Copyright in Computer-Composed Music: HAL Meets Handel. *Journal of the Copyright Society of the USA* 52, 281.

Ramalho, A. (2017). Will Robots Rule the (Artistic) World? A Proposed Model for the Legal Status of Creations by Artificial Intelligence Systems. *Journal of Internet Law* 21, 17–18.

Ritter, J., & Mayer, A. (2018). Regulating Data as Property: A New Construct for Moving Forward. *Duke Law and Technology Review* 16, 220.

Rosati, E. (2013). *Originality in EU Copyright: Full Harmonization through Case Law.* Edward Elgar Publishing.

Rosati, E. (2019). Copyright as an Obstacle or an Enabler? A European Perspective on Text and Data Mining and Its Role in the Development of AI Creativity. *Asia Pacific Law Review* 27, 198–217.

Saha, S. (2023, 27 January). Google Unveils MusicLM, A Music DALL-E. *AIM.* https://analyticsindiamag.com/google-unveils-musiclm-a-music-dall-e/?utm_so urce=rss&utm_medium=rss&utm_campaign=google-unveils-musiclm-a-music-dall-e

Samuelson, P. (1986). Allocating Ownership Rights in Computer-Generated Works. *University of Pittsburgh Law Review* 47(4), 1185, 1200–1205.

Samuelson, P. (1999). Privacy as Intellectual Property. *Stanford Law Review* 52, 1125.

Searle, J. (1984). *Minds, Brains and Science.* Cambridge University Press.

Selle v Gibb, 741 F.2d 896 (7th Cir. 1984).

Senftleben, M. (2022, 28 January). A Tax on Machines for the Purpose of Giving a Bounty to the Dethroned Human Author: Towards an AI Levy for the Substitution of Human Literary and Artistic Works. SSRN Research Paper No. 4123309. https://ssrn.com/abstract=4123309

Shenzhen Tencent v Yinxun, Nanshan District People's Court of Shenzhen, Guangdong Province [2019] No. 14010. https://mp.weixin.qq.com/s/jjv7aY T5wDBIdTVWXV6rdQ

Shynkarenka, V. (2022, 2 December). Don't Dismiss GPT-3/Stable Diffusion Use Cases if They Don't Work Right Away. *Vasili Shynkarenka Blog.* https:// vasilishynkarenka.com/dont-dismiss-ideas-for-gpt-3-stable-diffusion-use-cases-if-they-dont-work-right-away/

Simonite, T. (2022, 18 April). The Future of the Web Is Marketing Copy Generated by Algorithms. *WIRED.* www.wired.com/story/ai-generated-marketing-content

Solum, L. (1992). Legal Personhood for Artificial Intelligences. *North Carolina Law Review* 70, 1231.

Stamatoudi, I. (2016). Text and Data Mining. In Stamatoudi, I. (Ed.), *New Developments in EU and International Copyright Law.* Kluwer Law International.

Steinberg v Columbia Pictures Industries, Inc., 663 F. Supp. 706 (SDNY, 1987).

Strum B. et al. (2019). Artificial Intelligence and Music: Open Questions of Copyright Law and Engineering Praxis. *Arts* 8, 115–129.

Svedman, M. (2020). Artificial Creativity: A Case against Copyright for AI-Created Visual Work. *IP Theory* 9(1), 3.

Thompson, C. (2017, January). When Robots Take All of Our Jobs, Remember the Luddites. *Smithsonian Magazine.* www.smithsonianmag.com/innovation/ when-robots-take-jobs-remember-luddites-180961423

Three Boys Music v Michael Bolton, 212 F.3d 477 (9th Cir. 2000).

Toth, A. (2019). Algorithmic Copyright Enforcement and AI: Issues and Potential Solutions, through the Lens of Text and Data Mining. *Masaryk University Journal of Law and Technology* 13(2), 361–387.

Trade-Mark Cases, 100 U.S. 82 (1879).

Trapova, A., & Mezei, P. (2022). Robojournalism: A Copyright Study on the Use of Artificial Intelligence in the European News Industry. *GRUR International* 71(7), 589–602.

Triaille, J. P., De Meeûs D'argenteuil, J., & De Francquen, A. (2014). *Study of the Legal Framework of Text and Data Mining (TDM)*. European Commission. http://ec.europa.eu/internal_market/copyright/docs/studies/1403_study2_en.pdf

US Copyright Office. Compendium of U.S. Copyright Office Practices. 3rd edn. www.copyright.gov/comp3/comp-index.html

Weiss, S., Indurkhya, N., & Zhang, T. (2010). *Fundamentals of Predictive Text Mining, Texts in Computer Sciences*. Springer.

Wilkins, A. (2022, 15 November). How Will AIs That Generate Videos from Text Transform Media Online? *NewScientist*. www.newscientist.com/article/2346939-how-will-ais-that-generate-videos-from-text-transform-media-online

Wulff, A. (2019, 2 January). AI Is Incredibly Smart, but It Will Never Match Human Creativity. *TheNextWeb*. https://thenextweb.com/news/ai-is-incredibly-smart-but-it-will-never-match-human-creativity

Zimmerman, E. (2017). Machine Minds: Frontiers in Legal Personhood. *SSRN*. https://papers.ssrn.com/sol3/papers.cfm?abstract_id=2563965

13. The judicial system and the work of judges and lawyers in the application of law and sanctions assisted by AI
Karim Benyekhlef and Jie Zhu

INTRODUCTION

This is the best of times, or the worst of times; an age of wisdom or one of foolishness. In its pervasiveness and subtleties, the digital age raises wide-ranging challenges with lasting impacts on all aspects of society up to the work of our judiciary and legal professions. This is indeed a historical juncture where the evolving intricacies between society and technology are shifting the very foundations of our rule of law and established law practice. The ongoing revolution, experienced unwittingly yet irreversibly, may well be equal in magnitude to that memorable epoch from which Dickens derived his *Tale of Two Cities*.

But this will not be a tale within the confines of two cities, nor a work of (historical) fiction. It will instead be a realistic account of the evolving path of the law as we know it, and an audacious look into its foreseeable future. Legal professions are at a crossroads, with looming challenges ahead to the independence of the judiciary and securing due process of law against artificial intelligence (AI)-powered government abuse or interference. Emerging best practices may ultimately call for an in-depth reform of our evidentiary rules and concept of law.

GREAT EXPECTATIONS FROM AI: LEGAL PROFESSION AT A CROSSROADS

The gripping growth of AI research and applications does not take long to assert its pervasive influence over the dignity of law, encroaching upon the prerogatives of the legal profession and the sacrosanct precincts of the judiciary.

This vast and sprawling network of AI grip over the law as we know it can be apprehended through different lenses. One broad dividing line could be drawn between substantive and procedural law, a *summa division* that can roughly be equated to the contrast between software and hardware in computer science. The multitudinous challenges raised by AI-driven technologies to the traditional scope and conception of several of our fundamental rights, from e-privacy to e-reputation, have been widely discussed and hotly debated. Less so would be the extent to which some of our (anachronistic) ways to understanding the rule of law, practicing law, and holding trials are also being shaped by the advent of AI. Indeed, from a high-level (procedural) perspective, AI algorithms are on the way to transforming how our laws are made, constructed, and applied by providing AI-powered legal work (1) as means of proof, evidence analytics (2) to assist in case law analysis, and judicial analytics (3) investigating the courts' behavior itself.

AI-Powered Legal Work

The expression "machine learning evidence" – as some scholars (Nutter, 2019) use it – refers to any AI-assisted method used as a means to prove a fact asserted or merely to raise reasonable suspicion for further investigation. Robertson et al. (2020) distinguish between algorithmic surveillance technologies and predictive policing algorithms, to which we may add the targeted cross-analytics of aggregate data:

- Algorithmic surveillance technologies such as facial recognition (e.g. Clearview AI), automated license plate readers, and social media/network analytics, to assist crime investigators in identifying possible suspected individuals, vehicles, or behavioral patterns/relationships (e.g. gang membership or organized crime).
- Predictive policing algorithms (e.g. Predpol, Hunchlab, Civicscape, Patternizr) sifting through existing police records in order to discover patterns of criminal activity and predict crime hotspots that may warrant focused police patrolling.
- Targeted cross-analytics of digital (aggregate) data to detect cybercrimes (e.g. juvenile pornography), monitor traces of suspicious activity (e.g. proceeds of crime, money laundering, terrorist financing), backtrack the locations, movements, and even states of mind (e.g. fitness trackers, driver drowsiness detection systems) of victims and their alleged perpetrators.

AI enhances as well the accuracy and testing possibilities of specialized fields of expertise. In forensic DNA testing, AI enables the processing of "low level, degraded, or otherwise unviable DNA evidence that could not have been used previously" (Rigano, 2019, p. 5). In ballistics, AI and digital 3D models refine the non-invasive tracking of bullets' path so as to reveal critical information about the circumstances of a shooting such as the weapon used, the relative positioning of the victim to their shooter, and the shooter's bodily characteristics (Bain & Bassed, 2019). Other arenas of interest include accident reconstruction (Yilmaz et al., 2016), psychiatric diagnoses (Ćosić et al., 2020), forensic anthropology, and *postmortem* and substance identification (Dobay et al., 2020; Faisal & Khan, 2021; Takano et al., 2019).With the complex and analytic capabilities of AI, not only the evidence-gathering process is expedited by technologies, but also the automated analysis of complex or fragmented pieces of evidentiary value (Costantini et al., 2019).

These significant contributions of AI-powered tools to investigative power do not however account for the full extent of AI involvement in our evidentiary process. As an increasingly huge amount of information is directly generated, stored, updated, and processed in various electronic formats, our whole evidentiary process and discovery procedures may have to be revisited so as to not only facilitate, but also require the mandatory production of evidence via electronic means (e.g. intercepted communications, video/audio recording, web page extracts, electronic accounting registers). This is an area to watch in the future as the COVID-19 pandemic has drastically increased – and, to a large extent, encouraged – the use of video conferencing at trials, the virtual commissioning of affidavits, electronic witnessing, as well as remote hearing orders (Matyas et al., 2022).

As scholars challenge the continued relevance of the concept of "original records" in the digital environment (Duranti et al., 2010; Paciocco, 2013), the time will come when submitting the paper originals no longer complies with the "best evidence" rule. There may come a time when the "best evidence" rule would no longer equate with "unaltered" paper originals, but even require their being replicated on computers (Leonetti & Bailenson, 2010; Paciocco, 2013). Apart from the fact that voluminous documentation does not lend itself to superficial reviews through naked eyes, the best documentary and material evidence may have to be not only readable, but easily processable and the most informative (i.e. metadata, links to other documents, calculation formulas) as to its creation, chain of authorship, history, and successive manipulations.

In a futuristic mindset, it is not preposterous to envision whole trials taking place in an immersive virtual environment (IVE) through which technologies "recreate" to the juries the whole perceptual experience leading to the case at trial (Leonetti & Bailenson, 2010). The dividing line between true IVEs and computer animations is the ability to generate a cognitive feeling of embodiment and the potential to produce body ownership illusion (Bunker, 2019), as the result of which the distinction between actors and spectators becomes blurred. As the use of demonstrative evidence with limited immersive capabilities as well as several studies on mock trials have been reported across the United States (US) (Bunker, 2019), would it not be a better and more vivid percipient testimonial than contradictory oral renderings of dimly (and selectively) remembered past events?

As we will see later, whilst existing literature centers upon the prejudicial effects of data-driven policing on replicating social discrimination patterns and historical disadvantages, the advent of AI-powered trials as an invitation to adapt some of our key evidence rules has attracted comparatively less attention. One thing is certain: AI-powered evidence provides more than (incremental) assistance to e-crime investigation; instead, its far-reaching influence may indeed expedite the reform of our whole evidentiary process.

Legal Analytics

After the evidentiary stage, applying the proven facts to the applicable law is within the exclusive expertise of courts and attorneys. Up until recently.

When it comes to decision-making, AI leaps easily from the boundaries of evidence remodeling to legal analytics. Through the lens of data-fueled technologies, case law is but a collection of past data generated by courts, litigants, and counsels. From assessing the probative value of a particular piece of evidence, it does not take much for AI to include "legal" components in the course of data processing, be it applicable law, relevant jurisprudence, or commentaries.

In this respect, McGill and Salyzyn (2021) distinguish descriptive from predictive and prescriptive analytics on a spectrum of increased restrictions and pressure over the decision-making process of judges and the legal expertise of attorneys.

Descriptive analytics merely organizes and explains available data. Applied to the legal field, AI can help "automatically generate case law classification by practice area for decisions" (Law Society of Saskatchewan, 2021), or "automatically providing information useful to law professionals from … case reports" (Galgani & Hoffmann, 2010, p. 446). Furthermore, the added value that AI-assisted tools bring to documentary management can be of notable assistance in sorting out voluminous court records, managing case history, and facilitating litigants' exchanges of documentary evidence during the pretrial process (Reiling, 2020). Contract review, the drafting of routine documents, and regulatory watch are among other common applications of descriptive analytics in the legal practice (Campbell, 2020; Osbeck, 2018–2019).

Predictive or outcome analytics goes one step further. It not only uses history or existing data to understand the past, but aims at predicting the most likely outcome of a particular case from existing jurisprudence and known facts. In a sense, this is what litigators have been doing since the dawn of time: "Lawyers and judges generally are engaged in seeking to apply the principles or analogies of cases, statutes, and regulations to new situations" (Loevinger, 1963, p. 5; see also Osbeck, 2018–2019). Outcome prediction is crucial in legal practice, whether to advise clients about their proper course of action and the likely odds of success, to assist them in making settlement decisions, or to assess the likelihood of potential litigation. What about the application of scientific methods and statistical modeling to legal datasets? Since "Jurisprudence is primarily an undertaking of rationalism" (Loevinger, 1963, p. 8), legal reasoning should not be immune to scientific testing for consistency and statistical analysis (Nagel, 1965; see also Lawlor, 1963). This reminds us of those visionary words from American Justice Holmes as early as 1897: "For the rational study of the law the blackletter man may be the man of the present, but the man of the future is the man of statistics and the master of economics" (Holmes, 1897, pp. 11–12).

In Europe and elsewhere, several studies have highlighted the potential of AI-fueled predictive analytics in the legal domain. Aletras et al. (2016) define the task of predicting the outcomes of court cases as one of binary classification (applications granted versus denied). Applying a linear kernel to their support vector machine (SVM) model, an average accuracy of 79 percent has been reported as to automatically predicting the rulings rendered by the European Court of Human Rights, with the "facts" section of the cases being the best predictor. Those results are partially replicated by Medvedeva et al. (2020), using once again a SVM linear classifier to sort out whether there is any particular violation of the European Convention on Human Rights (ECHR) based on a textual analysis of the European Court of Human Rights' publicly available data. Medvedeva et al.'s model achieves an average accuracy of 75 percent, with a wide variability across different articles of the ECHR. Articles that encompass a large range of differing issues and circumstances (e.g. right to privacy, freedom of expression) may have a lower accuracy score than others of lesser scope (see also O'Sullivan & Beel, 2019). Compellingly, the data show that the names of the different judges are amongst the top outcome predictors for violations of Articles 13 (right to an effective remedy) and 14 (prohibition of discrimination) of the ECHR. Even higher performance (average accuracy of 90 percent and higher) has been reached "with relatively small data sets derived from well-structured court rulings" of the Turkish Constitutional Court (FatihSert et al., 2021), the French Supreme Court (Şulea et al., 2017), and the Brazilian Labor Court (Barros et al., 2018). Using a time-evolving random forest classifier, Katz et al. (2017) have been able to predict, with an average accuracy of 70.2 percent, the outcomes of over 28,000 US Supreme Court cases over nearly two centuries (1816–2015). In India, the SVM algorithm developed by Bhilare et al. (2019) reached the best accuracy of 78 percent – compared to other predictive models having being tested – with data collected from various legal Indian judicial sites. Comparative experiments with different machine-learning models (k-nearest, logistic regression, bagging, naïve Bayes, random forest, and SVM) show that the SVM outperforms the others across all metrics (Bhilare et al., 2019; Liu & Chen, 2017).

Despite laudable efforts, these seemingly encouraging results are nuanced. The above-mentioned algorithms do not so much predict the outcomes of future cases as simply learn to read through already published judgments up to the "conclusion" section, and then "infer" what the conclusion likely is. More fundamentally, the judicial arena warrants more than a yes–no answer. In the Canadian context, for instance, the balancing test requires not only proof of an established violation to a fundamental right or liberty interest guaranteed under the Constitution. An established violation can still be "demonstrably justified in a free and democratic society" (*Canadian Charter of Rights and Freedom*, s. 1). Only an unjustified violation may attract constitutional remedies over a wide specter ranging from an outright declaration of invalidity to temporary suspension thereof, including individual exemption in appropriate cases (Roach, 2013).

Furthermore, to the extent that these tools focus on replicating past patterns and behaviors, the artificially induced "Nietzschean" recurrence of the same bears the risk of fixating our constitutional living tree on a fossilized past, thus uncoupling our legal norms from changing social needs, circumstances, and values. Hence, according to AI-constructed "once prohibited, always prohibited" constitutional norms, (medically supervised) assistance suicide would never pass constitutional muster; our law will forever be hostile to same-sex marriage, and the concept of paternity leave/benefits – as opposed to its maternal equivalent – would never have been born.

That being said, aside from "trickier" socio-political issues or any others touching upon the "spirit of the time," there is unquestionably room for developing AI-driven analytic tools that can help facilitate the resolution of certain kinds of relatively low monetary disputes subject to statutory thresholds, where the applicable law is clear and straightforward. On March 29, 2020, the French government officially sanctioned the automated processing of litigants' personal data in order to train an algorithm (DataJust) to be used:

- in developing an indicative benchmark for bodily injury compensation;
- in assisting future litigants in the assessment of amounts claimed; and
- in informing judges called upon to rule on future bodily injury cases.[1]

This initiative, however, did not work out as planned due to incomplete datasets,[2] as well as the inherent complexity of the substantive law outlining differential compensation for bodily injury sustained in different contexts and fora.[3]

Elsewhere, the development has already prompted the rise of online dispute resolution tools assisted by AI to help inform prospective litigants on their rights and obligations, foster out-of-court settlements in low-intensity conflicts or routine cases (Benyekhlef & Zhu, 2018; Campbell, 2020; Lodder & Thiessen, 2003, Reiling, 2020), and augment our general trial intelligence (Vermeys & Acevedo Lanas, 2020).

Prescriptive analytics, on the other hand, involves more than predictions. It leaps from a mere description of the world as it is or will be to a normative level, as to how the world should be. We may grow accustomed to automated product/service recommendations; but what about the use of algorithmic tools thought to recommend a particular outcome in judicial settings based on established jurisprudence? Somehow such use of algorithmic prescriptive tools predates predictive legal analytics as we know it, as they have been widely used across US criminal jurisdictions since the mid-1990s to assess recidivism risk in pretrial custody, bail decision-making, and sentencing (Kehl et al., 2017). Despite occasional skepticism (Dressel & Farid, 2018) and public outcry (Angwin et al., 2016), algorithms do outperform humans in certain conditions (Lin et al., 2020), just as statistical (non-algorithmic) models surpass our clinical judgments in predicting a range of outcomes (Ægisdóttir et al., 2006),

---

[1]   France, Décret no 2020–356 du 27 mars 2020 portant création d'un traitement automatisé de données à caractère personnel dénommé, DataJust, J.O.R.F. no 0077 du 29 mars 2020.

[2]   Emile Marzolf, Exclusif: le ministère de la Justice renonce à son algorithme DataJust, *Acteurspublics*, January 14, 2022, https://acteurspublics.fr/articles/excl usif-le-ministere-de-la-justice-renonce-a-son-algorithme-datajust

[3]   Olivia Dufour interviewing Aurélie Coviaux, DataJust: "Plutôt que de faire de la justice prédictive, il faut engager une démarche d'indexation et de tri des décisions," *Actu-Juridique.fr*, January 27, 2022, www.actu-juridique.fr/civil/ responsabilite-civile/datajust-plutot-que-de-faire-de-la-justice-predictive-il-faut-engager-une-demarche-dindexation-et-de-tri-des-decisions/

including the prediction of violence (Hilton et al., 2006). Of particular note is that prescriptive legal analytics concerns not only the applicable law, but also applies the relevant facts (e.g. known risk factors) to the case at bar, subject to algorithmically driven discriminatory biases. This will be discussed in the next section.

Judicial Analytics

From what the facts are (machine-learning evidence) to what the law should be (legal analytics), AI may as well tell us what the judges would and must do. Indeed, judicial outcomes may be predicted either from "case-specific legal factors" such as the applicable law and the evidence tendered, or "extra-legal factors" ranging from the ideological preferences of individual judges to the dominant ideologies of the time (Shaikh et al., 2020). Whilst legal analytics based on "case-specific legal factors" has been relatively well received and remains for the most part unregulated, judiciaries and legal scholars have been experiencing some uneasiness in the prospect of their being subject to empirical analyses. This disfavor is best evidenced by the French ban, upon penalty of fine and imprisonment, on so-called judicial analytics, namely, the reusing of identity data from magistrates and members of the court registry in order to assess, analyze, and compare their actual or supposed professional practices.[4] That being said, as courts and attorneys are (generally) well versed in the analysis and weighing of known legal factors, the input of AI-fueled data-driven analytics can be the most valuable as a sociological discovery uncovering the relevance and interconnection of factors *a priori* extraneous to the applicable law itself (Chen, 2019), be it political allegiances and other idiosyncrasies of the decision-makers, litigants' (socio-economic) status, the identity of attorneys, systemic court delays, as well as non-doctrinal principles or "fact pressures" of cases (Llewellyn, 1931, p. 1243), i.e. every other fact circumstance that may influence the outcome of a case (e.g. media coverage, political pressure, costs of litigation). Again, this is not all foreign to common lawyerly experience nor to ingrained socio-political interests: beyond word-of-mouth gossip, empirical qualitative and quantitative studies abound on the effects of diverse trial participants' attributes (e.g. race, gender, political beliefs) and environmental constraints on court decisions (Barry, 2021; Boldt et al., 2021; Capurso, 1998; Posner, 2008; Songer & Johnson, 2007) and jury perception / decision-making

---

[4] France, Loi no 2019–222 du 23 mars 2019 de programmation 2018–2022 et de réforme pour la justice (1), s. 33.

(Hunt, 2015; Nelson, 2004). Hence, there is nothing inherently revolutionary in considering "extra-legal factors" that may intervene in any decision-making processes. The only thing really new is the same extralegal factors being subject to algorithmic filtering and data-driven analytics.

Potential Game Changers in Legal Practice

In practice there is much overlap between descriptive, predictive, and prescriptive analytics. Although some scholars tend to consider judicial analytics as "a sub-category of legal analytics" (McGill & Salyzyn, 2021, p. 255), legal analytics may encroach upon judicial analytics – some would say necessarily; neither would judicial analytics blindly ignore the state of applicable law and existing jurisprudence.

In all of its manifestations, AI excels in what human experts can't do, namely, the computing and analysis of vast amounts of "complex, potentially disparate, data in a realistic time frame" (Mitchell, 2010, p. 35).

From our cursory overview of the different encounters between AI and law, AI does seem to hold great promises to help improve the quality of evidence, the predictability of the application of the law and the consistency of court decisions, and the efficiency of (administrative) justice (Chohlas-Wood, 2020; Citron, 2008; Coglianese & Lehr, 2017).

AI has the uncanny ability to turn bulk data into meaningful information. Applied to the legal search, it provides a fine-grained pattern of the case law history and trends. As one Ontario judge noted:

> The reality is that computer-assisted legal research is a necessity for the contemporary practice of law and computer assisted legal research is here to stay with further advances in artificial intelligence to be anticipated and to be encouraged. Properly done, computer assisted legal research provides a more comprehensive and more accurate answer to a legal question in shorter time than the conventional research methodologies, which, however, also remain useful and valuable. (*Drummond v. The Cadillac Fairview Corp, Ltd.*, 2018, para. 10)

Besides up-to-date state of the law, judicial analytics sheds additional (quantitative) insight on the work of judges and court decision-making processes. As the analytics' focus turns from legal data to legal professionals and the judiciary, some would (at first) evince suspicion and even outrage. Mindful, however, of the judges' preferences, tendencies, and personalities that are being passed among lawyers by word of mouth for a very long time, a more structured review of those tendencies, personality traits, and overlooked individual biases may indeed increase transparency on judicial reasoning and help address systemic discrimination. Due to the insidious nature of systemic discrimination, algorithmic screening can elicit unconscious (individual) biases or institutional disadvantages against minorities and historically disadvantaged groups. One is quick to remember the failures of the COMPAS recidivism algorithm that is "biased against blacks" (Angwin et al., 2016). But way more serious would be to point out that the very risk factors recognized by current criminal justice and criminology literature may be biased against, among others, historically disadvantaged minorities (Eckhouse et al., 2019; Miller et al., 2021; Rogers, 2000). Since algorithms perform relatively well at modelling our (biased) impressionistic past in an (unbiased) quantitative manner, we should harness this potential and learn from the warning it gives as well as the insights it offers. McGill and Salyzyn (2021) go so far as to argue for an increased use of automated decision-making tools due to "emerging concerns about human fallibility" (p. 269).

Since long before the advent of AI, "Outcome prediction has always been a vital part of practising law" (Osbeck, 2018–2019, p. 101). Whilst it may be said that the "oracles of the law" (Holmes, 1897, p. 1) can now be pretty much taken up by AI, we should be mindful of our current AI hype being premised upon the illusory prospect of formalizing the whole of our legal reasoning and of filtering the intricacies of our law through the objective crucible of logical computations. Most of the promises revolve around providing for more powerful research and analytics tools, which do not equate to nor displace human scrutiny in the study and application of law. Human critics remain essential to carve out the allowable limits of algorithmic analyses.

Holmes' words from more than a century ago (*supra*) ought not be constructed out of context. His consequential approach on the study of law as "The prophecies of what the courts will do in fact" (Holmes, 1897, p. 4) was aimed at dissociating the practice of law from axiomatic morals, on the one hand, and pure rules of logic, on the other. "Statistics," in Holmes' view, meant more than a collection of quantitative measurements or metrics that would inevitably drive from cause A to effect B.

Rather, our "predictive" practice of law calls for a weighing of competing public policies, social imperatives not always apparent in the blackletter of published judgments, and (re)consideration of inarticulate grounds of public policy. Even though our legal systems place emphasis on judicial precedents, there is more to adjudication than consistency alone. The development of our (case) law does not follow incremental steps over a predictable linear path, but instead is driven by as many quantum leaps as called for in light of societal changes, technological innovation, politico-economic imperatives, precedent over-ruling, and law reforms. Where uncertain "foggy" data and non-quantifiable values leave room for discretionary judgments, AI would not help; nor are we ready to prefer simplified policy over a more nuanced approach (Citron, 2008), or foster standardized justice "at equitable justice's expense" (Re & Solow-Niederman, 2019, p. 246).

That being said, there remains a subset of questions that can be efficiently handled by AI-driven analytic tools. Whenever there is no "policy question" involved, that the applicable law is non-discretionary (e.g. standard calculations or minimum fines), and the relevant facts undisputed, AI-driven analytics and settlement tools can definitely help in reducing court backlogs, unnecessary legal costs, and delays (UK Civil Justice Council, 2015). This category would include a broad array of consumer protection frequently asked questions, residential tenancy disputes, joint divorce applications and alimony calculation, even traffic and parking tickets.

LOOMING CHALLENGES: LEGAL PROFESSION UNDER (ALGORITHMIC) SCRUTINY

Overall, the broadening use of AI raises two key challenges on the judiciary and the practice of the legal profession: the need to preserve judicial/attorney independence from AI processing (1) and to secure due process in the digital age (2).

Concerns over Preserving Judicial and Attorney Independence from AI Processing

We may welcome the advent of AI in judicial settings as a kind of percipient machine testimony enhancing the accuracy of the fact-finding process (Roth, 2017; Sites, 2018), or akin to (novel) expert evidence (Nutter, 2019). As amply demonstrated throughout our subsection "AI-Powered Legal Work," AI-generated data are gradually replacing human experts in their primary function of providing independent professional analysis and technical opinion to assist courts in the decision-making process (Costantini et al., 2019).

Envisioning AI evidence as a subcategory of expert evidence serves as a useful reminder to more familiar legal principles. As we reframe the inquiry as referring to the limits of expert evidence, the stakes are becoming clearer. So far, Canadian courts have been cautious to ensure that, as a general rule, no opinion (expert) evidence should touch upon the ultimate issue on trial, be it a finding of fact or the interpretation of the applicable law. In either case, expert (opinion) evidence is admissible on an *a priori* exceptional basis, on matters requiring specialized knowledge which go beyond the ordinary (legal) experience of the judge or jury.

Indeed, courts have been careful not to allow experts to "swallow whole the fact-finding function of the court" (*R. v. Abbey*, 2009, para. 71). There might be practical difficulties though in determining what constitutes an ultimate issue of which opinions and inferences can only be drawn by the judge or jury. The distinction becomes even trickier between inadmissible testimony on the "ultimate issue" per se and the failure to consider all relevant (and more accurate) evidence that would be material to the "ultimate issue." Concerns eventually boil down to the necessity of preserving the courts' gatekeeper function in assessing both the admissibility and the probative value of any (expert) evidence tendered. This gatekeeper function, which calls for "vigilance and healthy skepticism" (Goudge, 2008, p. 470), means for the courts to retain a (residual) discretion in considering all relevant evidence and not being bound by any particular expert/scientific/technological evidence or lay testimonies, and this, regardless of their reliability. Indeed:

- There may be a distinctive line to be drawn between what professionals consider they should do in a specific set of circumstances and what the duty of care should be in a negligence case.
- Algorithms may inform courts and litigants of the statistical distribution of the damage amounts that have been awarded in like cases. However, in deciding the "ultimate issue" of the amount to be awarded in the specific case at trial, the judge may take the average statistical distribution into account while also factoring in any other relevant considerations.
- Even DNA evidence, which well outperforms other evidence types in terms of accuracy, consistency, and individual characterization (Toncic & Silva, 2021), does not bind the courts as the latter may disregard it should it be established that the testing process had not been carried out properly, that the tested sample had been contaminated or tampered with, or that a particular piece of DNA evidence had been obtained through illegal means.

Even where expert evidence may be more accurate than lay judgments, the court should retain a reflexive attitude (and power) to discard any piece of expert evidence due to methodological flaws, inferences drawn from incorrect, incomplete, selective, or insufficient data/fact assumptions, or for any reason extrinsic to the probative value of the evidence *per se* (e.g. evidence unnecessary or obtained via illegal means).This is in line with the results of at least one field study in Marcy County and two other criminal courts located in metropolitan areas on the east and west US coasts, where Cristin (2017) found that "most judges and prosecutors did not use the analytics, dashboards, and risk-assessments tools at their disposal" (p. 8).

Concerning questions of (domestic) law, even less deference is due to extrinsic interpretation or (legal) opinions. Domestic law is indeed pleaded by attorneys retained by both parties as law experts, and divergent interpretations resolved through (aggressive) arguments in light of relevant facts. This general prohibition of expert opinion on questions of (domestic) law (Baker, 1992; Sopinka et al., 2018) is premised upon such opinions being unnecessary and the proper function of our trial system (Van Ert, 2005, p. 41).

The advent of AI would be no different. Beyond AI evidence gathering and digital expert evidence, reliance on algorithmic case law processing may result in securing an AI monopoly over the core of courts' expertise, i.e. analyzing relevant case law and approaching similar factual scenarios in the same way.

Indeed, if a mature technology is used in every instance to help determine both the relevant facts and the applicable law, why would the judiciary still exist? What would an independent judiciary mean in a foreseeable future? Would it need to be specified, from now on, that the right to a fair trial entails the right to a human judge? And that our "right to counsel" would be meaningless should counselling be no longer one of human prerogative (e.g. chatbots, legal virtual assistants, and analytics)?

With the onset of immersive demonstrative evidence, the risk of those testimonial aids "swallowing whole the fact-finding function of the court" is imminent. This is more than an issue of fairness or prejudice (Jackson et al., 2017). What would jury/judge independence mean should they be allowed to "feel" and "relive through" the whole traumatic experience of the victim and the accused in a truly immersive virtual environment? When judges and juries become "emotionally involved" to the same extent as the litigants, there will no longer be impartial decision-making.

The right to an (institutionally) independent and impartial (human) judiciary relates to concerns about the undisputed authority that may be granted to the "mystique of science" (*R. v. Béland*, 1987, para. 20). To bend under the "mystique of science" is to stop asking questions in the long run, unconditionally deferring to algorithmic results and findings under the pretense of higher accuracy, even where the judge is fully competent in drawing a proper conclusion from the facts tendered and the applicable law.

To be sure, with AI-powered analytics, courts and litigants may gain an unusual and (hopefully) accurate account of possible unfamiliar aspects of our law and the multitudinous ways by which social facts come to merge and interact with formal rules. But as with any other expert evidence, the gatekeeper function of the judiciary should nonetheless be retained to the extent necessary to raise apposite questions, to doubt the relevance of the same factors being (un)evenly weighed in different contexts, and to take into account any extrinsic considerations to the technology *per se* (e.g. exclusion of evidence obtained through illegal means). It is to preserve this gatekeeper function of our judiciary and the transparency of the judicial decision-making process that calls for securing human-led due process in the digital era.

Concerns over Securing Digital/Technological Due Process

Once again, drawing from our experience with expert evidence in general provides apt comparison. In its leading *R. v. Béland* (1987) decision, the Supreme Court of Canada warned against the use of polygraph results which, in the guise of objective science, are nevertheless conveyed through the mouth of the (human) operator: "Human fallibility is therefore present as before, but now it may be said to be fortified with the mystique of science" (para. 20). The same applies to AI-fueled analytics: "Machine evidence and expert testimony are inextricably linked due to the fact that AI-generated data must be explained" (Gless, 2020, p. 239).

Indeed, the "mystique of science" can readily be translated into the well-discussed "black-box problems," referring to the intrinsic opacity of AI processing. There are basically two levels of what we would call "intrinsic" opacity in AI algorithms:

- the (aggregate) input data taken into account in the algorithmic processing; and
- the exact operative reasoning behind the algorithmic processing itself.

Added to these black-box problems are a number of extrinsic contributing factors, such as proprietary information protection (e.g. patents, copyrights, and trade secrets), strategic withholding of relevant information, or even deliberate deception.

Without transparency and a minimum of intelligibility, adjudication by algorithm fosters incomprehensibility, datafication, disillusionment, and alienation with respect to, and within, our legal systems (Re & Solow-Niederman, 2019). Without adequate safeguards, AI bears the risk of overriding our "due process of law" (US, 5th and 14th Amendments), "principles of fundamental justice" (*Canadian Charter*, s. 7), or "rights to an effective remedy and to a fair trial" (*Charter of Fundamental Rights of the European Union*, s. 47). All these formally distinct expressions encompass at their core two sets of (constitutional) guarantees against abuse of government power, unlawful public interference in citizens' private affairs, or for resisting authoritarian states (Schaaf, 2021). It includes, but is not limited to, the right to a fair trial. Procedural safeguards or protections are concerned with how the decision (to prosecute or to convict) is reached and, more generally, the duty to act in a procedurally fair manner whenever a person's rights, privileges, or interests would be adversely affected. Our doctrine of natural justice is premised upon a basic assumption: the end result of a decision is more likely to be fair both in the broader public's and individual litigants' view if:

- adequate procedural steps have been followed to make sure that all relevant and the most reliable information can be taken into account; and
- prosecutorial investigations and the conduct of trial have not been carried out in so egregious a manner as to seriously undermine public confidence in the administration of justice.

In this regard, it is noteworthy that most of our current procedural safeguards were devised in the medieval era when our whole trial experience centered on the oral (cross-)examination of (adverse) witnesses (Baker, 1992; Paciocco, 2013), requiring from the trier of fact a careful weighing of contradictory versions of events and their respective credibility assessment. Thus:

- the general exclusionary rule against hearsay in the common law tradition and its functionally equivalent mechanisms to ensure the reliability of statements being used in an inquisitorial fact-finding process;
- the defendant's constitutional right to cross-examine or confront adverse/incriminating witnesses;
- the defendant's constitutional right to counsel so as to be informed of their rights and obligations in light of known circumstances;
- the defendant's constitutional right to present their own version of events and to be heard by an independent and impartial tribunal; and
- the constitutional right to obtain a reasoned decision that adversely affects one's rights and obligations.

Of course, procedural fairness involves not only timely and adequate notice, but also a decision to be reached without undue delays and cumbersome procedures on a cost-benefit analysis. Justice delayed is justice denied, even amounting to an abuse of process. Should the higher accuracy and precision of algorithmic analytics or tracing bring guilty defendants to negotiate, settle, or plead guilty, in that sense justice may be better served by aggressive algorithmic policing than traditional "days in court." That being said, whilst the bulk of our procedural safeguards is still centered upon the prospects of a staged trial and set for securing our "day in court," this prospect is fading, and fading fast so as to create an inherent disconnect between our legal priorities and technical possibilities.

Securing technological due process is concerned not only with the end results but also methodology designs and algorithmic process. Even where an all-knowing AI would give accurate results for every query, those results would never be procedurally fair unless adequate reasons for understanding, and a timely opportunity for questioning and challenging such results, are also provided. Whilst some lay opinions would be seemingly content with securing an "all-knowing AI," substantive fairness in itself does not equate to being procedurally fair, nor may in any way justify infringements to procedural safeguards devised for the proper administration of justice.

Again, we may drive our insights from established principles drawn from general rules applicable to all expert evidence. As some scholars have pointed out, "Expert evidence may negatively impact the integrity of the trial process if excessive deference is shown to the opinion of the expert, thus undermining the promise of impartial adjudication" (Bubela, 2004, p. 856). Whilst this apprehension applies to all expert evidence, the issue turns out to be particularly challenging due to (unconscious) overreliance on algorithms and machine-learning engineers and the difficulty to prevent data manipulation by algorithms.

Algorithmic biases, where they exist, are mostly attributed to (already) biased, inaccurate, unrepresentative, or incomplete input and training data (Coglianese & Lehr, 2017; Silberg & Manyika, 2019) when applied to the particular outcomes of individual cases. Much less discussed is the extent to which established theories on recidivism and other social phenomena contribute to those biases. Not all biases are algorithmic-driven. Some of our institutional biases reside within our "human-led" systems irrespective of algorithmic designs and even without any analytical input from the algorithms themselves. Human judges and prosecutors themselves are not immune to stereotypes and prejudices against targeted categories of litigants (Carmichael & Pereira, 2019; Steffensmeier et al., 1998; Wooldredge et al., 2015). Conversely, the individual attributes of judges and litigants significantly impact the latter's perceptions of justice and individuals' willingness to seek state justice (Shestowsky, 2016). To be sure, even where adequately constrained by legal or institutional factors, human decision-making is not bias-proof. More importantly, though, even with its air of objectivity and lack of intentionality, algorithm processing would not provide a definitive answer to human bias.

Together, these challenges underscore the interwoven relationship between procedural safeguards and substantive fairness. As the extent of the protection granted to both aspects of the "due process of law" is contextual and fact-sensitive, they come together in the overarching concern of safeguarding the gatekeeping function of the courts, both on the fairness of the end results reached (e.g. screening of unreliable expert evidence) and the way justice is served in the digital age.

EMERGING BEST PRACTICES: LEGAL PROFESSION AT WORK

In response to the above-raised concerns, emerging best practice as collected by thinking groups and law commissions around the world are beginning to be implemented. In this respect, it is worth noting that the COVID-19 pandemic has triggered increased interest in the prospect of "automated justice" and spurred novel initiatives in the "ethics of AI."

The European Union relies on a risk-based approach to fostering trust in AI. The most recent European Commission Proposal (2021) distinguishes between "unacceptable risk," "high risk," and "low or minimal risk":

- Systems that create "unacceptable risk," whose use is deemed to violate fundamental rights and a breach of Union values, should be prohibited. These include the use by public authorities of systems that can either:
  - evaluate or classify the trustworthiness of natural persons over a certain period of time based on a social score that may lead to detrimental/unfavorable treatment in unrelated contexts or that is unjustified or disproportionate; or
  - identify biometric characteristics in real time and publicly accessible spaces for the purpose of law enforcement, "unless and in as far as such use is strictly necessary for" the targeted search of specific victims of crime (e.g. missing children) or the prevention of a "specific, substantial and imminent threat to the life or physical safety of natural persons or of a terrorist attack" (art. 5(1)(d)). Even then, the use of AI systems should be subject to competent judicial or administrative authorization.
- Systems that pose "high risk" to their users (art. 6), that is, the use of which may entail fundamental rights implications such as:
  - biometric identification and categorization of natural persons;

- ○ employment and access to essential services;
- ○ law enforcement, migration, and border control; and
- ○ administration of justice, i.e. "AI systems intended to assist a judicial authority in researching and interpreting facts and the law and in applying the law to a concrete set of facts" (Ann. III (8)).
- Systems that entail "low or minimal risk" when used for interacting with humans, to detect emotions or determine social categories based on biometric data, or to generate or manipulate content that "appreciably resembles" existing persons or real entities (e.g. deep fakes) (art. 52).

High-risk systems are subject to several compliance requirements for risk management purposes (art. 9), including data governance (art. 10), record-keeping (art. 12), transparency to users (art. 13), and conformity assessment (arts 43–48), as well as human oversight (art. 14) and ensuring result accuracy (art. 15). On the other hand, "low or minimal risk" systems have to make their use known to the targeted users, unless it is necessary "to detect, prevent, investigate and prosecute criminal offences" or for the legitimate pursuit of arts and sciences (art. 52).

The legal framework will be implemented on both the European Union and national levels, with the European Artificial Intelligence Board being tasked to insure a smooth cooperation between national supervisory authorities.

More specifically as to the use of AI in judicial systems, the European Commission for the Efficiency of Justice's Ethical Charter (2018) lists five core compliance principles: (1) of respect for fundamental rights; (2) of non-discrimination; (3) of quality and security; (4) of transparency, impartiality, and fairness; and (5) "under user control." Following a review of different uses of AI in European systems, the European Commission for the Efficiency of Justice classifies them on a spectrum from "uses to be encouraged," "possible uses, requiring considerable methodological precautions," "uses to be considered following additional scientific studies," to "uses to be considered with the most extreme reservations."

It remains to be seen how these safeguards are taken into account without leading to major delays in trials and legal dispute resolutions.

In Canada, the Law Commission of Ontario (2020) proposed a "mix model of AI and algorithmic regulation" specifically for the use of algorithmic recidivism risk assessments in the criminal justice system.[5]

---

[5] The use of AI and algorithms in the civil and administrative systems was addressed in a subsequent Law Commission of Ontario paper: www.lco-cdo. org/en/our-current-projects/ai-adm-and-the-justice-system/ai-and-adm-in-the-civil-administrative-justice-system/

The mix model requires input from both federal and provincial regulation, with special emphasis on the "oversight role of courts and due process protections" (p. 40). Algorithmic accountability, in the Law Commission's view, should include technological due process, algorithmic transparency, ethical design standards, appropriate public participation/scrutiny (e.g. cross-validation by independent data scientists) and data literacy, and criminal justice-specific disclosure regulations. Most importantly, the Law Commission concluded that "widely deploying algorithmic risk assessments in the Canadian justice system at this time would be a mistake" (p. 41), absent a proper risk and quality management mechanism.

Similar concerns are echoed in the US, where experts urge for the need to conduct fundamental research on the impact of (meta)data analytics on the protection and scope of constitutional rights, and to develop best practice for assessing data quality, retention, disclosure, and correction (Jackson et al., 2017). In view of the increasingly intertwined relationships between justice and technology, the US expert panel suggested the need to build a justice system expertise for addressing complex technical concerns, beginning with the use of supporting technologies to enhance the quality of witnesses' testimony recordings and to facilitate the presentation of evidence at trial (from PowerPoint presentations to immersive virtual experiences).

Indeed, all of the above proposals for furthering technological due process can be best assessed in light of their traditional counterparts in safeguarding both our procedural and substantive due process of law (see also Citron, 2008; Coglianese & Lehr, 2017; Gless, 2020; Roth, 2017; Sites, 2018). As decisive evidence is shifting from oral testimonies to machine evidence and testimony, the functional equivalence may be sketched as in Table 13.1.

For reasons stressed above, it is pertinent to grant the same procedural safeguards to both pretrial investigations and during trial (see also Roth, 2017). In devising these new procedural safeguards for a digital age, inspiration may be drawn from technical expertise and training requirements for the use of approved screeners and breathalyzers in drug-impaired driving investigations. Whilst AI can be used as a means of command by the state, we should also be mindful of the subtle control of law enforcement processes by the private tech sector (Re & Solow-Niederman, 2019).

Indeed, unlike any other expert evidence, the long-term interplay between judicial systems and technology will not be sporadic or exceptional. From our fascination with numbers to (automated) governance by numbers and statistical analyses (Desrosières, 2010; Supiot, 2017), the prospects are daunting. Indeed, concerns have been voiced that the

Table 13.1   Comparing traditional evidentiary rules to their digital equivalents

Traditional evidentiary rules	Digital evidentiary equivalents
Exclusionary rule against hearsay or unreliable depositions	Exclusionary rule against the use of untested/unaudited technologies
Right to cross-examine adverse (fact) witnesses	Right to cross-examine expert witnesses on the design, development, and monitoring of technologies used in furthering adverse claims
Right to timely disclosure of incriminating evidence	Right to accessing data on which the prosecution case is built
Right to counsel so as to be informed of one's rights and obligations in light of known circumstances	Right to attorney at law and necessary technical counselling so as to be informed of one's rights and obligations in light of predictive policing and algorithmic surveillance
Right to present one's own version of events and evidence	Right to retain (and afford) necessary technical expertise to challenge adverse claims, or to request a second independent opinion related to the matter at hand
Right to be heard by an independent and impartial tribunal	Right to a decision not entirely based on algorithmic processing
Right to a reasoned (intelligible) decision that adversely affects one's rights and obligations	Right to information and transparent disclosure as to the extent of any algorithmic tools used or relied on by the court in support of its decision-making process

intrusion of AI-empowered technology into the courtrooms and legal practices will over time become indistinguishable with the essence of the rule of law itself. Some have already hinted to the advent of "self-driving laws" (Casey & Niblett, 2016) that, beyond evidence-based legislation/policing/policy, would blur the boundaries between formal laws and social norms, smooth the path from reactive to prospective policing, while obviating the unnecessary involvement of the (human) enforcement authorities. The advent of self-enforceable and instantly updated micro-directives (Casey & Niblett, 2016; Eliot, 2020; Ma, 2020) heralds an impending "legal singularity" (Alarie, 2016; Bennett Moses, 2020) that we don't know will ever be reached in a horizon of decades. We do know though that so long as the gatekeeper function of the courts and the rule of law remain of human agency and oversight, our immersion into a digitally enhanced reality and intelligence-led policing will foster valuable experience, expertise, and insights into a path of law never trodden before.

CONCLUSION

As a tool, AI might serve as a double-edged sword. The proven efficiency of computing and AI analytics in certain areas does not prejudge its adequacy on other issues less amenable to computing or quantitative analyses. Whilst AI-fueled analytics and data processing enhance law enforcement policing and crime detection efficiency, it is worth stressing that efficiency is not *per se* a constitutionally entrenched value and it must yield to other constitutional imperatives and human right concerns. Algorithmic law has its downsides in perpetuating patterns of systemic discrimination and prejudices against (members of) historically disadvantaged communities. AI-powered legal and judicial analytics threaten to swallow the core of legal scholars' and courts' expertise in the application of law. Over time, human judges and attorneys may even lose their legal expertise in case law analysis and decision-making to a point of no return. While being mindful of this prospect, we should not otherwise lose sight of the potential of AI in strengthening our constitutional safeguards to the rule of law and due process. Indeed, AI might help elicit unconscious biases that may cloud individual judgments or structural discrimination embedded in apparently neutral institutional designs and bona fide requirements. At the end of the day, AI will ultimately become what we make it. Only by acknowledging the potential and limits of technology can we retain control in our human-driven society and acknowledge the gatekeeper function of our judiciary in intelligence-led fair trials. Considering AI as a (novel) form of expertise requiring continued oversight and monitoring, while balancing healthy skepticism and measured optimism, seems the best workable solution.

REFERENCES

Ægisdóttir, S., White, M.J., Spengler, P.M., Maugherman, A.S., Anderson, L.A., Cook, R.S., Nichols, C.N., Lampropoulos, G.K., Walker, B.S., Cohen, G., & Rush, J.D. (2006). The Meta-Analysis of Clinical Judgment Project: Fifty-Six Years of Accumulated Research on Clinical Versus Statistical Prediction. *The Counseling Psychologist*, *34*(3), 341–382.

Alarie, B. (2016). The Path of the Law: Towards Legal Singularity. *University of Toronto Law Journal*, *66*(4), 1–13.

Aletras, N., Tsarapatsanis, D., Preoţiuc-Pietro, D., & Lampos, V. (2016). Predicting Judicial Decisions of the European Court of Human Rights: A Natural Language Processing Perspective. *PeerJ Computer Science*, *2*, e93.

Angwin, J., Larson, J., Mattu, S., & Kirchner, L. (2016). Machine Bias: There's Software Used across the Country to Predict Future Criminals. And It's Biased against Blacks. *ProPublica*. www.propublica.org/article/machine-bias-risk-assessments-in-criminal-sentencing

Bain, C., & Bassed, R. (2019). *Bullet Points: AI Forging a Path for Better Forensic Medicine*. Monash University. https://lens.monash.edu/@medicine-health/2019/11/19/1378233/ai-forging-a-path-for-better-forensic-medicine

Baker, T. (1992). The Impropriety of Expert Witness Testimony on the Law. *University of Kansas Law Review*, *40*, 325–364.

Barros, R., Peres, A., Lorenzi, F., Wives, L.K., & da Silva Jaccottet, E.H. (2018). Case Law Analysis with Machine Learning in Brazilian Court. In Mouhoub, M., Sadaoui, S., Ait Mohamed, O., & Ali, M. (Eds), *Recent Trends and Future Technology in Applied Intelligence* (pp. 857–868). Springer.

Barry, B.M. (2021). *How Judges Judge: Empirical Insights into Judicial Decision-Making*. Routledge.

Bennett Moses, L. (2020). Not a Single Singularity. In Deakin, S., & Markou, C. (Eds), *Is Law Computable? Critical Perspectives on Law and Artificial Intelligence*. Hart Publishing.

Benyekhlef, K., & Zhu, J. (2018). Intelligence artificielle et justice: justice prédic-tive, conflits de basseint en sité et données massives. *Cahiers de propriété intel-lectuelle*, *30*(3), 789–826.

Bhilare, P., Parab, N., Soni, N., & Thakur, B. (2019). Predicting Outcome of Judicial Cases and Analysis Using Machine Learning. *International Research Journal of Engineering and Technology*, *6*(3), 326–330.

Boldt, E.D., Boyd, C.L., Carlos, R.F., & Baker, M.E. (2021). The Effects of Judge Race and Sex on Pretrial Detention Decisions. *Justice System Journal*. https://doi.org/10.1080/0098261X.2021.1881665

Bubela, T.M. (2004). Expert Evidence: The Ethical Responsibility of the Legal Profession. *Alberta Law Review*, *41*(4), 853–870.

Bunker, K. (2019). From Presentation to Presence: Immersive Virtual Environments and Unfair Prejudice in the Courtroom. *Southern California Law Review*, *92*(2), 411–440.

Campbell, R.W. (2020). Artificial Intelligence in the Courtroom: The Delivery of Justice in the Age of Machine Learning. *Colorado Technology Law Journal*, *18*(2), 323–350.

Capurso, T.J. (1998). How Judges Judge: Theories on Judicial Decision Making. *University of Baltimore Law Forum*, *29*(1), 5–15.

Carmichael, J.T., & Pereira, C. (2019). Gender Disparity in Sentencing. In Bernat, F.P., & Frailing, K. (Eds), *The Encyclopedia of Women and Crime*. John Wiley & Sons.

Casey, A., & Niblett, A. (2016). Self-Driving Laws. *University of Toronto Law Journal*, *66*, 429–442.

Chen, D.L. (2019). Judicial Analytics and the Great Transformation of American Law. *Artificial Intelligence and Law*, *27*, 15–42.

Chohlas-Wood, A. (2020). *Understanding Risk Assessment Instruments in Criminal*

Justice. Brookings Institution. www.brookings.edu/research/understanding-risk-assessment-instruments-in-criminal-justice/

Citron, D.K. (2008). Technological Due Process. *Washington University Law Review*, 85(6), 1249–1313.

Coglianese, C., & Lehr, D. (2017). Regulating by Robot: Administrative Decision Making in the Machine-Learning Era. *The Georgetown Law Journal*, 105, 1147–1223.

Ćosić, K., Popović, S., Marko Šarlija, M., Ivan Kesedžić, I., & Jovanovic, T. (2020). Artificial Intelligence in Prediction of Mental Health Disorders Induced by the COVID-19 Pandemic among Health Care Workers. *Croatian Medical Journal*, 61(3), 279–288.

Costantini, S., De Gasperis, G., & Olivieri, R. (2019). Digital Forensics and Investigations Meet Artificial Intelligence. *Annals of Mathematics and Artificial Intelligence*, 86, 193–229.

Cristin, A. (2017). Algorithms in Practice: Comparing Web Journalism and Criminal Justice. *Big Data & Society*, 1–14. https://doi.org/10.1177/205395171 7718855

Desrosières, A. (2010). *La politique des grands nombres. Histoire de la raison statistique*. La Découverte.

Dobay, A., Ford, J., Decker, S., Ampanozi, G., Franckenberg, S., Affolter, R., Sieberth, T., & Ebert, L.C. (2020). Potential Use of Deep Learning Techniques for Postmortem Imaging. *Forensic Science, Medicine and Pathology*, 16, 671–679.

Dressel, J., & Farid, H. (2018). The Accuracy, Fairness, and Limits of Predicting Recidivism. *Science Advances*, 4(1), eaao5580.

Drummond v. The Cadillac Fairview Corp. Ltd., 2018 ONSC 5350.

Duranti, L., Rogers, C.M., & Sheppard, A.F. (2010). Electronic Records and the Law of Evidence in Canada: The Uniform Electronic Evidence Act Twelve Years Later. *Archivaria*, 70, 95–124.

Eckhouse, L., Lum, K., Conti-Cook, C., & Ciccolini, J. (2019). Layers of Bias: A Unified Approach for Understanding Problems with Risk Assessment. *Criminal Justice and Behavior*, 46(2), 185–209.

Eliot, L. (2020). Robustness and Overcoming Brittleness of AI-Enabled Legal Micro-Directives: The Role of Autonomous Levels of AI Legal Reasoning. arXiv: 2009.02243.

European Commission. (2021). *Proposal for a Regulation of the European Parliament and of the Council Laying Down Harmonised Rules on Artificial Intelligence (Artificial Intelligence Act) and Amending Certain Union Legislative Acts*. COM/2021/206 final, 2021/0106(COD), Brussels. https://eur-lex.europa.eu/legal-content/EN/TXT/?qid=1623335154975&uri=CELEX%3A52021PC0206

European Commission for the Efficiency of Justice. (2018). *European Ethical Charter on the Use of Artificial Intelligence in Judicial Systems and Their Environment*. Strasbourg. https://rm.coe.int/ethical-charter-en-for-publication-4-december-2018/16808f699c

Faisal, E., & Khan, Z. (2021). Golden Machines of Tomorrow: A Look into Machine Learning. *Voices of Forensic Science*, 1(1), 281–292.

FatihSert, M., Yıldırım, E., & Haşlak, I. (2021). Using Artificial Intelligence to Predict Decisions of the Turkish Constitutional Court. *Social Science Computer Review*, 1, 20.

Galgani, F., & Hoffmann, A. (2010). LEXA: Towards Automatic Legal Citation

Classification. In Li, J. (Ed.), *AI 2010: Advances in Artificial Intelligence* (pp. 445–454). 23rd Australasian Joint Conference, Adelaide, December. Springer.

Gless, S. (2020). AI in the Courtroom: A Comparative Analysis of Machine Evidence in Criminal Trials. *Georgetown Journal of International Law, 51*(2), 195–253.

Goudge, S.T. (2008). The Role of the Court. *Inquiry into Pediatric Forensic Pathology in Ontario, Vol. 3: Policy and Recommendations*, pp. 470–513.

Hilton, N.Z., Harris, G.T., & Rice, M.E. (2006). Sixty-Six Years of Research on the Clinical versus Actuarial Prediction of Violence. *The Counseling Psychologist, 34*(3), 400–409.

Holmes, O.W., Jr. (1897). The Path of the Law. *Harvard Law Review, 10*, 457.

Hunt, J.S. (2015). Race, Ethnicity, and Culture in Jury Decision Making. *Annual Review of Law and Social Science, 11*, 269–288.

Jackson, B.A., Banks, D., Woods, D., & Dawson, J.C. (2017). *Future-Proofing Justice: Building a Research Agenda to Address the Effects of Technological Change on the Protection of Constitutional Rights*. RAND Corporation. https:// dx.doi.org/10.7249/RR1748

Katz, D.M., Bommarito II, M.J., & Blackman, J. (2017). A General Approach for Predicting the Behavior of the Supreme Court of the United States. *PLoS ONE, 12*(4), e0174698.

Kehl, D., Guo, P., & Kessler, S. (2017). *Algorithms in the Criminal Justice System: Assessing the Use of Risk Assessments in Sentencing*. Harvard Law School. http://nrs.harvard.edu/urn-3:HUL.InstRepos:33746041

Law Commission of Ontario. (2020). The Rise and Fall of AI and Algorithms in American Criminal Justice: Lessons for Canada, Toronto. www.lco-cdo.org/ wp-content/uploads/2020/10/Criminal-AI-Paper-Final-Oct-28-2020.pdf

Law Society of Saskatchewan. (2021). New AI Generated Subject Classification for Saskatchewan Case Law Is Live! www.lawsociety.sk.ca/canlii/new-ai-gener ated-subject-classification-for-saskatchewan-case-law-is-live/

Lawlor, R.C. (1963). What Computers Can Do: Analysis and Prediction of Judicial Decisions. *American Bar Association Journal, 49*(4), 337–344.

Leonetti, C., & Bailenson, J. (2010). High-Tech View: The Use of Immersive Virtual Environments in Jury Trials. *Marquette Law Review, 93*, 1073–1120.

Lin, Z.J., Jung, J., Goel, S., & Skeem, J. (2020). The Limits of Human Predictions of Recidivism. *Science Advances, 6*(7), eaaz0652.

Liu, Z., & Chen, H. (2017). A Predictive Performance Comparison of Machine Learning Models for Judicial Cases. *IEEE Symposium Series on Computational Intelligence*. https://dx.doi.org/10.1109/SSCI.2017.8285436

Llewellyn, K.N. (1931). Some Realism about Realism: Responding to Dean Pound. *Harvard Law Review, 44*(8), 1222–1264.

Lodder, A.R., & Thiessen, E.M. (2003). The Role of Artificial Intelligence in Online Dispute Resolution. *Proceedings of the UNECE Forum on ODR*. www. odr.info/unece2003

Loevinger, L. (1963). Jurimetrics: The Methodology of Legal Inquiry. *Law Contemporary Problems, 28*(1), 5–35.

Ma, M. (2020). The Law's New Language? *Harvard International Law Journal Frontiers, 61*, 1–9. https://harvardilj.org/wp-content/uploads/sites/15/Ma-PDF- format.pdf

Matyas, D., Wills, P., & Dewitt, B. (2022). Imagining Resilient Courts: From COVID-19 to the Future of Canada's Court System. *Can Public Policy, 48*(1), 186–208.

McGill, J., & Salyzyn, A. (2021). Judging by the Numbers: Judicial Analytics, the Justice System an Its Stakeholders. *Dalhousie Law Journal, 44*(1), 249–284.

Medvedeva, M., Vols, M., & Wieling, M. (2020). Using Machine Learning to Predict Decisions of the European Court of Human Rights. *Artificial Intelligence & Law, 28*, 237–266.

Miller, W.T., Campbell, C.A., Papp, J., & Ruhland, E. (2021). The Contribution of Static and Dynamic Factors to Recidivism Prediction for Black and White Youth Offenders. *International Journal of Offender Therapy and Comparative Criminology*, 1–17. https://doi.org/10.1177/0306624X211022673

Mitchell, F. (2010). The Use of Artificial Intelligence in Digital Forensics: An Introduction. *Digital Evidence and Electronic Signature Law Review, 7*, 35–41.

Nagel, S. (1965). Predicting Court Cases Quantitatively. *Michigan Law Review, 63*(8), 1411–1422.

Nelson, M.S. (2004). The Effect of Attorney Gender on Jury Perception and Decision-Making. *Law & Psychology Review, 28*, 177–193.

Nutter, P. W. (2019). Machine Learning Evidence: Admissibility and Weight. *University of Pennsylvania Journal of Constitutional Law, 21*(3), 919–958.

O'Sullivan, C., & Beel, J. (2019). Predicting the Outcome of Judicial Decisions Made by the European Court of Human Rights. In Curry, E., Keane, M., Ojo, A., & Salwala, D. (Eds), *27th AI Irish Conference on Artificial Intelligence and Cognitive Science* (pp. 272–283), Galway.

Osbeck, M.K. (2018–2019). Lawyer as Soothsayer: Exploring the Important Role of Outcome Prediction in the Practice of Law. *Penn State Law Review, 123*, 41–102.

Paciocco, D.M. (2013). Proof and Progress: Coping with the Law of Evidence in a Technological Age. *Canadian Journal of Law and Technology, 11*(2), 181–228.

Posner, R.A. (2008). *How Judges Think*. Harvard University Press.

R. v. Abbey, 2009 ONCA 624.

R. v. Béland, 1987 2 R.C.S. 398.

Re, R.M., & Solow-Niederman, A. (2019). Developing Artificially Intelligent Justice. *Stanford Technology Law Review, 22*(2), 242–289.

Reiling, A.D. (2020). Courts and Artificial Intelligence. *International Journal for Court Administration, 11*(2). https://doi.org/10.36745/ijca.343

Rigano, C. (2019). Using Artificial Intelligence to Address Criminal Justice Needs. *NIJ Journal*, 280. www.ojp.gov/pdffiles1/nij/252038.pdf

Roach, K.W. (2013). *Constitutional Remedies in Canada* (2nd ed.). Carswell.

Robertson, K., Khoo, C., & Song, Y. (2020). *A Human Rights Analysis of Algorithmic Policing in Canada*. University of Toronto's International Human Rights Program and Citizen Lab at the Munk School of Global Affairs and Public Policy. https://citizenlab.ca/wp-content/uploads/2020/09/To-Surveil-and-Predict.pdf

Rogers, R. (2000). The Uncritical Acceptance of Risk Assessment in Forensic Practice. *Law and Human Behavior, 24*, 595–605.

Roth, A. (2017). Machine Testimony. *Yale Law Journal, 126*, 1972–2053.

Schaaf, S.D. (2021). Contentious Politics in the Courthouse: Law as a Tool for Resisting Authoritarian States in the Middle East. *Law & Society Review, 55*(1), 139–176.

Shaikh, R.A., Sahu, T.P., & Anand, V. (2020). Predicting Outcomes of Legal Cases Based on Legal Factors Using Classifiers. *Procedia Computer Science, 167*, 2393–2402.

Shestowsky, D. (2016). How Litigants Evaluate the Characteristics of Legal Procedures: A Multi-Court Empirical Study. *UC Davis Law Review, 49*(3), 793–841.

Silberg, J., & Manyika, J. (2019). Notes from the AI Frontier: Tackling Bias in AI (and in Humans). *McKinsey Global Institute.* www.mckinsey.com/featured-insights/artificial-intelligence/tackling-bias-in-artificial-intelligence-and-in-humans

Sites, B. (2018). Machines Ascendant: Robots and the Rules of Evidence. *Georgetown Law Technology Review, 3*, 1–27.

Songer, D.R., & Johnson, S.W. (2007). Judicial Decision Making in the Supreme Court of Canada: Updating the Personal Attribute Model. *Canadian Journal of Political Science, 40*(4), 911–934.

Sopinka, J., Lederman, S.N., & Bryant, A.W. (2018). *The Law of Evidence in Canada* (5th ed.). LexisNexis.

Steffensmeier, D., Ulmer, J., & Kramer, J. (1998). The Interaction of Race, Gender, and Age Is Criminal Sentencing: The Punishment Cost of Being Young, Black, and Male. *Criminology, 36*(4), 763–798.

Şulea, O.-M., Zampieri, M., Malmasi, S., Vela, M., Dinu, L.P., & van Genabith, J. (2017). Exploring the Use of Text Classification in the Legal Domain. *Proceedings of 2nd Workshop on Automated Semantic Analysis of Information in Legal Texts*, London. arXiv: 1710.09306.

Supiot, A. (2017). *Governance by Numbers: The Making of a Legal Model of Allegiance* (S. Brown, Trans.). Hart Publishing.

Takano, H., Momota, Y., Ozaki, T., & Terada, K. (2019). Personal Identification from Dental Findings Using AI and Image Analysis against Great Disaster in Japan. *HSOA Journal of Forensic, Legal & Investigative Sciences.* https://doi.org/10.24966/FLIS-733X/100041

Toncic, V., & Silva, A. (2021). The Contamination and Misuse of DNA Evidence. *Voices of Forensic Science, 1*(1), 47–57.

UK Civil Justice Council. (2015). *Online Dispute Resolution for Low Value Civil Claims.* www.judiciary.uk/wp-content/uploads/2015/02/Online-Dispute-Resolution-Final-Web-Version1.pdf

Van Ert, G. (2005). The Admissibility of International Legal Evidence. *Canadian Bar Review, 84*(1), 31–46.

Vermeys, N., & Acevedo Lanas, M.-F. (2020). L'émergence et l'évolution des tribunaux virtuels au Canada – L'exemple de la Plateforme d'aide au règlement des litiges en ligne (PARLe). *Sorbonne Law Review, 1*, 22–51.

Wooldredge, J., Frank, J., Goulette, N., & Travis III, L. (2015). Is the Impact of Cumulative Disadvantage on Sentencing Greater for Black Defendants? *Criminology & Public Policy, 14*(2), 187–223.

Yilmaz, A.C., Aci, C., & Aydin, K. (2016). Traffic Accident Reconstruction and an Approach for Prediction of Fault Rates Using Artificial Neural Networks: A Case Study in Turkey. *Traffic Injury Prevention, 17*(6), 585–589.

14. AI and national security

Saiph Savage, Gabriela Avila, Norma Elva Chávez, and Martha Garcia-Murillo

INTRODUCTION

Rapid technological change in the twenty-first century brought important challenges to the national security policies of many countries.[1] Rich, technologically advanced countries have strong national security policies whose role is directly linked to the development of the country and its economy. In this chapter, we describe how artificial intelligence (AI) is expanding the traditional boundaries of national security and address how to handle threats and mitigate risk in the relationships between a country's interrelated economic and political actors and in those among governments. We discuss how AI is being implemented for the purpose of national security, particularly at the strategic, tactical, and operational levels, and we describe the types of results that AI is expected to bring and what can be anticipated in the future.

This chapter is structured as follows. We begin by providing a history of how technology came to be embedded in the military and the role it has played in national security. Next, we describe how AI is being used in various national security contexts and the key actors involved in the creation and development of military AI. We go on to discuss how to design AI for the military, highlighting some key factors to consider. In the process, we address the role that AI is playing in the power relationships among countries, covering a few of the national strategies that some countries have adopted. We finish by presenting an agenda for AI in the military and highlighting key areas that bear looking into. In the end, this chapter should foster a wider understanding of how emerging technologies, in particular AI, have a direct impact on national security, of whether regulation is needed, and of how the COVID-19 pandemic disrupted the process of AI adoption by the military.

As we take a deep dive into AI and national security, it is key to recognize that AI is a core component of the United States (U.S.) Army's

[1]   The work in this chapter was partially supported by NSF grant FW-HTF-19541. Special thanks to Alberto Navarrete for his input to this work.

modernization strategy (Lawless et al., 2021). Today, AI can be considered a critical, "game-changing" strategic technology for every army in the world. It is expected that increased machine speed and processing power, as a core component of the *intelligentization* of warfare, will help improve military planning, operational command, and decision making (Kania, 2019). AI and data science will be applied on a large scale to obtain strategic advantages for the world's militaries and their related domains.

HISTORY OF TECHNOLOGY IN THE MILITARY

The use of technology in the military can be highly consequential for countries and the world because many past technologies started with military applications. A famous modern example took place in 1942, when the German Army first used closed-circuit television, a very basic black-and-white system that observed missile tests in preparation for long-distance military attacks (Times of India, 2015). At the time, the world couldn't imagine that this experimental technology would eventually become available to almost anyone for entertainment purposes in their homes, delivering images in color with high definition, and then becoming a component in mobile phones.

Since the First World War, the technological developments that have served in combat have given rise to technologies later used regularly by almost all societies, with cellular networks, digital photos, microwaves, and weather forecasting as a few examples. In recent decades, with a computing capacity that has doubled at least every two years (Cross, 2016), we will gradually see the emergence of new AI technologies in our daily lives that have been used in military operations worldwide.

National Security Components and AI

The concept of national security has two main aspects. The first is related to *military forces*, which are concerned with a number of different factors, such as the relative strength of opponents and the degree to which a given type of force should be used or whether it should even be used at all. The second component is *national defense*, which is the ability of armed forces to defend the sovereignty of a nation and the lives of its people. Understanding the tasks entailed by national security is key to understanding what aspects of the process could be enhanced or automated by AI. In the armed forces, some such tasks include command, administration, training, intelligence, communication, protection, and sustainment (Goldfarb et al., 2022). To fail at any of these tasks can be catastrophic and risk the lives of many people. Therefore, for armed forces to integrate AI successfully into their tasks, they must ensure the quality of the data that goes into AI and the transparency of the algorithms that determine the machines' decisions. Transparency will help the human operators to make better decisions with the AI and the associated data. However, part of the problem is that too much transparency can also put the military operation in danger if it is compromised by enemies. Consequently, one of the challenges of introducing AI for national defense purposes stems from a highly risk-averse culture in the military, one that tends to limit the development of technology that lacks transparency (which makes it hard for humans in the military to make strategic decisions) and has uncertainty. The problem is that while these concerns can help reduce harm, they can also curtail the scientific competitiveness of a nation's homeland security (Congressional Research Service, 2020).

National Security Agencies and Skepticism towards AI

The idea of using AI draws skepticism from national security agencies because their decision-making processes need consistent, high-quality results and a detailed level of interpretive power. One reason for their concern is that the results seen from AI so far have not reached the level of trustworthiness that state agencies unilaterally need to manage the operational risks they face. Consequently, AI designed for national security requires a heavy emphasis on preparation, tradecraft, and other considerations that guarantee predictability and certainty of action (Stone, 2021). Such safeguards are needed to gain a competitive advantage when adopting AI products for national security purposes (Office of the Chief Scientist of the U.S. Air Force, 2015).

The effective integration of emerging AI technologies into the military calls for testing, evaluation, validation, and verification by the leadership of the organization (Flournoy et al., 2020). This is especially true because of the military's highly hierarchical structure. One has to consider that the high command will use technology in their decision making differently than lower-level soldiers, who use technology for tactical, not strategic, purposes.

Another reason AI is faced with skepticism is because its processes often occur in a "black box" (Bathaee, 2018), with no perceptible mechanism, explanation, or way to validate trustworthiness. This triggers further hesitation on the part of the military to adopt AI (several AI models, such as deep learning, have difficulty in being transparent about how the model made the decisions it did, or why certain outcomes took place). An example of this is IBM's Watson system for medical oncology, which was used by over five countries. The system recommended treatments for patients with cancer, but after the results were analyzed, problems were found that resulted in recommendations for incorrect treatments (Abdala, 2019). Cases like this raise concerns and provide evidence that the analyses produced by AI are questionable, so AI tools are likely to be set aside due to a lack of understanding of how the output is produced. Information validation and tracing the details of output production are top concerns in national security communities.

Key Players in the Development of Military AI

For the most part, AI technologies for national security have been commercially produced (Allen, 2020), which has given developers in the private sector the upper hand. The development of AI can be very important to industry; it can make a company a key player in national and international markets and a key actor in data collection and deployment capacity, to the extent that national security frameworks have included industry in threat and risk assessments. However, a problem arises from the fact that industry actors do not always understand the goals and operations of national defense strategies, which unlike those of industry require cooperation among actors from different sectors with widely differing objectives. Military decision making calls for an evaluation of information unlike that of industry; it has to consider political priorities, as well as ways to deploy technology productively and safely (Congressional Research Service, 2020).

Because of the prominent role that the private sector has played in the development of defense technologies, to deploy AI successfully, the military will have to establish strategic partnerships with the private sector (Allen & Chan, 2017) and develop an understanding of corporate culture and its operations and innovation processes in order to align resources and priorities (Stone, 2021), and the private sector will have to converge with government to handle the challenges they face.

The divergence of organizational cultures and interests in AI between the private sector and the military can create tensions. Traditionally, the military functions more hierarchically and more bureaucratically than the private sector. Moreover, commercial and military organizations usually work in totally different contexts. The armed forces have jobs that are more sporadic and follow the temporary nature of events, as wars occasionally break out, and objectives like "security" are harder to define than "profit" or "shareholder value." In contrast, the private sector has its own mechanisms, laws, and norms for conducting transactions, which differ from those governing the military (Goldfarb et al., 2022).

Such differences between private companies and the military have resulted in a lack of trust between them, and failures often result when technologies developed in a civilian environment are transferred to a secure and restricted environment in the military (Scharre, 2017). In sum, when thinking about the military AI, it is key to recognize the differences in the ways the technology is deployed in commercial and military settings.

Improving Industry and Military Collaborations

One way that researchers have found to address the cultural differences between AI developers in the private sector and those at national security agencies is through the introduction of risk management techniques. Risk management provides a range of options, such as mitigation, that involve the acceptance, avoidance, and transfer of risk. It provides greater flexibility and a more realistic response to the exponential nature of emerging technologies such as AI (Du Mont, 2019).

Another strategy that can improve collaboration between industry actors and the military is the joint creation of guidelines for what is expected of military AI. To date, the lack of international policies and treaties governing emerging technologies has guaranteed that the technologies that have been developed so far align solely with the priorities of the private sector. The benefits and limits of new AI developments must be discussed and publicized in international forums with the objective of establishing international agreement on guidelines like those outlined in the Vienna and Geneva Conventions on diplomatic and consular relations.

DESIGN GUIDELINES FOR MILITARY AI

When designing AI in a national security context, the main players need to consider that a country provides security for the state and its citizens based on national security policies. Such policies seek to integrate and coordinate all related actors in response to the interests and threats deemed most important from both the domestic and international perspectives. Policy experts in the field need to consider multiple issues, as well as current and future changes in national security (DCAF, 2005). A way to start thinking about national security policies is to categorize them by strategic, tactical, and operational levels, which means basing them on certain aspects of the decision-making process within military settings and on the types of information that are needed. Considering these levels in design should help to better target the goals and expectations of military AI.

Designing Military AI at the Strategic Level

At the strategic level, we need a comprehensive understanding of emerging technologies, of the workings of bureaucracies in civilian and security establishments, and of the operational culture inside the intelligence community. For a military organization in combat mode, the data that inform operations include information on geographical terrain, weather conditions, an enemy's operational capabilities and interactions with civil society, as well as information on friendly forces. In the strategic decision-making process, the impact of AI will depend upon the reliability, trustworthiness, and quality of the analysis, as well as on the ability of the designers to explain all the possible outcomes that AI can generate (Stone, 2021).

An example of how strategy is integrated with the use of AI in the military is seen in Israel (Ahronheim, 2021). The Israel Defense Forces created an AI-based system that collects, stores, and analyzes intelligence data, and its military uses the curated intelligence to strategically inform its operations. With this system, the Israel Defense Forces were able to identify and neutralize more targets faster and more precisely than in prior conflicts. Utilizing an extensive network of electronic sensors on board unmanned aerial vehicles along with F-35 multi-mission aircraft and ground-based and subterranean seismic monitors along the border, the Israel Defense Forces collected billions of signals and other intelligence points on both Hamas' and the Islamic Jihad Movement of Palestine's orders of battle, military infrastructure, and daily routines, a task aided by Israel's near-limitless control of the borders and skies surrounding Gaza (Jewish Institute for National Security of America, 2021).

Designing Military AI at the Tactical Level

At the tactical level, AI can assist with predictions regarding alternative courses of action in a situation before the point of execution. Information superiority is a key type of support that AI can afford. It can offer more control of the operating environment and allow for a greater reliance on automated capabilities. However, if a critical failure occurs or the data used generate biased scenarios, trust can be compromised and lead to non-desirable outcomes or to the inefficient allocation of resources. In a national security context, officials are under great pressure and make decisions with widespread consequences; therefore, outcomes must be reliable and trustworthy. However, because it relies on probability models, AI cannot guarantee perfect scenarios; decision makers would prefer AI models that are more deterministic. Overall, those deploying AI at the tactical level tend to prefer the minimization of uncertainty in operations. Hence, it is expected that strategic-level decisions will be made by human beings, but AI can be used to help humans to better plan and execute at the tactical level (Congressional Research Service, 2020).

An example of how AI is being deployed within a military setting to tactical advantage is a case involving the U.S. Navy, which began to use an AI application for environmental analysis, collaborative search planning and force management, and sensor metrics. Known as the Undersea Warfare Decision Support System, it is an anti-submarine warfare command and control AI system that enables forces to network in order to collaboratively plan and execute tactical missions (Naval Sea Systems Command Office, 2021).

Another example of the tactical use of military AI is the British Army's use of AI during "Exercise Spring Storm" as part of "Operation Cabrit" in Estonia. The system provided tactical information on the environment and terrain through an AI engine based on automation and smart analytics (Ministry of Defense, 2021).

Designing Military AI at the Operation Level

At the operational level, AI has been primarily used in the development of lethal autonomous weapons systems, combined with operations such as surveillance and applied to the areas of logistics, cyberspace, information, command and control operations, semi-autonomous and autonomous vehicle operations, and predictive maintenance, among others (Bipartisan Policy Center & Center for Security and Emerging Technology, 2020).

An example of AI used for operational purposes in the military is a recent case involving the Ukrainian Army (Bhuiyan, 2022). Ukraine's Vice-Prime Minister told Reuters that when the 2022 war started, they used facial recognition software in their military operations to identify the bodies of Russian soldiers killed in combat so they could track down their families and inform them of their deaths.

Another example is the case of Abu Dhabi's Hunter 2, an AI-based swarming drone system for the military (Helou, 2022). The drones track and maintain the positions of fighter jets, convoys, and any other potential enemies to monitor and identify the right targets (Helou, 2022). Designed to ensure a decisive edge in combat, these ground-launched drones fly as a unit to perform a coordinated mission before overwhelming an adversary. Using advanced AI technology, the tactical drones share information to track and maintain their relative positions and effectively engage targets. With a maximum take-off weight of 8 kilograms per drone, the swarm of guided drones is agile and responsive en route to its target, providing countries with a sophisticated way to disable enemies.

When thinking about using AI to enhance military operations, a likely agenda item for the world's militaries over the next ten years will be the hybridization of operations, that is, combining machine and human capabilities in such a manner that physical operations are performed by AI systems that can predict and mitigate risk in all-terrain operations.

Moreover, intelligence and counterintelligence will play a fundamental role in the physical space in which these AI systems work to support physical combat, and machines will learn to make decisions within real-world combat situations.

Because of the many changes being made in the planning, execution, and improvement of army operations, from recruitment to logistics, it is necessary to generate scenarios in which AI can play a leading role in military operations. Today, militaries around the world have started to devise hybrid strategies, where machines and humans coordinate in military operations that encompass planning and the mobilization of forces, the collection and analysis of information to produce intelligence and counterintelligence, and the allocation of resources on the battlefield.

Broadening the Design Framework for Military AI

While the abovementioned guidelines provide a way to start to design AI for the military, the challenges of AI for national security require a broader framework that can provide a multidimensional perspective on security, one which considers non-traditional threats such as intra-state insurgencies; drug, gun, and human trafficking; terrorism; illegal migration; risks such as pandemics; natural disasters; violations of human rights; and extreme poverty and inequality (Ramacciotti, 2005). This broader framework points to a future where AI deployment is human-oriented and context-centered. Hence, the design of future military AI needs to consider the diverse conditions of individuals and their environments, which calls for a discussion of how emerging technologies can help address factors that have traditionally been omitted from a state's defense plans, such as climate change. The question is whether this can be done effectively, or if increases in energy production and consumption for a digital world are a limitation to tech evolution.

Within this broad framework, nations will need to consider how to apply AI in warfare. While the Department of Defense has adopted ethical principles for AI, there are still several limitations to these principles and the proposed frameworks. As of now, the principles are too general. When it comes to autonomous systems and weapons, policymakers need to consider more specific subsets of ethical principles. Likewise, attorneys need to understand how AI is changing the nature of legal practice relating to national security. An understanding of these issues can help shape the architecture of government decision making for military AI (Baker et al, 2020).

A NEW MILITARIZED AI WORLD ORDER

AI and the Redefinition of a Country's Power

When thinking about AI in the military, it is relevant to consider how AI can redefine a country's power. AI can expand capabilities by providing smaller countries with easier access to a growing number of actors, facilitating information exchanges, and affording superior processing powers (data collection, analysis, and creation), while fostering potential economic (new industrial revolution) and military superiority (Allen & Chan, 2017). This could lead to rethinking the traditional conceptualization of national power (Keohane & Nye, 1973), such that a country's population size (Daniels & Chang, 2021) would no longer be relevant in contrast to the impact of having highly developed AI systems. How countries understand and make emerging technologies thrive are factors that contribute to determining a nation's power, because AI can recalibrate the influence and relevance of any given country within the international system (Congressional Research Service, 2020). It is highly likely that in years to come, international organizations, when analyzing and defining the predominance and influence of any given nation, will take into account a country's AI capabilities and the potential of other emerging technologies (Daniels & Chang, 2021). Since 2015, over 20 countries have established committees or task forces to develop national AI strategies, which indicates their interest in enhancing their power through AI. However, not all strategies are equal, as they take a broad view of different elements like research and development, education, ethics, and data collection and sharing. Some countries have already launched their initial strategies, as can be seen in two cases: the U.S. and China.

AI Strategies in the United States, China, Russia, and Other Countries

The U.S. government's AI plan, outlined in an official policy document published in 2017, has three pivotal points: economic growth and jobs, national security, and government reform. Also, the U.S. Department of Defense is currently engaged in more than 685 AI projects, including some associated with major weapon systems, like the MQ-9 unmanned aerial vehicle and the joint light tactical vehicle. The Joint AI Center is working on a smart sensor that can identify threats and relay visual data to analysts (Demarest, 2022).

China launched a three-year action plan from 2018 to 2020 to strengthen its industrial development and the deployment and integration of AI. It intends to pursue a "first-mover advantage" to grow into the world's "primary AI innovation center" by 2030 (Saran et al., 2018). The goal of the first-mover advantage is to bring their AI to the global south and exert greater influence through technology. China has also increased AI research and development as the People's Liberation Army prepares for what they call "smart warfare." In recent years, the country has invested 150 billion dollars in this technology (Suarez, 2022).

Russia has pointed out that AI is the key to its defense strategy. The nation has dedicated itself to modernizing its army with state-of-the-art technology (which has also been present in the current war Russia has with Ukraine). In 2018, the government announced the creation of the Military Research Complex, whose objective is to research AI, cybernetics, and advanced computing systems for defense and security purposes (Suarez, 2022).

To better understand the role these types of national AI strategies can play in the world, the Spanish Institute for Strategic Studies determined that in terms of security and defense, countries are divided into advanced players (the U.S., China, Russia, and Israel) and emerging players (France, the United Kingdom, Germany, and the European Union) (Ministerio de Defensa, 2017). As a result, from a security perspective, the international balance of power will be determined to some extent by the technologically advanced actors and their strategic alliances. Less developed countries, like those in Latin America, have created participatory AI strategies by collaborating with non-governmental organizations (NGOs), universities, and federal government agencies. For instance, academics from the National Autonomous University of Mexico joined forces with NGOs and federal government ministries to create a national AI strategy. The strategy focuses not so much on military power as on using AI to empower underserved communities, which are a factor in a broad national security framework.

AGENDA FOR THE FUTURE OF MILITARY AI

Future studies about AI should consider the strategic implications of its deployment, as it could change how operations are conducted and how soldiers are trained and managed. In the following sections, we describe a few areas where AI in the military can be consequential.

Social Media and New Opportunities in Military AI

New threats in this rapidly changing technological environment have their origins in countries, organizations, individuals, etc. The involvement of these entities has enabled the rise of hybrid scenarios, some of which are combinations of different sources of threat; increasingly, cyberspace is emerging as a theater of operations. Information in cyberspace is loose, insecure, and can be disseminated by different actors (military, civilians, angry soldiers sharing unauthorized information). Information on social media as well has become a focus of national security policies; bad actors have used social media to launch non-existential attacks. To prevent threatening situations, AI plays a key role in the digital environment, using algorithms that can identify potentially threatening content (Nasser, 2022).

The denominated fifth space of war, cyberspace, should be considered neutral ground; however, countries in competition with the U.S. are working to establish a significant presence and to influence and dominate this space in order to engage in warfare. Russia and China are some of the main players, but other countries also enjoy a robust AI readiness in the digital world, particularly Australia, Canada, France, Israel, the United Kingdom, Germany, Japan, and the Nordic countries (Oxford Insights, 2019).

Pandemics as Another National Security Threat and Opportunities for Military AI

As seen with the onset of the COVID-19 pandemic, this type of health-related disaster cannot be ignored by national security strategists (White House, 2021). In 2019, the Annual Threat Assessment from the U.S. intelligence community listed pandemics as global threats, and in 2022, they became a top category within the human security context (Pollard & Kuznar, 2022). In the 2020 COVID-19 pandemic, AI was used to understand the spread of disease in a better way; for example, the Boston-based AI company DataRobot built an AI model to predict COVID-19 spread down to the country level, and the Canadian firm Bluedot detected the spread in Wuhan long before it was taken seriously elsewhere.

The Department of Defense, along with the U.S. Army, has augmented its JARVISS system, which is designed to manage threats, ensure readiness, and keep personnel safe. The agency now tracks the pandemic and maintains a COVID-19-specific dashboard to keep commanders informed. This type of platform provides data aggregation and fusion, with AI-enabled predictive analytics capabilities, to enhance resource allocation and support supply chain decisions.

Microelectronics and the Future of Military AI

Another relevant issue for the future of AI development is the production of microelectronics. Two of the most advanced countries are dependent on semiconductor production: the U.S. and China. The U.S. relies almost entirely on foreign microelectronics to produce its AI technologies. This dependency creates a strategic vulnerability involving the governments of microelectronics-producing countries; in addition, a natural disaster or other event could disrupt the supply chains for electronics and critically hurt the U.S. At the same time, China has made an enormous financial commitment to minimize, if not eliminate, its dependency on imported microelectronics (Schmidt, 2022).

CONCLUSION

AI poses both challenges and opportunities in the context of national security. The limited transparency and uncertainty associated with certain AI design approaches make it difficult for AI to be incorporated immediately into the U.S. national security structure.

The relationship between the AI industry and the military is complex and difficult to navigate because the military has a culture and values that are very different from those of industry. However, with appropriate public policy goals guiding the process, the potential outcomes can be positive, generating AI systems and knowledge that can make them key players within national and international security frameworks.

Governments should proceed carefully when considering the regulation of AI. From a national security perspective, misguided or cumbersome regulations could harm a country's capabilities and its national power structure; however, ethics must underline the analysis, design, development, and deployment of military AI applications and solutions.

Governments should consider passing laws that recognize the exponential nature of technological development, establish standards and implement flexible regulations that foster innovation in the sector, and continue to examine the sources of threats to their countries' national security. They could establish permanent bodies and direct funding for AI design and build frameworks to increase their competitiveness, aiming at the same time for international cooperation.

Given the rapid development of AI technologies, industry, academia, NGOs, and governments should cooperate and come to an agreement about their countries' national security priorities. Similarly, governments need to develop leaders with a deep understanding of AI, who recognize the impact that these technologies may have on the many sectors of the economy and society. They should work to develop sensitive tech policies that benefit their citizens, while maintaining an awareness of the limits of AI and other technologies.

REFERENCES

Abdala B. M., Lacroix S., & Soubie S. (2019, October). La política de la inteligencia artificial: sus usos en el sector público y sus implicancias regulatorias Just La IA como herramienta. www.cippec.org/wp-content/uploads/2019/10/185-DT-Abdala-Lacroix-y-Soubie-La-política-de-la-Inteligencia-Artifici....pdf

Ahronheim, A. (2021, May 27). Israel's Operation against Hamas Was the World's First AI War. *The Jerusalem Post*. www.jpost.com/arab-israeli-conflict/gaza-news/guardian-of-the-walls-the-first-ai-war-669371

Allen, G. (2020, April). Understanding AI Technology: A Concise, Practical, and Readable Overview of Artificial Intelligence and Machine Learning Technology Designed for Non-Technical Managers, Officers, and Executives. Joint Artificial Intelligence Center, Department of Defense. www.ai.mil/docs/Understanding%20AI%20Technology.pdf

Allen, G., & Chan, T. (2017, July). Artificial Intelligence and National Security. Belfer Center for International Affairs, Harvard Kennedy School. www.belfercenter.org/publication/artificial-intelligence-and-national-security

Baker, S. A., Wade, M., & Walsh, M. J. (2020). The Challenges of Responding to Misinformation during a Pandemic: Content Moderation and the Limitations of the Concept of Harm. *Media International Australia*, 177 (1), 103–107.

Bathaee, Y. (2018). The Artificial Intelligence Black Box and the Failure of Intent and Causation. *Harvard Journal of Law & Technology*, 31 (2), 890–938.

Bhuiyan, J. (2022, March 24). Ukraine Uses Facial Recognition Software to Identify Russian Soldiers Killed in Combat. *The Guardian*. www.theguardian.com/technology/2022/mar/24/ukraine-facial-recognition-identify-russian-soldiers

Bipartisan Policy Center & Center for Security and Emerging Technology. (2020, June). Artificial Intelligence and National Security. https://bipartisanpolicy.org/download/?file=/wp-content/uploads/2020/07/BPC-Artificial-Intelligence-and-National-Security_Brief-Final-1.pdf

Clark, C. (2017, August 8). Rolling the Marble: BG Saltzman on Air Force's Multi-Domain C2 System. *Breaking Defense*. https://breakingdefense.com/2017/08/rolling-the-marble-bg-saltzman-on-air-forces-multi-domain-c2-system/

Congressional Research Service. (2020, November 10). Artificial Intelligence and National Security. Congressional Research Service. https://crsreports.congress.gov/product/details?prodcode=R45178

Cross, T. (2016). After Moore's Law: Double, Double, Toil and Trouble. *The Economist Technology Quarterly*, 1. www.economist.com/technology-quarterly/2016-03-12/after-moores-law

Daniels, M., & Chang, B. (2021). National Power after AI. Center for Security and Emerging Technology. https://cset.georgetown.edu/publication/national-power-after-ai/

DCAF (Geneva for Democratic Control of Armed Forces). (2005). https://issat.dcaf.ch/download/17202/201862/bg_national-security%20(1).pdf

Demarest, C. (2022). Hundreds of AI Projects Are Underway as Defense Department Eyes Future Combat. C4ISRNet. www.c4isrnet.com/artificial-inte lligence/2022/02/22/hundreds-of-ai-projects-underway-as-defense-department-e yes-future-combat

Du Mont, M. (2019). Incorporating Risk into National Security Planning. Atlantic Council. www.atlanticcouncil.org/content-series/strategy-consortium/incorporating-risk-into-national-security-planning/

Flournoy, M. A., Haines, A., & Chefitz, G. (2020). Building Trust through Testing: Adapting DOD's Test and Evaluation, Validation and Verification (TEVV) Enterprise for Machine Learning Systems, Including Deep Learning Systems. CSET and WestExec Advisors. https://cset.georgetown.edu/wp-con tent/uploads/Building-Trust-Through-Testing.pdf

Goldfarb, A., & Lindsay, J. R. (2022). Prediction and Judgment: Why Artificial Intelligence Increases the Importance of Humans in War. *International Security*, 46 (3), 7–50.

Helou, A. (2022). Following the First Demonstration, Edge Unveils Swarming Drones Based on AI Technology. *Defense News*. www.defensenews.com/indus try/2022/02/22/following-first-demonstration-edge-unveils-swarming-drones-based-on-ai-technology/

Jewish Institute for National Security of America. (2021, October). JINSA's Gemunder Center Gaza Assessment Policy Project. https://jinsa.org/wp-con tent/uploads/2021/10/Gaza-Assessment.v8-1.pdf

Kania, E. (2019, June 7). Chinese Military Innovation in Artificial Intelligence. Center for New American Security. www.uscc.gov/sites/default/files/June %207%20Hearing_Panel%201_Elsa%20Kania_Chinese%20Military%20Innova tion%20in%20Artificial%20Intelligence_0.pdf

Keohane, R., & Nye, J. (1973). Power and Interdependence. *Survival*. https://doi.org/10.1080/00396337308441409

Lawless, W. F., Mittu, R., Sofge, D. A., Shortell, T., & McDermott, T. A. (Eds). (2021). *Systems Engineering and Artificial Intelligence*. Springer Nature.

Ministerio de Defensa. (2017). La inteligencia artificial, aplicada a la defensa. Documentos de Seguridad y Defensa Instituto Español de Estudios Estratégicos, Ministerio de Defensa.

Ministry of Defence. (2021, July 5). Artificial Intelligence was Used on Army Operations for the First Time. www.gov.uk/government/news/artificial-intelli gence-used-on-army-operation-for-the-first-time

Nasser, M. (2022). A Comparative Analysis of Information and Artificial Intelligence toward National Security. *IEEE Access*, 10, 64420–64434.

Naval Sea Systems Command Office. (2021, September 20). AN/UYQ-100 Undersea Warfare Decision Support System (USW-DSS). US Navy. www.navy.mil/Resources/Fact-Files/Display-FactFiles/Article/2166791/anuyq-100-un dersea-warfare-decision-support-system-usw-dss/

Office of the Chief Scientist of the U.S. Air Force. (2015, June). Autonomous Horizons, System Autonomy in the Air Force. U.S. Air Force. www.af.mil/Portals/1/documents/SECAF/AutonomousHorizons.pdf?timestamp=1435068339702

Oxford Insights. (2019). Government Artificial Intelligence Readiness Index. www.oxfordinsights.com/ai-readiness2019

Pollard, S. E., & Kuznar, L. A. (Eds). (2022). *A World Emerging from Pandemic: Implications for Intelligence and National Security.* National Intelligence University Press.

Ramacciotti, B. (2005, March). Democracy and Multidimensional Security: The Rising Need for Citizen Security in Latin America. Seminar on Security and Democratic Governability: Addressing Challenges in Latin America. https://pdba.georgetown.edu/Security/referencematerials_ramacciotti.pdf

Saran S., Natarajan N., & Srikumar, M. (2018). In Pursuit of Autonomy: AI and National Strategies. www.orfonline.org/wp-content/uploads/2018/11/Ai_Book.pdf

Scharre, P. (2017). The Lethal Autonomous Weapons Governmental Meeting, Part 1: Coping with Rapid Technological Change. *Just Security.* www.justsecurity.org/46889/lethal-autonomous-weaponsgovernmental-meeting-part-i-coping-rapid-technological-change/

Schmidt, T. A. (2022). *Silent Coup of the Guardians: The Influence of US Military Elites on National Security.* University Press of Kansas.

Stone, C. (2021). Artificial Intelligence in the Intelligence Community: Culture Is Critical. *Just Security.* www.justsecurity.org/77783/artificial-intelligence-in-the-intelligence-community-culture-is-critical/

Suarez, J. (2022). La Inteligencia Artificial Como arma de Guerra. *MIT Sloan Management Review Mexico.* https://mitsloanreview.mx/destacado-home/la-inteligencia-artificial-como-arma-de-guerra/

Times of India. (2015, April 6). Learning with the Times: Germans First Used CCTV in 1942 to Observe the V-2 Rocket Launch. https://timesofindia.indiatimes.com/india/learning-with-the-times-cctv-was-first-used-by-germans-in-1942-to-observe-v-2-rocket-launch/articleshow/46819159.cms

White House. (2021, January 21). National Security Memorandum on United States Global Leadership to Strengthen the International COVID-19 Response and to Advance Global Health Security and Biological Preparedness. www.whitehouse.gov/briefing-room/statements-releases/2021/01/21/national-security-directive-united-states-global-leadership-to-strengthen-the-international-covid-19-response-and-to-advance-global-health-security-and-biological-preparedness/

15. Governance, government records, and the policymaking process aided by AI
Andrea Renda

INTRODUCTION: AI AND THE FUTURE OF GOVERNMENT

Among the sectors that will be most heavily affected by the digital transformation, and specifically by the advent of sophisticated artificial intelligence (AI) applications, government stands out as one of the most controversial. AI applications in government promise enormous benefits, both in the modernization of public administration as well as in enabling innovative approaches to public policy and regulation. Such benefits can take the form of enhanced productivity, increased accuracy, as well as dramatic cost reductions. However, benefits may come with significant risks, both in terms of weaker protection of fundamental rights as well as loss of employment due to job automation. The former effect has been subject to significant research and ad hoc grey literature over the past years (see Renda et al. 2021 for a review of the major impacts). The latter, related to employment effects, will form the main subject of this chapter.

As often happens, global consultancy firms have been among the first to provide tentative forecasts of the impact of AI on government jobs. A few years ago, Eggers et al. (2017) estimated that in the United Kingdom 'up to 861,000 public sector jobs ... could be automated by 2030, saving some £17 billion annually in wages compared to 2015'. In 2018, Hawksworth et al. analysed a dataset of 29 Organisation for Economic Co-operation and Development (OECD) countries and identified three waves of transformation: an *algorithm* wave (until the early 2020s) focused on the automation of simple computational tasks and analysis of structured data, which is estimated to affect about 4 per cent of jobs in public administration and defence; an *augmentation* wave, affecting repeatable tasks and statistical analysis of unstructured data in semi-controlled environments (until the late 2020s), affecting about 26 per cent of jobs in the sector; and a third *autonomy* wave, in which physical labour and problem-solving in real-world situations will affect as many as 33 per cent of jobs, between now and the mid-2030s.

In reality, making predictions is extremely complex, not least because the extent of job automation in government will depend not only on progress in AI techniques but also on policy choices that will be made by governments going forward. In some countries, the temptation to automate both back-office and front-office government functions may become too strong to resist, also due to shrinking government finances and overall fiscal constraints, even more after the COVID-19 pandemic and economic recession triggered by Russia's invasion of Ukraine. The real challenge for government thus becomes how to harness the potential of AI and related technologies, without negatively impacting citizens, massively displacing and automating jobs, and without triggering a reduction in the overall quality and inclusiveness of public services.

Below, the issue of AI and public-sector jobs is explored in depth. The first section takes stock of the many ways in which AI is changing the nature, organization, and role of government. The second section explores the key use cases of AI-enabled solutions in government and discusses the future of public work. The chapter then briefly concludes by reflecting on the skills that will be needed for an adequate workforce in the public sector.

HOW AI IS CHANGING THE ROLE OF GOVERNMENT

In order to fully understand what AI can mean for governments, and how to maximize the possible benefits at the same time as minimizing the risks, a thorough reflection on the changing role of government is needed. In this respect, several research reports and grey literature contributions point to an evolving set of distinct roles that government will play in the coming years, due to the impact of the digital transformation. In particular, in addition to the traditional role of regulator and service provider, government will increasingly play the role of trusted intermediary and even act as a platform, providing data and support for third-party services. All these roles will require, in turn, new competences and skills.

The Government as Policymaker and Regulator

Apart from several emerging attempts to regulate AI applications and algorithms used by digital platforms (with countries like Canada, the European Union (EU), and the United States (US) currently being at the forefront of emerging regulatory approaches), governments are increasingly looking into the possibility of using AI in regulatory practice. This can encompass various phases of the policy cycle, including the establishment of secure data exchanges between regulators and regulated entities for monitoring purposes (so-called supervisory technologies, or SupTech); the use of AI to analyse and summarize submissions in open public consultations (e.g. the DORIS software used by the European Commission);[1] reliance on data-driven monitoring and inspections through the use of machine-learning techniques (OECD 2021); and even the introduction of experimental AI-based regulatory impact assessments. More generally, several new use cases are emerging in the space of algorithmic regulation (Ulbricht & Yeung 2022), including examples in which governments use AI to regulate AI (e.g. in the case of content moderation or in algorithmic inspections foreseen by new legislation such as the EU AI Act and Digital Services Act). Importantly, in some of these latter cases governments can also outsource algorithmic inspections to third parties, including academic and civil society, as in the case of the 'trusted flaggers' (specialized entities with dedicated structure and expertise in identifying illegal online content) and 'vetted researchers' in the EU Digital Services Act (Buri & van Hoboken 2021).

When it comes to governments' role as regulator, the use of AI is already a reality. A useful way to depict this development is to take as reference the 'regulatory governance cycle' as described by the OECD (2014) and map emerging uses of AI along the various phases of the life of a legal rule. As shown in Figure 15.1, AI is offering important solutions to policymakers, including forms of 'algorithmic regulation' including real-time monitoring of compliance (e.g. access to data on regulated entities' behaviour and application of anomaly detection software); real-time violation detections (e.g. image recognition used to detect cars that do not stop at a red light); and predictive policing (i.e. anticipating risks based on complex statistical software, for example estimating where in a city a crime is most likely to be 'about to happen'). A growing area of regulation makes use of data flows to enable more pervasive supervision and compliance verification. So-called RegTech solutions (or, in financial services, SupTech, or financial supervision through technology) are essentially data-driven and real time. Examples of RegTech approaches include: (1) establishing a secure data exchange agreement with regulated entities, so that they can monitor market conduct and regulatory compliance in real time, thus reaching complete regulatory compliance automation; (2) mandating that incumbent firms establish an open application programming interface (API), so that new entrants can access the data they need to viably compete in the regulated market (Open API solution, as in the EU Second Payment Services Directive); and (3) running machine-learning algorithms on the basis of reported data to enable anti-money laundering and tax fraud prevention.

---

[1]   https://joinup.ec.europa.eu/collection/doris/solution/doris/about

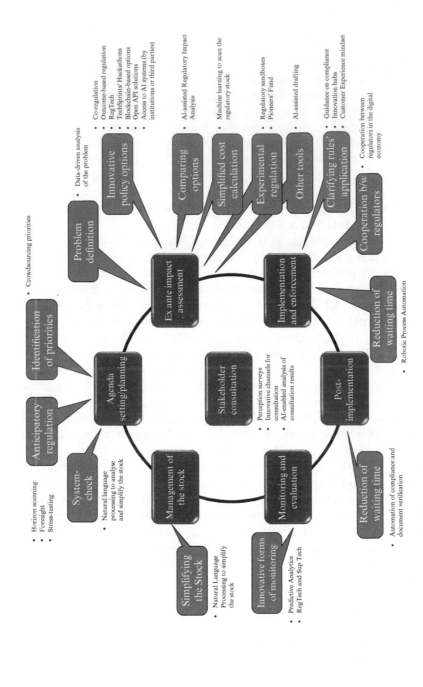

Source: Renda 2022, simplified.

Figure 15.1   New regulatory tools in the policy cycle

Government as Auditor

Through enhanced use of AI, governments can engage in real-time audits and inspections, by employing machine-learning techniques often referred to as 'anomaly detection'. Through this group of techniques, governments can increasingly reach formerly unthinkable levels of pervasiveness in controlling compliance, for example in the fields of unemployment insurance fraud and as tax fraud. Among the most often used techniques are simple statistical methods used to identify non-recurrent activities related to behavioural patterns of specific user groups; machine-learning techniques used to label users who display patterns that appear similar to known threats; anomaly detection to analyse suspicious activities such as actions taken on dormant claims; and the use of analytics such as network graphs, which can help determine exchanges between internal users and claimants and identify common attributes and hidden connections between claimants and users. That said, as will be recalled below, the use of sophisticated machine-learning algorithms to detect forms of fraud or lack of compliance can at once drastically reduce the need for personnel (if not at the outset when the AI systems need to be trained) and create important risks of profiling and discrimination of citizens and businesses.

Government as Service Provider

When providing services to businesses and citizens, governments increasingly use AI for a variety of use cases, from authentication (through facial recognition software) to processing information (AI-automated business license registrations, e.g. in Estonia) and providing help and advice to individuals (e.g. through conversational bots such as the Swedish 'Fredrik', on which see Henk & Nilssen 2021). AI-enabled government services can also be significantly enhanced by the optimization of back-office solutions, such as the use of image recognition for processing documents, and robotic process automation to quickly scan thousands of (similar) documents, as occurred during the early days of the pandemic in the US, as the number of applications for unemployment benefits skyrocketed in a matter of days. The use of AI and the deployment of 'agile' solutions through a quick iteration of experiments with public services is now dominating the scene in the study of public governance, with several countries forming an 'agile nations network' with a view to learning from software development what it takes to build a truly citizen-centric administration. Here too, however, the risk of discrimination and exclusion is a potential problem, as testified by reports of discriminatory uses of AI in public services in several countries, including highly developed and tech-savvy European countries like the Netherlands and Denmark.

Government as (or via) Trusted Intermediaries

In the age of data-driven governance solutions, governments increasingly collect personally identifiable data and act as trusted intermediaries, especially in all cases in which digital identity is used for public and private services. One key example is in the collection of biometric data for security purposes, with the underlying government commitment not to reuse data for other purposes than those they were originally collected for.[2] This requires new skills and competences in government, such as data stewardship skills and the ability to develop and deploy privacy-enhancing technologies governed by AI systems. Alternatively, governments can choose to endorse the establishment of separate, third-party data intermediaries to enhance citizens' trust that their data will not be reused by government. The EU Data Governance Act, for example, aims at creating this intermediate layer, which in turn requires that governments develop contractual and relational skills to handle data flows from and to intermediaries. Moreover, the emerging domain of business-to-government (B2G) data exchanges places government in the driver's seat when it comes to collecting information from businesses and citizens and then reusing it 'for good', for example in cases of emergency or for reasons of public interest. Finally, the explosion of machine-to-machine communication in the age of the Internet of Things forces governments to develop ways to monitor data exchanges in automated processes, for example in smart contracts. In all these cases, AI algorithms are applied to data exchanges, enabling privacy-enhancing government services, for example using cryptography or federated machine learning.

Government as a Platform

The digital revolution enables governments to become catalysts of innovation by pooling resources and offering large and small businesses the possibility to access open data to develop innovative public services, to the benefit of citizens and society. Early examples of government as a platform (GaaP), such as the Estonian X-Road, have shown a remarkable potential to simplify the life of citizens and businesses, as well as to untap the value

---

[2]   https://freedomhouse.org/report/report-sub-page/2020/false-panacea-abusive-surveillance-name-public-health

of data-driven innovation. At the same time, the GaaP revolution places governments' back office and service on cloud platforms (with varying degrees of centralization), and this in turn paves the way for 'agile' government, with a significant reliance on outsourcing public-service delivery to third parties. Such a massive platformization of government, similarly to what occurs with private platforms, also leads to a shrinking effect in terms of public employment.

All these developments are linked, in one way or another, to advances in AI and related digital technologies, such as edge/cloud computing and the Internet of Things. In all the roles illustrated above, governments have a variety of available use cases. The most common are illustrated below.

AI IN GOVERNMENT: KEY USE CASES, BENEFITS, AND RISKS

Several factors are pushing governments to increase their investment in AI solutions: beyond their overall promise, one must also consider the acceleration of digital transformation caused by the COVID-19 pandemic, as well as the need to find solutions to tight fiscal constraints for most governments around the world. In many countries, the stimulus plans adopted in the aftermath of the pandemic have often included strong incentives towards the modernization and digitalization of the public administration, which in turn has brought digital technologies and AI-powered solutions into regulatory agencies, courts, enforcement authorities, and other public institutions. The main use cases of AI in government can be grouped along a number of pillars, including support for democratic processes, tailored solutions (e.g. personalized public services), and more back-office solutions such as process optimization, predictive maintenance, inspection and enforcement, investigations, knowledge and archive solutions, and forecasting for policy development (Hoekstra et al. 2021).

Key techniques and use cases, as shown in Figure 15.2, include the use of chatbots or conversational agents; data mining; AI-powered collection and analysis of biometric data; computer vision and image recognition; geospatial AI; machine translation; and deep learning. In particular, the deployment of chatbots seems to be more advanced than all other applications in the 166 government administrations surveyed by Gartner in October 2021.

Furthermore, a report commissioned by the Administrative Conference of the United States (Engstrom et al. 2020) mapped the uptake of AI techniques in the federal and state administrations, showing interesting results which show a rapid spread of AI across a variety of use cases. The report found the highest number of use cases in the area of law enforcement,

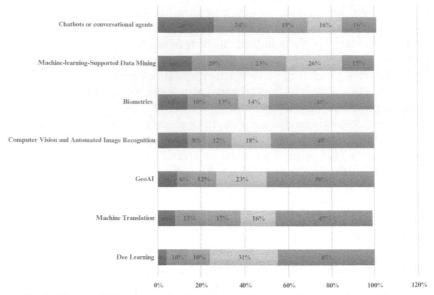

Note: Number of answers = 166. The question asked was: 'What are your organization's plans in terms of the following digital technologies and platforms?'

Source: Gartner 2021.

Figure 15.2 Type of AI adoption across government

followed by health and financial regulation. In terms of task performed by AI systems, the most common use is in 'regulatory research, analysis and monitoring', followed by 'enforcement', 'public services and engagement', 'internal management' and 'adjudication'.

Against this background, highly reputed institutions and academics have voiced significant concerns about the uncontrolled diffusion of algorithms in public administrations, with the Council of Europe observing that algorithmic decision-making 'is threatening to disrupt the very concept of human rights as protective shields against state interference' (Schulz et al. 2018, p. 33). This is also a likely reason why academics have turned to this issue over the past few years. For example, Desouza et al. (2020) observe that only roughly 4 per cent (59) of the articles published between 2000 and 2019 discussed applications of AI in the public sector. Sharma et al. (2020) find a slightly higher number of papers (74) in Web of Science and offer an organizing framework for the most common uses of AI in government.

Alongside the advantages, a number of concerns about possible downsides and misuses of AI are reported, including 'black box' problems (i.e. lack of transparency and/or predictability in the inner working of the algorithms used),[3] the amplification of biases of which users might be unaware (Wirtz et al. 2019), and the weakening of privacy protection 'due to the fact that many devices and services gather data without the user's full understanding of what is done with it afterwards' (Wirtz et al. 2019). A significant number of ongoing AI applications were found to lead to the compression of fundamental rights such as privacy, the right to a private life, and the right not to be discriminated against.

Perhaps the most telling examples are related to the application of predictive analytics to a variety of government functions, including predicting crime (e.g. predictive policing software, initially launched in California and then to many other cities in the world, but recently withdrawn in Los Angeles due to public concerns over discrimination); assessing risk of unemployment (see the Equinet report by Allen & Masters 2020); and determining the risk of tax fraud. A well-known case was the Systeem Risico Indicatie or SyRI model used in the Netherlands to determine the risk of fraud for social security/welfare, which was struck down in February 2020 by the District Court of the Hague (ECHR 2020, cited in NJCM 2020); or detecting children in vulnerable circumstances at an early stage. A famous case is the algorithm implemented in the Danish city of Gladsaxe in 2018, found to be profiling people and leading to possible discrimination (Alfter 2019).

Another controversial area of AI deployment in the public sector is in courts. Table 15.1 (from Renda et al. 2021, which in turn quotes Castellano 2021) summarizes emerging uses of AI in court by distinguishing between applications for case management, pre-trial use cases, trial phase, decision-making, and post-sentencing.

Moreover, AI deployment has become extremely widespread and controversial in the domain of border control and migration policy generally. Here, the collection and use of data through AI systems may lead to significant violations of fundamental rights, such as non-discrimination and the right to good administration. In the US, systems such as *SilentTalker*, *EyeDetect*, and *Discern* are being trialled privately or by public administrations, based on the assumption that lying is more cognitively demanding than telling the truth. Beduschi (2020) reports that Canada already

---

[3] The FAT/ML Research community established the 'Principles for Accountable Algorithms and a Social Impact Statement for Algorithms' (www.fatml.org/resources/principles-for-accountable-algorithms).

Table 15.1 *Uses of AI by courts*

Stages	Management of cases	Pre-trial	Trial	Judges' deliberation/ decision-making	Post-sentencing
(Potential) AI applications	Case management system	Plea bargaining – prosecutor's databases	Use of videoconference	Case law tools	Scoring of risks/ probability of recidivism/parole opportunities
	Electronic communications – digital platforms accessible for lawyers/clients		Automated transcription/ translation	Prediction technology	
	Automatic monitoring of procedures		Automated presentation of file document on screens during hearings	Legal research and analysis/ autonomous research	
	Automatic system for monitoring procedural delays		Case management (in a situation of complex cases)	Scoring of risks/assessment of the suspect (probability of recidivism)	
	Automatic system for completing procedural formalities		Use of emotional AI (e.g. affective computing, emotion detection)	Automated judgments (decision trees)	
	Automatic decisions on the progress of the case			Writing assistance tools and drafting judgments	
	Queue management			Decision-making systems	
	Automatic sorting of appeals			Intelligence assistant systems (identification of patterns, analysis of data, etc.)	

Main principles and issues to be taken into account

Principles				
Adversarial proceedings	Adversarial proceedings	Adversarial proceedings	Adversarial proceedings	Adversarial proceedings
Rule of law, due process, security	Equality of arms	Fair trial	Fair trial	Fair trial
No restriction of access to justice	Access to data by lawyers	Transparency neutrality (in profiling)	Transparency about use of AI by judge	Transparency of decision-making process
Equality of arms	Data protection and compatibility with fundamental rights	No use of emotional AI and videos are used during trial	Transparency of decision-making process	Algorithms and accountability
Transparency of decision-making			Algorithms and accountability	Right to appeal
Access to data by lawyers			Liability if errors occur	
			Access to evidence	
			Right to request a human intervention (judge)	

Source: Elaboration on Castellano 2021.

deploys algorithmic decision-making and AI technologies for immigration and asylum processes (Molnar & Gill 2018). Likewise, Switzerland is experimenting with an algorithm for the integration of refugees. However, as a downside, Beduschi underlines growing reservations about the emergence of a form of 'surveillance humanitarianism' (Latonero 2019).

Finally, the COVID-19 pandemic has led many governments to step up health data collection, with the underlying commitment to limit their activities to contact tracing for the purpose of containing the spread of COVID-19 (Renda 2022). However, in their role of trusted intermediary, many of them were tempted to use data for surveillance purposes, as testified by several reports.

Summing up, the promise of AI in government appears to be very significant, and at times even too tempting for governments, who may end up overlooking the risks generated by an improper use of AI in various functions of government. Among the risks, very often national AI strategies do not include important features such as: an *ad hoc* approach to the responsible deployment of AI solutions by government and, more generally, the public sector; attention to the possible loss of employment in the public sector, which could be mitigated through a human-centric approach to AI deployment; and a dedicated strategy to generate the skills that will be needed in the future to empower civil servants to make the most of AI solutions.

When and How to Use AI? Frameworks for the Responsible Development of AI in the Public Sector, at All Levels of Government

The first government to adopt a specific legislative framework for the use of AI in government was Canada, starting in 2018. Under the authority of the Financial Administration Act, the Treasury Board of Canada issued the Directive on Automated Decision-Making, which came into effect on 1 April 2020 and applies to the use of automated decision systems that 'provide external services and recommendations about a particular client, or whether an application should be approved or denied'. It includes an AIA designed 'to help [federal institutions] better understand and reduce the risks associated with Automated Decision System's', which should be carried out 'prior to the production of any Automated Decision System' by the federal authorities (Government of Canada 2018). The Directive imposed a four-tier risk classification and consequent algorithmic impact assessment for automated decision systems deployed by the government. Enhanced risk assessment is due whenever the system is likely to have very high impacts on the rights of individuals or communities; the health or wellbeing of individuals or communities; the economic interests of individuals, entities, or communities; or the ongoing sustainability of an ecosystem. No specific mention is made for what concerns the risk of job replacement, or the loss of agency among civil servants.

In the United Kingdom, the Office for Artificial Intelligence in collaboration with the Government Digital Service published the 'Guide on Using AI in the Public Sector' (UK Government 2019). This is a collection of guidance documents, including how to assess whether the use of AI will help an administration to meet user needs and how the public sector can best implement AI ethically, fairly, and safely. The key characteristics of the guidance documents include a broad definition of AI and a list of key factors to consider in the development of AI, including data quality (accuracy, completeness, uniqueness, timeliness, validity, sufficiency, relevancy, representativeness, consistency), fairness, accountability, privacy, explainability, and transparency, costs. Institutions are invited to consider how much it will cost to build, run, and maintain an AI infrastructure, train and educate staff, and assess whether the work to install AI may outweigh any potential savings.

In the US, the Government Accountability Office developed in 2021 an AI Accountability Framework for Federal Agencies and Other Entities, which introduces key approaches to governance, provides guidance on the responsible use of data, ensures adequate performance, and carries out appropriate monitoring of the outcomes and behaviour of AI systems. This framework was further developed by the National institute of Standards and Technology, in the US Department of Commerce, with the adoption of a broader risk management framework, and by the Office of Science and Technology Policy, which adopted in 2022 a blueprint for an AI Bill of Rights, which calls for a tailor-made definition of key principles and standards for AI by federal agencies (Engler 2022).

Perhaps the most comprehensive framework for the trustworthy development of AI to date is that provided by the EU Artificial Intelligence Act, proposed by the European Commission in April 2021 and still going through an extensive negotiation phase between co-legislators (the European Parliament and the Council of the EU). The AI Act introduces a risk-based regulatory framework, which identifies specific applications of AI that should be banned since they are unacceptably risky, and AI applications that should be regulated since they are high risk (Bogucki et al. 2022). Among these applications, several refer to typical government use cases, including migration, asylum, and border control management; the use of AI in the administration of justice and democratic processes; and the use of AI in law enforcement and the delivery of essential services. During the discussion in the Parliament and Council, several other applications have been identified for inclusion in the prohibited and high-risk categories. Prohibited applications may end up including the use of remote biometric identification in public places, predictive policing and algorithms to predict recidivism (similar to the COMPAS algorithm used, and fiercely criticized in the US); and high-risk applications may include access to public benefits, triage in healthcare, eligibility for life insurance, emergency response, and AI used in political campaigns.

International convergence on principles of responsible AI is likely to continue and even accelerate over the coming years. Importantly, principles of responsible AI are being developed at all levels of government, and perhaps not only at the national level. On the one hand, important frameworks have been discussed and approved at the international level (for example, UNESCO's Recommendation on the Ethics of AI, on which see Ramos 2022; the work of the OECD network of AI Experts as well as the work of the Global Partnership on Artificial Intelligence); and in the framework of bilateral agreements, such as the AUKUS trilateral security pact between Australia, the United Kingdom, and the US; the Indo-Pacific Quadrilateral Dialogue; and the EU–US Trade and Technology Council. On the other hand, at the subnational level, guidance on how to use AI in government is gradually becoming more widespread (good examples being the Canadian province of Ontario and the Australian province of New South Wales). Even more prominently, several cities (especially in the US) have taken action to regulate or even ban the deployment and use of AI for specific use cases. The latter development has given rise to what Verhulst et al. (2021) have defined as 'AI localism', a phenomenon in which public-sector uses of AI are discussed and regulated at the local level. A repository managed by New York University's Governance Lab distinguished several cases of prohibition of facial recognition, the establishment of AI registries, guidance and rules on how to procure AI systems, and initiatives related to the trustworthy governance of data. The quintessential example of localism on AI is the decision to shut down the project commissioned by the Toronto Harbor front to Sidewalk Labs (a subsidiary of Alphabet), which would have entailed a massive collection of citizen data, reportedly for the purpose of 'optimizing' the urban environment. Since then, dozens of initiatives have blossomed around the world, with local communities heavily involved in the definition of the limits and conditions of the use of AI by public authorities at the local level.

THE FUTURE OF PUBLIC WORK: MAPPING CIVIL SERVANTS' SKILLS

Recent developments in AI, especially in the domain of natural language processing and image recognition, offer important prospects for automating several government functions. Most authors and international organizations, in forecasting the future of jobs in government, have adopted a task-based approach, which does not directly focus on the number of jobs that will be lost but rather highlights those tasks within each job that will increasingly be carried out by machines, with or without human supervision. Accordingly, the net impact of AI on public-sector jobs depends on several factors, including: (1) how many existing tasks will be automated; (2) whether some job positions will see all tasks automated, and will therefore be eliminated; (3) whether the overall impact of such automation will lead to the reallocation of workers to non-automated tasks; and (4) the number of new tasks that will be created as a result of the modernization and the transformation of government (see the first section above). Many of these factors, in turn, depend on the criteria that will be adopted by governments in assessing whether a job should be automated: governments focused on the need to reduce costs, irrespective of quality and overall employment targets, may end up replacing more tasks and jobs in their administrations; governments that, for example, place employment or, more broadly, the Sustainable Development Goals at the core of their action and agenda may end up deciding to automate fewer jobs.

Undoubtedly, without suitable education of the public workforce, governments may end up being unable to harness the potential of the use of AI in their administrations, and may ultimately lose their role to the private sector. The shrinking of government size was somehow predicted by early analyses such as PwC (2018), but this is not an inevitable consequence of the rise of AI. On the contrary, the need for fair, transparent, efficient, and accountable public services and regulation calls for the development of a new generation of skilled civil servants who can significantly promote the trustworthy diffusion and use of technology. Looking at the new roles of government described in the first section above, the following consequences may emerge for government employment and related skills.

New Skills for Policymaking and Regulation

Policymakers will have to gradually develop new skills, which range from data governance and stewardship to the ability to deploy and monitor the operations of machine-learning systems, or at least procure trustworthy AI applications. Given the features of data-hungry AI techniques such as machine learning, policymakers will have to complement the effectiveness and efficiency of AI with domain knowledge and the ability to exercise human oversight. Moreover, the optimization of a given function through AI may not always occur in a way that is fully compliant with the existing legislation: for example, cases of discrimination that an AI system (and most economists) would find to be efficient, including some forms of social credit scoring and predictive policing, may fall under the prohibited uses of AI or at least the 'high-risk' or 'high-impact' applications that will be subject to regulatory requirements in some legal systems. Against this backdrop, the ability to follow the process and interpret and monitor the outcome of AI systems' actions or recommendations is, and will continue to be, an essentially human competence in the development and implementation of legal rules.

One reason why regulators should not entirely delegate to AI systems the design and implementation of regulation is the likelihood that, once the algorithmic nature of regulation is known, regulated entities 'game' the system by exploiting the lack of situational awareness and overall intelligence of current AI systems, or by directly attacking them to cause malfunctioning or manipulate the behaviour of the AI system. The ability to attack an AI system to test its robustness over time and stress-test it against possible attacks becomes, therefore, a key competence of future government teams (so-called 'red teams' and 'pen-testing' processes).

Going forward, the acceleration of the pace of AI innovation will challenge regulators to adopt increasingly adaptive, agile regulatory approaches. In a growing number of cases, regulation will be 'of technology, with technology', as in the case of emerging approaches to regulate smart contracts, as well as in all other cases of 'law as code'. This, in turn, will have important consequences on the role of humans in regulatory management and oversight. In some countries, a new generation of what used to be called 'responsive regulation' (Ayres & Braithwaite 1992) is emerging, leading to the establishment of 'innovation hubs', where regulated entities can receive clarification and guidance on how to comply with regulatory requirements, and experimental spaces such as regulatory sandboxes and regulator-led pioneer funds, in which rules and prospective regulatory reforms can be tested and prototyped with the help of regulated entities.

These innovative regulatory approaches portray a future in which humans oversee self-executing regulatory frameworks, use AI solutions to detect anomalies in compliance patterns, and exercise uniquely human skills in providing assistance and guidance to regulated entities whenever needed. In a world like this, pervasive monitoring poses the problem of potential intrusion into the private sphere of citizens and the confidential operations of businesses, leading to forms of social credit scoring, like that in China, that are currently raising eyebrows in the EU but are increasingly tempting for authoritarian and even some democratic regimes. Accordingly, in the future regulation should be accompanied by adequate skills and solutions related to the governance of data, and the rise of government as trusted intermediary.

In later phases of the policy cycle, the implementation, monitoring, and enforcement of legal rules will increasingly rely on the support of AI systems. Examples proliferate around the world. OECD/CAF (2022) described uses of machine learning in the Italian regions of Lombardy and Campania, where AI is used for inspections of construction sites and for food safety and veterinary inspections. In Vietnam, the tax authority is reportedly seeking to build up and upgrade applications to automatically check tax returns at tax offices, automate some of the field inspection/audit steps by using electronic tax management platforms, and automatically connect data with third-party databases (for e-invoice verification, digital reconciliation, etc.) (Rödl & Partners 2022). Sophisticated image analysis is being used in Washington, DC to automate inspection of sewers (Intel 2022) and the French Directorate for Food Quality is using AI to automate restaurant hygiene inspections (DGAL 2019).

New Skills in Public Services

Besides adopting new tools and approaches in regulation, governments will increasingly transform the way they offer public services. In Europe, the AI Watch group, located in the European Commission's Joint Research Centre, collected as many as 143 cases of AI use in government across the EU 27 member states (JRC 2022). OECD and CAF (OECD2022) collect use cases around the world, particularly for Latin American countries. The World Bank reports several cases of successful implementation of AI solutions in public services, as well as in the back office through robotic process automation (Farooq & Solowiej 2020). The World Economic Forum (Kirkham 2021) identified, as part of the 2021 Davos agenda, seven ways the use of AI can restore trust in the delivery of public services: (1) reducing fraud and error in tax and benefits systems; (2) detecting grant fraud; (3) finding errors in public finance data; (4) examining service delivery processes; (5) automating public services; (6) predicting public health crises; and (7) efficiently allocating resources. The benefits of personalized public services are certainly significant, especially if one imagines future combinations of Internet of Things, AI, and edge/cloud services. Image capture/recognition/analysis, natural language processing, and more versatile systems combining different AI models are finding their place in a myriad of public services.

Another area in which civil servants may be called to new tasks in the future is that of data management and governance. This is even truer today, as the hoarding of data in the hands of a few tech giants is being met with increased distrust by end users around the world, and governments are actively seeking to 'liberate' data by enabling more competition and trust-enhancing governance models in the storage, processing, and use/reuse of this essential resource. A good example is the EU's data strategy, centred around data unbundling and interoperability obligations (included in the forthcoming Data Act and Digital Markets Act); the launch of sector-specific and horizontal, cross-cutting data spaces; and a federated cloud ecosystem (Renda 2020).

Most citizen-facing applications of AI will require adequate data management and stewardship, and this is an area in which most of the competences appear to be lacking in governments around the world. Van Ooijen et al. (2019) show the cycle of data management in the public sector, highlighting the various activities that will be needed throughout the process, from the collection and generation of data to storing, securing, and processing data; sharing, curating, and publishing data; and using and reusing data. Many of these activities will require a combination of human skills and AI. At the same time, obstacles to a successful completion of the data governance cycle include the lack of data sharing inside administrations; the lack of access to data held by the private sector (B2G); the lack of data management and stewardship skills; and the lack of a legal framework that is adequately conducive to optimal data reuse.

In some countries, the ability of government to handle data and enable their reuse (in full respect of privacy legislation) has led to a transformation of government into an enabling platform. A good example in this respect is Estonia, a small country that managed to leapfrog in the adoption of good practice by investing in a secure internet-based data exchange layer that enables states' different information systems to communicate and exchange data with each other. X-Road serves as a platform for application development by which any state institution can relatively easily extend their physical services into an electronic environment. For example, if an institution, or a private company for that matter, wishes to develop an online application it can apply to join X-Road and thereby automatically get access to any of the following services: client authentication (either by ID card, mobile ID, or internet bank authentication systems); authorization, registry services, query design services to various state-managed data depositories and registries, data entry, secure data exchange, logging, query tracking, visualization environment, central and local monitoring, etc. These services are automatically provided to those who join X-Road and they provide vital components for the subsequent application design. Therefore, X-Road offers a seamless point of interaction between those extending their services online and different state-managed datasets and services.

CONCLUSION: FUTURE JOBS AND SKILLS IN THE AI-DRIVEN PUBLIC SECTOR

The previous sections took stock of the ongoing transformation of government in the age of AI. This transformation is going to be pervasive, and its impact on the future of public-sector jobs will depend on the extent to which governments manage to acquire new skills, embracing the technological revolution in a human-centric, trustworthy way. The magnitude of the challenge is significant: in the US, according to Accenture (2020), between 20 and 45 per cent of the working time of civil servants is dedicated to tasks that can be automated, and between 45 and 60 per cent of their time corresponds to tasks that can be complemented by technology. In Latin America, Weller et al. (2019) estimated that the average probability of technological substitution in public administration and defence sectors is 43.2 per cent, and approximately 30 per cent of the public administration labour force works in occupations with a high risk of substitution.

It should be noted that these estimates consider the number of public jobs susceptible to automation, but not the number of new public jobs that could be created in the context of AI adoption, nor the number of workers in positions at risk of automation that could be relocated to other government positions. To face this challenge, governments must prioritize efforts to develop new soft and hard skills in public workers. Chinn et al. (2020), in their analysis for McKinsey, estimate that in the next three years the governments of the EU will have the challenge of training close to 9 million workers in digital skills, digital citizenship skills, and traditional soft skills. They estimate the need for an additional 1.7 million employees with technological skills in the EU-28 (including the United Kingdom) by 2023, including approximately 1.1 million people with advanced and complex data analytic skills. For complex data analysis alone, France, Germany, and the United Kingdom will each require more than 100,000 additional skilled employees in the public sector by 2023. Interestingly, the authors add that certain classical skills like problem-solving and creativity will maintain or increase their importance, requiring further development.

As a matter of fact, the scholarly understanding of the skills that will be needed in government in the future is increasingly veering away from traditional coding or science, technology, engineering and mathematics skills, towards more foundational critical and analytical thinking capabilities, as well as skills that enable flexibility and adaptability to changing circumstances, and are therefore compatible with the 'agile governance' paradigm at a time in which resilience (intended as the ability to adapt to unpredictable, or unpredicted, shocks) becomes a key feature of institutions. The main pillars of a strategy to enable government resilience in the age of multiple risks and the rise of AI as a general purpose technology are thus the following:

- *Data governance and stewardship skills* will be needed for governments to fully enable their role as platforms, intermediaries, and regulators. A good data steward needs to be able to rely on a suitable legal framework for data governance and possess skills in ensuring data quality, data definition, and compliance with privacy standards; ensuring data completeness, accuracy, and integrity; managing metadata and processes; ensuring data security; and carrying out adequate monitoring.
- *Complementary skills to machine learning, to be coupled with domain knowledge.* Rather than pure coding or software development skills, government officials will have to master abilities that enable full cooperation with AI systems, either on a 1:1 basis or in so-called 'superteams', in which one AI system interacts with several individuals. For example, in 2021 the Deloitte 'Human Capital Trends' report observed that one of the key trends to watch is US federal agencies' incorporation of AI agents and functions directly into the work of human teams, in what are called AI-infused superteams: this requires long-term effort to both reskill employees and change their organizational culture to better incorporate AI tools.
- *Constant reskilling and upskilling of workers*, in what appears to become a definitive feature of the future of work, i.e. the need for a suitable 'work-retrain-life' balance. Several governments around the world are now launching programmes to reskill their workforce, from Australia to India, Europe, the US, and several developing countries.
- *The ability to monitor the job market and carry out horizon scanning* to understand where future jobs may be, and what skills may be needed to fill the related vacancies. In this respect, the current Fourth Industrial Revolution paradigm appears to be insufficient to guide governments on where skills may be needed. The paradigm is almost exclusively related to technological deepening in value chains and industrial plants; on the contrary, an 'Industry 5.0' approach such as that adopted by (parts of) the European Commission ensures that the digitization of industry contributes to a human-centric, resilient, and sustainable industrial transformation in the coming years (Renda 2022).

In summary, absent a coordinated, comprehensive strategy to transform government, the impact of AI on public-sector jobs is likely to be negative.

However, governments that can step up their efforts and their 'situational awareness' with respect to the impact of digital technologies in the public sector will be able to pave the way for a brighter future for the public workforce. In this brighter future, humans perform non-repetitive tasks in government and, thanks to updated skills and the support of AI systems, provide high-quality public services and regulations to the benefit of society as a whole.

REFERENCES

Accenture. (2020). Technology Vision report. At https://www.accenture.com/us-en/insights/technology/_acnmedia/Thought-Leadership-Assets/PDF-2/Accenture-Technology-Vision-2020-Full-Report.pdf

Alfter, B. (2019). Automating Society 2019: Denmark, AlgorithmWatch. Available at: https://algorithmwatch.org/en/automating-society-2019/denmark/

Allen, R. Q. C., & Masters, D. (2020). *Regulating for an Equal AI: A New Role for Equality Bodies*. EQUINET, Brussels.

Ayres, I., & Braithwaite, J. (1992). *Responsive Regulation: Transcending the Deregulation Debate*. Oxford University Press, Oxford.

Beduschi, A. (2020). International Migration Management in the Age of Artificial Intelligence. *Migration Studies*. https://tinyurl.com/ydwan3de

Bogucki, A., Engler, A., Perarnaud, C., & Renda, A. (2022). *The AI Act and emerging EU digital acquis. Overlaps, gaps and inconsistencies*, CEPS In-Depth Analysis 2022-02.

Buri, I., & van Hoboken, J. V. J. (2021). The Digital Services Act (DSA) Proposal: A Critical Overview. Universiteit van Amsterdam – Instituut voor Informatierecht. https://dsa-observatory.eu/wp-content/uploads/2021/11/Buri-Van-Hoboken-DSA-discussion-paper-Version-28_10_21.pdf

Castellano, P. S. (2021). Inteligencia artificial y Administración de Justicia: ¿Quo vadis, justitia? *IDP: Revista de Internet, Derecho y Política*, 33.

Chinn D., Hieronimus S., Kirchherr J., & Klier J. (2020). *The Future Is Now: Closing the Skills Gap in Europe's Public Sector*. McKinsey & Company.

Desouza, K. C., Dawson, G. S., & Chenok, D. (2020). Designing, Developing, and Deploying Artificial Intelligence Systems: Lessons from and for the Public Sector. *Business Horizons*, 63(2), 205–213.

DGAL (French General Directorate for Food). (2019). Activity Report.

Eggers, W. et al. (2017). AI-Augmented Government. Deloitte. www2.deloitte.com/us/en/insights/focus/cognitive-technologies/artificial-intelligence-government.html

Engler, A. (2022). The AI Bill of Rights Makes Uneven Progress on Algorithmic Protections, *Lawfare*. www.lawfareblog.com/ai-bill-rights-makes-uneven-progress-algorithmic-protections

Engstrom, D. F., Ho, D. E., Sharkey, C. M., & Cuéllar, M.-F. (2020). Government by Algorithm: Artificial Intelligence in Federal Administrative Agencies. Report submitted to the Administrative Conference of the United States. www.acus.gov/sites/default/files/documents/Government%20by%20Algorithm.pdf

Farooq, K., & Solowiej, B. J. (2020). Artificial Intelligence in the Public Sector: Maximizing Opportunities, Managing Risks. World Bank report 157501.

http://documents1.worldbank.org/curated/en/809611616042736565/pdf/Art
ificial-Intelligence-in-the-Public-Sector-Maximizing-Opportunities-Managing-R
isks.pdf

Gartner. (2021). https://www.gartner.com/en/newsroom/press-releases/2021-10-
26-gartner-survey-finds-more-than-half-of-digital-govern

Government of Canada. (2018). Directive on Automated Decision-Making. At
https://www.tbs-sct.canada.ca/pol/doc-eng.aspx?id=32592

Hawksworth, J., Berriman, R., & Goel, S. (2018). Will Robots Really Steal
Our Jobs? An International Analysis of the Potential Long Term Impact of
Automation. PricewaterhouseCoopers. www.pwc.co.uk/services/economics-
policy/insights/the-impact-of-automation-on-jobs.html

Henk, A., & Nilssen, F. (2021). Is AI Ready to Become a State Servant? A Case
Study of an Intelligent Chatbot Implementation in a Scandinavian Public
Service. Proceedings of the 54th Hawaii International Conference on System
Sciences. http://hdl.handle.net/10125/71290

Hoekstra, M., Chideock, C., & Veenstra, A. F. van (2021). Quickscan AI in publieke dienstverlening II, Quickscan AI in publieke dienstverlening II. Report,
Rijksoverheid.

Intel. (2022). Streamlined Sewer Pipe Inspection Analysis with Intel AI
Technologies. Case Study. www.intel.com/content/dam/www/central-libraries/
us/en/documents/2022-11/dc-water-wipro-ai-case-study.pdf

Kirkham, R. (2021). 7 Ways AI Can Restore Trust in Public Services. World
Economic Forum. www.weforum.org/agenda/2021/01/ai-trust-public-services/

Latonero, M. (2019). Stop Surveillance Humanitarianism. *New York Times*, 11 July.

Molnar, P., & Gill, L. (2018). *Bots at the Gate: A Human Tights Analysis of
Automated Decision-Making in Canada's Immigration and Refugee System*. The
Citizen Lab, Toronto.

NJCM (Nederlands Juristen Comité voor de Mensen-rechten). (2020).
Consultation EU White Paper on Artificial Intelligence. https://njcm.nl/wp-
content/uploads/2020/06/Outline-reactie-internetconsultatie-AI-2.pdf

OECD. (2021). *Data-Driven, Information-Enabled Regulatory Delivery*. OECD
Publishing, Paris. https://doi.org/10.1787/8f99ec8c-en

OECD & CAF. (2022). *The Strategic and Responsible Use of Artificial Intelligence
in the Public Sector of Latin America and the Caribbean*. OECD Publishing,
Paris. https://doi.org/10.1787/1f334543-en

Ramos, G. (2022). AI's Impact on Jobs, Skills, and the Future of Work: The
UNESCO Perspective on Key Policy Issues and the Ethical Debate. *New
England Journal of Public Policy*, 34(1), Article 3.

Renda, A. (2020). Making the Digital Economy 'Fit for Europe. *European Law
Journal*, 26(5–6), 345–354. https://doi.org/10.1111/eulj.12388

Renda, A. (2022). Beyond the Brussels Effect: Leveraging Digital Regulation for
Strategic Autonomy. FEPS policy brief, March.

Renda, A., Arroyo, J., Fanni, R., Laurer, M., Sipiczki, A., Yeung, T., et al. (2021).
Study to support an impact assessment of regulatory requirements for Artificial
Intelligence in Europe. European Commission. At https://op.europa.eu/en/
publication-detail/-/publication/55538b70-a638-11eb-9585-01aa75ed71a1

Rödl & Partners. (2022). ASEAN Newsflash, 4Q/2022.

Schulz, W. et al. (2018). *Algorithms and Human Rights: Study on the Human Rights
Dimensions of Automated Data Processing Techniques and Possible Regulatory
Implications*. Council of Europe, Brussels.

Sharma, G. D., Yadav, A., & Chopra, R. (2020). Artificial Intelligence and Effective Governance: A Review, Critique and Research Agenda. *Sustainable Futures*, 2, 100004.

UK Government. (2019). https://www.gov.uk/government/collections/a-guide-to-using-artificial-intelligence-in-the-public-sector

Ulbricht, L., & Yeung, K. (2022). Algorithmic Regulation: A Maturing Concept for Investigating Regulation *of* and *through* Algorithms. *Regulation & Governance*, 16, 3–22.

van Ooijen, C., Ubaldi, B., & Welby, B. (2019). A Data-Driven Public Sector: Enabling the Strategic Use of Data for Productive, Inclusive and Trustworthy Governance. *OECD Working Papers on Public Governance*, 33. https://doi.org/10.1787/09ab162c-en

Verhulst, S., Young, A., & Sloane, M. (2021). The AI Localism Canvas. 1 September. *Informationen zur Raumentwicklung*, 48(3), 86–89.

Weller, J., Gontero, S., & Campbell, S. (2019). *Cambio tecnológico y empleo: una perspectiva latinoamericana. Riesgos de la sustitución tecnológica del trabajo humano y desafíos de la generación de nuevos puestos de trabajo*, Macroeconomics of Development series, No. 201 (LC/TS.2019/37), Santiago, Economic Commission for Latin America and the Caribbean (ECLAC).

Wirtz, B. W., Weyerer, J. C., & Geyer, C. (2019). Artificial Intelligence and the Public Sector: Applications and Challenges. *International Journal of Public Administration*, 42(7), 596–615.

PART III

THE LABOR IMPLICATIONS OF ARTIFICIAL INTELLIGENCE AT WORK

16. Recurrent memes and technological fallacies
David Heatley and Bronwyn Howell

The belief that technological change is accelerating, and that it will cause devastating effects on the labor market, has a very long history (Mokyr et al., 2015). Current anxiety about a dystopian "future of work" caused by advances in artificial intelligence (AI) is merely the latest outbreak of a remarkably persistent meme.

Memes are ideas, behaviors, or styles that spread by means of imitation from person to person within a culture, often carrying symbolic meaning representing a particular phenomenon or theme (Wikipedia, 2021). They propagate because they are appealing (to many), appear to be logical, and take effort to refute. These characteristics, however, do not make such memes correct.

We outline a brief history of the 2010s "future of work" meme outbreak. We trace the outbreak to forecasters that made strong predictions about the rate of AI development and adoption, adopted strong assumptions about how those technologies would affect specific jobs, and how effects on specific jobs would affect the wider labor market.

These forecasts have morphed into "fact." And the burden of proof appears to have shifted from their proponents to their opponents. We believe this justifies our "meme" characterization. However, forecasts are testable. They can, and should, be tested against reality. And when tested, these ones fail. The evidence against them is overwhelming (NZPC, 2020).

Why then is the future of work meme so persistent? We suggest that the logic that supports it is based on economic fallacies. One – the lump of labor fallacy – has a long history. We explore other contributing fallacies and biases in human judgment that facilitate memes becoming falsely established as "facts."

What policies should governments adopt to deal with the future of work? Predicting technology is hard and predicting the labor-market effects of technology is foolhardy. Governments will inevitably need to adjust labor-market policy in response to change, but they should wait until evidence of change and its direction materialize before deciding how to act. Trying to "get ahead of the game" and protect workers' interests is laudable, however, acting on predictions rather than data risks harming the interests of those they seek to protect.

OLD ANXIETIES AND CONFIDENT PREDICTIONS

Technological anxiety appears to surface at least once a generation. Commentators typically report a heightened, accelerating, or unprecedented rate of change, and infer negative labor-market consequences. Examples are plentiful, including:

> We are being afflicted with a new disease of which some readers may not yet have heard the name, but of which they will hear a great deal in the years to come – namely, technological unemployment. This means unemployment due to our discovery of means of economising the use of labour outrunning the pace at which we can find new uses for labour. (Keynes, 1930)

> machines will be capable, within twenty years, of doing any work a man can do. (Simon, 1960)

> [Technological change is occurring at] a breath-taking pace, and such a pace cannot but create new ills as it dispels old, new ignorance, new problems, new dangers. (Kennedy, 1962)

> it was very evident that some sections of the community were seriously concerned at the likely impact of micro-processors and new technologies on employment opportunities and the control of the economy itself. (Young, 1980)

Although periods of technological progress can disrupt specific sectors and occupations, they have not led to lasting and widespread unemployment (Autor, 2015). People found new work elsewhere, and resources flowed to new firms and industries. Looking at history, Keynes' "technological unemployment" has proved to be a mirage. Yet the meme persists.

The 2010s "Future of Work" Outbreak

Breakthroughs by AI researchers starting around 2007[1] – and subsequent increases in research and development investment from the early 2010s – resurfaced these anxieties:

---

[1]   Breakthrough technical papers include Hinton (2007), Raina et al. (2009), and Krizhevsky et al. (2012).

Digital technologies change rapidly, but organizations and skills aren't keeping pace. As a result, millions of people are being left behind. Their incomes and jobs are being destroyed, leaving them worse off. (Brynjolfsson & McAfee, 2011)

[Accelerating progress in AI could lead to] sustained periods of time with a large fraction of people not working [and to a fall in] both the labor force participation rate and the employment rate. (Furman, 2016)

The most influential recent predictions of labor-market change were those of Frey and Osborne (2013). That study has been widely interpreted as concluding that 47 percent of United States (US) employment would be automated over the next 10–20 years. It was followed by a slew of other studies that, to varying degrees, reused Frey and Osborne's assumptions, methods, and datasets. Figure 16.1 shows the headline results from 14 such studies.[2]

These "jobs at risk" forecasts rely on models that incorporate many assumptions about the rate of AI development and adoption: how that technology will affect specific jobs and how effects on specific jobs will change the wider labor market. Those assumptions are, ultimately, a matter of judgment by the study authors, and differing judgments will lead to variance between the model outputs. Such variance can be seen in Figure 16.1. It is also possible that the models are out of step with reality.

While concerns about job automation have been the backbone of the future of work meme, we acknowledge that other concerns about the effects of specific technologies on workplaces and employer–worker relations have arisen over a similar timeframe. Examples include technology that monitors worker performance, and digital platforms that match or allocate work. In some cases, these concerns have become grouped under the "future of work" banner, in others they are being pursued independently. This chapter does not address these concerns.

TESTING THE PREDICTIONS AGAINST REALITY

It is now nine years since Frey and Osborne's 2013 study – 90 percent of the way to the near end of their forecast period (2023) and nearly halfway

---

[2]   See Heatley (2019a) and NZPC (2019) for full references to the studies in Figure 16.1.

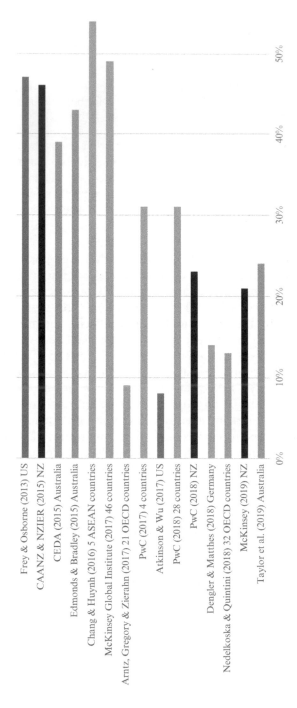

Source: Heatley, 2019a; NZPZ, 2019.

Figure 16.1 Jobs at risk from automation over the following 10–20 years, selected models

to the far end (2033).[3] If their predictions were correct then the effects should be obvious by now. An economy with rapid or increasing technological change would exhibit measurable changes in various economic and labor-market indicators. These indicators fall into two broad groups: (1) the pace of technological change; and (2) the labor-market effects of technological change.

Evidence of change in and across these indicators consistent with the predictions would support the methodology of the models and the validity of the assumptions and datasets on which the models rely. Conversely, a lack of such evidence (or contrary evidence) would cast significant doubt over these models.

The Pace of Technological Change

Many contemporary studies claim that the pace of technology development and adoption is "accelerating," or that today's emerging technologies are "exponential" in a way that distinguishes them from earlier ones. Ideally, such claims could be tested against a metric of the pace of technological change that met three criteria: robustness, wide acceptance, and the availability of long-run data. However, no metric meets these criteria. Here we look at two proxies: driverless vehicle adoption and productivity growth. In neither case do the data support the claims.

Driverless vehicle adoption is way behind "schedule"

Frey and Osborne (2013) reported "most workers in transportation and logistics occupations, together with the bulk of office and administrative support workers, and labor in production occupations" to be particularly at risk. Indeed, AI replacing vehicle drivers makes an outsized contribution to projected job losses in all the studies in Figure 16.1. In addition, a "driverless car" removes a currently clearly defined job entirely – an effect easier to distinguish than those from many other potential applications of AI. (An example with unclear effects is a chatbot on a website on which there has already been some substitution of the human salesperson's task with web features such as a frequently asked questions (FAQ) page. It is

---

[3]   The world economy and labor markets have been significantly disrupted by the SARS-CoV-2 pandemic, and by collective and individual responses to the pandemic. This disruption started in February 2020 and the world is yet to return to a "new normal" (as of September 2022). For this reason, we ignore labor-market data after 2019 in this chapter. We note, however, that most advanced economies are currently experiencing labor shortages – rather than the surpluses one would expect from technological unemployment.

not clear whether the substantive effect of the chatbot is on the supply side (marketing task), thereby impacting on paid work tasks, or the demand side (decreasing the (search) time taken for the customer to ascertain information already provided in the FAQ), in which case the effect on paid work tasks is negligible.)

Driverless cars – somewhat a poster child for advanced applications of AI – would make us "permanent backseat drivers" from 2020, according to a 2015 *Guardian* article (Adams, 2015). Tesla chief executive officer Elon Musk tweeted in 2016 that the company would demonstrate a cross-country automated drive by "next year." In 2019, he tweeted that "everyone with Tesla Full Self-Driving" would be able to make such a journey by 2020 (Barry, 2021).

That widely predicted future has not come to pass. AI and related technologies have not advanced so quickly (Glaser, 2019; Lee, 2018; Naughton, 2019).

Austroads (2021) documented continuing downwards revisions of forecasts around the world:

> During the last 18 months there has been a significant adjustment in comparative forecasts ... One example that typifies the updates to forecasts can be seen in comparing the UK Connected Places Catapult (2021) to the Transport Systems Catapult (2017) market forecast ... There is a clear downward shift right across the forecast period from 2025–2035, representing both later introduction and slower growth.

Austroads (2021) forecasted that at most 1 percent of the Australian vehicle fleet will be capable of "Highly Automated Driving for many rural journeys, defined as vehicles capable of operating without a driver on rural roads as well as motorways" by 2031.[4] Litman (2020) was similarly restrained, predicting that driverless vehicles will not be common and affordable until the 2050s or 2060s.

There is no consensus about the pace of current and future progress in AI. Some commentators are highly skeptical. Marcus (2018), for example, posited that AI "may well be approaching a wall" due to inherent limitations. AI has previously experienced large increases in investment and activity, only to be followed by "winters" during which funding and interest in AI research dried up (specifically 1974–1980 and 1987–1993). Rather than a smooth curve of improvement, the development of AI in the past is more a process of "fits and starts" (Snow, 2018).

---

4   This definition aligns with level 4 of the Society of Automotive Engineers levels of driving automation (SAE International, 2021). Level 4 falls somewhat short of level 5, "full driving automation," in which there is no role whatsoever for a human driver.

Kahneman et al. (2021) suggest that data-driven AI models are better than human-mediated models, but not by much, as they still rely on human judgment in their specification. Their chief benefit is that, because they are not subject to human errors and biases, they are more consistent than humans in interpreting and processing data and taking action. However, neither are they able to respond to unprecedented circumstances (Howell & Potgieter, 2021), or take account of legitimate variations in human expectations. One impediment to widespread adoption of autonomous vehicles is varying human perceptions of morally acceptable actions to take. An example is the "trolley problem": should a vehicle be programmed to avoid striking (say) five adults or one child when confronted with that stark choice (Heatley, 2019b; Roff, 2018)?

Productivity growth is down, not up
The rate of technological change cannot be measured directly, as there is no systematic way to measure the relative importance of different technologies.

Firms adopt technology to improve their performance – to increase profits, grow their market, or further their mission. Decisions that improve firm performance typically also raise national productivity – the ability to produce more or better goods and services with the same or fewer inputs. So, productivity growth is a useful proxy indicator of the long-run rate of technological change (US National Commission on Technology, Automation, and Economic Progress, 1966).

Labor productivity is defined as economic output per worker. Accordingly, replacing a worker with a machine capable of the same output results in an increase in measured labor productivity. If such replacement had accelerated, then labor productivity should similarly accelerate. This is not borne out in the data (Figure 16.2). Rather, labor-productivity growth since 2011 has been in the doldrums.

Multifactor productivity (MFP) growth, a related metric, measures changes in output that cannot be attributed to changes in the amount of capital or labor input. MFP growth reflects factors such as advances in knowledge and improvements in management and production techniques. All else equal, technological progress leading to better and cheaper machines should spur MFP growth. Yet the data for advanced economies shows anemic MFP growth in recent years (Figure 16.3).

It is plausible that productivity improvements have occurred but are either not being measured accurately or pertain to inherently unmeasurable factors (e.g. intangible capital; Brynjolfsson et al., 2021). While this cannot be discounted, it is not a new phenomenon, having dated from at least Robert Solow's (1987) observation that "you can see the computer age everywhere but in the productivity statistics" (Solow, 1987).

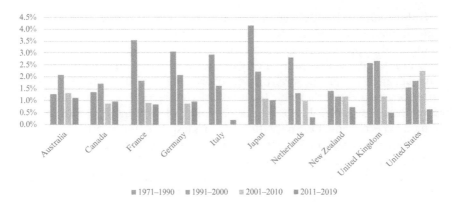

Source: OECD.Stat, https://stats.oecd.org/viewhtml.aspx?datasetcode=PDB_
GR&lang=en#

Figure 16.2   *Labor productivity: average annual growth rates, selected*
OECD countries, 1971–2019

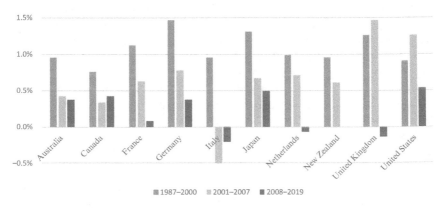

Source: OCED.Stat, https://stats.oecd.org/viewhtml.aspx?datasetcode=PDB_
GR&lang=en#

Figure 16.3   *Multifactor productivity: average annual growth rates,*
selected OECD countries, 1985–2019

Yet equally plausible arguments suggest that the potential productivity
effects of computerization – and hence AI which is derived from them –
have been overestimated (e.g. Gordon, 2000; Triplett, 1999). It may be
that despite expectations, these technologies are just not as transformative
as was originally expected.

The Labor-Market Effects of Technological Change

In an economy with rapid or increasing technological change, measurable changes in a variety of labor-market indicators would be expected. These include:

- Unemployment and labor-market participation rates. Fast rates of technological change create frictional unemployment, where an increased number of people are displaced from their current jobs, and time between jobs adds to the average unemployment rate.
- Rates of occupational churn.[5] New technology creates new occupations (elevator operators in the 1920s) and eliminates old ones (elevator operators in the 1970s). More generally, it shifts the relative proportions of occupations demanded by employers.
- Exit rates for older workers. Older workers are more likely to have their skills made obsolete by new technologies and have much less to gain by retraining. So, they would be likely to leave the labor market in greater numbers.
- Shifting boundaries between jobs performed within and outside of firms. Technology can change what jobs are more efficiently done in house or contracted out. These effects might show up in changes to rates of self-employment and temporary work compared to rates of permanent employment.
- Average length of job tenure. Job tenure should be measurably shorter, as a result of a change in one or more of the above indicators.

NZPC (2020) examined New Zealand labor-market indicators to see if they supported claims of accelerating technological change. It also considered international trends, particularly for Australia (as its labor market is to some extent linked to New Zealand's) and for the US (as it is a significant developer and early adopter of emerging technologies).

NZPC (2020) found no evidence for these three countries consistent with accelerating technological change. Highlights include:

- Low unemployment rates and high participation rates in New Zealand, Australia, and the US.

---

[5] We note the distinction between an *industry*, a collection of related entities in national statistics, and *occupation*, which transcends industries. The application of AI does not necessarily affect all occupations within an industry equally. For example, accountants and taxi drivers (occupations) may both work in the transport industry, but driverless vehicles would affect these occupations differently.

- Occupational churn, which measures shifts in the proportions of occupations demanded by employers in an economy, is a direct measure of the labor-market effects of technological change over extended time periods.[6] Drawing on 150 years of US data, Atkinson and Wu (2017) concluded that "the rate of occupational churn in recent decades is at the lowest level in American history – at least as far back as 1850." New Zealand (Maré, 2019) and Australian (Office of the Chief Economist, 2018) studies, covering shorter periods, similarly found no recent increase in occupational churn.
- Older workers are staying in the workforce for longer. Older workers would likely find their skills becoming redundant if technological change was accelerating. And as older workers have less to gain from retraining than younger workers, it might be expected that older workers would drop out of the workforce at increasing rates. However, labor-force participation by people aged 55–64 has been rising across the Organisation for Economic Co-operation and Development (OECD) over the past two decades (OECD, 2019). Other factors – rising educational attainment, improving health, and increases in the age of eligibility for government-provided retirement income – are encouraging older people to remain longer in the labor market. The rate of technological change has not been rapid enough to offset these factors.
- New Zealand data show that the proportion of temporary and casual work has remained broadly stable over the past decade. Self-employment rates have also been stable or have declined in New Zealand, and trends in other countries have been mixed. These data do not support claims that New Zealand's employment arrangements are being significantly affected by technological change.
- Australian (Borland & Coelli, 2017) and US (Hyatt & Spletzer, 2016) data show increasing average length of job tenure.

Summary: No Evidence of Technological Acceleration, Nor Labor-Market Disruption

In summary, NZPC (2020) found no labor-market data supporting the idea that technological change was accelerating, nor that labor markets

---

6   The logic behind this observation is that shifts between occupations are often costly to workers, so they will generally only make such shifts in an economy that is itself changing significantly (and thus changing what jobs are offered and rewarded). Technological change is the most common cause of such economic changes.

were being disrupted by technological change.[7] Technological change – as measured by productivity growth, business dynamism, and labor-market change – is static or slowing. While no single indicator on its own provides strong support for this conclusion, together the evidence is strong. This conclusion casts significant doubt on the predictions of the jobs-at-risk-from-automation models. It would be imprudent to plan based on the predictions of one, or a group, of these models.

TECHNOLOGICAL FALLACIES AND THEORIES OF LABOR MARKET

Why have the jobs-at-risk-from-automation models performed so poorly in predicting the future? We believe they embody several fallacies.

The Lump of Labor Fallacy

The lump of labor fallacy is the misconception that both the amount of work to be done in an economy (and hence supply of jobs from employers) and the number of people who want work (and hence demand for jobs from workers) are inflexible (Schloss, 1891). People holding this misconception have tried, at different times and with varying degrees of success, to keep immigrants, women, and machines from competing with existing workers, theorizing that increased competition for a fixed number of jobs must inevitably lead to higher unemployment and/or lower wages.

The unstated assumption behind the fallacy is that demand for products and services is inelastic (i.e. price changes do not affect the quantity the producer can sell). But should machinery lower the cost of production of a product or service whose demand is elastic, it will in many cases make sense for business owners to lower their prices and expand production – which tends to increase their demand for workers. (This is why, according

---

[7] Another possible effect of rapid technological change might be seen in changes to the proportion of jobs offered through job-mediating platforms. US evidence suggests that platform-mediated work such as ride-share driving for Uber, or click-work for Amazon Mechanical Turk, remains a small proportion of all work. In the US, approximately 1 percent of households earned income through such work in 2018. Most of these households are doing so for short periods, and not as a primary source of income. For example, a US bank study found that 60 percent of transport work earners (e.g. Uber) and nearly 70 percent of other platform earners in the year to July 2017 received platform income in three or fewer months of that year (Farrell et al., 2018).

to Kestenbaum and Goldstein (2017), spreadsheet software expanded the market for accountants. Spreadsheets dropped the price of running what-if accounting scenarios, and customer demand for those scenarios was very responsive to price.) A further effect is that lower prices benefit consumers directly, allowing them to spend money on other things, thus creating jobs elsewhere in the economy.

Another assumption underpinning the lump of labor fallacy is that machines are primarily a direct replacement for human labor in the production process. But machine introduction can have other effects. A machine-enabled increase in product quality, for example, can have the same effect as a decrease in price. Machines can also perform dangerous or unpleasant tasks that are socially useful but might not otherwise be performed.

The Luddite Fallacy

The luddite fallacy is the idea that new technology destroys jobs (Tabarrok, 2003). If it were generally true, then the new technology of the past few centuries would mean that there were no jobs today.

History shows that apparently labor-replacing technologies have wider effects on the economy that increase the demand for labor. In practice, technology adoption tends to reduce prices, which increases demand; and new technology makes it possible to service previously unmet demand.

The No-Change Baseline Fallacy

Even if technological unemployment is highly unlikely, technology adoption can still cause frictional unemployment, the costs incurred as people and regions adjust to changes in the products and services demanded, and in the skills needed to produce them.[8] Indeed, such changes will almost certainly occur – as they have in the past.

The headline "47% of US employment would be automated over the next 10–20 years" has the implicit message "half of you will lose your jobs to a machine." This is an incorrect interpretation. Most people can expect to spend no more than 45 years in the workforce (e.g. between ages 20 and 65). Over 15 years (the half-way point between 10 and 20), 33 percent of people will retire from the workforce. If we assumed instead that the

---

[8]   Frictional unemployment is unemployment "that occurs because, as people change jobs when some sectors of the economy grow and others contract, it is not practicable to dovetail precisely leaving old jobs and starting new ones. At times of fairly full employment, frictional employment may form an appreciable fraction of total unemployment" (Black et al., 2013).

burden of job-replacing automation in any particular year fell on those about to retire for other reasons, then 47 percent over 15 years becomes a much less scary 14 percent over 15 years. If we assume further that every worker chooses, on average, to upskill or retrain mid-career, then the "jobs automation problem" might largely disappear.

While reality sits somewhere between these extremes, this does illustrate the importance of carefully choosing a baseline. Assuming a no-change baseline is another fallacy.

The Just a Small Step from Innovation to Ubiquity Fallacy

There is no shortage of cool technological innovations. But very few make it through the difficult hurdles of technical and commercial viability. Even fewer become ubiquitous, comprehensively replacing prior technologies. Yes, there is everyone's go-to example, the smartphone. But even this took decades to become ubiquitous, if one starts the clock at earlier attempts (e.g. Apple Newton, Palm Pilot, Windows CE, Blackberry). For every smartphone there is a flying car. And a jetpack. Not to mention fusion power …

Empirical studies have shown that the diffusion of most successful technologies follows an S-shaped "technology diffusion curve" (Rogers, 2003 [1962]). Figure 16.4 depicts this curve, with its three crucial parameters: (A) the point of market saturation; (B) the time taken to reach market saturation; and (C) the time taken to reach the inflection point, when exponential growth switches to exponential decline. While these are all measurable ex post, they are unknowable ex ante. It is not until one reliably observes the inflection point (C) that it is reasonable to forecast (A) and (B).

The long life of existing assets means that even if new technology becomes ubiquitous for new sales, it will take many years for them to form a majority of the stock. For example, even if, starting tomorrow, every vehicle sold in the US was autonomous, it would still take approximately six years to reach 50 percent fleet penetration.[9]

The Very Long-Run Fallacy

Susskind (2020) found that technological unemployment is highly unlikely in the foreseeable future:

---

[9]   The average age of US cars and light trucks was 12.1 years as of January 1, 2021 (IHS Markit, 2021). This is a slight increase from an average of 11.9 years as of January 1, 2020. IHS Markit attributed the increase to Covid-19.

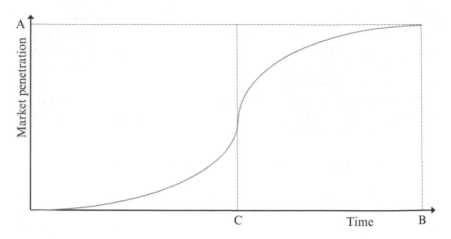

Figure 16.4   The technology diffusion curve

> Current fears about an imminent collapse in the demand for the work of human beings are overblown. In the short run, society's challenge will be in avoiding frictional unemployment: in all likelihood, there will be enough work for human beings to do for a while yet, and the main risk is that some people will not be able to take it up.

Susskind further explored a scenario for the more distant future – a "world without work." In this scenario AI becomes better and cheaper to employ than *all* types of human labor. "But in the longer run … we have to take seriously the threat of structural technological unemployment, where there is simply not enough demand for the work of human beings."

Susskind's analysis leaves two open questions. Is this "world without work" scenario realistic? And, if so, is there anything useful that could be done about it today? Given that technological unemployment is historically unprecedented, a high burden of proof falls on those who believe that *this time* is different. An even higher burden of proof falls on those who think individuals and society can respond effectively today to a theory that *next time* will be different.

In the very long run almost anything is possible. We cannot rule out that people in the future may face Susskind's structural technological unemployment. But they will have a better understanding of the situation they face, and no doubt better tools to deal with it, than the current generation. We use the term very long-run fallacy to describe the idea that the current generation can choose effective responses in the face of such high levels of uncertainty.

The "We Can Predict the Future of Technology" Fallacy

"The only two certainties in life are death and taxes," according to Mark Twain. Or Benjamin Franklin or Daniel Defoe, depending on your source. Which goes a long way towards proving the point. There is only one past, though the details are sometimes unclear or contested. But there are many possible futures, so prediction is fraught. In some cases, it is reasonable to extrapolate from past data. In others, the interaction of a limited number of factors can be modeled, offering forecasts with a reasonable level of reliability. But these techniques fail when predicting technological progress. Society lacks crucial information about yet-to-be-invented, yet-to-be-commercialized, and even yet-to-be-widely-adopted technologies.

WHY IS THE "FUTURE OF WORK" MEME SO PERSISTENT?

Work is central to people's lives, so a threat to work is an existential threat. It not surprising that people react to threats-to-jobs headlines. But why is this meme so persistent in the face of consistent evidence to the contrary? We can speculate about possible reasons, and further research should narrow the field. However, psychological, political, and social factors may provide better explanations for individuals' responses and the prevalence of the meme than economic and technical factors.

A Predisposition towards Pessimism

Psychology and neuroscience research have shown that human beings are predisposed to respond predictably to uncertainty and existential threats by according pessimistic scenarios far greater weight than is justified objectively.

Under prospect theory (Kahneman & Tversky, 1979), individuals respond differently to uncertain losses and gains. A scenario in which jobs will be lost is feared by much more than a scenario with the gain of the same number of jobs is welcomed. That is, the loss of (say) 100 jobs incurs a much larger expected utility loss than the expected utility gain from 100 new jobs (Figure 16.5). Similarly, the loss of something already held is felt more keenly than the loss of the same item anticipated but not yet obtained: losing $100 from one's wallet is regretted more than losing a lottery where the expected winnings were $100. Thus, losing one's current job to AI is feared much more than losing the prospect of a future one created by AI; so logically more effort is put into worrying and whipping up fear about job losses to AI than into advocacy for the potential employment benefits created by the technology.

The way the scenario is "framed" can also influence risk-averse decision makers. When choices are framed in terms of losses, individuals tend to prefer the option that minimizes risk (i.e. the more certain – or arguably less uncertain – status quo) over an uncertain future "gamble." Yet when the same outcome is framed as a gain, then the "gamble" is preferred. Together, these characteristics of human psychology appear to explain preference for no change (the apparent certainty that no jobs will be lost) over the "gamble" of introducing new technology (where a large number of jobs could be lost – even though a large number may also be gained). Given this bias, narratives emphasizing the negative consequences gain greater traction in popular perception and, if repeated often enough, can become the prevailing memes. Narratives outlining the gains are by comparison much less prevalent in the historic record, because job losses were feared more than job gains were valued.

Prospect theory also illustrates the "anchoring effect" of the status quo. When assessing the anticipated payoffs of an intervention, individuals

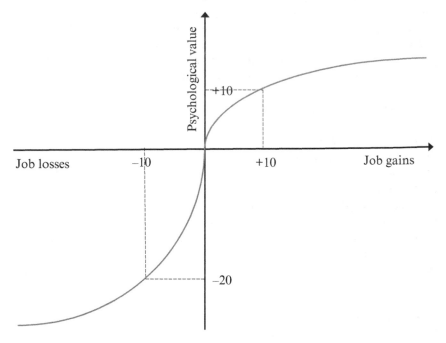

Figure 16.5   Prospect theory S-curve

frequently assess it against the status quo outcome as it is currently, not as the status quo is expected to be in the future. Consequently, ex ante expected gains are overestimated if the status quo ante trend is an increase, while losses will be overestimated if the underlying trend is downward. Yet when the effects of the intervention are considered ex post, individuals tend to measure the effects not in comparison to their actual ex ante state but against some relative comparator. When the outcome is worse relative to the comparator at the outset, then the individual will feel a loss has been incurred, even though they may be materially better off than when they started. This can lead to a magnification of the weight attributed to losses in a prospect theory assessment – the same numerical loss is seen to incur a much more negative effect. A succession of negative outcomes over time can lead to the same outcome being successively more and more negatively valued.

Thus, at a policy level, any evidence of loss attributed to AI can fuel the fear, but assessments of gains are not adjusted in the same manner. The prospect theory utility curve becomes increasingly more asymmetric as the negative weights grow but positive ones remain unchanged; the negative perceptions of those left worse off can come to crowd out the perceptions of gains to those left better off, even though the overall effect is positive.

A Reluctance to Look beyond First-Round Effects

A further reason for the narrative of large job losses from AI can be attributed to the complexity of labor markets, and the human desire for simplicity. The reality of complex environments is that events seldom play out linearly, with direct cause-and-effect explanations. There are many different contexts and influences at play, and many interactions and feedback effects. Yet human minds are primed to look for simple cause-and-effect relationships, which seldom come to pass (Kahneman, 2011). The tendency is to look for simple explanations that conform to well-established narratives and abstract away (ignore) any trails of evidence that do not fit a predetermined pattern (Taleb, 2008). Thus, despite the (inconvenient) evidence that past technological changes have not led to massive system-wide labor market disruptions, the simple historic narrative persists. This suits the agenda of risk-averse individuals who prefer the (apparent) certainty of no change.

Yet another bias comes from using simple models to make predictions in complex environments. Simple models economize on the number of variables and tend to use simple linear relationships. This leads to the problem of WYSIATI – what you see is all there is (Kahneman, 2011) in modeling – modelers overlook underlying factors and interactions that are not immediately obvious. What appears to be happening at a high level may conceal multiple and highly time- and context-dependent lower-level interactions that can together lead to very different outcomes than those imagined possible at the simple higher level. And because such multiple interactions can lead to a very wide range of different outcomes, and the relationships are not always linear, the ability to make confident predictions is severely constrained. The "simple" model is "certainly" not what plays out – and averaging the aggregate of a range of lower-level interactions is rarely satisfactory either, as averages conceal a vast array of individual outcomes that can occur (Savage, 2002). Forecasts made from simple models – such as the broad projections of the overall effect of AI on labor markets – should thus be treated with extreme caution.

Easy to Repeat, Difficult to Refute

Humans prefer simple, cause-and-effect narratives to explain complex scenarios because they appear to confirm evidence observed personally (e.g. everyone knows someone who lost a job because of new technology) and no loose ends are left around to confound belief in the narrative (e.g. the young person with a job in the animation industry doesn't feature in the story). The simplicity of the narratives lends them to easy repetition and portrayal in popular media. They are easy to repeat.

By contrast, making sense of the loose ends is a specialist task for expert researchers, not one best delegated to storytellers or the Greek Chorus. But once the meme is established, it is very difficult for new knowledge to make an impact on the dominant narrative or influence decision-making. Hence it can take quite a long time for decision-makers, notably in the political and social spheres, to replace old ideas with new scientific knowledge and technological advances in their decision-making. For example, in Victorian London, John Snow painstakingly mapped the incidence of cholera amongst consumers of water from the Broad Street pump to demonstrate his theory that water-borne pathogens were responsible. Yet despite the evidence of reduced infection when the pump was closed, public officials persisted in their belief that miasma (bad air) caused the infection and refused for many years to address Snow's other concerns about the city's drains and cesspools causing excessive illness (Tuthill, 2003). It is likely to be just as difficult, 200 years on, to use evidence to unseat policymakers' established beliefs about the effects of AI on the labor market.

Motivated Supporters and Disinterested Objectors

New technology does not happen without optimists. Innovations need research funding and seed capital. And attracting money in noisy, competitive environments requires a relentlessly positive message – one that downplays time constraints, costs, and difficulties, while overselling latent demand and social benefits.

Meanwhile, technology pessimists and catastrophists identify social harms overlooked or downplayed by optimists. Fearing the worst, they accept the aggressive timeframes and adoption rates promoted by the techno-optimists as fact. A near-term and certain threat, after all, is a much more compelling call to arms.

Those with other, perhaps more realistic, views of the likely success and adoption timeframes of new technology have little incentive to participate in these debates. These disinterested stakeholders are less likely to get involved than those with a larger stake.[10] And, no doubt, they find it difficult to be heard in the ensuing din.

CAN GOVERNMENT ACT NOW TO AVERT A FUTURE OF WORK CRISIS?

A government that took the 2016 headline "Robots could replace 1.7 million American truckers in the next decade" (Kitroeff, 2016) at its word would have had a good reason to be concerned. 1.7 million was 100 percent of truckers – and they would all lose their jobs within just ten years. Or, according to Roberts (2016): "Maybe it's two years, maybe five, maybe 10, but either way, the trajectory is toward drivers being put out of business, and 1.8 million truck driving jobs (not to mention all the other jobs they support) is a lot to lose in that short a period of time."

If these claims were credible, an urgent policy response was justified back in 2016. The US Government might have considered, for example, a ban on new driver training and licensing, an early retirement program, and devoted significant resources to retraining truck drivers. Or it might have restricted the sale of autonomous trucks, to prevent or slow their adoption.

But as time has borne out, such policy responses would have been premature. As of late 2022 – six years after the headlines – no US truck drivers have been replaced by autonomous vehicles. Rather than the widely predicted surplus, the US is facing a severe shortage of drivers:

> The American Trucking Associations (ATA) estimates that the US is short 80,000 truckers – an all time high for the industry. And if nothing changes, the shortfall could reach 160,000 over the next decade. (Fleury, 2021)

---

[10] This is an example of the concentrated benefits, diffuse costs problem (Olsen, 1971 [1965]).

> Truck drivers have been in short supply for years, but a wave of retirements combined with those simply quitting for less stressful jobs is exacerbating the supply chain crisis in the United States, leading to empty store shelves, panicked holiday shoppers and congestion at ports … Mr. Biden said last month that he would consider deploying the National Guard to alleviate the trucker shortage. (Ngo & Swanson, 2021)

A seemingly "justified" urgent policy response in 2016 would have been damaging to drivers, and to the wider economy.

Predicting technology is hard. Predicting the labor-market effects of technology is foolhardy. To implement policy based on such predictions is fraught. The COVID-19 pandemic is illustrative: the Global Health Index assessing the pandemic preparedness of OECD countries in 2019 had no predictive power in identifying which countries would turn out to be better managers of the COVID-19 epidemic (COVID-19 National Preparedness Collaborators, 2022). Whatever the preparedness index measured, it was not well matched to the actual challenges of the COVID-19 pandemic. So, one might assume that costly actions taken had no effect, and that actions that could have been effective were not undertaken, because those responsible had unreliable information.

Governments will inevitably need to adjust labor-market policy in response to technological change. But they should wait until reliable evidence of adverse consequences materializes before deciding how to act. Trying to "get ahead of the game" and protect workers' interests is laudable, however, acting on predictions rather than fact risks harming the interests of those they seek to protect. As the "bad news principle" cautions when making decisions under uncertainty (Abel et al., 1996), acting when one should have waited (exercising an option to intervene) is more costly than waiting for more information to become available, because the action is irreversible. If the subsequent information indicates action is required, then it can still be taken, but undoing the effects of the action if it turns out to be wrong is usually impossible.

REFERENCES

Abel, A., Dixit, A., Eberly, J., & Pindyck, R. (1996). Options, the value of capital and investment. *Quarterly Journal of Economics*, 111(3), 753–777.

Adams, T. (2015, September 13). Self-driving cars: From 2020 you will become a permanent backseat driver. *The Observer*. www.theguardian.com/technology/2015/sep/13/self-driving-cars-bmw-google-2020-driving

Atkinson, R.D., & Wu, J. (2017). False alarmism: Technological disruption and the US labor market, 1850–2015 (@Work Series). Information Technology and Innovation Foundation. www2.itif.org/2017-false-alarmismtechnological-disruption.pdf

Austroads (2021). Future Vehicles Forecasts Update 2031. AP-R654-21. https://austroads.com.au/publications/connected-and-automated-vehicles/ap-r654-21

Autor, D. (2015). Why are there still so many jobs? The history and future of workplace automation. *Journal of Economic Perspectives*, 29(3), 3–30.

Barry, K. (2021). Elon Musk, self-driving, and the dangers of wishful thinking: How Tesla's marketing hype got ahead of its technology. *Consumer Reports*. 11 November. www.consumerreports.org/automotive-industry/elon-musk-tesla-self-driving-and-dangers-of-wishful-thinking-a8114459525/

Black, J., Hashimzade, N., & Myles, G. (2013). *A dictionary of economics*. Oxford University Press.

Borland, J., & Coelli, M. (2017). Are robots taking our jobs? *Australian Economic Review*, 50(4), 377–397.

Brynjolfsson, E., & McAfee, A. (2011). *Race against the machine: How the digital revolution is accelerating innovation, driving productivity, and irreversibly transforming employment and the economy*. Digital Frontier Press.

Brynjolfsson, E., Rock, D., & Syverson, C. (2021). The productivity J-Curve: How intangibles complement general purpose technologies. *American Economic Review: Macroeconomics*, 13(1), 333–372.

COVID-19 National Preparedness Collaborators. (2022). Pandemic preparedness and COVID-19: An exploratory analysis of infection and fatality rates, and contextual factors associated with preparedness in 177 countries, from Jan 1, 2020, to Sept 30, 2021. *The Lancet*, 399, 1489–1522.

Farrell, D., Greig, F., & Hamoudi, A. (2018). The online platform economy in 2018: Drivers, workers, sellers and lessors. JPMorgan Chase Institute. www.jpmorganchase.com/corporate/institute/report-ope-2018.htm

Fleury, M. (2021, November 8). How will the US deal with a shortage of 80,000 truckers? *BBC News*. www.bbc.com/news/business-59136957

Frey, C.B., & Osborne, M.A. (2013). The future of employment: How susceptible are jobs to computerisation? Oxford Martin School Working Paper, University of Oxford. www.oxfordmartin.ox.ac.uk/publications/the-future-of-employment/

Furman, J. (2016). Is this time different? The opportunities and challenges of artificial intelligence. Presented at AI Now: The Social and Economic Implications of Artificial Intelligence Technologies in the Near Term, New York University. July. https://obamawhitehouse.archives.gov/sites/default/files/page/files/20160707_cea_ai_furman.pdf

Glaser, A. (2019, June 13). How close are we to self-driving cars, really? *Slate*. https://slate.com/technology/2019/06/selfdriving-car-chris-urmson-aurora-interview.html

Gordon, R. (2000). Does the "new economy" measure up to the great inventions of the past? *Journal of Economic Perspectives*, 14(4), 49–74.

Heatley, D. (2019a, July 17). What to do when forecasts diverge? Blog, New Zealand Productivity Commission. www.productivity.govt.nz/futureworknz blog/what-to-do-when-forecasts-diverge/

Heatley, D. (2019b, October 2). Biased algorithms – a good or bad thing? Blog, New Zealand Productivity Commission. www.productivity.govt.nz/future worknzblog/biased-algorithms-a-good-or-bad-thing/

Hinton, G.E. (2007). Learning multiple layers of representation. *TRENDS in Cognitive Sciences*, 11(10). www.cs.toronto.edu/~hinton/absps/tics.pdf

Howell, B.E., & Potgieter, P.H. (2021). Uncertainty and dispute resolution for blockchain and smart contract institutions. *Journal of Institutional Economics*, 17(4), 454–559.

Hyatt, H.R., & Spletzer, J.R. (2016). The shifting job tenure distribution. *Labour Economics*, 41, 363–377.

IHS Markit (2021, June 14). Average age of cars and light trucks in the US rises to 12.1 years, accelerated by COVID-19, according to IHS Markit. Media release. https://news.ihsmarkit.com/prviewer/release_only/id/4759502/

Kahneman, D. (2011). *Thinking, fast and slow*. Random House.

Kahneman, D., & Tversky, A. (1979). Prospect theory: An analysis of decision under risk. *Econometrica*, 47(2), 263–292.

Kahneman, D., Sidony, O., & Sunstein, C. (2021). *Noise: A flaw in human judgement*. Penguin Random House.

Kennedy, J. F. (1962, September 12). Address at Rice University on the nation's space effort. Speech. www.jfklibrary.org/learn/about-jfk/historic-speeches/addr ess-at-rice-university-on-the-nations-space-effort

Kestenbaum, D., & Goldstein, J. (2017). Episode 606: Spreadsheets! Podcast. *Planet Money*. www.npr.org/sections/money/2017/05/17/528807590/episode-60 6-spreadsheet

Keynes, J.M. (2030). Economic possibilities for our grandchildren. In *Essays in persuasion*. Harcourt Brace, pp. 358–373.

Kitroeff, N. (2016, September 25). Robots could replace 1.7 million American truckers in the next decade. *Los Angeles Times*. www.latimes.com/projects/la-fi-automated-trucks-labor-20160924/

Krizhevsky, A., Sutskever, I., & Hinton, G.E. (2012). ImageNet classification with deep convolutional neural networks. *Proceedings of the 25th International Conference on Neural Information Processing Systems*, 1, 1097–1105.

Lee, T.B. (2018, December 31). The hype around driverless cars came crashing down in 2018. *Ars Technica*. https://arstechnica.com/cars/2018/12/uber-tesla-and-waymo-all-struggled-with-self-driving-in-2018/

Litman, T. (2020). *Autonomous vehicle implementation predictions: Implications for transport planning*. Victoria Transport Policy Institute. www.vtpi.org/avip.pdf

Marcus, G. (2018). Deep learning: A critical appraisal. ArXiv: 1801.00631.

Maré, D. (2019). Occupational drift in New Zealand: 1976–2018 (Motu Working Paper No. 19–22). Motu Economic and Public Policy Research. http://motu-www.motu.org.nz/wpapers/19_22.pdf

Mokyr, J., Vickers, C., & Ziebarth, N.L. (2015). The history of technological anxiety and the future of economic growth: Is this time different? *Journal of Economic Perspectives*, 29(3), 31–50.

Naughton, K. (2019, January 1). Self-driving cars keep tapping the brakes. *Bloomberg Businessweek*. www.bloombergquint.com/businessweek/self-driving-cars-a-main-event-at-ces-keep-tapping-the-brakes

Ngo, M., & Swanson, A. (2021, 9 November). The biggest kink in America's supply chain: Not enough truckers. *New York Times*. www.nytimes.com/2021/11/09/us/politics/trucker-shortage-supply-chain.html

NZPC. (2019). New Zealand, technology and productivity. Technological Change and the Future of Work: Draft report 1. New Zealand Productivity Commission. www.productivity.govt.nz/assets/Documents/16fbd1875d/Draft-report-1_NZ-technology-and-productivity.pdf

NZPC. (2020). Technological change and the future of work: Final report. New Zealand Productivity Commission. www.productivity.govt.nz/assets/Documents/0634858491/Final-report_Technological-change-and-the-future-of-work.pdf

OECD. (2019). OECD employment outlook 2019: The future of work. www.oecd-ilibrary.org/employment/oecd-employment-outlook-2019_9ee00155-en

Office of the Chief Economist. (2018). Industry insights: Future productivity. Australian Department of Industry, Innovation and Science. https://publi cations.industry.gov.au/publications/industryinsightsjune2018/documents/Indu stryInsights_3_2018_O NLINE.pdf

Olsen, M. (1971 [1965]). *The logic of collective action: Public goods and the theory of groups.* Harvard University Press.

Raina, R., Madhavan, A., & Ng, A.Y. (2009). Large-scale deep unsupervised learning using graphics processors. *Proceedings of the 26th International Conference on Machine Learning*, Montreal. http://robotics.stanford.edu/~ang/ papers/icml09-LargeScaleUnsupervisedDeepLearningGPU.pdf

Roberts, D. (2016, August 3). 1.8 million American truck drivers could lose their jobs to robots. What then? *Vox.* www.vox.com/2016/8/3/12342764/autono mous-trucks-employment

Roff, H. (2018). The folly of the trolleys: ethical challenges and autonomous vehicles. Brookings Institution, December 17. www.brookings.edu/research/the-folly-of-trolleys-ethical-challenges-and-autonomous-vehicles/

Rogers, E.M. (2003 [1962]). *Diffusion of innovations* (5th ed.). Free Press.

SAE International. (2021). Taxonomy and definitions for terms related to driving automation systems for on-road motor vehicles. J3016, April.

Savage, S. (2002). The flaw of averages. *Harvard Business Review*, 80(11). www. researchgate.net/publication/291793661_The_Flaw_of_Average

Schloss, D.F. (1891). Why working-men dislike piece-work. *The Economic Review*, 1(3), 311–326.

Simon, H.A. (1960). *The new science of management decision.* Harper & Row.

Snow, J. (2018, October 18). An A.I. glossary. *New York Times.* www.nytimes. com/2018/10/18/business/an-aiglossary.html

Solow, R. (1987, July 12). We'd better watch out. *New York Times Book Review*, 36.

Susskind, D. (2020). *A world without work: Technology, automation and how we should respond.* Penguin Books.

Tabarrok, A. (2003). Productivity and unemployment. *Marginal Revolution*, Blog, December 31. https://marginalrevolution.com/marginalrevolution/2003/12/pro ductivity_an.html

Taleb, N. (2008). *The black swan: The impact of the highly improbable.* Penguin.

Triplett, J. (1999). The Solow productivity paradox: What do computers do to productivity? *Canadian Journal of Economics*, 32(2), 309–334.

Tuthill, K. (2003). John Snow and the Broad Street pump: On the trail of an epidemic. *Cricket*, 31(3), 23–31.

US National Commission on Technology, Automation, and Economic Progress. (1966). Report of the National Commission on Technology, Automation and Economic Progress. US Government. https://files.eric.ed.gov/fulltext/ ED023803.pdf

Wikipedia. (2021, December 12). Meme. https://en.wikipedia.org/w/index. php?title=Meme&oldid=1059890758

Young, J. (1980). *The acceleration of technological change and its implications for employment and industrial relations.* Industrial Relations Centre, Victoria University, Wellington.

17. AI and income inequality: the danger of exacerbating existing trends toward polarization in the US workforce
Dan Sholler and Ian MacInnes

INTRODUCTION: AI ON TWO SIDES OF THE INCOME SPECTRUM

Dr. Richardson sits alone at a computer workstation in a 100-square foot room off the main hallway of her urban healthcare clinic. She is about to see her last patient for the day, a 67-year-old woman who has experienced discomfort while breathing. Dr. Richardson is reviewing scans of the woman's lungs done by a clinic technician just a couple of days ago. She looks first at the original image, scanning it for abnormalities. "Hmm, not seeing anything," she mutters to herself. She then closes the image and opens a second image, this one with three areas of the lungs marked by small green squares. She focuses her eyes on the areas enclosed by green boxes, which a new artificial intelligence (AI) program has identified as "abnormal." She sees nothing that her experience-based rubric would flag as problematic. Still, she gets up from her wheeled chair, walks a few feet to the next door, and asks another doctor to look at the images. They spend 10 minutes discussing possible reasons for the AI-generated annotations – discolorations invisible to the naked eye, differences from previous imaging results, and technical errors – before deciding that additional tests are necessary to determine the cause of the annotations and, possibly, the patient's breathing difficulties. Dr. Richardson signs into the electronic medical record for her patient to order the tests. She then calls for the patient to enter the room and advises the patient to schedule appointments for the additional tests.

Over a thousand miles away from the healthcare clinic, Sophia holds up her pedometer to show that she has walked 8 miles through a clothing retailer's warehouse floor so far today. She accrued these miles zooming through rows and rows of 5 foot-high shelves to pick items ordered by online shoppers, reaching into open boxes of shirts, pants, facemasks, and undergarments. Her route through the warehouse is calculated and dictated by software running on a mobile phone-like device strapped to her arm. The software plans a route that prevents traffic jams and co-worker small talk by preventing any two workers being within 10 feet of one another, ensuring that Sophia takes the fastest path to her next pick. She looks at the device for path instructions, uses it to scan each item she picks, and consults it to see how much work she has left to complete on her shift. She looks away from the device only while walking or placing an item into the wheeled cloth cart she rolls around in front of her. If her two years of warehouse work are any indication, she will walk two to four more miles before her shift ends at 2:00 p.m., each step guided by the device. She is tired, but her night classes at the local community college begin next month, and the $1 per hour increase she received for working through the pandemic will be a good head start toward the costs of books and a new laptop she needs for her education. So she presses on.

Once her cart is full, Sophia empties it onto a spiral conveyor belt that leads to a mechanical sorter on the floor below. Just down a set of stairs from the picking area, George tends to a line of six AI-enabled robots that again sort the clothing items into orders destined for online shoppers. Items of clothing fall from the mechanical sorter belt into a holding bay encircling a robotic arm. The arm picks up each item by its plastic packaging with a suction gripper, rotates the item so that a set of 360 degree barcode scanners can identify the item, and places it into one of 40 cubbies, each cubby corresponding to a single customer's multi-item order. George walks down the row of robots looking for green lights on any of the 240 cubbies, indicating that all items in an order are present. He removes the items from green-lit cubbies and places them in a plastic tote on a wheeled baker's rack, scanning a barcode on the tote to confirm all items are present. Once his baker's rack is full, he wheels the rack to a station where his co-worker will scan the tote barcode, pack the orders into boxes, and apply a shipping label. When George started his job at the warehouse, he was responsible for sorting these items himself, standing at a wall of cubbies and scanning each item as he placed it into the correct location. Tending to the robots is easier work, he tells us, requiring more walking but less arm movement and even less cognitive attention.

Sophia and George have different jobs in the warehouse, but both make the same wage, a dollar per hour above the state minimum. Both hope to become supervisors for their areas once peak season – the months leading up to the winter holidays when orders are at a fever pitch – rolls around and they have an opportunity to prove their worth in a seasonal supervisor role. Last year, neither Sophia nor George was able to keep their supervisor role after the holidays ended. "It's such a short period of time and everyone, the workers, the managers, everyone is working so hard that they aren't paying attention to how I'm performing. Unless I screw up, then they pay attention," George tells us.

Both the warehouse and the urban healthcare clinic are sites of deployment for advanced AI. For Sophia and George, AI helps to organize and administer their work; for Dr. Richardson, AI introduces complexity and uncertainty to diagnosing patient conditions. Both settings might also be viewed as sites of deskilling: work contexts in which a larger share of the analytical work once done by humans is being done by machines. Yet warehouse workers and doctors, as we know, do not face the same level of risk and opportunity when it comes to navigating the changes introduced by AI. Warehouse workers will not, for example, be sued for malpractice if their AI-enabled devices lead them astray in their picking path, while doctors must still sign off on diagnoses and treatment decisions recommended by AI. Likewise, Sophia and George did not receive formal education to perform their work duties and therefore have little reason to question or consult with one another about the decisions made by the devices and robots that organize their work.

The employment and income consequences of AI deployment, though, quite clearly threaten Sophia and George more than they do Dr. Richardson. Doctors will not, in the near term, lose their jobs to AI-enabled automation; even if job loss was a risk, doctors have powerful professional organizations and lobbying groups at their disposal to shape the trajectory of technological futures (Sholler, 2020). Warehouse workers, on the other hand, may start to see hiring quotas and shift hours shrink at their automated workplaces, with little to no collective bargaining power available to them to affect change (Rosenberg & Greene, 2021). In this chapter, we ignore the autonomy problems facing the highly trained professionals who are increasingly asked to use AI in their everyday work. We instead focus on the causes and consequences of the predicament low-wage workers find themselves facing as AI gains popularity and technical maturity in workplaces such as warehouses. We take this stance because, in our estimation, the worsening income inequality in the United States (US) is driven more by shrinking opportunities for workers in the low- and mid-wage end of the income spectrum than it is by autonomy threats to those in the high-wage end of the spectrum. We support this claim by first demonstrating that "low-skill" workers have, for decades or more, lost the most in terms of income and employment compared to mid- and high-skill workers. We then summarize the possible organizational and policy avenues for avoiding the continuation of trends that have, to date, been detrimental to income equality in the US.

AI IN HISTORICAL CONTEXT: ONGOING SKILL- AND TECHNOLOGY-BASED POLARIZATION IN THE US ECONOMY

Scholars, technologists, politicians, and futurists often focus on AI's transformative potential to flexibly automate entire classes of cognitive and physical work. For all the hype, though, we have little reason to expect that mass AI deployment will play out any differently from previous technologies in terms of its impact on income inequality. The primary reason is straightforward: all new workplace technologies are embedded in an array of historical, economic, political, and social systems that shape their impact on work and workers regardless of technical capabilities. Accordingly, AI, like many other general purpose technologies, will likely contribute to higher productivity, efficiency, and growth for companies that have implemented it (Bahrin et al., 2016; Prettner, 2016). Indeed, today's AI – robots, chatbots, and the like – stands to continue a pattern of technology-enabled growth that has roughly been consistent since the Industrial Revolution in the 1700s.

The trend we focus on here, job and income polarization, has likewise been a consistent trend in at least the last two decades, with information technology (IT) playing a role in the accumulation of wealth in the top percentiles of earners. Evidence from the early 2000s, for example, indicates that the introduction of IT affected the demand for labor, sometimes substituting for manual and cognitive labor by encoding work in explicit rules that can be translated into algorithms; in other cases, technology complemented labor by enabling humans to take on non-routine, complex tasks. Autor et al. (2003) estimated that from 1960 to 1998 these shifts in labor demand and the resulting skill profiles of jobs favored college-educated workers: the labor market rewarded and proliferated high-skill composition jobs, a phenomenon sometimes referred to as skill-biased technological change.

The mass implementation of IT over the last few decades provides a cautionary tale as we move forward with AI. There is no doubt that the loss of jobs in the 1980s – a result of IT-enabled outsourcing and automation in manufacturing and other industries – created tremendous hardship for workers who lost reliable and high-paying jobs where they were able to grow within the company from entry-level operators to specialist and management positions. Positions with pathways to higher incomes like these are less abundant, leaving workers with few on-the-job avenues through which to build marketable skills. Worse yet, people in such positions who lose their jobs or see advancement pathways disappear end up in psychological and financial circumstances that deeply threaten their health and welfare (O'Brien et al., 2022). This trend appears to continue today: according to Acemoglu and Restrepo (2017), there is "mounting evidence that the automation of a range of low-skill and medium-skill occupations has contributed to wage inequality and employment polarization" (p. 3).

Polarization often occurs as industries automate or otherwise alter work processes with new technology, transformations driven by market pressures, labor dynamics, or simply isomorphism. In the process of mass technology implementation at the industry level, a worker can experience at least two outcomes depending on where they are positioned at the time of the transition (Goyal & Aneja, 2020). They can either move to a better position that provides more opportunities for professional growth and income or be relegated to another similar task, potentially with lower wages, if it is not being eliminated altogether. The distinction between these two moves depends on education, experience, and skills. In the absence of these qualifications, low-wage workers face dire consequences: fewer opportunities to make upward moves and, given that they are already positioned in the lowest-paying occupations, limited opportunities to move laterally. In other words, few marketable skills and greater supply of low-skill labor can increase the probability that the next job will also be low skill, lower pay, and with few, if any, supplementary benefits.

It is for these same reasons that AI stands to exacerbate income inequalities. Yet analyses of recent AI deployment has tended to focus only on reduction in employment rather than the other, equally dire consequences such as reduction in skill-building opportunities and erosion of advancement pathways. To be sure, recent analyses suggest that scholars and commentators are at least partially justified in their focus on AI's potential to reduce employment. In the US, labor participation of low-skilled workers has declined by 2.34 percent and of medium-skill workers by 2.56 percent (Fersht, 2016; Petropoulos, 2018).

We believe a stronger research agenda focused on how AI might affect job skill profiles and job quality is needed to supplement studies of employment reduction. The reasons, again, are historical: early in the history of computing, changes in demand for skilled labor have accelerated from minimal in the 1960s to much more prevalent in the subsequent decades (Autor et al., 2003). We know that AI will be increasingly capable of taking on more and more complex tasks. As far back as the 1960s, for example, Polanyi and Sen (1960) wrote in the Tacit Dimension that "the Skill of a driver cannot be replaced by a thorough schooling in the theory of the motorcar" and, even 50 years later (Autor et al., 2003), still listed driving a car as a complex task that would be difficult to replace with computers. However, today we see an increasing number of car manufacturers developing autonomous vehicles and trucks, some of which are already on the road (Ackerman, 2021). This is to say that the set of tasks that computers can undertake is widening; as a result, the skills and quality of jobs in the mid-range of the income spectrum may be in danger of degradation in the same way low-wage jobs have been for decades.

We know that work is changing as a result of technology and it affects people differently depending on demographics, experience, skills, and education. Economists have called this skills-biased technological change. Inequalities emerge when technologies require companies to hire high-skill workers who would command higher salaries, thus resulting in wage inequality (Autor et al., 2003). Perhaps the most well-known cases of the technology and income inequality relationship are professions replaced by computers. Computers can perform better than humans as they are able to store, retrieve, and act upon information better. These capabilities have made obsolete professions such as bookkeepers, telephone operators, cashiers, and many other routine occupations (Bresnahan, 1999).

Decoupling of Wages and Productivity

The potential of mid-level job degradation is particularly concerning given the ongoing, sustained trend of productivity-driven profits accruing to the very highest earners at the expense of mid- and low earners. When organizations adopt any IT, they seek one or both of two effects: saving labor (displacement effect) or enhancing labor (productivity effect) (Chiacchio et al., 2018). Contextualizing the polarization of jobs and wages requires assessing whether polarization emerged in response to the success of these efforts. Employers, in other words, may be keeping wages low for a substantial portion of the workforce to accommodate downward trends in their productivity. Economic data from the Federal Reserve, though, suggests that the period from 1950 to today has been marked by a steady increase in output per employee in the US, growing by over 250 percent. Real hourly compensation, on the other hand, grew by just over 115 percent and was concentrated in the top percentiles of earners (Bureau of Labor Statistics, 2021). It appears that wages in the US, then, are decoupled from productivity, and/or that productivity gains are being reinvested into the top end of the workforce, such as by the creation of "superstar" firms (Autor et al., 2020). The latter explanation aligns with observations of high-quality, high-wage job growth outpacing mid- and low-quality jobs.

Additional research on the general trend of wage-productivity decoupling lists technological development and globalization as possible causes (e.g. OECD, 2018). As discussed above, technological innovation tends to be skill-biased (Berman et al., 1998; Card & DiNardo, 2002;

Fernandez, 2001), meaning that new production technologies increase the demand for educated, experienced labor over unskilled labor as cause and consequence of skilled workers' technology-enabled productivity gains (and a greater share of work being done by technologies rather than mid- and low-skill labor). The globalization argument for wage-productivity decoupling suggests that the availability of low-wage labor and inputs at the global scale produces cost and productivity benefits that do not translate into higher wages locally. In reality, "The Great Decoupling" in the US is likely the result of a combination of factors (Brynjolfsson & McAfee, 2012). No matter the cause of decoupling, it is essential to understand how increasingly capable AI systems might contribute to increasing decoupling and, in turn, polarization in the US job market.

From an economic perspective, the calculations being made thus far regarding decoupling are about whether the introduction of technology leads to greater productivity and whether it is labor saving or not. This argument fails to take into consideration that those calculations are dynamic and change depending on the price of technology and labor. The year 2021, for example, saw an increase in inflation related to increased spending after a reduction in Covid-19 restrictions. With limited opportunities for travel and entertainment many workers, and even the unemployed receiving enhanced benefits, were able to save money. This led to an increase in prices, including for labor. Once vaccinations began in early spring and restrictions were starting to ease around the US, hourly workers experienced a 3.9 percent real average increase in their weekly earnings (Bureau of Labor Statistics, 2021). With greater demand for goods and services, commodities also experienced shortages and increased prices. The introduction of AI will result in what Hicks (1963) called labor saving (displacing effect), where at any given wage the introduction of a technology will reduce the demand for labor. It was also during the height of the Covid-19 pandemic that delivery of products became necessary, making workers at warehouse distribution centers essential. It remains to be seen, however, if their productivity during this period of global upheaval will result in sustained increases in wages.

HOW AI STANDS TO EXACERBATE POLARIZATION AND INCOME INEQUALITY

Without intervention, AI will exacerbate a problem that has plagued the US workforce for decades: wage increases will go to the highest earners, while the lowest earners will have modest to no growth in their incomes. There is no reason to believe things will happen any differently, as the trend has been ongoing for over 20 years alongside the development of automation technologies. An additional factor that will contribute to the social and economic inequalities we experience with AI is the speed at which these changes are happening. Several studies (Chiacchio et al., 2018; Friedman, 2016) have alluded to the faster pace at which technology is being introduced. A report by McKinsey Global Institute (Dobbs et al., 2015) indicated, for example, that technological advance is now ten times faster and 300 times the scale of what it was during the Industrial Revolution in the eighteenth century, thus resulting in 3,000 times the impact. While there are indications that integration of new technology to old systems is not always fast, if their predictions are correct and AI is implemented much faster than in prior technological revolutions, it will not provide enough time for the population to adapt, find alternative positions for their skills, or find the time to invest in acquiring new skills to integrate smoothly into a more technologically driven economy. Rapid changes and the competitive pressure companies face to keep up with the advances they face can result in rapid and significant increases in income and wealth inequality (Korinek & Stiglitz, 2021b).

One of the main challenges for low-skill, low-paid populations is that some of their job tasks are repetitive and can be easily automated with the use of more intelligent machines and robots. At the low end of the AI spectrum simpler machines are replacing workers through automated kiosks, materials-handling robots, and service machines. As these technologies mature, they are starting to replace other functions that are more routine in nature, such as fast food that has simple ingredients and steps for preparation. Regarding the way technologies like robots affect the labor market, early studies (Graetz & Michaels, 2017) that used the industrial robots database estimated that it reduced low-skilled labor and negatively affected the position of these workers. Moreover, algorithmic management technologies (Duggan et al., 2020; Lee, 2018) threaten to reduce the skill requirements and skill-building opportunities of mid-level jobs in the same fashion. There are, nonetheless, jobs toward the mid- and high levels of the wage distribution that can benefit from computers as they cannot yet be done by these systems. Searches and research about patents or legal cases, for example, can significantly increase the productivity of lawyers, while market information can improve managerial decision making.

While this analysis focuses on the effects in the US, they are likely to be felt in other countries as well. The long-term trends in income inequality among rich English-speaking countries (the US, the United Kingdom, Canada, Ireland, and Australia) shows that since about 1980 the share of income going to the richest 1 percent has gone up almost to the levels of 1920. The effect has been much less pronounced in continental Europe and

Japan, which indicates that this effect is not inevitable. Institutional and political frameworks play a role in shaping inequality of incomes (Roser & Ortiz-Espina, 2016).

AVERTING INCREASING INEQUALITY: LABOR MOVEMENTS, TECHNOLOGY DEVELOPMENT, AND POLICY MEASURES

The question becomes, then, how we can produce policies and technologies that reduce income inequality as AI deployments increase? We begin to develop ideas for how to do so via an examination of the causes of the current polarization we see, rooted in economic and political systems that have de facto governed technology development over at least the past 15 years. We argue that the increasing capabilities of technology – namely, AI and related technologies – demand a more active approach to using AI to reduce job polarization and resulting income inequality.

Labor Movements

A commonly cited reason for increasing polarization is an overall reduction in the collective bargaining power of US workers. Union membership in the US has declined substantially since the 1950s, and this decline is linked to polarization. Probability of low wage employment, for example, is reduced by 39 percent with union membership, compared to a 33 percent reduction among college degree holders (California Future of Work Commission, 2021). Aside from negotiating higher pay and better benefits, unions also play a critical role in retraining workers when economic cycles or technological change interrupt the normal operation of a given occupation. Likewise, unions have driven changes to pregnancy and parental leave regulations, working hours and conditions, unemployment insurance, and wrongful termination laws, each of which supports workers' ability to transition into and out of jobs with less risk to meeting basic needs.

Despite the decline in union membership in previous decades, the US is showing signs of a labor-organizing revival. Service and industrial workers are organizing unionization efforts at some of the nation's largest employers. Similarly, the 2020 vote on Proposition 22 in California prompted discussion about the need for collective action among workers in gig-economy contract positions (Hiltzik, 2021). The revival of unionization efforts is not relegated to low-wage occupations, either: recent developments in the IT industry, for example, demonstrate US high-wage workers' willingness to reengage their collective bargaining power. The formation of the Alphabet Workers Union, a group of Google engineers and other workers who organized to gain some control over the company's global influence, suggests that the reemergence of unions may be seen across the income spectrum (Conger, 2021).

Recent union membership data add support to the anecdotal examples listed above. California's union membership, for example, increased for the first time in many years in both 2019 and 2020, rising by 99,000 in 2019 and 139,000 in 2020 to a rate of 16.5 percent of the labor force (Bureau of Labor Statistics, 2021). While still well short of the membership levels from decades past, these numbers give reason to pay close attention to labor organizing and its potential impact on polarization in the near future.

Unions and professional organizations have always been a primary tool workers use to shape the trajectory of technological change. There are implications for labor during this transition period that can lead to increased inequality. With diminishing bargaining power in recent decades, workers have been unable to coordinate to demand better wages and conditions. An example of the weakening of labor power in America was the effort by Amazon workers to unionize, which was counteracted with aggressive anti-union efforts from the company (Streitfeld, 2021). Their weakening power, however, is not only manifested in their inability to negotiate directly with the company but also in political arenas. In countries like the US, where political campaigns are financed by large contributions, corporations and wealthy individuals will likely exert more power than workers. As Korinek and Stiglitz (2021a) state, "in a political system dominated by money, the innovators, increasingly rich, may use their economic and political influence to resist redistribution" (p. 13). In the US, labor protections are weak. Entities like the National Labor Relations Board do not have the power to impose sanctions on aggressive anti-union campaigns by companies facing unionization efforts.

Universal Basic Income, EITC, and Incentives through Subsidies

The US and its state governments have several policy avenues available for averting deepening income inequality in the wake of AI. Universal basic income (UBI) has been suggested as a policy proposal for averting technology-driven income inequality (Miller, 2021). Giving people a source of income that is not linked to employment can serve to increase their bargaining power. They would be less likely to choose the first job available and could focus more on how a job will foster their long-term goals. Having income that would cover basic needs, including food and housing, gives workers some bargaining power. They have the option to refuse a job but no disincentive to seek one, because any new income would not be taken away through graduation from traditional safety net programs, such as welfare and unemployment insurance. Previous research also suggests that consumption patterns under a UBI are unlikely to be wasteful (Garcia-Murillo & MacInnes, 2021).

While UBI has advantages, policies involving cash linked to incentives are also desirable and should perhaps form the bulk of the assistance. An example is the earned income tax credit (EITC), which works as a subsidy for wages provided directly to lower-income workers, encouraging people to seek jobs. The current program in the US is, in our view, insufficient: too few people qualify and most families get their credit at the end of the year, which may not be when they need it (Greene, 2013). It should be expanded to a wider range of incomes and phased out gradually as income increases. The taxation system should be integrated with subsidies such as EITC and UBI, and then simplified for those at lower income levels to ensure that everyone files a tax return, and that all people who qualify receive tax subsidies.

These subsidies should include tax credits for seeking education and training. In this way, people would be more likely to invest in their long-term income rather than taking the first job that comes available. This process could be assisted on the demand side of the labor market by giving subsidies to employers that offer apprenticeships. The government should also address childcare, another impediment to labor force participation. It may make sense for some people to not take full-time jobs so that they can take care of children but there should also be options for those who want to be formally employed. Providing a tax credit to those with young children could help them pay for childcare if they choose to be employed.

Unemployment Policy and Benefits

With limited education a person may be unemployed for several months. Lack of perfect mobility may prevent workers from looking in more economically vibrant markets. A person with employment gaps is also likely to receive a lower wage and be more vulnerable to discharge given their short tenure (Hall et al., 1995). One of the most concerning empirical results about the impact of robotization on employment is that it resulted in the loss of jobs while no evidence was found that employment was created somewhere else in the economy in any occupation or education group (Acemoglu & Restrepo, 2020). The history of technological change has not yet shown a long-term trend toward persistent unemployment. This is, perhaps, not surprising as it is possible to find things for people to do, even if they are not paid as much as they were prior to the advance.

It is a mistake, in our view, to focus on unemployment as an outcome of technological change. Job quality and mobility matter more. Many of the people in jobs made obsolete by AI advances will not immediately find comparable employment at similar wages. To the extent that this type of displacement becomes common, more will have to be done to find productive things for these people to do and ensure that they have sufficient income to ensure mass market demand. In the past, technological advance was slow enough that people would not have to change careers multiple times in their lives. If AI advance accelerates this will likely require much more investment in retraining than has occurred in the past.

The lack of universal benefits providing basic protection to people also impedes the movement of workers from one job to another. In a payroll-based insurance and benefits model, people are more likely to stay at their jobs for longer than they should simply to maintain those benefits. As a result, they do not give themselves the opportunity to update their skills before they become obsolete, making the transition to a new job much more difficult. Some unemployment programs worsen this problem by incentivizing people to take any job, rather than focusing strategically on new skills that could be in demand.

Lack of social protection during transition periods and employment arrangements that are not covered by benefits or labor regulation protections will exacerbate the inequities between those in non-traditional employment settings or unemployed/in transition compared to those with higher education and experience with higher incomes and benefits. In recent years, the US is experiencing an expansion from traditional to non-traditional freelance-type work that provides limited benefits or labor protections. From 2014 to 2019 4 million more people in the US have become freelancers, amounting to 35 percent of the workforce (Upwork, 2019). This movement requires a redesign of the benefits system. To the extent that freelancing is good for the economy, it is necessary to ensure that workers choosing this type of employment have access to comparable benefits at similar cost. Perhaps it is necessary to move to a portable system where benefits are not linked to a particular employer. Employer-based health insurance in the US, for example, was established by accident due to labor market conditions facing employers after the Second World War, and it seems suboptimal, particularly in the context of the growth of freelancing and the increasing frequency that people are now changing jobs.

Reskilling Initiatives

Labor, unlike machines, cannot be easily "programmed" to take on other tasks. While one could argue that humans are to an extent a "general purpose technology," the switching costs of moving from an obsolescent profession to a growing one are substantial and, it is often the case that such unemployed workers may not be able to find another job at a similar wage.

Both in developed and developing countries there is a risk of having a wave of unemployed and low-educated people who, in the absence of support, could resort to addiction and crime. During these transition years when companies are adopting AI more broadly, both the private and the public sector need to implement policies that facilitate a move by workers to better positions.

This may involve governments requiring companies installing these technologies to implement training that can facilitate a transition to higher-paid and more professionally challenging/rewarding tasks. Because the private sector has not faced incentives to increase its labor costs either in wages or training, governments need incentives or laws in place that provide a better alignment between the company and the larger interests of the nation to have incomes that will meet the needs of a modern economy. Governments need to invest in education by supporting the research and development enterprise of their countries while also making education more economically accessible. Among low-skilled workers some will be unable to make the transition and could lose their livelihood entirely.

Rewards for Workers Contributing to AI Development

Workers who continue to toil in low- and mid-wage jobs regardless of eroding pay and benefits are actively contributing to the development of the very AI that stands to worsen or eliminate their jobs. Consider, for example, the doctors and warehouse workers introduced at the beginning of this chapter: each action they take in working with AI offers the developers of the technology opportunities to learn, improve their technology, and sell better versions of it down the line. This is particularly true of new, experimental technologies often sold by startup vendors. No such technology is successful immediately after introduction: organizations and workers must adapt to technology-driven changes and vendors must revise their solutions to accommodate the day-to-day realities of the work environment, a process that is often slow and costly (Garcia-Murillo & MacInnes, 2019). Indeed, it is only when workers begin to directly interact with the new technology that organizations can adapt and wring productivity out of new processes.

Yet we do not see examples of organizations and AI vendors rewarding workers for these development efforts. Roboticists, computer scientists, engineers, and others employed by AI vendors receive enormous rewards for their contributions to AI (e.g. high pay, equity in the company, skill building, career opportunities). In other words, the very development of AI actively contributes to polarization. This need not be the case. The workers who use newly deployed AI and help to develop it should be rewarded in a similar fashion, whether by their employing organization or the technology vendor. Such an initiative would likely require coordination between all parties to ensure that those who contribute the most are rewarded accordingly, and that these rewards are sustainable in terms of skill building and career advancement.

Globalization and Remote Work

Labor markets are global, which tends to put downward pressure on wages. Technologies that reduce the cost of labor can also reduce the costs of goods and services, which also causes companies to keep wages low. Inequality is manifested at the local level with workers at the bottom of the economic ladder having little bargaining power and opportunities to grow their skills to meet the demands of the global business environment. Inequalities across countries are also emerging. Companies from developed countries are entering less-developed countries, bringing with them technologies that dominate those markets, leaving any local technological development difficult to achieve. When a nation is unable to develop technology of its own and becomes instead an adopter it can (1) limit investments in technological development, (2) reduce investment in innovation, (3) reduce spending on Internet of Things infrastructure, and (4) fail to pass laws or regulation around AI that could provide protections or foster education in science, technology, engineering, and mathematics (Goyal & Aneja, 2020).

There are factors that will challenge our governments' ability to respond to the digital transformation of work that can negatively affect workers. One of them is taxation of global digital companies that do not need to have a physical presence for the provision of their services. The global nature of their operations can allow them to find locations that give them tax advantages. The same is true for workers and there has already been a pattern of production where products and services are made in nations with low wages and labor standards. This could add pressure on wages for developed nations that now compete with the drastically lower wages of developing nations. A global world with different economic contexts leads to two impact paths. In poor nations the existence of these digital platforms with low barriers to entry can afford them greater freedom, independence, and a higher wage to what they obtain in their own countries under potentially exploitative labor conditions. In developed nations they get the same benefits of freedom and flexibility regarding location and time, but their wages are impacted by the presence of workers with significant lower wages willing to perform digital tasks at minimal pay.

There are many countries in the world with inadequate welfare systems that could protect a person when they are unemployed. According to the World Bank, in developing nations, eight in ten people receive no social assistance and six in ten work without health insurance (World Bank, 2019). A similar problem prevails in the US, where health insurance coverage is tied to employment and larger entities tend to have the resources necessary to provide coverage. There are now many more work arrangements that lack health protection, leaving people vulnerable and potentially open to bankruptcy if they suffer from an unexpected illness or accident. It has also been estimated, for example, that 50 percent of the income of multinationals is reported in jurisdictions that levy a tax rate of less than 5 percent (Clausing, 2016). Treaty negotiations will likely be necessary to improve conditions and reduce the incentives for countries to undercut each other.

CONCLUSION: WHAT DO WE WANT THE FUTURE TO LOOK LIKE?

Because AI is implemented in various industries, inequality, which is normally defined in economic terms, can also be present in other areas, such as healthcare. The use of AI for clinical as well as administrative decisions by doctors and insurers can negatively affect people in the absence of frameworks or principles that can prevent unequal treatment of individuals (Takshi, 2021).

Labor costs also need to be compared to both the type of labor needed as well as the cost of technology. It is possible that the changes that companies undertake when implementing AI in their operations and services are a response to market forces, where the motivation to use emerging technologies is not necessarily driven by the desire to reduce costs but much more by the pressure to use or offer state-of-the-art technologies. If some companies are introducing AI, it could generate concerns in others that they also need to do so to remain competitive.

During this transition, however, companies will be experimenting and, in the process, taking advantage of low-wage labor, which, in the US and in some other developed countries, is poorly protected. Companies can now take advantage of technologies that can provide labor on demand for short-term projects. They can issue a call for proposals and give the work to the lowest bidder, thus reducing the total number of workers on their payroll.

With some implementations of AI, such as more intelligent robots at work that take on more currently human responsibilities, the demand for some types of labor decreases. The impact of technology on work affects countries differently. Developing nations which have lower levels of education and technological skills will likely suffer greater economic consequences when technology begins to replace labor as costs increase.

Regardless of arguments in favor of or against mass deployment of AI, it is undeniable that AI will shape the future of work across a wide variety of industries and occupations. We believe it is essential to consider all available avenues to avert the income inequality we have seen in the wake of previous technological change, and that the options listed above are just a few possibilities with precedent. An array of stakeholders must work together to give all workers a stake in successful AI development and deployment. Low-wage workers are already doing their part; it is incumbent upon the rest of us – policymakers, scholars, educational institutions, corporations, small businesses, and technology vendors – to do ours.

REFERENCES

Acemoglu, D., & Restrepo, P. (2017). Robots and jobs: Evidence from US labor markets. NBER Working Paper, w23285.

Acemoglu, D., & Restrepo, P. (2020). The wrong kind of AI? Artificial intelligence and the future of labour demand. *Cambridge Journal of Regions, Economy and Society*, *13*(1), 25–35.

Ackerman, E. (2021). *This Year, Autonomous Trucks Will Take to the Road With No One on Board*. IEEE Spectrum. https://spectrum.ieee.org/this-year-autono mous-trucks-will-take-to-the-road-with-no-one-on-board

Autor, D. H., Levy, F., & Murnane, R. J. (2003). The skill content of recent technological change: An empirical exploration. *Quarterly Journal of Economics*, *118*(4), 1279–1333.

Autor, D. H., Dorn, D., Katz, L. F., Patterson, C., & Van Reenen, J. (2020). The fall of the labor share and the rise of superstar firms. *Quarterly Journal of Economics*, *135*(2), 645–709.

Bahrin, M. A. K., Othman, M. F., Azli, N. H. N., & Talib, M. F. (2016). Industry 4.0: A review on industrial automation and robotic. *Jurnal Teknologi*, *78*(6–13).

Berman, E., Bound, J., & Machin, S. (1998). Implications of skill-biased technological change: International evidence. *Quarterly Journal of Economics*, *113*(4), 1245–1279.

Bresnahan, T. F. (1999). Computerisation and wage dispersion: An analytical reinterpretation. *The Economic Journal*, *109*(456), 390–415.

Brynjolfsson, E., & McAfee, A. (2012). Jobs, productivity and the great decoupling. *New York Times*.

Bureau of Labor Statistics. (2021). Real weekly earnings up 3.9 percent for year ending March. www.bls.gov/opub/ted/2021/real-weekly-earnings-up-3-9-percent-for-year-ending-march-2021.htm

California Future of Work Commission. (2021). The future of work in California: A new social compact for work and workers. www.labor.ca.gov/wp-content/uploads/sites/338/2021/02/ca-future-of-work-report.pdf

Card, D., & DiNardo, J. E. (2002). Skill-biased technological change and rising wage inequality: Some problems and puzzles. *Journal of Labor Economics*, *20*(4), 733–783.

Chiacchio, F., Petropoulos, G., & Pichler, D. (2018). The impact of industrial robots on EU employment and wages: A local labour market approach. www.bruegel.org/wp-content/uploads/2018/04/Working-Paper-AB_25042018.pdf

Clausing, K. A. (2016). The effect of profit shifting on the corporate tax base in the United States and beyond. *National Tax Journal*, *69*(4), 905–934.

Conger, K. (2021). Hundreds of Google employees unionize, culminating years of activism. *New York Times*. www.nytimes.com/2021/01/04/technology/google-employees-union.html

Dobbs, R., Manyika, J., & Woetzel, J. (2015). The four global forces breaking all the trends. *McKinsey Global Institute*, *11*(4), 1–5.

Duggan, J., Sherman, U., Carbery, R., & McDonnell, A. (2020). Algorithmic management and app-work in the gig economy: A research agenda for employment relations and HRM. *Human Resource Management Journal*, *30*(1), 114–132.

Fernandez, R. M. (2001). Skill-biased technological change and wage inequality: Evidence from a plant retooling. *American Journal of Sociology*, *107*(2), 273–320.

Fersht, P. (2016, July 4). Automation Impact: India's services industry workforce to shrink 480,000 by 2021 – a decline of 14%. Horses for Sources. www.horsesforsources.com/indias-services-industry-set-to-lose-640000-low-skilled-jobs-to-automation-by

Friedman, F., & Thomas L. (2016). *Thank You for Being Late: An Optimist's Guide to Thriving in the Age of Accelerations*. Picador.

Garcia-Murillo, M. A., & MacInnes, I. P. (2019). AI's path to the present and the painful transitions along the way. *Digital Policy, Regulation and Governance*, *21*(3), 305–321.

Garcia-Murillo, M. A., & MacInnes, I. P. (2021). Consumption patterns under a universal basic income. *Basic Income Studies*, *16*(2), 257–298.

Goyal, A., & Aneja, R. (2020). Artificial intelligence and income inequality: Do technological changes and worker's position matter? *Journal of Public Affairs*, *20*(4), e2326.

Graetz, G., & Michaels, G. (2017). Is modern technology responsible for jobless recoveries? *American Economic Review*, *107*(5), 168–173.

Greene, S. S. (2013). The broken safety net: A study of earned income tax credit recipients and a proposal for repair. *NYU Law Review*, *88*, 515.

Hall, R. E., Farber, H., & Haltiwanger, J. (1995). Lost jobs. *Brookings Papers on Economic Activity*, *1*, 221–273.

Hicks, J. (1963). *The Theory of Wages*. Springer.

Hiltzik, M. (2021). Column: A California judge pinpointed the biggest problem with Prop. 22 – its greediness. *Los Angeles Times*. www.latimes.com/business/story/2021-08-24/proposition-22-worker-rights

Korinek, A., & Stiglitz, J. E. (2021a). Artificial intelligence and Covid-19: Covid-19 driven advances in automation and artificial intelligence risk exacerbating economic inequality. *The BMJ*, *372*.

Korinek, A., & Stiglitz, J. E. (2021b). Artificial intelligence, globalization, and strategies for economic development. Working Paper No. 28453. National Bureau of Economic Research. https://doi.org/10.3386/w28453

Lee, M. K. (2018). Understanding perception of algorithmic decisions: Fairness, trust, and emotion in response to algorithmic management. *Big Data & Society*, *5*(1).

Miller, K. (2021). *Radical Proposal: Universal Basic Income to Offset Job Losses due to Automation.* Stanford HAI. https://hai.stanford.edu/news/radical-proposal-universal-basic-income-offset-job-losses-due-automation

O'Brien, R., Bair, E. F., & Venkataramani, A. S. (2022). Death by robots? Automation and working-age mortality in the United States. *Demography*, *59*(2), 607–628.

OECD. (2018). Decoupling of wages from productivity: What implications for public policies? In *OECD Economic Outlook*, 2 (pp. 51–65). https://doi.org/10.1787/eco_outlook-v2018-2-3-en

Petropoulos, G. (2018). The impact of artificial intelligence on employment. www.bruegel.org/wp-content/uploads/2018/07/Impact-of-AI-Petroupoulos.pdf

Polanyi, M., & Sen, A. (1960). *The Tacit Dimension.* University of Chicago Press.

Prettner, K. (2016). The implications of automation for economic growth and the labor share of income. Working Paper No. 04/2016. ECON WPS. www.econstor.eu/handle/10419/141275

Rosenberg, E., & Greene, J. (2021). The union's defeat at Amazon is shaking up the labor movement and exposing a rift between organizers. *The Washington Post*. www.washingtonpost.com/technology/2021/04/18/after-amazon-bessemer-union-fight-labor-movement/

Roser, M., & Ortiz-Espina, E. (2016). *Income Inequality.* Our World in Data. https://ourworldindata.org/income-inequality#within-country-inequality-in-rich-countries

Sholler, D. (2020). Infrastructuring as an occasion for resistance: Organized resistance to policy-driven information infrastructure development in the US healthcare industry. *Computer Supported Cooperative Work*, *29*(4), 451–496.

Streitfeld, D. (2021, March 16). How Amazon crushes unions. *New York Times*. www.nytimes.com/2021/03/16/technology/amazon-unions-virginia.html

Takshi, S. (2021). Unexpected Inequality: Disparate impact from artificial intelligence in healthcare decisions. *Journal of Law and Health*, *34*(2), 215–251.

Upwork. (2019). Freelancing in America: 2019 survey. www.upwork.com/i/freelancing-in-america/

World Bank. (2019). *World Development Report 2019: The Changing Nature of Work.* World Bank. https://elibrary.worldbank.org/doi/pdf/10.1596/978-1-4648-1328-3

18. The impact of AI on contracts and unionisation
Michael Walker

INTRODUCTION

When we talk about artificial intelligence (AI) the first question that must be answered is one of definition. AI refers to a range of emerging technologies. In the sense of machine learning, it has been around for over 50 years. Discussion around AI in the workplace in the past few years often refers to algorithmic management but this, too, is a form of machine learning and is not the fully autonomous notion of AI. Since full AI is still a way off, for the purposes of this chapter, the discussion will mostly relate to algorithmic management systems which are increasingly being adopted in workplaces today, even more so in response to the rise of remote working during the COVID-19 pandemic (De Stefano, 2020).

The introduction of AI in the workplace presents numerous challenges to unions that are similar to the long-experienced challenges of automation generally: task displacement, the use of technology for surveillance, and the need to establish mechanisms for consultation and joint decision-making that will ameliorate the worst of the adverse impact on workers. Evidence suggests that, where this happens, outcomes improve not just for workers but for firms also which become highly competitive.

Negative impacts of algorithmic management have been extensively discussed (Kellogg et al., 2020; Moore & Woodcock, 2021), including in other contributions to this volume (Benyekhlef & Zhu, Chapter 13; Koeszegi et al., Chapter 2; Theodorou & Aler Tubella, Chapter 3). Two streams of the discussion are, first, around the highly negative impact of algorithmic management, particularly on workers in gig employment who have been the first to experience it (Rosenblat, 2018; Wood et al., 2019) and, second, around potential policy solutions (De Stefano, 2020; Kellogg et al., 2020). Both of these streams deal mainly with non-union contexts. Despite recent inroads by unions, the gig economy remains a mostly non-union environment. Similarly, policy solutions are directed mostly at lawmakers and regulators often in the United States and make little reference to a role for unions that, as intermediaries between workers and management, can shape the implementation of technologies including

Table 18.1   How AI impacts unions

	Micro	Macro
Impact on workers	Task displacement Surveillance Lack of transparency Discrimination	Layoffs at unionised firms No union culture in new firms
Impact on unions themselves	Potential for task displacement (WorkIt)	Online collective action as a competitor

AI in the workplace. As we will see, the high-union context of the Nordic countries has proven critical in the way that AI is being implemented there in a manner that is more positive for workers (Pérez Ortiz et al., 2021). It is questionable whether proposals for co-determination (formal systems of workplace democracy with worker and employer representation) can be achieved in Anglo-American economies where unions generally have significantly less workplace power outside a few highly unionised sectors such as the British public service.

AI can be construed as having a macro and micro impact both on workers and on unions themselves, as set out in Table 18.1.

MACRO IMPACTS

Below I will move on to a discussion of perhaps the sharpest impact of AI on work, where it takes the form of electronic performance monitoring. Before getting to that, it is worth first discussing the macro impact of AI on industries where AI-enabled technology companies move in and displace incumbent firms.

A familiar example is Amazon, which began life as an e-commerce bookseller that eventually out-competed bricks-and-mortar stores such as Borders which closed in 2011. Amazon has since gone on to become an e-commerce giant that sells nearly any kind of consumer good, as well as cloud computing. At its heart, the initial success of Amazon was its recommendation algorithm that drove increased sales by suggesting similar books based on past purchase behaviour (Singh, 2020).

The result was a significant shift in employment: a reduction in bookstore retail clerks and an expansion of warehouse and delivery jobs. Workers in Amazon warehouses are subject to intense monitoring (more of which below). What can unions do about this? Not a whole lot, except organise workers in these new workplaces. Amazon is the subject of a major international organising campaign led by UNI Global Union that, at the time of writing, has seen the most success in Italy, where Amazon has been made subject to a binding tripartite agreement (Reuters, 2021). In the United States, recent efforts to organise Amazon have been much less successful, in large part due to the difficult threshold of obtaining a majority vote (Rhinehart, 2021).

A second familiar example is Uber which, similarly, entered the point-to-point transportation industry intending to disrupt taxis. An important factor was its algorithm that efficiently matched drivers with passengers. It must also be said that another element of Uber's success is that it claims its drivers are not employees, which allows it to save on overheads relative to its competitors in the taxi industry because it doesn't have to pay for sick leave, holiday pay, or even intra-shift waiting time. The taxi industry was never particularly unionised to begin with but, again, unions and other worker advocates have mobilised to push back against Uber and other platform companies around the world (Vandaele, 2018, 2021).

AI and algorithms are also starting to make their way into white-collar work, with some administrative aspects of even complex fields of work such as law and accounting being reconfigured by task automation (Rani et al., 2021). A caveat here is that sometimes minor tasks that appear to be automated are in fact being outsourced to gig workers (Marvit, 2014), many located in the developing world (Rani et al., 2021), which is not so much technological displacement as it is a white-collar version of the more familiar phenomenon of offshoring. Unlike in manufacturing or call centres, this form off offshoring does not seem to be accompanied by any political outcry, perhaps due to a popular misunderstanding of the nature of the displacement.

In all, companies that adopt algorithmic management technologies tend to have lower costs than those that don't and have been steadily gaining market share. Unions, meanwhile, need to make inroads into newer firms if they are to avoid obsolescence. Limited progress has been made so far.

Union Substitution and Counter-Strategies

Unions, for the most part, have not had a lot of success in organising new industries and in many countries are absent from the majority of workplaces. In the absence of this 'channelled' form of worker voice, there has been a proliferation of other responses, ranging from 'coping' (Bucher et al., 2021; Galper, 2020) to online chatter (Walker et al., 2021) to collective action (Bronowicka & Ivanova, 2021). Additionally, the year 2021 saw a wave of strikes not seen in many years (Kerrissey & Stephan-Norris, 2021).

This is one of the scenarios predicted by Visser (2019). If unions cannot organise new workplaces, they will be substituted for other forms of voice. He posits four possible futures for unions:

1. Marginalisation – in which workers voice as expressed through unions continues to retreat and the balance of power swings further to employers.
2. Dualisation – in which unions share their traditional role with new actors.
3. Substitution – in which the new actors replace the role traditionally played by unions.
4. Revitalisation – in which unions do eventually experience another upswing and regain a level of influence comparable to that experienced in the twentieth century.

As Visser notes, it is difficult to predict at this moment which future will best describe what happens in the years ahead, and it may well differ in different jurisdictions. Certainly at this point marginalisation seems to be the dominant theme as a shrinking minority of workers belong to unions. Density isn't destiny, however, and because the additional extent of union 'reach' (Haynes et al., 2006) means that unions often play an outside role in workplace regulation, they may still be able to shape the deployment of AI in workplaces even where they do not have significant numbers of members.

Union Tech

AI could also play a role in the fate of unions themselves, as organisations. Like all workplace technologies, including email and mobile phones, AI is now something that unions can consider introducing internally. An example is the WorkIt app: a peer-to-peer platform designed to facilitate worker resistance initially in Walmart but now also in Amazon. The app itself is powered by AI. Advocates discovered, however, that they needed to alter the workings of the app in order to make it effective. One surprising discovery was that the app did not work as an automated 'problem-solver' but rather uncovered hotspots of workplace disgruntlement that union officials were able to organise around (Flanagan & Walker, 2021).

WorkIt is a smartphone app that allows workers to discuss issues in their workplace. It has an FAQ section for questions and answers and a more open-ended forum section. The creators of the app, Organization United for Respect, were a very small group of worker advocates seeking to organise a massive company, Walmart, with over 1 million workers, and had to think about how to scale their organisation. They hit on the idea of using IBM's Watson AI to answer the most commonly asked questions in the FAQ section, thus allowing their limited resources to stretch further. As of 2020, the original version of the app had over 10,000 active users and had been licensed to several other worker organisations, including AFT Texas, National Domestic Workers Alliance, and Center for Community Change.

The adoption of WorkIt in one union provides an interesting vignette of the changing nature of work and tech adoption generally. Australia's United Workers Union (UWU) is one of the licensed users of WorkIt. While there was some unease that the introduction of AI would reduce employment at the union's telephone call centre, by answering members' questions automatically, UWU officials found that the app actually identified workplaces and issues that were 'hotspots' and thus organising opportunities for the union. This knowledge had never been so readily available before. It also created a new kind of work in that UWU's activists often had to probe a little further to discover what was behind a person's question: whether the enquiry was a person checking up on their rights or was a result of an ongoing situation of exploitation, and whether it was experienced just by that one person or perhaps by many others at the same workplace. Following this line of enquiry from the app was a new kind of task for the union's activists. As a result, the introduction of AI through WorkIt actually increased rather than decreased the amount of work that had to be done, but only because of the purposeful restructuring of work by the union's leadership.

WorkIt is not alone, there are now a number of similar apps that exist either alongside or in support of unions. Others include Unit, Frank, and Breakroom. An aspect that is yet to be explored is the extent to which sorting algorithms have an impact on what issues become highlighted and thus become more talked about by workers. It is likely that the same dynamics on social media platforms that reward user engagement (whether favourable or unfavourable) and therefore promote more extreme viewpoints, leading to political polarisation, would also play out in these worker-organising platforms. This would suggest that worker-organising platforms would tend to highlight comments expressing more militant, anti-employer views and thus drive the current upswing in worker activism and strikes. More research is needed to investigate the extent to which AI sorting algorithms are playing a part.

MICRO IMPACTS

The second level in which AI impacts workers and unions is more directly at the level of tasks. This can take place in two ways: through task loss due to automation and through electronic performance monitoring. Unions in many jurisdictions have access to consultation provisions, either in collective agreements or in legislation, which notionally exist to ameliorate the impact of the introduction of automation, however, it is difficult to find examples where this has happened in practice.

An important distinction to make is that task loss is not the same thing as job loss (Bannò et al., 2021), even though one often follows the other. Workers generally perform a variety of tasks in their daily work and while automation might remove a particular task, the majority of a role survives the change. In an ideal world, employers would reskill their staff to fill the gap in their week with other tasks. This is what provisions for consultation around the introduction of technology were originally designed to do. In reality, these changes are introduced in workplaces where there is no union present, or where the union does not have the leverage to push back, except in some high-minded employers or in the Nordic system where union membership is very high (Kjellberg, 2017).

It needs to be said that there is an employment upside to all this digitisation: it is also creating new employment for software engineers and for entirely new jobs relating to the management and commercialisation of data – jobs that are for the most part well paid. Even the unionists using the AI-enabled WorkIt app, discussed above, found that the AI created new tasks just as fast as it made others obsolete. On the whole there is not a consensus over whether digitalisation is a net plus or minus for employment, with some studies suggesting that the substitution effect will be outweighed by the invention of new tasks, while others remain more pessimistic, believing that AI and robotisation will lead to runaway job losses (Pérez Ortiz et al., 2021). All that can be said with certainty is that automation is as old as the Industrial Revolution and, despite two centuries of task substitution, human beings have been steadily working fewer hours (Lucassen, 2021, pp. 369–370) but are not working 15 hour work weeks as John Maynard Keynes predicted in 1930. Moreover, the reductions that were secured in working hours in the twentieth century were achieved only by legislation that placed limits on working time. This difference in regulatory environment explains the differences in working time that persist to this day between Western Europe and the United States.

In a twist on the job loss narrative, Prassl argues that the people with the most immediate cause to fear job loss through AI are not actually frontline workers but rather middle managers, whose supervisory functions can be done more efficiently by algorithm (Prassl, 2019).

ELECTRONIC PERFORMANCE MONITORING

The most hotly contested area today is not task *loss* and redeployment, which employers and unions alike agree is inevitable, but rather the task *intensification* resulting from electronic performance monitoring. There are a range of technologies used to monitor performance, and their deployment has only increased during COVID-19 (De Stefano, 2020; Nissim & Simon, 2021).

The use of algorithms for monitoring is merely the latest in a long history of electronic surveillance going back decades (Sewell, 1998). It can even be seen as a continuation of the desire for constant efficiency improvements based on measurement that began a century ago with scientific management (Akhtar & Moore, 2016). Workers and unions expressed very similar misgivings in the 1970s when computers were first introduced into workplaces, not so much about task displacement but about the fear of opaque decisions made by computer programs rather than human beings (Engblom, 2021).

This long history is sometimes lost in the present-day discussion around AI and its 'black box' nature that renders decisions inscrutable, which sometimes gives the impression that AI is a new and game-changing barrier for worker advocates. Firstly, it is helpful to remember that complex technology has been in the workplace for most people's entire working lives. Secondly, it is not always necessary to have direct access to the decision-making process in order to understand its impact (although it does help). Whistleblowing researchers at Google famously proved that the language model used by the company's AI was discriminating against people of colour. They did this not through access to the code but by demonstrating its differential impact in the visible world, where systems were discovered to be disadvantaging female and non-white job applicants (Buolamwini & Gebru, 2018).

Unions have also emphasised that AI represents the latest in a long line of work-intensifying technologies that pose psychosocial risks to workers (Akhtar & Moore, 2016), as the sense of constant surveillance, the ratchet effect, and the failure to make allowance for individual energy levels and work capacity all add to a sense of stress.

Even the apparently novel capacity of AI to reach further than a human manager into an employee's life is not as new as it seems. The introduction of automated scanning of internal chat and email, computer usage, and even spoken tone of voice and sleep patterns (De Stefano, 2020) is novel and intrusive but still nowhere near as oppressive as the master and servant laws that unions resisted in the nineteenth century.

Provisions for consultation around the introduction of technology are written into many union contracts and have been for decades. Unions have shown an interest in recent years in breathing new life into these clauses, which have been relatively dormant, as a bulwark against intrusive electronic monitoring.

In the United Kingdom, the peak union body Trades Union Congress (TUC), which speaks collectively for around 5.5 million union members, released a manifesto in early 2021, *Work and the AI Revolution*, setting out the British union movement's priorities in tackling AI at work.

With respect to AI, the TUC report calls for:

- a *legal* duty to consult trade unions on the introduction of AI (that is, a statutory rule rather than a negotiated one);
- a legal right to have AI decisions reviewed by a human; and
- the prohibition of discriminatory algorithms of the kind discovered at Google.

The manifesto also calls for 'data reciprocity', asserting that data on workers are of monetary value to employers and are currently being extracted for free from the contributing workers, who are often not even aware of what data are being collected.

While it is aspirational and contains very few examples of successful curbs on AI, TUC's manifesto is an important document as it gives an indication of the priorities that unions in the Anglo-American world will pursue in the years ahead.

A little stronger is the Joint Declaration on AI signed in 2021 between UNI Global Union, Insurance Europe, BIPAR, and AMICE regarding the responsible use of AI in the insurance sector. Unlike TUC's manifesto, which represents unions' preferred position, this declaration is a bilateral agreement between a global union federation and industry associations that represents in-principle agreement. Unsurprisingly, it is much less ambitious in scope but does at least recognise the potential for AI bias and the importance of the principle of transparency. Consistent with the TUC manifesto, the joint declaration also explicitly includes a provision for 'ensuring that those concerned are able to challenge the outcome, decision or recommendation produced by AI'.

On the other hand, the joint declaration also acknowledges the potential for positive benefits flowing from the introduction of AI, including the opportunity for higher-quality jobs. The partners also agree that AI can be used for personnel-related tasks 'such as coordinating holiday and working times of employees, organising shift systems or service times'. This is a significant concession for a union body to make. People elsewhere have pointed to the potential of AI scheduling systems to contribute to the 'gigification' of traditional work as workers can be placed on minimum or zero-hour contracts and are automatically offered shifts at very short notice (Jamal, 2021).

While rare, there are some instances where unions have successfully prosecuted or negotiated limits on the introduction and use of AI in the workplace. We will now turn to two case studies, one in the Anglo-American context in which the regulatory environment is unfavourable to unions and one in the Nordic context in which the regulatory environment is more favourable to unions.

Teacher Evaluations in Houston

In 2017 the Houston Federation of Teachers successfully pursued a legal strategy against its members' employer, the Houston Independent School District. The issue went to machine decision-making. Unbeknownst to them, teachers were being evaluated by algorithm and ultimately either rewarded or even fired based on the algorithm's determinations. The teachers' union successfully challenged the system in court on behalf of seven teachers who been adversely affected by the opaque rating system (Webb & Harden, 2017).

While this was not a ground on which the court case was lodged, a further issue with the evaluation decision is that it evaluated teachers according to their student results, relative to the state average. It is inevitable that half of all students will get a result below the average, meaning that the system was effectively culling teachers based on their students' performance. It did not weight the results based on socioeconomic factors that make particular schools perform better than others, or a myriad of personal-level impacts that are not part of the calculation but that a human manager would be aware of and could take account of.

The District Court upheld the challenge on due process grounds under the Fourteenth Amendment (that binds the government which, in this case, was the teachers' employer). The judge found that the algorithmic evaluations had two fatal deficiencies and struck them down on the basis of procedural due process, specifically that they deprived teachers of sufficient information to meaningfully challenge a low score.

GPS Tracking in Sweden

In Sweden, the union IF Metall successfully pushed back against intrusive uses of GPS monitoring in the workplace. The union ran a very creative argument that allowed the technology to continue to be used but in a way that did not adversely affect the union's members (Bender & Söderqvist, 2021).

The company involved was a mining company that used GPS tracking to monitor the location of its workforce. Ostensibly, this was for safety reasons, however, it was not long before the technology was being used to rate the speed at which people were working and thus to monitor performance, for example by timing the duration of workers' bathroom breaks. IF Metall did not push back directly against the use of the technology for performance monitoring, however, they did negotiate that the monitoring and performance would be visible only at the level of the business unit rather than at the level of individual workers. As a result, location anonymisation has since been built into the system. This means that individuals were not being singled out for working on a particular task slower than average, and thus finding themselves at risk of termination. At the same time, the union did not question management's arguments in favour of productivity, but merely disagreed that it was necessary to monitor individuals to achieve that goal. Management, for its part, argued that its goal was not punitive but merely to use data-gathering to further develop its lean manufacturing principles. The outcome of negotiation is that managers have the most need to worry about AI, as their metrics are now subject to much closer scrutiny. It is their job, armed with these data, to identify opportunities to improve performance, rather than to turn it into an opportunity for punitive action.

What happened in this case is consistent with an overall preference of Anglo-American companies to deploy technology in the form of data analysis that improves production, which leads to layoffs, while Nordic companies favour robotisation (Pérez Ortiz et al., 2021). The authors suggest this flows from the industrial relations cultures of the Nordic countries, which operate on a model of organised corporativism with high union density and collective bargaining coverage. By contrast, Anglo-American companies operate on company-level collective bargaining. What this case surprisingly demonstrates is that high-union, high-consultation Nordic countries actually have higher rates of introduction of technology because fears are allayed and resistance is lower.

In securing this outcome, IF Metall had two advantages: first, the regulatory environment in Sweden obliged the company to consult. The specific instrument was the Codetermination in the Workplace Act. This law was designed and introduced to place guardrails around the implementation of technology in general and not AI monitoring specifically, but it proved to be an effective source of leverage for the union. The union's second advantage was that this company had an extremely high unionisation rate which gave the union workplace influence. Had either not been the case, the negotiation might not have happened. So co-determination over technology is not just a problem-solving issue, it is also fundamentally a power issue and it is questionable whether policy solutions alone will resolve power imbalances wrought by AI.

Unions are of course only one actor in employment relations regulation. In many jurisdictions the unions' requests have been incorporated into labour laws. Italy's Civil Code now prohibits surveillance of workers by default (De Stefano, 2020). Addressing such issues through legislation rather than workplace-level consultation is a rather blunt instrument that may not be the best way of governing the day-to-day operation of surveillance equipment. The way such equipment is used can vary considerably from one workplace context to the next (De Stefano, 2020; Engblom, 2021).

Lastly, a particular aspect of electronic surveillance that is also a new iteration of an old problem is the capacity of this technology to be used to target union activists, or even *potential* union activists (in much the same way that WorkIt does, except with the opposite intention of firing or disciplining them). There are AI tools that market themselves to employers for their ability to identify influencers and change-makers and to sanction people who may be participating in protected action (De Stefano & Taes, 2021). While union-busting is not new, the fact that these technologies can be deployed to prevent workers organising at such an early stage, rather like in Philip K Dick's science-fiction novel *The Minority Report*, would be very difficult to prove as the affected worker themselves may be completely unaware of the reason they have been sanctioned.

DISCUSSION

The issues around algorithmic management that unions have shown the most opposition to are intrusive monitoring, transparency, the lack of human oversight, and, flowing from this, the potential for algorithms to exhibit discriminatory forms of bias.

The evidence is that employers are broadly in agreement about the right of appeal and about combating discrimination; not so much about automated monitoring which is a cost-saving measure. Perhaps surprisingly, one group that stands to be disadvantaged by automated monitoring are middle managers for whom it amounts to task displacement. That is little consolation to the monitored workers, however, who face increased stress from the panoptic effect of being always under a watchful eye and whose employers inevitably ratchet up their expectations of performance.

What is perhaps the most surprising is just how familiar all these issues are. None are specific to AI or algorithmic management. Decisions made by inscrutable computer programs have been a source of unease for at least 50 years. While early computers were feared as a form of deskilling and today's because they remove accountability, fundamentally both new and old reflect concern at the loss of control by workers to machines that make decisions in a manner that the human brain cannot directly comprehend. The issue of transparency in machine decision-making is a lot older than AI.

With respect to monitoring, this, too, has a longer history that predates algorithmic management. Workers 20 years ago complained that the use of surveillance tools was pushing them to the limit (Akhtar & Moore, 2016).

It is only the problem of automated discrimination that appears to be novel; however, issues of gender and racial discrimination in general are not new. Unions have been pushing for gender equity in the workplace for 100 years (maternity protection was one of three conventions passed at the International Labour Organization's first sitting in 1919) and racial discrimination in the workplace has been a live concern since the 1960s.

Algorithmic management, then, is perhaps best seen as a continuation of trends that have been in place for many decades. The challenge for unions is not that this is a new kind of challenge; it is the normal challenge that solutions that make sense will not be adopted unless workers have power in their workplaces.

The contrast between the Nordic and Anglo-American experiences is instructive on this point. In the Nordic system, where union membership is high and where their participation in workplace governance is backed by legislation, unions have been able to play a role in ameliorating the adverse impacts of algorithmic management. Moreover, firms in this milieu are able to adopt technology more readily and be more competitive. In the Anglo-American experience, unionism is lower and they have fewer rights enshrined in legislation. The result is that employers have a free hand to introduce automation but experience has been that they have done so out of a cost-saving mentality that workers resist out of a well-founded fear of layoffs (Pérez Ortiz et al., 2021).

The path forward for unions is to make themselves relevant. If the experience of work deteriorates through the adoption of algorithmic management in Anglo-American jurisdictions, the opportunity is created for unions to channel the associated grievances of workers. The challenge is how to push back when there are few levers to pull. In that respect, the creative legal challenge mounted by the teachers' union in Houston may indicate a pathway for unions wishing to promote decent working conditions while facing lower density and an unfavourable regulatory environment.

Backing such campaigns would certainly be a rational course of action for aggrieved workers.

CONCLUSION

Overall, the picture is not an encouraging one for unions in most jurisdictions, where they do not have sufficient leverage to push back against the more odious aspects of AI. Left to their own devices, workers will continue to respond in other, less constructive ways, from seeking escape or other forms of coping, through to new forms of collective resistance.

Electronic performance monitoring has become very widely adopted during the COVID-19 pandemic. If it is as intrusive as commentators allege, then unions have an opportunity to make themselves relevant by organising over this issue and pushing back against it. The AFT case in Houston demonstrates that this can be achieved even in an unfavourable regulatory environment. Of course, intrusive surveillance is not the only problem workers face in contemporary workplaces and sits amongst other issues, not the least of which is low wages and income inequality. Whether surveillance rates are high enough for unions to make it a priority remains to be seen. If unions do not pursue it, other advocates may step in to fill the gap, either at a firm level or at the political level. Or the experience of work may simply continue to deteriorate for many people if no one pushes back against the power of the employer.

REFERENCES

Akhtar, P., & Moore, P. V. (2016). The psychosocial impacts of technological change in contemporary workplaces, and trade union responses. *International Journal of Labour Research, 8*(1/2), 101–131.

Bannò, M., Filippi, E., & Trento, S. (2021). Risk of substitution of European workers: How is it influenced by socio-demographic and job characteristics? Paper presented at the 19th ILERA World Congress, Lund.

Bender, G., & Söderqvist, F. (2021). How to negotiate an algorithm: A case study on voice and automation in Swedish mining. Paper presented at the 19th ILERA World Congress, Lund.

Bronowicka, J., & Ivanova, M. (2021). Resisting the algorithmic boss: Guessing, gaming, reframing and contesting rules in app-based management. In J. Woodcock & P. V. Moore (Eds), *Augmented Exploitation: Artificial Intelligence, Automation and Work* (pp. 149–162). London: Pluto Press.

Bucher, E. L., Schou, P. K., & Waldkirch, M. (2021). Pacifying the algorithm: Anticipatory compliance in the face of algorithmic management in the gig economy. *Organization, 28*(1), 44–67.

Buolamwini, J., & Gebru, T. (2018). Gender shades: Intersectional accuracy disparities in commercial gender classification. Paper presented at the Conference on Fairness, Accountability and Transparency.

De Stefano, V. (2020). 'Masters and servers': Collective labour rights and private government in the contemporary world of work. *International Journal of Comparative Labour Law and Industrial Relations, 36*(4).

De Stefano, V., & Taes, S. (2021). Algorithmic management and collective bargaining. *Foresight Brief*, 10. Brussels: European Trade Union Institute.

Engblom, S. (2021). Algorithms, trade unions and effective workers voice. Paper presented at the 19th ILERA World Congress, Lund.

Flanagan, F., & Walker, M. (2021). How can unions use artificial intelligence to build power? The use of AI chatbots for labour organising in the US and Australia. *New Technology, Work and Employment, 36*(2), 159–176.

Galper, A. (2020). *Accommodation-through-Bypassing: Overcoming Professionals' Resistance to the Implementation of Algorithmic Technology*. Massachusetts Institute of Technology.

Haynes, P., Boxall, P., & Macky, K. (2006). Union reach, the 'representation gap' and the prospects for unionism in New Zealand. *Journal of Industrial Relations, 48*(2), 193–216.

Jamal, U. (2021, 27 August). Gig apps for a pandemic economy: Part time, no commitment. *Associated Press*.

Kellogg, K. C., Valentine, M. A., & Christin, A. (2020). Algorithms at work: The new contested terrain of control. *Academy of Management Annals, 14*(1), 366–410.

Kerrissey, J., & Stephan-Norris, J. (2021, 11 November). US workers have been striking in startling numbers. Will that continue? *Washington Post*. www.washingtonpost.com/politics/2021/11/11/us-workers-have-been-striking-startling-numbers-will-that-continue/

Kjellberg, A. (2017). Self-regulation versus state regulation in Swedish industrial relations. Paper presented at the International Conference in Honour of Professor Ann Numhauser-Henning: Flexibilisation, Non-Discrimination and Ageing Societies.

Lucassen, J. (2021). *The Story of Work: A New History of Humankind*. New Haven: Yale University Press.

Marvit, M. Z. (2014). How crowdworkers became the ghosts in the digital machine. *The Nation, 5*(2).

Moore, P. V., & Woodcock, J. (2021). *Augmented Exploitation: Artificial Intelligence, Automation and Work*. London: Pluto Press.

Nissim, G., & Simon, T. (2021). The future of labor unions in the age of automation and at the dawn of AI. *Technology in Society, 67*, 101732.

Pérez Ortiz, L., Heredero de Pablos, M., Ruesga, S. M., & Baquero, J. (2021). Digitalisation and unionism in Europe under the varieties of capitalism. Paper presented at the 19th ILERA World Congress, Lund.

Prassl, J. (2019). What if your boss was an algorithm? Economic incentives, legal challenges, and the rise of artificial intelligence at work. *Comparative Labor Law and Policy Journal*.

Rani, U., Kumar Dhir, R., Furrer, M., Göbel, N., Moraiti, A., & Cooney, S. (2021). *World Employment and Social Outlook 2021:* The role of digital labour platforms in transforming the world of work. www.ilo.org/wcmsp5/groups/public/---dgreports/---dcomm/---publ/documents/publication/wcms_771749.pdf

Reuters. (2021). Amazon reaches agreement with trade unions in Italy. www.reuters. com/business/amazon-reaches-agreement-with-trade-unions-italy-2021-09-15/

Rhinehart, L. (2021). The Protecting the Right to Organize (Pro) Act: A major step toward restoring the right to organise for US workers. *International Union Rights*, *28*(2), 3–5.

Rosenblat, A. (2018). *Uberland: How Algorithms Are Rewriting the Rules of Work*. Oakland: University of California Press.

Sewell, G. (1998). The discipline of teams: The control of team-based industrial work through electronic and peer surveillance. *Administrative Science Quarterly*, *43*(2), 397–428.

Singh, S. (2020). *'Why Am I Seeing This?' How Video and E-Commerce Platforms Use Recommendation Systems to Shape User Experiences*. New America.

Vandaele, K. (2018). *Will Trade Unions Survive in the Platform Economy? Emerging Patterns of Platform Workers' Collective Voice and Representation in Europe*. European Trade Union Institute.

Vandaele, K. (2021). Collective resistance and organizational creativity amongst Europe's platform workers: A new power in the labour movement? In J. Haidar & M. Keune (Eds), *Work and Labour Relations in Global Platform capitalism*. Cheltenham, UK and Northampton, MA, USA and Geneva: Edward Elgar and ILO.

Visser, J. (2019). Trade unions in the balance. www.ilo.org/actrav/info/pubs/ WCMS_722482/lang--en/index.htm

Walker, M., Fleming, P., & Berti, M. (2021). 'You can't pick up a phone and talk to someone': How algorithms function as biopower in the gig economy. *Organization*, *28*(1), 26–43.

Webb, S., & Harden, J. D. (2017, 12 October). Houston ISD settles with union over controversial teacher evaluations. *Chron*. www.chron.com/news/houston-texas/ education/article/Houston-ISD-settles-with-union-over-teacher-12267893.php

Wood, A. J., Graham, M., Lehdonvirta, V., & Hjorth, I. (2019). Good gig, bad gig: Autonomy and algorithmic control in the global gig economy. *Work, Employment and Society*, *33*(1), 56–75.

Index